P9-EML-629

# POLITICS OF FRUSTRATION

# Books by Holger H. Herwig

THE GERMAN NAVAL OFFICER CORPS 1890–1918: A Social and Political History

POLITICS OF FRUSTRATION: The United States in German Naval Planning 1889–1941

# POLITICS OF FRUSTRATION

## The United States in German Naval Planning, 1889—1941

HOLGER H. HERWIG

Little, Brown and Company—Boston–Toronto

FIRST EDITION
T 04/76

The author is grateful to the following publishers for permission to reprint previously copyrighted materials:

The University of Chicago Press, for "Prelude to Weltblitzkrieg" by Holger H. Herwig, as published in *Journal of Modern History*, Vol. 43, No. 4, December 1971. Copyright © 1971 by The University of Chicago.

*The Historian*, for the article "The Failure of Imperial Germany's Undersea Offensive Against World Shipping" by Holger H. Herwig and David Trask, Vol. 33, No. 4, August 1971. Copyright © 1971 by Phi Alpha Theta.

*Central European History*, for the article "Admirals versus Generals: The War Aims of the Imperial German Navy 1914–1918" by Holger H. Herwig, Vol. 5, September 1972. Copyright © 1972 by Emory University.

*Militärgeschichtliche Mitteilungen*, for the article "Naval Operations Plans Between Germany and the United States of America 1898–1913" by Holger H. Herwig and David Trask, 2/1970, S 5–32.

LIBRARY OF CONGRESS CATALOGING IN PUBLICATION DATA
Herwig, Holger H
Politics of frustration.

Bibliography: p.
Includes index.
1. United States — Foreign relations — Germany.
2. Germany — Foreign relations — United States.
3. United States — History, Naval. 4. Germany —
History, Naval. 5. European War, 1914–1918 — Causes.
6. World War, 1939–1945 — Causes. I. Title.
E183.8.G3H44 327.73'043 75-43997
ISBN 0-316-35890-8

Designed by Susan Windheim

*Published simultaneously in Canada*
*by Little, Brown & Company (Canada) Limited*

PRINTED IN THE UNITED STATES OF AMERICA

*For Lorraine*

"Contrariwise," continued Tweedledum,
"if it was so, it might be;
and, if it were so, it would be;
but as it ain't, it ain't.
That's logic."

—Lewis Carroll, *Through the Looking Glass*

# Author's Note

A NUMBER OF PEOPLE HAVE GIVEN GENEROUSLY OF THEIR TIME AND KNOWLEDGE to this study. First and foremost, I would like to thank Professor Andreas Hillgruber of Cologne University for discussing this subject with me during several visits, and for making available to me then unpublished manuscripts dealing with this topic. Dr. Jost Dülffer of the same university was kind enough to share his work on the "Raeder" period prior to the outbreak of the Second World War. Professor David F. Trask of the State University of New York at Stony Brook has collaborated with me on a number of specialized researches on German-American naval history, and has unselfishly shared his own research on the United States Navy during the First World War. Several of my colleagues at Vanderbilt University, especially J. León Helguera and Melvyn P. Leffler, read segments of this manuscript and rendered critical evaluations. Their judicious comments greatly benefited this study; the shortcomings remain my own.

I would like to express my gratitude to the Alexander von Humboldt-Stiftung in Bonn, West Germany, for financial aid, to the Vanderbilt University Research Council for extending summer fellowships and grants-in-aid, and to Roger Donald of Little, Brown and Company for his generous encouragement.

Finally, I owe a great deal to my undergraduate students, who by the simple devices of friendship and honesty have buoyed me up over the past three years.

H. H. H.

*San Marcos, California*
*July 1975*

# Contents

*Contents*

# POLITICS OF FRUSTRATION

# Introduction: The Newcomers

To success through breeding.
*Motto of the German Navy League*

ON 24 APRIL 1971 THE *New York Times* REPORTED IN A FRONT-PAGE STORY the discovery of a German contingency war plan to invade the United States around the turn of the century. Based on an article that Professor David F. Trask and I published in 1970 in the West German historical journal *Militärgeschichtliche Mitteilungen*, the *Times* story evoked considerable response, ranging from the enthusiastic support of New Englanders who knew of the numerous German spy and reconnaissance activities in their area to the indignant protests of retired German naval officers, some of whom had served both Kaiser Wilhelm II and Adolf Hitler. Later, in *The German Naval Officer Corps: A Social and Political History 1890–1918* (Oxford 1973), I analyzed the social, political, religious, and educational characteristics of the Imperial German naval officer corps, and in working on that analysis I came across repeated statements by German naval leaders on American affairs and particularly the United States armed forces. These experiences have led me to develop this extended study of German-American relations as shown in German naval policies toward the United States in three crucial periods between 1889 and 1941, which provides broader background and perspective for the arguments in the above-mentioned article.

The study of German-American relations has found surprisingly few takers, with the notable exception of Alfred Vagts. It is only in the wake of the National Socialist holocaust and the American experience in Vietnam that scholars have begun to plow this rich field. The relative glut of investigators over the last two decades arose partly because numerous archives only recently opened their records for this period. For example, the British have now made available those documents relating to the entry of the United States into the Second World War; the American "Black" war plan of 1913–1914 remained classified until the 1950s. And since about 1967 the Bundesarchiv-Militärarchiv (Federal Military Archive) in Freiburg, West Germany, has allowed scholars access to the holdings of the former Marinearchiv (Navy Archive), now returned to West Germany by the British and Americans. Numerous sets of personal papers belonging to important naval leaders were deposited in Freiburg after 1945, and they supplement the records of official government agencies. This wealth of material has made research for this study feasible. Unfortunately, the German army files did not fare so well: almost all were destroyed during air raids on Berlin, especially in 1942 and 1945.

This book in no way presumes to represent a general history of German-American relations between 1889 and 1941. Rather, it is a composite of three studies on critically important historical periods: the era of colonial rivalry from 1889 to 1905; the German-American conflict from 1917 to 1918; and the National Socialist period to 1941, culminating in the German declaration of war against the United States. In essence, this work is an *essai*, an attempt to unearth some of the basic themes that run through these three time spans. I have tried to address myself especially to the currently popular notion of continuity, that is, the continuity — or lack thereof — of ideas and concepts from the Wilhelmian to the Hitlerean periods. A number of questions emerge at once. Why did Germany and the United States enter the naval race at almost identical moments in the 1890s? What were these newcomers seeking in far distant areas such as Samoa and the Philippines? What were Germany's intentions in the Western Hemisphere? Why did the Reich opt for unrestricted submarine warfare in January 1917, knowing full well that such a policy would put her on a collision path with the American republic? Why did American naval officers — led by Admiral George Dewey — view Germany as their most probable enemy? And finally, what prompted Adolf Hitler in December 1941 to repeat what he considered to have been the cardinal error of the First World War: conflict with the United States?

In answering these questions, I have knowingly chosen to omit certain vital areas and topics. These are self-evident and I leave them for future scholars. Nor have I opted to investigate the creation of the modern German and American navies. And I might also point out that my major concern has been the study of Germany's attitude toward the United States, and specifically what role the latter assumed in German strategic deliberations in the twentieth century; the sections dealing with the American republic are designed first and foremost as background material to complement the German side of the picture.

On the other hand, the issue of imperialism consumes much of the following. The revisionist, or "New Left," interpretation of American history by, among others, William A. Williams, Walter LaFeber, Lloyd C. Gardner, Thomas J. McCormick, and Bruce M. Russett has found its German counterpart in Volker R. Berghahn, H. Böhme, Fritz Fischer, Immanuel Geiss, Dirk Stegmann, Hartmut Pogge von Strandmann, and, most frequently, Hans-Ulrich Wehler. Wehler especially has depicted the period prior to 1914 as one dominated by social imperialism and colonialism. The former was designed, according to him, to suppress reform movements at home, and the latter to provide lucrative and guaranteed outlets for German industrial production. Winfried Baumgart has vehemently attacked this interpretation — which has been extended back into the pre-Wilhelmian era — and thereby launched a debate among German scholars that threatens to rival that between Fritz Fischer and the late Gerhard Ritter over the origins of the First World War, both in quantity of books and articles produced and in personal recriminations. As a result, I have had of necessity to take up this overly plowed and highly emotional field, but only to the extent that it concerns German-American relations.

It has not been my intent to take away completely the economic interpretation of imperialism, but to point out that other factors were also at least equally at work. Trade surpluses, armaments windfalls, merchant shipping monopolies, and territorial aggrandizement are integral components of the larger issue. And not to be overlooked is the crude Darwinistic "survival of the fittest" argument put forth, for example, by Chancellor Bernhard von Bülow: "The question is not if we want to colonize, but that we must colonize whether we want to or not." The Kaiser's new "Bismarck" equated colonial with national issues and called for an end to the practice whereby Germans had become the "cultural fertilizer" for other nations, particularly the United States. Colonization, Bülow concluded, was the very "struggle for one's survival."[1] Moreover, one also has to include in any study of imperialism matters such as national pride, prestige, expansion, military and naval strategy (bases), international power politics, and the like. General Lothar von Trotha, the governor of German South-West Africa, at the turn of the century rendered his analysis of colonialism: "It was neither political because we lacked the enthusiasm, nor economic because initially we lacked the capital. . . . It was simply pure speculation."[2] The combination of all the factors outlined above, I suggest, makes up the complex phenomenon of late nineteenth-century imperialism. Nor should one overlook that much of this analysis is made possible primarily through the benefit of historical hindsight. The Kaiser's "World Marshal," Count Alfred von Waldersee, wrote shortly before his departure for China to suppress the so-called Boxer rebellion in July 1900: "We are supposed to pursue *Weltpolitik* [world politics]. If I only knew what that is supposed to be."[3]

Finally, it should not be forgotten that according to the Imperial German constitution of 14 April 1871, the Kaiser was accorded virtually a free hand in determining the Reich's foreign and military policies. In other words, this study deals first and foremost with the ruling circles in Germany: the Kaiser, the Foreign Office, and the various branches of the military and naval establishments; to wit, the people who formulated and often dictated Germany's foreign and military postures vis-à-vis the United States. I therefore consciously accept the risk of incurring the wrath of my colleagues for not including in this work the attitudes of the various Germans who were pro-American, who desired no colonial expansion and much less confrontation, who sought arbitration for overseas disputes through the International Court at The Hague — in short, all the "good" Germans. The Hitler period was hardly known for its democratic procedure or collegial decision-making process; hence here once more the primary focus has of necessity to rest with the Führer and his military and naval paladins.

And what about the two main protagonists of this book? A cursory glance at Germany and the United States in 1889 reveals a surprising degree of at least commercial equality. While the Reich handled 11.1 percent of the world's trade, the United States was not far behind with 10.1 percent. The total of exports and imports of the two nations was roughly the same at around $1.5 billion per annum. Whereas American exports to Germany amounted to 9 percent ($68 million) of her total, Germany's exports to the United States came to 11 percent ($82 million) of hers. Nor were the populations of the two lands overly disproportionate in 1889: the United States consisted of 61.8 million people and Germany of 46.9 million, while the annual rate of population increase by the turn of the century was 1.9 percent in the U.S. and 1.5 percent in Germany. Moreover, Berlin and New York each housed about 1.5 million people, though other American cities took a decided advantage with 1.1 million for Chicago and 1 million for Philadelphia, while the Reich could counter only with 0.6 million for Hamburg and 0.3 million for Munich. Boston, the object of much German strategic speculation and planning, in 1889 possessed a population of 448,000.

The sheer physical dimensions of the United States, of course, greatly outdistanced those of Germany. The Reich's 208,732 square miles were paltry in comparison with America's 2,974,000. Yet much of the republic's land was uninhabited, and this accounts for the tremendous diversity in population density: around 21 people per square mile in the United States and 225 in Germany. The size variable also accounts for the much larger railroad network in the U.S. (approximately 170,000 miles) than in the Reich (27,000 miles). And in terms of natural resources and industrial capacity, the United States was just beginning to tap her vast potential. By 1889 she outproduced Germany in coal 140 million to 85 million metric tons, and in pig iron 9.4 million to 4.5 million metric tons. On the other hand, the Reich's manpower drain to the United States was rapidly coming to an end. Overall annual German emigration had by 1889 dropped to 90,250 people, of whom 84,424 (93.5 percent) went to the United States, from a high in 1881 of 210,547; by 1900 emigration was to decline further to a relative trickle of about 30,000 per annum. Nevertheless, in 1890 there were 2.784 million German-born residents in the United States, and this figure sufficed to prompt German economists and popular writers to clamor for overseas colonies — particularly in South America — in order to halt completely this "cultural fertilization" of the United States.

Neither country in 1889 possessed a navy of great importance, and both lay well behind Great Britain, France and Russia in this respect. Germany had twenty-six elderly armored vessels and twenty-three small cruising ships either in service or under construction, while the United States had nine (first-class) armored and fifteen unarmored ships either in commission or building. The republic's need to base her small fleet along two major oceans accounts partly for her greater naval expenditures ($21.4 million for 9,921 men) than those of the Reich ($8.5 million for 16,116 men). Conversely, Germany's continental location among three major land powers (Russia, Austria-Hungary and France) forced her to maintain a much larger army (491,759 men at a cost of $88.1 million per annum) than the United States (27,759 men at $44.4 million). The republic's vast surface area here accounts in all likelihood once more for the relatively higher costs of maintaining even this minuscule land force.

Germany and the United States were both newcomers upon the colonial scene in the 1880s. Whereas the republic had throughout much of the nineteenth century concentrated her energies on westward expansion into former Spanish and English holdings, the Reich under Chancellor Otto von Bismarck had in the mid-1880s laid the basis for a colonial empire overseas. Bismarck, exploiting the Anglo-French colonial rivalry in Egypt and the Sudan, managed to acquire four African colonies (Togoland, the Cameroons, German South-West Africa, and German

East Africa) as well as far-flung island possessions in the South Seas (New Guinea, the Bismarck Archipelago, the North Solomon and the Marshall islands). The total area of this empire amounted to only 1.17 million square miles, of which the African lands accounted for 85 percent, or one-quarter of the African holdings of Britain and France. Much of the German territory consisted of barren, almost desert stretches that no European powers had wanted. But it was to be Germany's dream for the next half-century to create a so-called Central African colonial empire by connecting the triangle of German East Africa, German South-West Africa and the Cameroons-Togoland with the territories of "dying" empires: Portuguese Angola to the west, Portuguese East Africa (Mozambique) to the east, and the Belgian Congo in Central Africa. If these new additions — according to German plans — could be further complemented by territorial concessions wrung from Britain in Rhodesia, British East Africa or even British South Africa, as well as strips of the French Congo, then the Reich would realize her dream of a Central African colonial empire stretching from the Atlantic to the Indian Ocean, connected by a system of railroads, and serving as the vital land link for a projected worldwide German telegraph cable.

But these plans remained on the drawing board. Bismarck in the late 1880s dropped the colonial issue once it had served its purpose and coldly rejected further African conquests with the claim that his "map of Africa" lay in Europe; that is, with the need to maintain a favorable diplomatic balance among Russia, Austria-Hungary, France, and Italy. And the period after 1890 was to bring but small gains. Kaiser Wilhelm II by 1900 had added the Caroline, Marshall and Mariana islands as well as Upolu and Savaii in the Samoan group and Kiaochow in China to the Reich's overseas empire, a paltry increase of 2,000 square miles (a net gain of 0.18 percent). Kiaochow was administered directly by the navy and was designed to become a model colony. German settlers were encouraged to come here, business concerns were given special tax incentives to relocate in Kiaochow, German steamship companies received government subsidies for the China trade, and separate schools for Germans and natives were set up to reveal to the latter the benefits that accrued from colonial rule. Kiaochow rapidly became known as the "Brighton of the Far East," and in fact became the model that German planners hoped at a later date to establish elsewhere, particularly in South America (southern Brazil). But the colonial venture proved to be costly, and instead of "milking" the territories of raw materials, Berlin by 1900 annually poured about $6.5 million in direct — and an equal or greater amount in indirect — subsidies into her overseas territories. None of the latter became the object of German emigration; only one of every one thousand Germans leaving the homeland by 1900 went to the colonies.

The United States, on the other hand, in 1889 did not possess an overseas empire in the traditional sense. However, she arrived on the colonial scene with a vengeance between 1898 and 1904, annexing Hawaii (1898), Guam (1899), Puerto Rico (1899), Tutuila and Pago Pago in Samoa (1900), and the Panama Canal Zone (1904). If one adds to this Cuba in 1901 (by virtue of the Platt Amendment) and the Philippines by 1902, the total American territory either acquired or controlled in these six years amounted to no less than 127,385 square miles. And when compared with the Kaiser's scant gains during the same period (about 15 percent of the republic's additions), it is not difficult to gauge the degree of jealousy, rivalry, and disappointment that permeated the deliberations of German planners through the 1890s and beyond. In fact, German-American relations in the Far East and South America between 1889 and 1905 must be seen in this light in order to appreciate their intensity and importance.

# I

# The Weltpolitik of Wilhelm II and the United States (1889–1906)

ONE

# Competition in the Pacific (1889–1899)

After twenty years, when it [the fleet] is ready, I will adopt a different tone.

— WILHELM II *to Bülow*
*29 October 1899*

GERMAN-AMERICAN RELATIONS HAD BEEN RELATIVELY AMICABLE AND SURprisingly devoid of strife before the 1890s. The American Revolutionary War had found German public opinion, such as could be registered, not on the side of the Hessian mercenaries and their British employers. In 1781 Prussia's Frederick the Great was the first ruler of a major European power to recognize the new republic. But the "age of navalism," as William L. Langer labeled the era commencing with the 1890s, brought Germany and the United States into conflict over colonial territories, trading rights, harbor facilities, and the like, primarily in Samoa, the Philippines, and South America. It is hoped that by our examining these three areas, light may be shed upon German-American relations, and some old myths and shibboleths concerning imperialism — and especially the economic "motive" usually associated with it — revised. Anyone desiring a more embracing treatment of this subject need only consult Alfred Vagts's magnum opus.[1]

The subjects chosen for special analysis will be treated only with regard to their importance, and often their *alleged* importance, in the broad spectrum of German-American relations. In dealing with Germany's attitude toward Samoa, the Philippines, and South America, the important matter is not always so much what occurred, or what Berlin's official policy was, as what others *thought* Berlin was up to and, conversely, what Berlin *thought* others, especially the Americans, were up to. For with the emergence of a mighty daily newspaper business in the western nations, the *vox populi* often tended to drown out the voice of the government, or at least to shape it. Thus in the period we are concerned with, people in Germany who had not the slightest inkling, for example, of what or where Samoa was suddenly found themselves defending its virtues as a German colony — usually at the local beer hall. It was a new factor in international relations and one that only Germany's Iron Chancellor, Prince Otto von Bismarck, was able to ignore. As we shall see, the men who succeeded him were deeply infected with what Thomas Carlyle called "ballot box influenza," aided, abetted, and sometimes directed by the public press.

## Samoa I (1889)

German and American business interests first clashed seriously in the 1880s over the Samoan Islands, "that miserable archipelago," as Sir Thomas Sanderson, permanent undersecretary of the British Foreign Office, put it. Germany (1877 and 1879), the United States (1878), and Great Britain (1880) had all concluded special treaties with Samoan rulers; each nation desired at least coaling stations on one or more of the islands. The Australians, too, were anxious to adopt an independent stance in this region, which they regarded not without reason as being in their backyard. The situation was further compounded by a civil war over the kingship of the islands between the Malietoa and Tupua families, a "Samoan War of the Roses" as the Foreign Office in Berlin termed it.[2] The United States backed the Malietoas in this struggle, while Germany supported the Tupuas. Not surprisingly, the conflict soon progressed to the point where neither country could justify its involvement on the basis of possible gains to be realized.* This was even more tragically brought out on 15 March 1889 when a hurricane demolished numerous warships that had been dispatched to this tropical trouble spot. Of the German vessels *Adler*, *Olga*, and *Eber*, and of the American ships *Trenton*, *Nipsic*, and *Vandalia*, only the *Olga* and the *Nipsic* escaped destruction; the storm drove them onto the beaches and not the coral reefs. A high price indeed for what Henry Adams called "wretched little lava-heaps." Unfortunately, the obvious lesson was lost. The public press in the United States joined House and Senate leaders in demanding a firm American stand on the Samoan issue.

* While Germany had cornered almost 70 percent of the trade in the South Seas, in the case of Samoa this amounted to a mere $600,000 in the year 1885. America's trade with Samoa was a paltry $120,000 that year. Alfred Vagts *Deutschland und die Vereinigten Staaten in der Weltpolitik* (New York 1935), I, 637.

As early as 31 December 1888 the *New York World* had demanded that an American protectorate be proclaimed over the Samoan Islands. The *Chicago Tribune* supported this position on 8 April 1889, while the *New York Herald* (24 January 1889) trumpeted shrilly against OUTRAGES BY GERMAN AUTHORITIES UNREDRESSED, and informed its readers HOW AMERICAN RIGHTS WERE NEEDLESSLY SURRENDERED BY THE STATE DEPARTMENT. Finally, the *San Francisco Examiner* on 8 March 1889 reported on proposed British naval expenditures, lamenting that "if only we had them we could reduce Bismarck's armada to a pile of iron filings."[3]

Both House and Senate were outraged by alleged German affronts in Samoa. In January 1889 the Republican Congress offered President Grover Cleveland (whose term would end on 4 March) a war chest of $500,000 and an additional $100,000 to construct an American port facility at Pago Pago harbor — the "Gibraltar of the Pacific." Moreover, America's naval budget immediately ballooned by over five million dollars annually. Congressman William McAdoo (of New Jersey) solemnly pronounced the Samoan question to be "germane to the naval question"; only "sufficient naval power" could protect the United States against foreign insults. "If the United States were a naval power . . . Bismarck would never have allowed the landing of a single German soldier on the Samoan Islands." Discussions in the Senate were equally passionate. Senator Joseph N. Dolph of Oregon proposed that the Monroe Doctrine be extended to include Hawaii and Samoa. Senator William P. Frye of Maine depicted German involvement in Samoa as "one of the greatest insults against the United States that she was ever subjected to." His colleague from Maine, Senator Eugene C. Hale, was convinced that the German government was behind the Samoan troubles. However, the most inflammatory rhetoric came from Senator John H. Reagan of Texas. While making it painstakingly clear that he in no way was supporting northern "Nigger friends" in their efforts on behalf of the Samoans, Reagan nevertheless asserted that he would not tolerate any insult to American interests abroad. "Sir, there is something worse than the calamities of war; and that is the sacrifice of honor of a great nation, the sacrifices of the rights of citizens, the humiliation of its officers in the face of an arrogant power." It was hardly a unique stand.[4] Cleveland's successor Benjamin Harrison apparently seconded Reagan's oratory. On 18 March 1889 he sent three special envoys to investigate conditions in Samoa with instructions that

. . . in any questions involving present or future relations in the Pacific, this government cannot accept even temporary subordination and must regard it as inconsistent with that international consideration and dignity to which the United States, by continental position and expanding interests must always be entitled.[5]

America was coming of age in the best European tradition.

The German government in Berlin, still firmly in the hands of Bismarck, refused to let the Samoan question be exploited for the sake of increased naval expenditures. On the one hand, Bismarck would not accept insults or pressure from America, while on the other hand he declined to succumb to colonial or naval pressure groups at home. The entire Samoan question smacked to him too much of the "new world" of trade, commerce and industry in which he felt ill at ease. When Ambassador Count Paul von Hatzfeld cabled from London that the United States might join with France and thereby pose a direct threat in Europe, Bismarck casually replied that such a move could be checked effectively by a German–British rapprochement.[6] The Junker chancellor was irritated, but not moved to precipitate action, by a haughty, almost threatening letter on the Samoan tangle from former Senator Carl Schurz on 3 February 1889. In the letter, sent through the German embassy in Washington (Count Emmerich von und zu Arco-Valley), Schurz cautioned Bismarck not to risk war with the United States over Samoa. He specifically warned that not even the destruction by Germany of New York, Philadelphia, and Boston would force the United States to the peace table. Instead, American cruisers would sweep Germany's merchant marine from the seas and the resulting "war of attrition" would end in disaster for Germany in about two years, that is, when America completed construction of a mammoth battle fleet. France, Schurz claimed, would come to the aid of the United States. Bismarck was content to reject this impassioned note with a few realistic observations. He informed Schurz that a Franco-American alliance could result only in an Anglo-German counterpart and that America's war resources were hardly unlimited; he flatly denied that the United States could construct a battle fleet in two years. In an accompanying letter to Count Arco, Bismarck adopted a statesman-like tone. He dismissed the possibility of a German-American war caused by slighted "military sense of honor" as "irresponsible." In addition, he would not hear of naval saber rattling between the two newcomers on the colonial scene. "The commanders of our navy have strict orders to avoid every [possible] conflict with American warships."[7]

Baron Friedrich von Holstein, the secretive, ambitious "gray eminence" of the Foreign Office, was also brought to heel by Bismarck, who reprimanded his aide in September 1888 for telling the American chargé in Berlin that Germany did not care which "Nigger Chief" ruled in Samoa.[8] Holstein, in turn, dutifully informed General Count Alfred Waldersee, chief of the Prussian General Staff, the following year: "A war with America — now — would be horrible."[9] And the old chancellor put Germany's official position on the Samoan question in a nutshell in January 1889 when he confided to the British ambassador, Sir Edward Malet, that Samoa was "not worth the evils which might result from a collision of the armed forces of Germany and the United States." This consideration as well as the chancellor's belief that "we have no *political* interests in Samoa" was largely responsible for the Berlin Samoan Conference, the first international meeting conducted in the English language, which by its Final Act on 14 June 1889 established a tripartite administration over Samoa.[10]

But Bismarck's studied calm and serenity belied the general feeling in Germany. Nationalism, chauvinism, navalism, colonialism, and the like dictated against a peaceful relationship between Germany, Great Britain and the United States. Count Waldersee publicly urged the country to use the American "danger" as a pretext to increase Germany's readiness for war.[11] And German naval leaders quickly seized the opportunity to make themselves heard. So ominous did they consider the events in Samoa that on 23 February 1889 the acting chief of the Admiralty, Vice Admiral Baron Max von der Goltz, requested a memorandum on how a war with the United States could best be waged. Rear Admiral Guido Karcher, chief of staff of the Admiralty, on 13 March replied that Germany could only conduct such a war by "annihilating the enemy's war fleet [and] destroying his merchant fleet." Moreover, Karcher argued that peace could be forced only by "damaging the enemy's land and exerting pressure on the public . . . through [naval] bombardment" of his principal coastal cities. The admiral recognized that the German fleet was still too small effectively to carry out an invasion of the United States, and therefore concluded that the German navy would have to limit itself to cruiser raids against American shipping designed to interrupt maritime trade on the eastern seaboard. He was adamant on this point. "The war will be conducted primarily as a cruiser war."[12]

The British naturally were well aware of the militant anti-American feeling prevalent in some German ruling circles as a result of the Samoan tangle. Prime Minister Lord Salisbury was informed by the Foreign Office on 15 June 1889:

> There has not been a time since 1870–1 in which the soldiers and sailors who surround and flatter the military pride of H.I.M. [Wilhelm II] have had more

influence than now. The Emperor has more than once, in presence of persons whom I know, expressed his impatience at the studied peaceful attitude of the Chancellor [Bismarck].[13]

However, the British Foreign Office was hardly ruffled by the Samoan issue, enveloping its official stance in customary condescension. "It is for Germany and the U.S. to agree and for us to bless them."[14]

For Bismarck the Samoan conference marked his final days in office. They were bitter ones. The German press, from the conservative *Kreuzzeitung* to the liberal *Vossische Zeitung*, denounced the final treaty as the "work of the departing Bismarck dynasty." The *Berliner Tageblatt* went so far as to compare the document with Prussia's diplomatic humiliation by Austria in the question of German leadership at Olmütz in 1850.[15] It was all too much for the country squire Bismarck. What did the palm trees of Samoa mean to him in his beloved Saxon forest? He was unable to generate any enthusiasm for the bustling activity in Hamburg's harbor whenever he made the short trip there from his nearby retreat in Friedrichsruh. And of course it was the merchants of Hamburg who were most active in the Samoan trade. As a final gesture of contempt, Bismarck supported his erstwhile enemy, the Progressive Party, to block proposed government subsidies for the Samoan Steamship Line. On 20 March 1890 Kaiser Wilhelm II dropped his famous "pilot." A new era dawned for Germany. Her future was now proclaimed to "lie with the seas." She would seek her rightful "place in the sun." She would become a truly *world* power (*Weltmacht*). And with regard to German-American relations, Bismarck's cautioning hand was gone. The road was now open for a more energetic policy of confrontation.

## The American "Danger'

Years later, in retirement in Doorn, Holland, Wilhelm II claimed that as early as 1897 Great Britain and the United States had concluded a secret "gentlemen's agreement" designed to keep Germany strictly a European continental power and away from the major trade markets of the world.[16] In fact, the Kaiser was convinced by the turn of the century that especially in the field of economic competition the United States posed the greatest threat to Germany. Alfred Vagts concluded after a meticulous investigation of this topic that there never existed serious German–American economic rivalry for third markets — indeed, on the contrary, that there was a great deal of mutual cooperation especially on these third markets — and that much of the hullabaloo stemmed from imaginary fears and emotional illusions. Vagts noted that the German stock market was hypersensitive "to the appearance of even a phantom."[17] It is, of course, beyond the scope of this study to analyze the alleged American "danger" to Germany in the field of economic competition. Suffice it to say that whatever the validity of the charges of economic warfare that were hurled across the Atlantic, the issue aroused animosities and heated sentiments on both sides. Of special interest for our purpose is Vagts's observation that the basically feudal mentality of German diplomats, steeped in antiquated mercantilist philosophy, equated any economic or financial depression at home with a corresponding loss of power on the international scene. Thus, by the turn of the century the booming American economy had to entail a commensurate increase in that nation's diplomatic and military status. Conversely, since the German economy was experiencing a temporary period of recession, her value on the international scene was falling and she would have to adopt drastic measures to halt the downward trend. In other words, importance was attached to economic issues not for their own merits in terms of profits and balance of trade but because they were considered indicators of a nation's power and international status.

This realization helps put into perspective the Kaiser's veritable obsession with the "danger" that the American economy posed to Europe. The specter of American economic domination caused Wilhelm to turn repeatedly to his fellow European rulers for support. Specifically, he sought to create a pan-European economic bloc under German leadership directed against the United States — with or without Great Britain — modeled upon Napoleon Bonaparte's Continental System (against England) of 1806.

The German emperor gave what was perhaps the clearest expression of his obsession with the American "danger" during a meeting with his cousin Czar Nicholas II of Russia in September 1896 in Görlitz, Silesia. On 7 September, two days before the monarchs met, Germany's foreign secretary, Baron Adolf Marschall von Bieberstein, exchanged notes on the subject with a special envoy of the Russian Foreign Office (Chichkine) during a preparatory meeting in Breslau. Marschall announced that both Chile and Uruguay had canceled their trade agreements with Europe. As President, William McKinley would further cajole them into signing reciprocity trade treaties providing American business interests with a virtual trade monopoly in these countries. "Europe at this time looks on helplessly because it is divided." Marschall suggested that the Continent should unite "to fend off the common danger." A first step along this line would be higher tariffs against American grains, a measure designed to appeal to the Russians. Some might denounce such a European union as "phantasy," but Marschall preferred to view it as "futuristic politics" that eventually would be forced upon Europe by dire necessity later, if not by voluntary agreement now. The Russians, according to the German reports, agreed "with every word." When the two emperors met on 9 September, the road was clear for quick agreement: "Union of Europe in a common protective tariff league for the struggle against McKinley and America — be it with or without England." Nicholas II agreed to present the case to his French ally and to call on France to bury past grievances (Alsace-Lorraine was still in German hands) in order to "defend the European continent hand-in-hand with the German Emperor." Wilhelm was ecstatic. "The French will look pretty silly."[18]

Chancellor Prince Chlodwig von Hohenlohe-Schillingsfürst was not overly fond of the notion of a "tariff league," preferring instead "a sort of Continental Blockade." But the German ambassador in Vienna, Count Philipp zu Eulenburg, reported on 14 September 1896 that Count Agenor Goluchowski, Austria-Hungary's foreign minister, "enthusiastically endorsed the idea of a European union directed against America."[19] Still better tidings came from Nicholas II, who informed his royal cousin on 20 October that he had discussed the matter with the French and that the idea had found favor especially with Minister President Jules Méline. Russia, Germany, and France agreed to exchange notes on the issue.[20] Three days later the German ambassador in Paris, Count Herbert Münster, wired that leading circles in the French capital were generally agreed that American money was already having an adverse effect on Europe.[21]

The matter lay dormant until the following spring. In February 1897 Marschall discovered that Count Michael Muraviev, Russia's new foreign minister, agreed with him that Europe was being threatened primarily by "growing British and American cooperation." While the Russian did not see the necessity for immediate countermeasures, he nonetheless agreed that "the increasingly brutal actions of the United States would one day force Europe to unite." But without Great Britain.[22]

By this time Wilhelm II had worked himself into a veritable fit. The cancellation of the trade agreements with South America he equated to "the beginning of a war to the death" between Germany and the United States. Specifically, he predicted that the German people would now finally realize their folly in having accepted over the past decade the socialists' parliamentary opposition to naval increases. A strong fleet now, the Kaiser counseled, would have prevented the South American action. Wilhelm admonished the Foreign Office, and especially its new

head, Bernhard von Bülow,* to spare no effort on behalf of a vigorous naval construction program.[23]

On 11 August 1897 Wilhelm and Nicholas again took up the issue of a European tariff league against the United States, this time in St. Petersburg. The czar demanded a "confidential memorandum" on how best to counter the American economic "threat," "with, possibly without, and even against, England." Count Muraviev again stressed that it was absolutely imperative that Europe prevent "a trade agreement between England and the United States."[24] These words already contained the germs of what German leaders throughout the twentieth century would refer to as the "Anglo-Saxon capitalist conspiracy."

A practical example of how the proposed continental league might function against the United States cropped up in the Cuban crisis of September 1897.† Wilhelm at once argued that Cuba was a "European state" by virtue of having belonged to Spain "for centuries." Thus, the United States seemed determined to rob Europe of part of its territory "by fair means or by foul — seemingly the latter." "Yankee money" and "Yankee audacity secretly supported by John Bull" threatened Spain. Cuba was about to be absorbed by what Wilhelm termed the "Anglo-American Limited Company for International Theft and War Incitement." He called upon continental Europe to rally to Spain's defense, to keep Cuba out of the clutches of Great Britain and the United States, and especially for European monarchs not to succumb to "the snobbism of republican money." Moreover, and most importantly, a common front now "would enhance and solidify the Continental Union that the Tsar and I have planned against America." Fortunately Foreign Secretary von Bülow, normally a vain and arrogant operator, finally managed to persuade Wilhelm to leave the initiative to other European states, preferably Catholic Austria and France.[25] It is fair to state that the Kaiser's proposed treatment of the Cuban question smacked less of the envisaged continental tariff league and more of the Congress of Vienna's Holy Alliance, that "international fire brigade" as Heinrich von Treitschke so aptly described it.

* Bülow's star rose meteorically: he was foreign secretary 1897–1900 and chancellor 1900–1909; in June 1899 he was made a count and in June 1905 a prince.

† A civil war in Cuba over constitutional liberties had since 1895 reduced the population by 400,000 and destroyed much of its wealth. Spain, on the other hand, deployed over 200,000 troops to crush the rebellion and used the severest measures: civilian detention camps, barbed wire enclosures, and lines of blockhouses across the narrowest part of the island. While the struggle brought Spain almost to economic collapse, it more importantly outraged American public opinion. President McKinley, though opposing recognition of the insurgents, in the fall of 1897 raised the possibility of American intervention.

The Kaiser's position was vociferously supported by the German ambassador in Washington, the crotchety Theodor von Holleben. In lengthy annual reports on German-American relations he constantly drew attention to the current economic competition for world markets, viewing this contest primarily in terms of international power politics. A sample report will suffice to convey Holleben's attitude. On New Year's Day 1898 he submitted a résumé that can be regarded as fairly typical. The ambassador was certain that economic rivalry with Germany was the dominant issue in the United States, regardless of whether the Democrats or the Republicans were in office. "Thus the future is not a happy one for Germany." Holleben discerned that of late the economic competition had reached an almost unbearable stage. He concluded from an examination of newspapers and public opinion that Germany was regarded by most Americans as "the most hated land." In fact, it was the press that had transformed economic factors into political terms. "They believe us capable of anything, especially the worst." Since this sentiment rested upon Germany's ability to compete successfully with the United States in the markets of the world, there could be no easing of tensions. The Kaiser noted "Correct" on the document. Holleben earnestly advised Berlin not to rely upon German-Americans to improve this image; they were rapidly becoming Americanized and their sympathy for their native land was limited to singing the German national anthem. Above all, the envoy counseled that America understood only strength. Germany must never back down in the face of "American braggadocio." Wilhelm again agreed and not surprisingly concluded that the United States would only respect Germany when the latter possessed a mighty battle fleet.[26]

Holleben was at other times even more specific — as well as more pessimistic — in his prognosis of German-American relations. In 1900 he reported that members of the American armed forces were convinced that the two nations would eventually go to war. He informed Berlin that Germany could not avoid a confrontation with the United States if it wanted to be a world power; his special concern was that the United States had become the world's leading producer of gold and that her balance of trade amounted to a huge $649,000,000 profit. The ambassador chastised those at home who still did not believe that a German-American economic struggle was inevitable. The only possible antidote to American industrial and financial expansion lay in an alliance with Great Britain "while it is still possible to face America jointly."[27] It shall be seen later that Adolf Hitler developed similar convictions — though obviously for different reasons.

These twin notions of a "pan-European" tariff league against the United States and of an Anglo-Saxon "conspiracy" against Germany died only slowly. In retrospect, one can say that the Spanish-American War in 1898 and the resulting failure of Europe to unite against "Onkel Sam" proved to be the high-water mark of this idea.[28]

But the old convictions never totally disappeared. In March 1900 Holleben again warned of the alleged Anglo-Saxon "alliance," and the Kaiser noted: "Coming events cast their shadows before!"[29] Prince Hugo von Radolin cabled from St. Petersburg in July 1900 that a "very high ranking Russian official" (probably the finance minister, Count Sergei Witte) had again approached him concerning a Russian-German-French league against Great Britain and the United States. Money thus saved on land troops could be poured into fleets designed to keep the Anglo-Saxon maritime powers at bay.[30] In January 1901 Holleben once more called for an "economic defensive stance against the United States"— including Great Britain.[31] Two months later Germany's naval attaché in London, Lieutenant Commander Carl Coerper, warned that the Americans (J. Pierpont Morgan) were purchasing the British Leyland Line in order to gain a monopoly over passenger travel in the Atlantic. The Kaiser was not surprised. "Only a union of all Continental [steamship] lines, including the English, can counteract this."[32] In June Holleben relayed rumors that the United States might seize the Azores; Europe must react and establish an "anti-Monroe Doctrine."[33] That same month a German official in South America, Wilhelm Staudt, warned Chancellor Hohenlohe "that the United States are our greatest enemy." Staudt pointed out that the United States would not be content with cornering markets in Asia and Latin America; Europe itself would fall to American industrial and financial expansion unless a "European tariff league" was formed. In almost contemporary terms, Staudt cautioned that Russia was Germany's political, the United States her economic, enemy. It was the duty of her statesmen to keep these two future giants at a distance.[34] The main obstacle to the tariff league, as the Foreign Office in Berlin lamented in August 1901, was the refusal of the British to participate.[35]

As late as 1903 Wilhelm II approached the French with yet another suggestion to renew Napoleon's Continental System.[36] The following year he continued to warn against the "approaching American economic hegemony," and in 1906 he finally convinced Count Witte of the growing American "danger."[37] And in 1907 the Kaiser made one final plea to Eugène Etienne, one of the leaders of the Colonial Party in France, at the Kiel naval review, pressing him with the need for a Franco-German alliance against "the great common perils, the Japanese and the Americans."[38] Was Wilhelm really serious?* The American senator Chauncey Depew returned from a trip to Europe convinced that the United States

* Certainly Japan's crushing victories over Russia's fleets in the Far East in 1904–1905 prompted Wilhelm to raise the specter of the "yellow peril."

was widely regarded as the "white terror" and that she must at all times be prepared for war with a European power. The Kaiser fully agreed. "Right and properly seen." And the notion never quite died. Wilhelm saw himself as late as 1912 as the "leader of the policies of the United States of Europe." He informed Walther Rathenau, head of Germany's largest electrical firm (AEG) and destined to become economic czar during the First World War, that he planned in 1912 to create "the United States of Europe against America." Germany, Austria-Hungary, France, Great Britain, and Italy would have to forget past grievances in order to face the economic and military challenge of the two new powers, the United States and Japan.[39]

In the final analysis, one should not overestimate this notion of economic rivalry and talk of a "pan-European" tariff league. It reflected mainly the mood of European stock markets in a period of temporary decline as against an upswing in the United States. Moreover, countless intra-European rivalries and conflicting ambitions militated against such common action against a non-European foe. Baron von Holstein realized from the start that the issue of Alsace-Lorraine stood between Germany and France, and Bülow noted that the Russians could not agree with Germany to close the Baltic Sea in the event of war with the Anglo-Saxon maritime powers.[40] They might have added, too, that Germany was undermining the proposal by challenging the Russians in China and in the Balkans, the French in North Africa, and the British in the Middle East. In short, economic factors simply were not powerful enough to determine a nation's course — even in this golden age of imperialism. Other factors dominated everywhere: prestige, national pride, military strategy, social Darwinism, survival of the fittest arguments, expansion, international power politics, and the like.[41] Perhaps the most relevant meaning of the economic "danger" thesis lies in the fact that it was so readily translated into political terms. It created an atmosphere of rivalry and suspicion which turned poisonous in 1898 when the United States and Spain clashed over Cuba and the Philippines — the latter a region in which German trade did not even amount to one million dollars annually, and with a capital, Manila, that housed a mere eighty-five German nationals.

## Spain's Heirs Fall Out (1898)

In September 1897 Assistant Secretary of the Navy Theodore Roosevelt informed Secretary of the Navy John D. Long that Germany and Japan were rapidly becoming the main antagonists of the United States. According to Roosevelt, the United States should strive to create what another Roosevelt was to call a "two-ocean navy"— that is, a fleet sufficient to dominate Japan in the Pacific without opening the door to a German assault in the Atlantic. The energetic young undersecretary reminded his chief that in 1894 the then Captain Alfred Tirpitz had singled out the United States as Germany's potential rival in his Service Memo No. IX, Germany's naval Magna Carta.[42] Captain A. S. Crowninshield, chief of the Bureau of Navigation, went a step further. He cautioned Secretary Long that Germany's seizure of Kiaochow in China in November 1897 was sufficient evidence of her hostility toward the United States, that this move foreshadowed future German advances into the Western Hemisphere.[43] German acquisition of the Carolines and the Marianas in October 1899, and of most of the Samoan Islands in March 1900, could only strengthen such suspicions and fears.

Teddy Roosevelt's belief that Germany planned to seize territory somewhere in the Western Hemisphere became almost an obsession, "a veritable nightmare," with him. "He was absolutely convinced that the Kaiser would one day start trouble somewhere in this hemisphere."[44] Although he obviously could not know it, there was some justification to Roosevelt's "obsession." For in Berlin statesmen and naval men alike anxiously awaited the death knell of the Spanish colonial empire. As early as January 1897, in his capacity as chief of the German Cruiser Squadron in East Asia, Tirpitz had wired Berlin that Spain could not hold the Philippines much longer and that Germany's naval planners would do well to study the geography and military potential of the islands. This was the recommendation of a most ambitious naval officer, of a man who had only recently scoured the Chinese coast for a suitable German naval base and who was destined within the year to become the "father" of the Imperial German Navy. The Kaiser seconded this stance two months later. "I am determined, when the opportunity arises, to purchase or simply to take the Philippines from Spain — when her 'liquidation' approaches."[45] The fact of the matter is that Wilhelm II was becoming increasingly apprehensive regarding American naval and colonial aspirations. When the United States ambassador in Berlin, Andrew D. White, congratulated Foreign Secretary von Bülow in December 1897 on the latter's speech to the Reichstag supporting German naval expansion, adding his hope for "sympathy and cooperation" between the two nations, the Kaiser curtly remarked: "Ahem! if we are *strong* and therefore worthy of being cooperated with!"[46] And when news reached Wilhelm on 2 March 1897 that American warships were heading for Manila, he immediately informed the Spanish ruler of this development. "Those

Yankee scoundrels want war!" Worse yet, three days later Ambassador von Holleben wired from Washington that the United States planned to seize the Philippines as a bargaining counter to use at the peace table. Wilhelm was outraged. "The Yankees cannot do that! Because one day we will require Manila."[47] And for once "grandmama" agreed; Queen Victoria condemned the American action against Spain with equal fervor. "It is monstrous of America."[48]

The Kaiser was initially inclined to accept a Spanish invitation to Germany to dispatch warships to Manila as a symbol of protest against the United States. But cooler heads prevailed and he soon realized that his pet project of an anti-American continental bloc was doomed to failure because Great Britain would never join. "Perfidious Albion," the Kaiser complained, would strive to maintain her independent status "between the Continent and America or Asia."[49] In fact, such wishful grand strategy soon gave way to more sober analysis, primarily from the clever, entrepreneurial Tirpitz.

On 16 March 1898 Foreign Secretary von Bülow asked Rear Admiral Tirpitz what possible benefits Germany might derive from an American-Spanish conflagration. Tirpitz flatly announced his regret that "*the Spanish-American conflict came politically too early for him*"; that is, before Germany had developed sufficient naval power "to play a decisive role." Nonetheless, Tirpitz urged that German warships be sent to the Philippines to represent her interests in that region.* The admiral assured Bülow that naval officers had made a careful study of American "chauvinism"; there was no doubt that the United States would annex Cuba. Tirpitz urged action upon Bülow. "With this comes the *last opportunity* for us to purchase Curaçao and St. Thomas." Failure to take advantage of the present international constellation, to act before the Panama Canal was completed, could only mean the loss of South America as a market for Germany's industrial production. This consideration was especially crucial because Tirpitz was convinced that Germany could not retain a major share of the North American market much longer. Nor was the Caribbean the only area to be exploited. Tirpitz recommended that the Reich complement its Kiaochow colony with a "settlement" on the Yangtze River, preferably at Woosung or Canton. If the government provided protection, German merchants could trade with impunity up and down the Yangtze River.[50] Such was the new *Realpolitik* of Bismarck's successors.

* Admiral von Tirpitz claimed, in his *Erinnerungen* (Leipzig 1920, p. 141), that he was not informed of the decision to send the warships to Manila, that the matter took him by surprise.

In the coming days Rear Admiral Tirpitz flooded the German government with advice. He informed Wilhelm II through Bülow that although the Spanish fleet was slightly superior to that of the United States, in the long run America would prevail over Spain because of her larger population and greater financial power. This, in turn, would lead to more active and direct American political and economic involvement in Europe. The American "danger" was obviously alive and kicking. On 24 April Tirpitz reminded the Kaiser that it was not enough merely to defend German fisheries and coastal trade. Instead, the admiral viewed it as his historic mission to increase Germany's colonial holdings, particularly "to create a chain of overseas maritime naval bases." He reminded the Supreme War Lord of the special task that the latter had set for him: "to link the fatherland with the Greater Germany"— those Germans domiciled beyond the Reich's territorial boundaries.[51] This notion, as shall be seen later, was not unique either to Tirpitz or to the Wilhelmian period.

German naval planning was also given concrete form and a sense of reality. On 10 April 1898 the Reichstag passed the First Navy Law calling for the construction of nineteen battleships, eight armored cruisers, twelve large and thirty light cruisers by 1 April 1904 at a cost of 409 million marks. The heavy ships were to be automatically replaced after twenty-five years of service. The Kaiser rather prematurely began to sign his correspondence with the czar as "Admiral of the Atlantic."

Tirpitz found himself in agreement with Admiral Eduard von Knorr, the navy's commanding admiral. On 20 April 1898 Knorr sent the Kaiser a lengthy memorandum discussing the possibility of overseas territorial aggrandizement as a result of the Spanish-American War. The naval officer felt that the time was ripe for Germany to seize a naval base in the West Indies. The United States was tied down in the Far East and, provided that she was allowed to retain Cuba, would acquiesce in such a German move. Knorr stated that it was absolutely essential "for now and especially for the future" that the Reich obtain "a number of naval bases in all the seas." He then reiterated a standard argument. The world was almost "wholly divided among the major powers"; there was no virgin territory to be claimed. Thus it was "essential" that Germany "seize" suitable naval *Stützpunkte* (bases) at any opportunity. Specifically, Knorr pressed for future bases in the West Indies, possibly one of the Dutch (Curaçao, Aruba, Buen Ayre) or Danish islands (St. Thomas, Ste. Croix, St. John). He reminded Wilhelm II that no less an authority than Captain Alfred Thayer Mahan had recently pointed out that a naval base in the West Indies would dominate the growing trade in the Gulf of Mexico as well as the Panama Canal — when constructed.[52]

But it proved difficult to pinpoint exactly where Germany might acquire territory. Early in May 1898 the matter was taken up during an audience with the Kaiser. The Admiralty again mentioned Curaçao and St. Thomas as suitable *Stützpunkte* and repeated its peacetime as well as wartime need for a chain of naval stations girdling the globe. "We lack a secure base almost everywhere in the world." Yet it warned against depending on opportunities provided by wars between foreign powers. Spur of the moment decisions would lead nowhere; only "systematic planning" could bring results. Thus the Admiralty decided to investigate the question in all earnest with the Foreign Office as well as with the Naval Office. It identified as possible objectives the entire Samoan group, the Carolines, part of the Philippines (Mindanao), and Fernando Po on the west coast of Africa.[53]

But the horizon soon darkened. Commodore George Dewey scored a quick and complete triumph over the Spanish fleet off Cavite on 1 May 1898. In Berlin, Bülow received the bleak tidings that Great Britain and the United States might divide the Philippines between them. Events would pass Germany by. Bülow hastily cabled London to inform Lord Salisbury that Germany was firmly resolved not to be left out of the Spanish "liquidation"—there "should be no doubt that the German government expects . . . not to go empty-handed at any new division of the globe."[54]

Events in the Philippines came to Bülow's rescue. A native rebellion compounded and prolonged the Spanish-American War and thereby delayed any decisions regarding the future of the islands. The German consul in Manila, Friedrich Krüger, now saw his chance. On 12 May he enthusiastically recommended that Berlin select a German prince to head a Philippine monarchy and reported that the natives apparently favored this development. But Krüger's entrepreneurial fervor in the field of diplomacy was not shared by Bülow. The latter not only rejected the notion of a German prince as king of the Philippines, but further refused to listen to similar and related projects, such as a German protectorate over the islands. While he preferred "division" of the islands among the chief interested powers, Bülow thought a neutrality agreement such as the major European powers had extended to Belgium in 1839 most readily attainable. Hasty unilateral action by Germany would only drive the Americans into the waiting arms of the British. Above all, Germany lacked sufficient naval power to back her claims. The advantage of the neutrality proposal lay in the fact that it would postpone a "final decision" over the Philippines until a later date, when Germany possessed the sea power necessary to enforce her demands. The Kaiser agreed. He proved most unreceptive to the idea that a fellow German prince might gain a crown in the Pacific.[55] He decided on 18 May 1898 to send Vice Admiral Otto von Diederichs, commander of the cruiser squadron in East Asia, from Kiaochow to Manila in order to gain firsthand knowledge of the situation.[56] However, final sailing orders did not reach Diederichs until 2 June.

The Kaiser's prevailing mood was one of frustration and bitterness. He saw — or professed to see — new evidence of the alleged Anglo-Saxon "gentlemen's agreement" all around him. In Hong Kong the British Eastern Telegraph Company forsook neutrality and allowed Dewey to communicate with Washington at will. American ships were permitted to use British bases and take on coal, while a second Spanish fleet, en route to Manila, encountered numerous British obstacles, especially at Suez. Captain Edward Chichester, the British commander at Manila, proved most accommodating to Dewey.[57] It was too much for Wilhelm II to bear. By 20 May he could no longer contain his anger and frustration: "The naval increases [of 1898] came too late. We are now incredibly weak at sea. In one year we will be stronger, in three significantly stronger. I hope that we will have peace until 1901 so that we can then put forth demands and seize the initiative."[58]

The American victory over the Spanish fleet in Manila and the subsequent blockade of that city attracted a host of foreign spectators. Great Britain, Russia, Germany, and France sent warships to the Philippines; only Japan refrained from such action. The German presence was most keenly felt by Dewey. Between 12 and 20 June 1898 Vice Admiral von Diederichs assembled a force greater than that of the blockading Americans: the cruisers *Kaiserin Augusta*, *Kaiser*, *Prinzess Wilhelm*, *Irene*, and *Cormoran*.[59] Ambassador von Holleben soon reported from Washington that the American press was extremely annoyed with the overpowering German contingent in Manila. This, in turn, further irritated Wilhelm. "No one has ever before bothered about this! And it is totally immaterial to me!"[60] The tragic fact of the matter is that no one in Berlin grasped the danger inherent in the Dewey-Diederichs confrontation in Manila Bay. The summer vacation season had left the German capital almost totally devoid of responsible senior officials and naval authorities: Bülow was enjoying the Austrian alpine air at Semmering, Tirpitz was at St. Blasien in his beloved Black Forest, and Wilhelm was on board the royal yacht *Hohenzollern* on his customary annual northern cruise. Moreover, the Foreign Office was not even notified — much less asked — about Diederichs's actions in the Far East. It was, as Wilhelm curtly put it, "a naval matter."[61]

On 1 July 1898 Admiral von Knorr drafted a second lengthy review of the international situation in general, and German naval policy in particular. The Spanish-American War, according to this officer, had made the question concerning German naval stations in East Asia most acute. Now was the time to acquire new territory. The admiral recommended as such particularly Mindanao — except for Luzon the largest island in the Philippines — along with the Sulu Archipelago and Palawan. These lands would supplement Germany's present possessions in New Guinea and Oceania.[62] That very day Bülow cabled ominously to Holleben in Washington: "His Majesty the Kaiser considers it the primary task of the German government not to leave unexplored any possible opportunity resulting from the Spanish-American conflict to acquire naval bases in East Asia."[63] The mounting inability of the United States to solve its problems with both Spain and the Philippine rebels encouraged Germany to press her claims in the Far East.

The Germanophile American ambassador in Berlin, Andrew White, attempted to calm troubled waters with a Fourth of July speech in Dresden calling for continued German-American friendship and peaceful competition. But to no avail. The Prussian envoy at the Dresden court, Count Carl Dönhoff, informed Chancellor Hohenlohe that he regarded America's recent triumph over a European power (Spain) as a first step toward American interference in European affairs. The Kaiser hardly needed this new confirmation of old suspicions. His response was: "Right! Therefore quickly a strong fleet. Then the rest will fall into place!"[64]

What fell into place instead was the single most destructive event in German-American relations prior to the First World War. In mid-July 1898 Admirals Dewey and Diederichs nearly came to blows in Manila Bay. Almost overnight newspapers around the world flashed headlines announcing a German-American war in the near future. The Manila "incident" somehow never died. After the First World War it was rekindled by Baron Hermann von Eckardstein's memoirs. Eckardstein, an official of the German embassy in London in 1898, claimed that Count Herbert Münster had confided to him in April 1898 that the "adventurous" policy in the Pacific of German naval and colonial fanatics had "brought a German-American war within a hair" of reality. Eckardstein further stated that only "pure chance" had prevented a German-American war in the wake of the Dewey-Diederichs confrontation in the Philippines and that the Samoan question in 1899 once more brought Germany to the brink of war with the United States. In fact, the baron asserted that in 1911 a high-ranking American naval officer had shown him a telegram from President McKinley to "US Admiral Caribbean" that reportedly read: "Don't risk a single ship, war with Germany imminent."[65] Although Eckardstein's account has largely been discredited, it remains necessary to take a brief glance at the events in Manila in

July 1898 which, though in retrospect they seem trivial, poisoned German-American relations.

The basic problem at Manila seems to have been a clash of personalities between Dewey and Diederichs, enhanced by mutual mistrust. The German admiral later acknowledged that the concentration of such a large German flotilla had been a diplomatic blunder, and Captain Chichester later suggested that the Americans had regarded German actions in the Philippines as bluff.[66] Whatever the case, relatively petty incidents involving international blockade regulations, especially the *droit de visite* (inspection rights), soon cropped up. One German vessel failed to display her colors until an American gunboat fired a shot across her bow; another German warship failed to heave to while approaching Dewey's squadron by night until likewise threatened; and Dewey especially disliked German ship movements at night, which forced him to train spotlights on them and thereby reveal to the Spanish his own positions. Diederichs accepted Dewey's dominant position as commander of the blockade, but he firmly rejected any *droit de visite*. On 10 July the German commander sent his flag lieutenant, Paul von Hintze, to Dewey's flagship *Olympia* to protest the boarding of the cruiser *Irene* by an officer of the American revenue cutter *McCulloch*. It was during this meeting that Dewey lost his temper. According to German naval records, the American admiral insisted upon his right to board any vessel, military or merchant, and "to make the inquiries necessary to establish [her] identity." At this point, following a detailed discussion of specific points in dispute, Dewey apparently grew angry:

> Why, I shall stop each vessel whatever may be her colors! And if she does not stop, I shall fire at her! And that means war, do you know, Sir? And I tell you, if Germany wants war, all right, we are ready. With the English I have not the slightest difficulty, they always communicate with me.

Diederichs reported that Hintze excused himself as soon as Dewey uttered the words "If Germany wants war." The German admiral claimed that he paid no attention to Dewey's outburst and simply attributed it to "American lack of manners."[67]

Vice Admiral von Diederichs poured out his bitterness over the events in the Philippines in several communications to the Admiralty. The most acid of these, dated 28 August 1898, sarcastically claimed that American troops went into battle wearing their toothbrushes as hat decorations, and that it would be "a long, long time" before the American republic would constitute "a respectable" military power. "It appears, therefore, that right now neither the officers nor the men of the American army seem to be equal to European opponents. It will require many years of training before the mercenaries and the generals will have been transformed into useful soldiers and military commanders. For the present, a European army deployed ruthlessly according to our traditions would be certain of victory against the hesitating, groping tactics of the Americans."[68]

Diplomatic discussions in Berlin paralleled the unpleasant proceedings in the Far East. The German Foreign Office initially hoped to pressure Ambassador White into urging his government to make concessions to Germany with regard to naval bases in the Philippines. Baron Oswald von Richthofen, acting head of the Foreign Office, presented White with a sweeping appraisal of events on 10 July 1898. "The historical development of the world in the coming century hinges to a large degree upon the regulation of German-American affairs." According to Richthofen, the United States was at the crossroads: she must choose between Germany and Great Britain. Rapprochement with the latter would result in the creation of a union of continental states against the "Anglo-American alliance." On the other hand, amicable relations with Germany could be had for a slight fee: Samoa, the Carolines, the Sulu islands, and parts of the Philippines.[69] Two days later White inquired just exactly what Richthofen had in mind when he used the terms "coaling stations" and "naval stations." The aristocrat replied that he meant "naval stations with sufficient hinterland." Specifics began to emerge. "I see the matter much like Kiaochow. The requisite hinterland for each station in the Philippines means the entire island."[70]

But Baron von Holstein was less assertive. On 25 July 1898 he drafted a worried letter to Bülow. A recent emotional outburst by the Kaiser against Lord Salisbury convinced Holstein that still more naval expenditures were planned for the immediate future, and this could only mean parliamentary discussion of the Manila episode. Holstein was apprehensive. The Foreign Office did not possess a clear conscience. "We," meaning Consul Krüger in Manila, Admiral von Diederichs, the Foreign Office in Berlin, and the Kaiser, were "courting the insurgents" in the Philippines "with the hope of thereby getting something positive"—a naval station—"out of the entire affair." He wished that the German flotilla in Manila would "evaporate," but realized that Wilhelm II would never entertain such a notion. He surmised that the Americans suspected, "and probably not without justification," that the German warships in the Philippines were there "to seduce the Filipinos into believing that other Gods besides the Americans could be had." But Holstein could see no easy solution. He shared the popular belief that the Americans recognized only strength in the shape of battleships and that any German retreat in Manila would produce "far-reaching detrimental consequences."[71] In short, not even Holstein's fertile brain could produce a blueprint either for gaining German naval stations or for easing tensions with the United States. Failure to adopt one course or the other could only deepen American suspicions of German duplicity over the Philippines.

The American naval attaché in Berlin, Commander Francis Barber, was clearly alarmed over the situation in that capital. He informed his government on 12 July of Germany's ambitions in the Far East. "I advise immediately doubling Dewey's squadron." Only force, he argued, impressed the German emperor, who regarded the Monroe Doctrine as "gall and wormwood."[72] Such sentiments were grist for the mill for American naval enthusiasts. In Manila the United States had found a convenient *causa sine qua non;* naval appropriations could be obtained almost at will whenever the specter of Germany's "threat" to the Western Hemisphere was raised. Roosevelt perhaps put it best: "As an American I advocate keeping our Navy at a pitch that will enable us to interfere promptly if Germany ventures to touch a foot of American soil."[73] The captain of the American warship *Kearsarge* expressed his desire to face Germany before that country had completed her fleet program, and Secretary of War Elihu Root warned of the German "menace."[74] The worst sort of public display was reserved for Captain John B. Coghlan, commander of the *Raleigh* at Manila, upon his return to the United States in April 1899. This officer publicly revealed Dewey's altercation with Hintze, specifically mentioning that Dewey had told the Germans that he would never back down at the sight of their flag "which one could buy in every State for half-a-dollar." During a banquet in New York's posh Union League Club, Coghlan climaxed his boorish behavior with a satirical rendition of the German national anthem. Although official apologies soon came from Secretary of the Navy John Long (6 April), Secretary of State John Hay (24 April), and President McKinley (26 April), the issue rankled among many Germans. The naval envoy in Washington, Lieutenant Hubert von Rebeur-Paschwitz, called Coghlan's actions an affront to the German naval officer corps. And Wilhelm II was not about to maintain silence. "*Il y a des canailles même en Amerike* [*sic*]!" (That is your American riffraff!)[75]

The American press naturally adopted a violently anti-German stance. On 18 September 1898 the *Morning Oregonian* described Germany as "our bitter, relentless, uncompromising enemy." The *Chicago Daily Tribune* on 5 October ran the headline: MAY HAVE WAR WITH

GERMANY. CONFLICT WITH UNITED STATES IS THOUGHT IN BERLIN OFFICIAL CIRCLES TO BE NEAR. On 25 November the *Washington Post* declared: "We know . . . that in the German Government the United States has a sleepless and insatiable enemy." In fact, throughout much of the following year American newspapers such as the *New York Herald* specialized in keeping the likelihood of a German-American war in the public eye. Most of these reports made their way to Berlin.[76] McKinley's decision to annex Hawaii, Guam, Wake Island, Cuba, and Puerto Rico, and to accept the Philippines "as a gift from the gods" in order to "uplift and civilize and Christianize" it, spurred the Kaiser on in his frenzied efforts on behalf of a mighty battle fleet.[77]

Wilhelm II was most resentful that no diplomatic pressure could be brought to bear against the republic that challenged German colonial and economic expansion. In July 1898 he grumbled that the Americans would quickly have discovered limits upon their freedom of action if Germany had possessed a powerful fleet. "Once our navy has passed through the danger period perhaps the moment will come for the final reckoning with the USA."[78] But for the time being he could only hurl invectives across the Atlantic. "The egoism of the Americans is limited only by their vanity."[79] The Kaiser pronounced the United States a land fit only for Social Democrats, and he regarded the energetic Theodore Roosevelt as Germany's most dangerous potential foe. "The future military dictator! Europe beware?!!"[80] Only battleships would help against the United States. When the *Scientific American* warned its readers that the United States Navy would soon be outstripped by its German counterpart, Wilhelm noted with egotistical relish: "I fervently hope so."[81] Fault for the present lack of requisite sea power naturally lay with "those dumb, asinine Reichstag delegates."[82]

But the tide would change. On 29 October 1899 the Kaiser told Bülow that there would be no repeat of Germany's present misery once the fleet was built. "After twenty years, when it is ready, I will adopt a different tone." His present impotence vis-à-vis the United States, Wilhelm told Bülow, very much reminded him of the time when his father was interrupted by the Duke of Hesse while on the toilet at the train station in Cologne and could only reply: "Never finished!" (*Pas encore fertig!*)[83] And no one could transform serious diplomatic difficulties into petty personal issues as neatly as Wilhelm II. When Sir Thomas Lipton asked in August 1899 if he could borrow skipper Ben Parker and the crew of the Imperial Yacht *Meteor* to compete against the *Columbia* in the America's Cup race, the Kaiser immediately replied that he could not afford rivalry with America "even in the field of sports" because it would cause new "bad blood" between the two nations. Moreover, Wilhelm's suspicious mind quickly surmised that the entire thing was only a screen "to advertise Lipton's tea" and he would have none of that.[84]

Germany's naval officers were, like their Supreme War Lord, deeply disappointed that she had come empty-handed out of the reapportioning of Spain's possessions. They were resolved not to permit a repetition of this error in the future. Diederichs, it appears, became interested in the Philippines immediately after his quarrel with Dewey. By August 1898 he hoped that the islands would be declared officially neutral so that Germany could flood them with merchants, engineers, and scientists. In October he occupied himself with thoughts of the Anglo-American "trade monopoly brotherhood." America's "violation of Spanish possessions" and Great Britain's "rape of the Transvaal" were ominous; only a union of the European seafaring nations could effectively oppose the two western maritime giants. "We cannot direct our eyes to future needs too soon, and these demand a good secure harbor on the southern extremity of our East Asian station." Diederichs especially coveted the Dutch East Indies as well as the Carolines and the Marianas. Time and again he sent cables to Berlin calling for a continental union, headed by Germany, Russia and France, against the "Anglo-Saxon world."[85] The Kaiser's brother, Admiral Prince Henry, temporarily under the illusion that Germany had actually annexed the Philippines, with bluster declared it was "a new happy indication of the expansionist forces of the Reich."[86] Admiral Tirpitz, on the other hand, kept his glance riveted on the Caribbean. He reminded Foreign Secretary von Bülow of the value of a German base at St. John, and Chancellor Hohenlohe of the need for increased naval appropriations. "Not now, but in 1901." An increase could easily be justified in parliament on the grounds of the increased "danger" posed by Great Britain and the United States. Tirpitz mused that a continental league, including Russia and France, would be most desirable, "were it not for Alsace-Lorraine."[87] The admiral also contemplated purchasing the Langkawi Islands from Siam, which would allow "our further advance into East Asia." And he talked once more about creating a system of German naval bases girdling the globe. The admiral was merely biding his time until Germany possessed sufficient sea power "to take energetic steps against England and America." Until then, German diplomacy would have to "dance on eggs."[88]

Bülow adopted a rather cautionary stance in these matters. Initially he favored an international conference to decide the fate of the Philippines, believing that Germany would obtain a coaling station in the process. At other times he envisaged peaceful acquisition of Ponape, Yap, Kusaie, the Ladrones or Marianas, and even one of the Canary Islands. But he was resolved not to antagonize the United States at this juncture, even passing up an alleged opportunity to gain a foothold in the Dominican Republic.* In any event, Bülow cabled Friedrich Krupp in May 1898 "the keen and pressing desire" that the weapons king complete "His Majesty's warships at the quickest pace possible."[89] Holleben in Washington stressed that the United States would respect and observe only strength. He hoped that the time would soon come "when we can adopt a different tone."[90] Words indeed designed to flatter his imperial master. But Bülow was not granted time to heal the wounds inflicted upon German-American relations at Manila.

## Samoa II (1899)

No sooner had the waves stirred up by the Spanish-American War subsided than a new storm broke over the horizon. Or rather, an old one reappeared. The uneasy truce created by the Samoan tripartite agreement in June 1889 was broken early in 1899. A civil war among the Samoans once again erupted over the issue of kingship, and this time Germany found herself opposed by both the United States and Great Britain. Wilhelm II was extremely sensitive in this matter, especially since the German consulate at Apia was accidentally shelled by an American warship. Foreign Secretary von Bülow, however, sought to settle the issue peacefully. As early as 14 March 1899 he instructed Admiral Prince Henry, commander of the cruiser squadron in East Asia, to avoid all incidents with the United States. "An armed conflict with the great North American Republic . . . at this time would be extremely unwelcome."[91] A fortnight later Bülow even contemplated making overtures to the Americans regarding a possible alliance against the British, but he quickly abandoned this unlikely project so soon after Manila. In any case, he urged restraint upon the Foreign Office as well as the German press, because a German-American conflict would delight the British at a time when they were bogged down in South Africa. And Bülow realized, of course, that Germany, alas, possessed few "diplomatic levers" vis-à-vis the United States.[92]

Above all, the new Samoan trouble once again brought to light Germany's need for battleships. Bülow was ready. "The events in Samoa constitute further proof that overseas policies can only be executed with

* On 30 August 1898 the Dominican president, General Ulysses Heureaux, asked the German resident minister (Michahelles) for "protection" in return for a coaling station. Both Bülow and the Kaiser rejected the invitation for fear of alienating the United States.

sufficient naval power." Wilhelm agreed. "What I have daily preached for ten years to those oxen Reichstag deputies."[93] Both men were under great pressure at home, particularly from the Berlin chapter of the German Colonial Society, which sarcastically cheered the United States on in its claim to Pago Pago harbor:

A favorable opportunity to establish themselves at Samoa has been seized — by the Americans. Not by us Germans, whose interests in these splendid islands are by far the greatest. . . . We look quietly on, and when America and England share the booty, and — perhaps — magnanimously give us a crumb or two, we rejoice at the success! Why did we not take advantage of the situation . . . why this delay, why are fears and misapprehensions allowed to spread, why does no word come from an authoritative source?[94]

An "authoritative source" finally spoke, but it hardly pleased the Colonial Society. In April Bülow instructed the German press to curb its anti-American outbursts. When the *Deutsche Zeitung* failed to heed this advice, the foreign secretary exploded: "Do we already possess a strong fleet?! And is such an instrument replaced by the naval tables in the *Deutsche Zeitung?* May the *Deutsche Zeitung* give us 50 armored ships." The Catholic press of South Germany proved especially difficult to handle; the *Augsburger Postzeitung* revived still fresh memories of Uncle Sam as "the hangman of Spain."[95]

On 14 April 1899 Bülow took up the Samoan question in the Reichstag. He conceded that the "great Christian peoples of Europe" would never allow war to break out over "an island group in the South Sea of whose 30,000 inhabitants barely 500 were Europeans, and with an annual trade of less than three million marks." But there were other issues at stake: the protection of German trade, property, and life as well as the maintenance of treaty rights and obligations.[96] To a trusted aide, the foreign secretary was more candid: "The entire Samoan question has absolutely no material but only ideal and patriotic interest for us."[97]

Bülow's toughest battle, however, was with the secretary of the Naval Office, Rear Admiral Tirpitz.* The admiral was not only an ardent advocate of navalism according to Mahan and an enthusiastic exponent of German *Weltpolitik*, but also a clever manipulator of public opinion and of parliament. Moreover, he was vain, ambitious, ruthless, and immune to criticism, in short, a man tailor-made for the peculiar Prussian-German constitutional system created by Bismarck. While parliament was debating the Samoan issue, Tirpitz urged the foreign

* Although the Naval Office was responsible primarily for naval funding and construction, Tirpitz managed to usurp strategy matters by force of personality and dominance over the Kaiser.

secretary to exploit "the hostile stance of England and America" in order to wring additional naval appropriations from the Reichstag. The admiral bluntly asserted that Great Britain and the United States were determined "to seek a war with Germany and destroy her before the fleet is built."[98] On 11 October Tirpitz formally informed Bülow that Samoa was "already today of the greatest strategic value for the German navy as an important station on the route from Kiaochow to South America." The future would only enhance the strategic significance of the Samoan Islands "because the Panama Canal will create new sea routes for world trade and thus also new strategic military routes." Moreover, the islands were vital for the planned "German world cable" that would be laid from South America to Samoa, from there via New Guinea to East Africa, and across the continent to the German colonies in West Africa.[99] That same day the chief of the Admiralty (Admiralität), Rear Admiral Felix Bendemann, reiterated to Bülow Tirpitz's dictum that "the military point of view" necessitated German control of Samoa. The admiral, whose office was responsible for naval strategy and deployment of ships, wanted the island group primarily as a further link between Germany's South Sea possessions and South America.[100]

In the end, this second Samoan crisis was also resolved without recourse to arms. Admiral Tirpitz eventually abandoned his aggressive position, vacillating between the "mailed fist" and retreat, between "energetic countermeasures against England and America" and a policy of "dancing on eggs" while naval construction proceeded.[101] War with the United States over Samoa in 1899 would be premature; the mighty battle fleet would not be ready for at least another decade. The peace settlement in the fall of 1899 gave Germany most of the Samoan Islands, although the United States kept the main island, Tutuila, with its valuable harbor at Pago Pago. Great Britain received the Tonga group, Savage Island, Lord Howe Island, most of the German Solomon Islands, and other minor concessions.

Perhaps the most significant and lasting outcome of the crisis was Germany's fervent resolve to expand her navy. In mid-October 1899 the Kaiser announced in Hamburg: "We have bitter need of a powerful German fleet." Bülow, defending the Samoan settlement before parliament on 11 December, enlightened the deputies with a sweeping historical survey. Every century, he philosophized, had witnessed "conflict, a giant liquidation, in order to reapportion influence, power, and possessions in the world anew." In the sixteenth century Spain and Portugal had divided the world; Holland, France, and Great Britain entered the race in the following hundred years; the eighteenth century had seen the British triumph over Holland and France; and the nineteenth century experienced a reemerging France and the newcomer Russia. The twentieth century, Bülow predicted, would find Italy, Russia, the United States, Japan, and France creating mammoth fleets in order to be prepared for the new "giant liquidation." Germany could not afford to miss this historic moment.[102]

The century closed with Joseph Chamberlain's ill-fated proposal for an Anglo-American-German agreement to rule the world, an Anglo-Saxon–Teutonic alliance. The British colonial secretary had realized that as a result of Britain's involvement in the Boer War, "splendid isolation" had ceased to be valid. In a number of speeches — particularly on 13 May 1898 at Birmingham and on 30 November 1899 at Leicester — he called for "a new Triple Alliance between the Teutonic race and the two great branches of the Anglo-Saxon race"; that is, between Germany, Great Britain and the United States. However, the proposal was stillborn. Bülow rejected the idea because he thought he detected behind it Chamberlain's desire to keep Great Britain and Germany out of South America, "although very promising strips of land for the future are to be found there."[103] Holleben reported from Washington that the Americans would reject the proposal because they did not trust Germany. "Leading Americans" and especially President McKinley found Germany as distasteful as ever. "A permanent rapprochement with America is thinkable only as the result of Germany's economic demise."[104] On 24 November 1899 Bülow informed Holstein that he desired no alliances, be they with Great Britain, the United States, or both. "The future task of the German government is to create a strong fleet . . . and then to await future developments with patience and poise."[105] In fact, at that very moment German naval officers were turning their attention to possible "future developments."

TWO

# Contingency War Planning: Berlin (1899–1900)

Whenever war occurs in any part of the world, we in Germany sit down and make a war plan.

— WILHELM II *to A. J. Balfour*
*22 November 1899*

"THE PERIOD WHEN GERMANY LEFT THE EARTH TO ONE OF HER NEIGHBORS and the seas to the other while reserving heaven — where pure theory is enthroned — for herself . . . is over." Foreign Secretary von Bülow's bold pronouncement, greeted with delight and shouts of "Bravo!," introduced Germany's first major naval program to the Reichstag in December 1897. Bülow herewith announced Germany's search for "a place in the sun." The issue was clear-cut: "Either world power [status] or demise." Admiral Tirpitz presented the requested naval appropriations as "a question of life or death." Failure to pass the legislation would lead to "economic and then political defeat" for the Reich.[1]

The Reichstag agreed. In April 1898, as previously mentioned, it passed the First Navy Bill, calling for seventeen battleships, eight armored cruisers, nine large and twenty-six light cruisers, to be supported by a material reserve of two battleships and seven cruisers.[2] We have already noted to what degree the Spanish-American War influenced the issue of naval expansion, and that already in 1897 Tirpitz envisaged and planned future naval increases. Passage of the Navy Bill was facilitated by clever naval propaganda directed by Tirpitz's Naval Office. No stone was left unturned, no path untried, in this masterful manipulation of public opinion. German children, including the Kaiser's sons, were clothed in sailor suits and fed a steady diet of romantic sea yarns. In 1890 Alfred Thayer Mahan's *The Influence of Sea Power Upon History* was read in German naval officer circles, and by 1894 Wilhelm II was "devouring" it. Mahan was thereupon translated and, at government expense, serialized.

Leading historians and economists were also called upon to provide a framework of cultural, economic, political, military, and vulgar Darwinistic timber for the new institution. They included Hans Delbrück, Otto Hintze, Erich Marcks, Gustav Schmoller, Werner Sombart, Max Weber, and many others. Tirpitz's journal *Nauticus* frequently published gems of wisdom from Heinrich von Treitschke on behalf of the fleet program:

> It is highly probable that a nation without colonies, regardless of how strong it is, will not long belong to the Great European Powers. . . . We see today how Europe's Great Powers are creating a mass aristocracy of the white race around the globe. Whoever does not play a role in this mighty competition will not enjoy a happy future. . . . And we are here talking about our existence as a Great Power overseas.[3]

In 1900, one year after these words were quoted in *Nauticus*, the economist Gustav Schmoller perhaps most precisely defined what many middle-class Germans cherished: "In the coming century we must desire at all costs a German colony of some 20 to 30 million people in South America. . . . This is impossible without warships, which provide secured maritime communications and a presence backed by force."[4] A recent historian has concluded that this naval propaganda established in Germany "a practical if not nominal Propaganda Ministry" almost thirty-five years before Joseph Goebbels.[5] Few bothered at the turn of the century to examine more closely the likely repercussions that such a measure would ultimately exert on Germany's relationship with her European neighbors as well as with her American rival.

The creation of a mammoth battle fleet was officially justified by the "risk theory" (*Risikogedanke*) behind it: its ultimate strength would deter any naval opponent from risking an all-out naval encounter with Germany, to be left, even after a victorious outcome, at the mercy of a strong third naval power or coalition. Moreover, it was argued that the fleet would increase Germany's appeal as an ally (*Bündnisfähigkeit*) to other relatively minor sea powers in search of "a place in the sun." The late Gerhard Ritter has described this official reasoning as "a gruesome mistake" and the entire German naval policy under Wilhelm II as "gigantic misspeculation."[6] Certainly the fleet contributed heavily to the growing antagonism between Germany and Great Britain. Ludwig Dehio went so far as to depict Tirpitz's naval policy as "a sort of cold war directed against England's world empire."[7] And finally, it cannot be overlooked that this fleet was basically an offensive weapon. Bülow's promise to the Kaiser that the fleet would permit him to pursue "a great overseas policy" entailed armed collision with established colonial powers. After all, German naval officers were the first to complain that no virgin land was available for peaceful colonization. And Tirpitz's statement that Germany must acquire a world empire or be reduced to a backward European agrarian nation suggests that talk of empire and naval stations was no idle boast.[8] Peaceful competition, entailing protection of colonies and trade primarily against the natives, necessitated overseas cruisers. But Tirpitz firmly rejected such "*jeune école*" notions. As Volker Berghahn has put it: "In contrast to the war of attrition envisaged by cruiser warfare, the war of battleships was designed with a single blow to decide control of the seas."[9]

The Spanish-American War in 1898 provided German naval enthusiasts, flushed with their recent success in the Reichstag, with an example of the importance of sea power for *Weltpolitik*. As early as 24 October 1897 the *Münchner Allgemeine Zeitung* had published a statement by a member of the Catholic Center Party supporting the pending Navy Bill in the Reichstag. The anonymous writer assigned the future navy the task of abolishing the Monroe Doctrine by actively assisting Catholic Spain in the impending war against the United States. The American secretary of state, John Sherman, was informed of this point of view by his envoy in Denmark.[10] And the confrontation between Dewey and Diederichs in Manila Bay fanned the flames of navalism in both countries. Admiral Dewey theorized: "It is indecent to fight Spain anyhow. Now, if France could come in too, we could save our faces, but best of all if Germany would come in. If only Germany could be persuaded to come in."[11] In fact, Dewey in 1898 flatly predicted that the next war of the United States would be in fifteen years with Germany. These dire prophecies were not ignored in Germany. The United States was now regarded as a most dangerous competitor in the pursuit of colonial possessions and naval coaling stations. Germany's political and military leaders therefore turned their attention to the likelihood of an armed clash with this new rival.

## Invasion Strategies I (1898–1900)

"Whenever war occurs in any part of the world, we in Germany sit down and make a war plan."[12] These Imperial words were recorded by the British statesman Arthur James Balfour in November 1899; and indeed it later became known that during the winter of 1897–1898 a young lieutenant in the supreme command of the navy (Oberkommando der

Marine), the future official naval historian Eberhard von Mantey, had indeed turned his attention to the formulation of a contingency war plan against the United States.

Theoretical naval studies — called *Winterarbeiten* after the season in which the subjects were handed out — were designed either to test the overall planning abilities of certain promising officers or to shed light on current naval problems. They have all too often been dismissed by historians as insignificant *essais* by junior staff officers anxious for recognition and promotion. On the contrary, they often formed the basis for, and reflected the direction of, official Admiralty planning. This is especially true if one keeps in mind that the senior Admiralty officers did not take an active role in at least the formative stages of planning, preferring instead to save their talents and energies for the *Immediatvorträge*, the Imperial audiences, in which they had to present and defend these plans before the Supreme War Lord, Wilhelm II.* The relevance and importance of the *Winterarbeiten* become evident in the case of the contingency war plan against the United States.

Before 1897 the *Winterarbeiten* assignments usually were related to the British Royal Navy, but in 1897–1898 they reflected the mounting German-American rivalry at sea; the first five topics assigned dealt with Cuba, the Philippines, the Monroe Doctrine, Central America, and the American mainland.[13] And in 1898–1899 the questions assigned were on possible landing sites in the United States (Chesapeake Bay and Long Island), the bombardment of New York City, and other related matters. In 1901–1902 Admiral von Diederichs asked for studies on the "strategic and tactical value of American naval matériel" and the "military geography" of the United States, the West Indies, and South America. The following winter (1902–1903) the Admiralty requested discussion of the "military geography" of the islands and coastlines of the Caribbean Sea and the Gulf of Mexico, the military status of American possessions in the West Indies, the probable value of the future Panama Canal to the United States Navy, the navy's caliber, the value of the Virgin Islands as a German base, and how a European power could best defeat the United States at sea. In 1903–1904 Admiral Büchsel once more asked for an evaluation of the United States Navy, of the West Indies, and of the Virgin Islands for American naval stations. The next year only one topic

* Thirty years after formulating his plan, Mantey reflected: "Moltke, Schlieffen, even Waldersee made their great O[perations] Plans all alone. With us [the navy] the O-Plans were made by some intelligent, young, junior people and the chief of the Admiralty Staff gave them his blessings and presented the O-Plans to the Kaiser." Bundesarchiv-Militärarchiv, Freiburg im Breisgau, West Germany, F 7590, Nachlass Hollweg, vol. 4, Mantey to Vice Admiral Karl Hollweg, 16 April 1929.

was listed regarding the United States: the extent of maritime commerce on the eastern seaboard. It will be seen later that these assignments reflected the various stages of Admiralty thinking on a possible German-American war.[14]

Mantey's study of 1897–1898 on the feasibility of a naval offensive against the United States laid the basis for all future considerations regarding this matter. In stark contrast to the 1889 study of Rear Admiral Karcher, which had restricted German naval operations to cruiser warfare, Mantey recommended a naval assault upon the area between Portland, Maine, and Norfolk, Virginia. "Here is the heart of America and here the United States can be hurt most critically and forced to the peace table most easily." Since the United States could not be blockaded into surrender due to its unlimited natural resources, the war would have to be won "through [military] successes on the mainland of the United States itself." In short, Mantey recommended a decisive naval battle with the United States Navy off the eastern seaboard, to be followed by a joint naval-military occupation of Norfolk, Hampton Roads, and Newport News (later this was expanded to include Gloucester, Massachusetts). The German invasion would be climaxed by a thrust up Chesapeake Bay in the direction of Baltimore and Washington. Finally, Germany had to be prepared to face the American Pacific Fleet approximately one month after the aforementioned points had been taken.

Yet Mantey was generally optimistic. He noted particularly the peaked condition of the United States Navy. Congress seemed extremely niggardly with its funds, thereby forcing the navy to copy existing, and hence antiquated, European designs. American democracy further hampered development. "It is highly detrimental to the navy that every citizen is allowed a voice [in naval matters] and, should his voice be rejected, is free to raise the greatest possible noise in the public press." Moreover, the armored plates for warships still had to be purchased abroad because the local industry did not yet possess "the necessary experience and sufficient production capabilities." The American army was also pretty much a negligible quantity. The only tried troops available in case of foreign invasion were some cavalry regiments that had been kept in combat readiness fighting Indians out West! The militia was not even on a level with German reserves. "Militia service is pure fun and games." And finally, morale in the armed forces was far below German standards. "They make life for the soldiers as easy as possible, provide them with excellent accommodations and food, [and] give them almost no duty. The result is lax discipline, pathetic drills, and numerous desertions." It is interesting to note that Mantey paid no attention to the vital problem of supplying this expeditionary force across three thousand miles of open sea. Such mundane considerations were left for later stages of planning.[15]

The question naturally comes to mind of who assigned this topic, which headed the list in 1897–1898. There is no clear answer. The commanders of the two naval stations at Kiel and Wilhelmshaven usually asked the director of the navy's Education Department (Inspektion des Bildungswesens der Marine), at that time Rear Admiral Iwan Oldekop, who was concurrently head of the Naval Academy, to recommend subjects for study. Only the most qualified and useful *Winterarbeiten* were utilized by the Admiralty for official business. Thus it is highly probable that the topic was handed out by Oldekop, who also evaluated it, passed it on to Admiral Karcher, who in turn sent it to Admiral von Knorr, the navy's commanding admiral. Captain Friedrich Forstmeier of the West German official Military-Historical Research Center in Freiburg states that the operation plans were "developed personally by the Chief of the Admiralty Staff under Imperial direction." Moreover, Forstmeier was informed by Eberhard von Mantey's son in 1971 that the *Winterarbeit* of 1897–1898 was chosen by the young lieutenant after two urgent letters from his father (a general in the German army) advised him to select a work of especially topical interest which stood a chance of reaching the Admiralty. General von Mantey was convinced that this was the case with the "attack against the United States."[16] Whatever the case, Mantey's work quickly made its way to the top of the command structure. Admiral Hans von Koester, chief of the Baltic Naval Station (Kiel) and designated inspector-general of the navy, noted: "Agreed. An ambitious study which provides a lucid, overall picture of the American coast and therefore is most interesting at this particular moment."[17] The latter part of the verdict leaves no doubt that the possibility of war with the United States was very much in the minds of some of Germany's leading naval officers. Were they already looking towards greater horizons than Great Britain and the North Sea?

In the United States such an adventurous scheme was not thought possible. In 1898 Commodore G. W. Melville, chief of the navy's Bureau of Engineering, estimated that an enemy risking operations in American waters would need a fleet twice the size of the United States Navy.[18] This could only mean the Royal Navy; even on paper the German fleet did not qualify. And Melville could hardly be accused of being a Germanophile. He belonged to the group close to Theodore Roosevelt and Henry Cabot Lodge that believed the Kaiser "capable of anything," especially in the Western Hemisphere.

In the meantime the command structure of the German navy underwent streamlining and modernization. On 14 March 1899 the supreme command of the navy was dissolved and the Kaiser personally assumed command (Oberbefehl der Marine). Rear Admiral Felix Bendemann was appointed first chief of the newly created Admiralty Staff (Almiralstab). That same month the ambitious Mantey submitted a second *Winterarbeit*, probably ordered by Admiral Oldekop or Admiral Koester, which formed the basis for much of the subsequent work on the contingency operations plan against the United States.

It far outdid the 1898 work in boldness of scope and daring of execution. No less a target than New York City was selected. Mantey expected the United States to spread its troops in a thin line between Newport and Norfolk, with either New York or Norfolk serving as the navy's mobilization center. The American battleships would probably be drawn into battle formation near New York because it was not only America's largest city but also her industrial center. Mantey dismissed Cape Cod, Nantucket Island, Martha's Vineyard, Block Island, and Cape May as possible bases because of generally prevailing adverse weather conditions, deciding instead on Norfolk. The success of this bold plan would lie in the speed of its execution. Requisite supplies would have to be stored and ready in German ports, so that immediately following a declaration of war, both men and matériel could be shipped to the eastern seaboard of the United States. Because of the unexpectedness of such a strike, the invaders "could hope to find the mine barriers not yet completed, the naval sappers not yet properly trained, coastal batteries not yet fully armed, and munition supplies not yet fully stored." The Spanish-American War buttressed these assertions. "One has only to be reminded of conditions in Havana and in American ports after the outbreak of last year's war, of how long it took to make those harbors even relatively defensible." As examples of successful naval initiative Mantey cited Lord Nelson's seizure of Copenhagen in 1801, the Union fleet's entry into New Orleans harbor in 1862, and Admiral Farragut's "damn the torpedoes" entry into Mobile harbor in 1864. Last but not least, civilian panic would assist naval operations. "In New York large-scale panic will result from just the mention of a possible bombardment."[19]

In this second study Mantey estimated that by 1900 the United States Navy would consist of seven battleships, fourteen cruisers, and fourteen armored cruisers. Therefore, Germany would need seventeen battleships, thirty-three cruisers, and four auxiliary cruisers for successful operations off the east coast of the United States. Three thousand tons of coal would be consumed daily. By cruising for twenty-five days at an average hourly speed of eight to nine nautical miles, it was estimated that 75,000 tons of coal, to be transported in forty to sixty freighters, would be required. The problem of supplying this force with coal, ammunition, food, medical supplies, water, and the like for an extended period in American waters was once again ignored. In fact, Mantey's greatest worry was that the United States Navy might refuse a decisive naval encounter.

Basing his information upon intelligence reports received by the Prussian General Staff from Captain Count G. Adolf von Götzen, Germany's military attaché in Washington, Mantey decided to deploy two separate naval units. A blockade fleet would be stationed at the exit of Long Island Sound (between Orient Point and Connecticut) and a main assault fleet, assigned to overpower the New York City forts, would arrive in New York at the same time. Entry into the harbor would be forced on the very day of arrival. If army troops ("2 to 3 battalions infantry and 1 battalion engineers seem fully sufficient") were to be taken along, they would be landed on Long Island and the main attack postponed until the morning following arrival in American waters. Once entry into New York's Lower Bay was forced, Forts Tompkins and Hamilton would be engaged and, if possible, downtown New York shelled by naval artillery. If this frontal attack failed, the force would withdraw and occupy Block Island, which would afford good telegraph communication with Germany. Mantey estimated that in order to overwhelm both the United States Navy and New York's coastal defenses, Germany would need "33⅓ percent naval superiority." New York's fortifications, except for the newest installations at Sandy Hook (New Jersey), were well known because Count Götzen had regularly furnished exact descriptions of them. Above all, Mantey admonished German naval planners "to pursue the war with the greatest possible energy in order to conclude it in the *shortest* possible time." Obviously, he was afraid that a war of attrition would prove detrimental to Germany by allowing the United States time to mobilize its vast war potential.

This bold plan was submitted to Vice Admiral August Thomsen, chief of the First (and only) Battle Squadron. Thus the *Winterarbeit* progressed from "the green baize table" through the offices of the Naval Academy, the Baltic Naval Station, and the Admiralty Staff to Germany's highest-ranking active commanding officer. Thomsen at once recognized the merits of the plan but discounted Mantey's reliance upon the element of surprise. New York City could not simply be "overrun," and the long trip over three thousand miles of open ocean would not escape the attention of American intelligence forces. By the time the German armada reached New York it would find "barriers, forts, and fleet" in its path. Applying a "reverse risk" theory, Thomsen concluded:

> The proposed direct assault upon New York will not be possible in the foreseeable future so long as the navy of the United States of North America exists, and when it no longer exists, ours will also be so weakened that we will probably not be able to carry out the attack against [New York City's] fortifications.

Furthermore, Thomsen dismissed Mantey's worries that the United States Navy might dodge an all-out sea battle. American "egoism" and "search for glory" would cause that country's military planners "to seize every chance to do battle."[20]

But Thomsen had an alternate plan. Instead of occupying Norfolk as a naval base, he suggested "Puerteriko," the seizure of which "would pose only minor difficulties." If the United States fleet engaged the German invasion forces here, this would be only to Germany's advantage, because the enemy would then also be far removed from his home base. From Puerto Rico operations against the mainland of the United States could be carried out at any time with impunity. Especially Newport, Rhode Island, and Hampton Roads, Virginia, seemed suitable targets. The older German warships would secure the base at Puerto Rico while the newer vessels would land the German army regulars on the continental United States. Thomsen was not sure, however, that the capture of New York, Washington, Baltimore, and Philadelphia would convince "the country between the East and the West" to sue for peace. The admiral admitted that he "was not familiar with the size" of the land "between the East and the West." Yet this was not crucial. "I should like to believe, nonetheless, that much will have been accomplished when we have taken and hold the American northeast." And finally, Thomsen acknowledged the timeliness of Mantey's study, "because at this moment every thinking German naval officer is busy studying . . . the consequences of an armed conflict between Germany and the United States of North America."

Two interesting observations emerge from Admiral Thomsen's remarks. First, as had Admiral von Koester the previous year, Thomsen clearly recognized that a naval conflict between the United States and Germany was a distinct possibility and not merely wishful thinking by junior officers, not mere "routine considerations." It is revealing to note that in this "age of navalism" colonial disputes in far distant Samoa and the Philippines sufficed to turn the attention of Germany's leading naval planners to the likelihood of maritime operations against the United States. Second, Thomsen's inability to spell Puerto Rico and his lack of information on the size and industrial-military-financial capabilities of a potential enemy argue little for the thesis, expounded by former naval officers and accepted by many historians at face value, that Germany's naval officers were especially "cosmopolitan" and "knowledgeable of world matters."[21]*

* Mantey later complained that naval officers had thought too much in terms of "*Continental* politics" and that especially the officers of the Admiralty Staff were merely "an unfortunate imitation of the [army] General Staff . . . the staffs thought

This notwithstanding, the new Admiralty Staff proceeded full steam with the operational planning for a war against the United States. By utilizing Mantey's two studies, it was possible to put on paper the first detailed "plan of advance" (*Marschplan*) during the same month as Mantey's second study, March 1899. Thus the *Winterarbeiten* had now become official Admiralty Staff business. In its basic execution, Mantey's plan of March 1899 remained the model for a German advance to the east coast of the United States; later versions merely streamlined Mantey's concept.

Admiralty planners in March 1899 concluded that if Germany did not want to sacrifice her overseas trade at the outset of a war with the United States, "our fleet must as quickly as possible assume the offensive against the American [east] coast with the aim of encountering and annihilating the enemy fleet." The route of attack was to be as follows:

> The cruising radius of our ships necessitates a coaling station for the advance. As such we must regard the western Azores — Topes [or] Flores. During the worst season of the year, i.e. winter, the advance must proceed via Flores to the northeastern Antilles and only from there to the east coast of the United States; in the summer, i.e. the best time of the year, in a straight line from Flores to the American coast.

Puerto Rico was dismissed as a possible station because it was too far from the main theater of the war. Instead, Frenchman Bay, Maine, and Long Bay, South Carolina, were suggested. The enemy fleet was expected to gather at Hampton Roads or in Long Island Sound. Good supply depots could be established in the region of Cape Cod and Nantucket Island.[22]

The main German armada would be ready to sail from Wilhelmshaven on the seventh day of mobilization, while the supply ships would be ready two days later and would join the main fleet on the twelfth day. Then, once united, the convoy would pass from the North Sea through the English Channel to Flores in the Azores at a cruising speed of nine knots. The older ships of the *Siegfried* class (S.M.SS. *Siegfried*, *Beowulf*, *Hildebrand*, etc.) would initially steam ahead at twelve knots and recoal on the northern coast of France or Spain. If this proved to be impossible, they would be towed the rest of the way to Flores by the more modern warships once their coal supplies had been

---

that they were half-gods." He bitterly asserted that the naval officers "were a Prussian army corps transplanted into iron barracks." Bundesarchiv-Militärarchiv, Freiburg im Breisgau, West Germany, F 7590, vol. 4, Mantey to Hollweg, 16 April 1929.

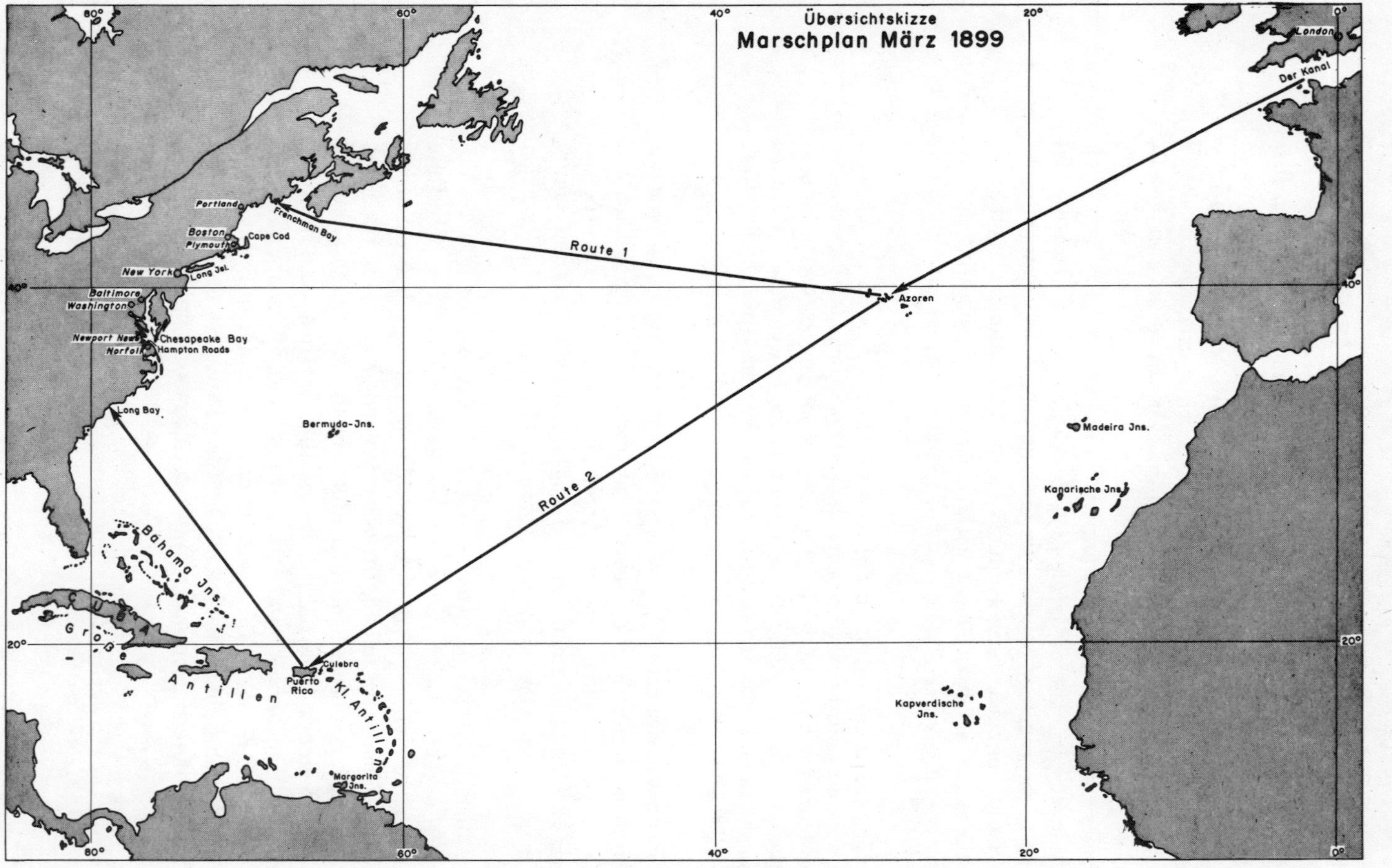


*The 1899 Invasion Plan:* German title: Outline Map, Line of March, March 1899. Antillen: Antilles. Azoren: Azores. Der Kanal (The Canal): English Channel. Grosse: Greater. Ins.: Islands. Kanarische: Canary. Kapverdische: Cape Verde. Kl.: Lesser. Route 1 is for a summer invasion plan; Route 2 for the winter. The map is from Holger H. Herwig and David F. Trask "Naval Operations Plans Between Germany and the United States of America 1898–1913. A Study of Strategic Planning in the Age of Imperialism," in *Militärgeschichtliche Mitteilungen*, 10 (1970), 5–32. Courtesy of *Militärgeschichtliche Mitteilungen*

exhausted. This leg of the journey would take ten or eleven days. Recoaling in the Azores would last only one or two days.

In the summer season, the march across the Atlantic to Frenchman Bay would proceed at seven knots and the ships of the *Siegfried* class would be towed most of the way, weather permitting.* Travel time was estimated at between eleven and twelve days. On the other hand, should the advance occur during the winter, thirteen or fourteen days would be required to traverse the distance between Flores and Puerto Rico, with a further five or six days needed to reach Long Bay, in this case at a pace of nine knots. The coaling stop at Frenchman Bay or Long Bay would last only one day. Therefore the decisive fleet engagement with the United States Navy would take place in the summer between the thirty-first and thirty-fourth day of mobilization; in the winter between the thirty-ninth and the forty-fourth day.

In December 1899 the man who had carried out the seizure of Kiaochow and who had confronted Dewey in Manila Bay was appointed chief of the Admiralty Staff. He was immediately involved in the evolution of the operations plan against the United States. On 3 December 1899 Tirpitz asked Vice Admiral von Diederichs to supply the Naval Office with information on this subject:

> In the debates in the budget commission I will be required to provide precise information concerning the advent of war with England or America in order convincingly to prove the necessity of our planned new increases for the battle fleet.

Tirpitz did not want "a technical Admiralty Staff study," but stressed that he required a memorandum "which in lay terms comprehensible for members of the budget commission persuasively proves just how extraordinarily unfeasible, yes, hopeless, our situation would be in such a war." In other words, a study designed to panic parliamentary delegates into granting immediate naval increases. Particularly, Tirpitz asked Diederichs to detail the inability of the German fleet to deal with the United States Navy "because in order to be at all effective we must advance to America's shores."[23]

Diederichs's reply came on 20 January 1900. "An effective blockade of the American coast is not possible with the *matériel* of the Navy Bill of 1898." But the admiral was not content merely to provide support for Tirpitz's planned naval appropriations; he took the possibility of war with the United States seriously and in detailed fashion elaborated upon the issue. Admiral von Diederichs urged combined naval and military operations on the eastern seaboard of the United States. "The most ef-

* The *Siegfried* class were "coastal armored cruisers" of 3,500 tons displacement.

fective method of forcing peace" in any future German-American conflict would be "the acquisition of valuable maritime cities in the New England states." For this, however, it was first necessary to defeat the United States Navy at sea. "Our only means of defense lies in an offense." Diederichs also complied with Tirpitz's request to provide justification for a new naval increase by demanding thirty-eight battleships as well as twelve large and thirty-two light cruisers for the German navy. "The fleet must be doubled."[24]

This estimate was precisely what Tirpitz hoped to wring from the Reichstag, but the consideration of war with the United States could not be utilized as leverage by the Naval Office in light of the fact that the Admiralty Staff was already contemplating offensive operations in American waters with the forces provided for in the Navy Bill of 1898. Moreover, Tirpitz obviously did not wish to set a final number (thirty-eight) for the ultimate battleship strength of the fleet. It was more prudent to leave this question open and he preferred, instead, to use the British Royal Navy for comparison "because the further development of our fleet is designed to allow us to face the most powerful enemy at sea."[25]

Having aided Tirpitz in his endeavors on behalf of added naval appropriations, the Admiralty Staff returned to its own problems of strategic planning. Diederichs's first step in the formulation of the operations plan against the United States was to make absolutely certain that the cruisers stationed overseas possessed instructions in the event of a German-American war. On 1 February 1900 the cruiser squadron in East Asia received official orders, in case of a war declaration: "to engage enemy naval forces near the Philippines as fast as is humanly possible." The strategy was designed to tie the American forces down "and thereby indirectly protect our trade." Here, also, German naval leaders saw no choice but to assume the offensive. "Every favorable opportunity must be taken advantage of to inflict damage upon the enemy." The cruisers deployed in East African, West American, and Australian waters were instructed to come to the aid of the East Asian naval flotilla. The Kaiser noted on the orders: "Agreed. Wilhelm I. R."[26] The main theater of operations, however, was to be the east coast of the United States.

The offensive-oriented stance of the Admiralty Staff was stiffened by reports from the German naval attaché in Washington. On 26 January 1900 Lieutenant Hubert von Rebeur-Paschwitz submitted a lengthy memorandum to Tirpitz wherein he concluded that operations into the interior of the United States would be hopeless and that "an occupation of the nominal capital Washington would make no impression whatsoever since neither trade nor industry are of any significance here." Instead, the naval attaché recommended "unsparing, merciless assaults against the northeastern trade and industrial centers," specifically against Boston and New York. Provincetown at the tip of Cape Cod would provide an excellent *Stützpunkt*.[27] Rebeur-Paschwitz had personally inspected the region around Cape Cod and his report greatly facilitated Admiralty Staff planning in Berlin. Moreover, Tirpitz granted Diederichs permission to communicate directly with the Washington naval envoy, and the latter was soon ordered to undertake a new inspection tour of the coastline between New York and Boston in search of a suitable landing site.

On 26 February 1900 Diederichs was granted his first audience with the Kaiser on the subject of naval operations plans against the United States. He reviewed past planning for the monarch, informing Wilhelm that Germany did not possess a contingency war plan against the United States. The admiral then presented the main features of Mantey's March 1899 study, recommending offensive naval operations on the east coast of the United States in the event of war "so that we will not voluntarily leave control of the seas in our enemy's hands."* Only an offensive stance could prevent "destruction of our trade and our fleet" by the Americans. The entire German fleet, including the ships of the dated *Siegfried* and *Baden* classes† as well as the antiquated armored frigates *König Wilhelm*, *Friedrich Karl*, *Preussen*, and *Friedrich der Grosse*, would be deployed, thus giving Germany at least numerical supremacy over the United States Navy. Such an expedition, the chief of the Admiralty Staff noted, would not avoid difficulty. "To match these ships against modern armored vessels with rapid-fire cannon in battle three thousand miles from their home bases is more than 'risky.' " Still, it was calculated that enough initial as well as subsequent coal and supplies could be delivered by weekly supply convoys. There existed no shortage of supply ships. The route of attack remained: "Coaling depot on the Azores, advance in winter time to the American West Indies, in summer time directly to the New England states." Diederichs harbored strong reservations regarding the feasibility of such an undertaking at the present time but expressed confidence for the future. "The comparative relative strengths [of the two fleets] in battleships will shift in our favor in 1901 and 1902 to such an extent that we can plan to conduct offensive operations by the fall of 1902."[28] In the end, Diederichs held back from drawing up a final operations plan against the United States to be submitted to the Kaiser, "because only after passage of the pending [Second] Navy Bill can we

* The Admiralty Staff documents for the Imperial audience (see note 28) indicate that the first work on the operations plan against the United States was received on 1 December 1899, and that the plan of March 1899 had formed the basis for it.

† The *Baden* class were "armored cruisers" of 7,411 tons displacement.

possibly count upon sufficient means with which our navy can conduct an offensive against the United States."[29]

The chief of the Admiralty Staff did not have long to wait. On 14 June 1900 the Second Navy Bill was approved, providing for a German battle fleet of thirty-eight battleships, twenty large cruisers, and thirty-eight light cruisers.[30]* Tirpitz had planned just such an increase — in fact doubling — almost from the moment that the First Navy Bill was passed in 1898.[31] The new bill provided even more warships than Diederichs had requested in his report to Tirpitz on 20 January 1900. Such a dramatic doubling of the fleet was easily explained as having been necessitated by the worsening of the international situation since 1898 — the Spanish-American War and the Boer War — and was vociferously supported by the German Navy League, founded on 30 April 1898, just weeks before the Dewey-Diederichs confrontation in Manila Bay. Germany's future, as Tirpitz was overly fond of saying, now truly lay "with the seas." The major industrial nations of the world were committed to a new, highly intensified stage in the armaments race. There could be no turning back, no return to normalcy. Navies are not built overnight. A minimum of two decades is needed for construction and personnel training. Thus, if all went according to plan for Germany and she passed safely through the "risk" period, she would be ready to assume her place among the world's major maritime powers by about 1920. Then would come a time, as the Kaiser hinted during a speech in Cuxhaven in 1900, to inspect the globe anew for "points where we can drive in a nail."[32] Foreign Secretary von Bülow was swept off his feet by the historicism of the moment. Parliament was told precisely what this bill meant to Germany in terms of decades. "The times of powerlessness and submissiveness are gone and shall never return. . . . In the coming century the German people will become either hammer or anvil."[33] Bülow could hardly have dreamed how prophetic this citation from Goethe would be. In fact, the combination of the creation of a mammoth battle fleet second only to that of Great Britain and the passing of the nineteenth century caused Germany's leaders to pause a moment and to reflect upon her projected course in the coming century.

## Thoughts for a New Age (1 January 1900)

The counterpoint to Bülow's "hammer or anvil" speech of December 1899 was the Kaiser's proclamation of 1 January 1900 in the Hall of Honor in the Berlin Armory (Zeughaus). With countless foreign digni-

* Compare this with Diederichs's recommendation of 20 January 1900 (see page 52).

taries and correspondents in attendance, Wilhelm II adopted the familiar tone of the officers' mess hall. The "glorious German Army," he announced, would continue to be the rock "upon which Germany's power and greatness rests," especially since "providence" would probably force his sons to take up the sword once more. The nineteenth century had seen how his grandfather (Wilhelm I) had reorganized the Prussian Army and raised it to the highest pinnacles of honor and glory; the next century would witness a similar development of the German navy "so that the German Reich might be in a position to realize abroad all that has not yet been attained." This allusion to future expansion was strengthened by Wilhelm's closing citation of Friedrich Wilhelm I, Prussia's "Soldier King": "When one wants to decide anything in this world with the pen it can be done only if the power of the sword stands behind it."[34]

The speech is more interesting than the many famous marginal notes that the Kaiser scribbled on documents that passed across his desk because he was well aware of its significance. He was here addressing himself not to isolated incidents or reports but to future developments spanning decades. His frequent references to major events in Prussian history during the preceding two centuries were purposely designed to give added weight to his remarks. It was not mere coincidence that the most frequently recurring words were *Weltmacht*, *Weltreich*, *Weltgeltung:* words intended to emphasize Germany's future role in *world*, as opposed to strictly European, affairs.

The Kaiser's manifesto did not fall upon deaf ears. Publicists such as Eduard von Hartmann quickly announced that Germany aspired to take her place among the other "Great Powers," the United States, Great Britain, and Russia. Max Lenz, a pupil of Leopold von Ranke, dedicated a book to his teacher's concept of "Great Power" status. And the radical Pan-Germans naturally welcomed the speech in their *Alldeutsche Blätter:* "The new century places Germany before a crucial dilemma: do we want to sink down to the level of a power of, at best, secondary rank . . . or do we want to become . . . a superior people [*Edelvolk*], a master people [*Herrenvolk*] destined to become the harbinger of culture for all of humanity?" Former court chaplain Adolf Stöcker's *Evangelische Kirchenzeitung* also took up the Imperial standard. Bismarck's genius, Stöcker asserted, had raised Germany from a nation of "poets and thinkers" to one of "doers and conquerors," thereby providing Germany with hegemony in Europe. "Now we are about to create a powerful navy in order to protect our greatly expanded trade, to increase our still relatively worthless colonial empire, and to grant us a voice in the struggle for world domination [*Weltherrschaft*]."[35]

The various New Year's proclamations are doubly interesting because they often contain sentiments and attitudes not generally found in the official documents. The *Frankfurter Zeitung*, which can hardly be accused of radicalism, provided a good sample. In a lead editorial on 30 December 1899 it drew a parallel between 1800 and 1900 in pseudo-Hegelian dialectics. By 1800 the prevailing cosmopolitanism was being challenged by a new virile nationalism. In 1900 that nationalism was under attack by imperialism and a synthesis, cosmopolitanism, already at hand. It seemed to be a squaring of the circle. But the cosmopolitanism of 1900 that the paper spoke of was not ethereal, not of the intellect, but very real and physical in the sense of world empires. Could Germany afford to stand idly by and watch as others marched towards this goal? The paper thought not. History would soon see three or four superpowers dominating the globe. "We hope and wish that Germany will be one of these world empires." The "foundation and expansion" of "world empires" was singled out by the *Frankfurter Zeitung* as the salient issue in the coming century. Finally, the satirical *Kladderadatsch* in its final issue of the nineteenth century expressed a widespread fear when it "reported" the arrival of a new century in which "much of Europe will go into the private ownership of the Rockefellers and Vanderbilts."[36] Pictures of German battleships adorned many a newspaper front page and magazine cover.

There also existed a general feeling that the "Romance" nations were in a state of decline and that the "Germanic" countries were the natural heirs. Perhaps Joseph Chamberlain had been close to the mark with his proposed Anglo-American-German alliance — at least in theory. The rector of the Charlottenburg Technical College in Berlin, a person enjoying imperial patronage, touched on this theme in his New Year's declaration: "The end of the century finds the Romance peoples in decline [and] the German culture in the process of conquering the world. It finds Germany as the leading political and economic power, protecting this process with a mailed fist."[37]* Others, although not agreeing on exactly what "peoples" were "declining," took up the theme. Ludwig Stein wrote that especially the Persian, Indian, and Chinese empires were ready for reapportioning, and Theodor Ziegler predicted that Great Britain's "defeats in South Africa" foreshadowed a new "division of the world."[38] The latter notion concerning the fall of the British Empire naturally appealed to Admiral von Tirpitz. It was his firm belief that

* Theodore Roosevelt informed Professor Hugo Münsterberg of Harvard in 1903: "The future totally belongs to a cooperating Germany, England and the United States; the Slavs are still one hundred years behind and the romance nations are finished." Cited in Alfred Vagts *Deutschland und die Vereinigten Staaten in der Weltpolitik* (New York 1935), II, 1597.

Great Britain had seen her best days and that Germany would have to be ready when the time came to divide the spoils with Japan, Russia, and the United States.[39]

## Invasion Strategies II (1900–1902)

Germany's leaders remained preoccupied throughout 1900 with naval appropriations as an expression of German power and purpose. Bülow assured the parliamentary budget committee in March that only battleships commanded respect. The crisis in Manila might have been prevented, he suggested, if Germany had been able to support Diederichs with a mighty battle fleet. Moreover, the future would surely bring a new confrontation, probably in Venezuela or Guatemala. German trade, steadily increasing in East Asia and South America, required warships for protection. Naval funds, Bülow stated, "were designed first and foremost to provide security at sea against England and America."[40] He cleverly inverted Bismarck's arguments from 1889 against naval expenditures. Then, the chancellor had reasoned that Germany needed only a fleet sufficient to protect her interests in Samoa against the minuscule United States Navy. But now the Americans were laying the foundations for "a great fleet." Thus Germany was forced to keep pace with American naval construction if she wanted to maintain the parity recommended by the legendary Bismarck.[41] A perfect vicious circle.

Admiral von Tirpitz assured Reichstag critics that his battleship concept did not rule out cruiser construction. In fact, he went on record with a promise of large overseas cruisers in the near future in order to protect German maritime trade in Asia and South America, "where we can accomplish little through diplomatic means but only through the might of our ships."[42] And the Reich's naval envoy in Washington kept Berlin informed of local developments. His reports had a single purpose: to spur naval planners on in their quest for a fleet second to none. Rebeur-Paschwitz particularly stressed that the United States had a head start on Germany in terms of battleship construction, but he felt certain that Germany could overcome this initial lead by superior organization, construction, and personnel training.[43]

The Kaiser, of course, remained for Americans the most reliable source regarding Germany's alleged hostile intentions overseas. At the public launching of the battleship *Wittelsbach* in Wilhelmshaven in July 1900, he again rattled the saber, warning that in the future no decision could be made "upon the ocean or in faraway lands without the German

Emperor." He announced that it was solely *his* duty and *his* privilege to create the necessary—"and if it must be, the most powerful"—means to enforce this bold claim. The self-styled "Admiral of the Atlantic" further warned that he would deploy his battleships "without mercy."[44] Needless to say, the speech was hardly designed to calm American apprehensions concerning German designs—especially upon the Western Hemisphere.

This public rhetoric was paralleled by continued staff planning for the operational plan against the United States. In the formulation of this contingency plan, Admiral von Diederichs had placed special emphasis upon close cooperation between the Admiralty Staff and the General Staff of the army. The Kaiser's marginal instructions—"joint report Admiralty Staff – General Staff"—on Rebeur-Paschwitz's cable to Tirpitz of 6 January 1900 served as the official basis for joint talks.[45] Diederichs first approached Count Alfred von Schlieffen, chief of staff of the Prussian army, on this matter on 28 November, after passage of the Second Navy Bill, and on 1 December the general conveyed his willingness to commence work. Throughout the remainder of 1900 both planning agencies turned their attention to the plan. Naval staff work had been slowed down somewhat by Tirpitz's request of December 1899 for information on the operations plan against the United States, to be used to justify the desired naval expansion to the Reichstag. This delay was further compounded by the necessity of converting the March 1899 strategic operational *Marschplan* into a detailed mobilization plan for both fleet and train.

On 10 December 1900 Diederichs presented the results of these long months of Admiralty Staff planning in still another audience with Wilhelm II on the state of the American contingency plan. He again recommended Boston and/or New York as the most suitable targets, with Provincetown serving as *Stützpunkt*. He estimated that by 1901 Germany would have twenty-two battleships against eighteen for the United States, a total of 172,145 tons of floating warships as against 141,893 tons, and a German advantage of 138 to 114 pieces of heavy naval artillery. "Germany's armored fleet is numerically superior to that of the United States." In ships available and suitable for duty on the Atlantic Ocean, Germany also held a favorable edge: fifteen to eleven battleships, 136,088 to 113,634 in total tonnage, and ninety-seven to ninety in heavy naval cannon. Hence the offensive could only lie with Germany. "An American expedition into German waters, however, would be utterly unsuccessful."[46]

But Wilhelm II proved, desipte all his bombast, to be a more sober military planner. He did not accept the optimistic calculations of his naval leaders, and instead ordered that "with respect to the impossibility of transporting enough troops to the American mainland at the start of a war, we should take the island of Cuba under consideration as a preliminary target in our advance against North America." Diederichs was hardly pleased by this turn of events. On 25 February 1901 he asked Schlieffen to calculate the number of troops needed for an occupation of Cuba, but at the same time he reminded the general that Cuba was not the final goal and that the army should also figure out how many troops it required for land operations against Boston and New York. "It thus appears to me as necessary as ever to extend our preliminary studies on the basis of the Imperial audience to cover the mainland areas [of the United States], independent of the cursory work on the occupation of Cuba (and Portorico)."[47]

Schlieffen proceeded cautiously. He took the Kaiser's position as Supreme War Lord at face value; open disregard of an Imperial decision was anathema to him. On 13 March 1901 he sent his calculations to Diederichs. The letter is a model study in vagueness. Schlieffen obviously did not want to commit himself in writing. He agreed to Cape Cod as "a base for operations against Boston as well as against New York," but insisted that the troops would have to break out of this narrow peninsula, preferably to Plymouth, as soon as possible after landing. The strength of the American regular army was estimated at 100,000 men, of which number perhaps 30,000 to 40,000 would be available for duty on the east coast at the time of a German landing. The general cautioned Diederichs not to pay too much attention to examples from the Spanish-American War — an obvious reference to Mantey's second study. In 1898 it had taken the United States four weeks to assemble 125,000 men and three months later there were still only 223,000 men in uniform. But this figure was misleading, Schlieffen warned, "because a [German] landing upon American soil will stir patriotism much more than the [Spanish-American] war did." And of the eleven million men eligible for military service in the United States, the general estimated that 106,000 had received "scanty military training" and that the United States could therefore have some 100,000 men — "of which one-third are well trained, two-thirds not properly trained" — available at the point of attack. He was even more cautious in estimating the number of German troops required for the operation, guardedly stating that this would depend on the number of troops the United States could muster immediately after the outbreak of hostilities. "One cannot give precise figures because the Americans possess no organized mobilization plans, preferring instead to base their defenses upon the creation of large volunteer armies that will first have to be organized and trained militarily once war is proclaimed." In any case, Schlieffen estimated one army corps for securing the landing site (Cape Cod) and even greater numbers to break out of the peninsula. "Thus it becomes clear that at the outset 100,000 men will have to be transported to the Cape Cod peninsula. This number would probably also suffice for operations against Boston." An attack upon New York City, on the other hand, would require an even greater force because of "the significantly longer lines of communication" and the mounting danger of American flank attacks as their reserve and volunteer units were mobilized. Obviously, time and quickness of movement were the keys to any possible operations on the eastern seaboard. Schlieffen did not bother to discuss the relative merits of Cuba and Puerto Rico as landing sites, "because His Majesty has decided that Cuba shall be the preliminary target for an attack upon North America." He merely expressed concern that the Cubans might prove hostile to the German invaders. Consequently, 50,000 soldiers would be needed to secure the island as a base of operations; 100,000 additional troops would be required for the jump to the American mainland. But the general warned that even this quantity would not be sufficient for operations into the interior of the United States.[48]

Diederichs was furious. To Schlieffen's evasive reply that the requisite German force would depend on enemy resistance encountered, the admiral sarcastically commented: "That is most ingenious!" At the foot of the letter Diederichs added: "Since, in the view of the General Staff, we are unable to accomplish anything on the mainland with the number of troops that we can transport there, we *must* advance *against the islands* [West Indies] or else declare our [military] bankruptcy vis-à-vis the United States." The admiral resolutely refused to abandon his plans for a direct landing on the east coast of the United States. Three days after Schlieffen's disappointing reply he stated anew: "We must continue to contemplate a landing in Cape Cod Bay."[49] It should be remembered, as Captain Forstmeier has pointed out, that the navy was overly anxious to show the prestigious Prussian army what sea power could accomplish — if only the army would go along and offer its vital support.

Berlin planners relied heavily upon reports submitted by Germany's naval attaché in Washington. In February 1901 Rebeur-Paschwitz had wired Schlieffen's office regarding the urgency of an operations plan against the United States. The communication bordered on insolence. The envoy noted that by now not even the Prussian army could afford to ignore the fact that the United States posed as much of a "danger" to Germany as any of her continental neighbors (Russia and France). He especially reminded the General Staff that it would do well to reread a manuscript entitled "World History in Outline," written by a man "very close to the General Staff"— Yorck von Wartenburg. Rebeur-Paschwitz quoted at length from this work: "Despite the fact that the West Atlantic world [America] is still totally dependent intellectually upon the East Atlantic [Europe], it desires to annihilate it economically *and the final showdown will not be of a peaceful nature*" (my italics).[50]

On 20 March 1901 Admiral von Diederichs asked Rebeur-Paschwitz to inspect all possible landing sites in the Boston–New York area once more. He deviously informed the naval attaché that Schlieffen had answered his queries regarding the possibility of a German landing in the Cape Cod area in a "generally very positive manner."[51] Specifically, Diederichs asked Rebeur-Paschwitz to board the cruiser S.M.S. *Vineta*, which was coming up from South America for an inspection tour of Boston under the guise of a routine repair stop. The admiral obviously still cherished the direct invasion project, despite an official veto from the Kaiser and an unenthusiastic response from the General Staff.[52]

Rebeur-Paschwitz and Captain Baron R. von Kap-herr, a special military member of the Washington embassy, completed a survey of possible landing sites in the Boston area in March 1901. Their joint findings recommended two sites north of the city, Rockport and Gloucester, Massachusetts.[53] Rebeur-Paschwitz took this opportunity once more to impress upon Schlieffen the climate of opinion in the United States, stressing:

> . . . that at least for the navy there exists every reason clearly to contemplate the necessity of operations against the United States. I have at various times . . . pointed out how [American] confidence and feelings of superiority vis-à-vis Europe have drastically increased and how such sentiments have found expression in the press, in the speeches of parliamentarians, and everywhere else to a degree which, I believe, is hardly imaginable by us [at home].

The envoy asked specifically that the gentlemen of the General Staff be constantly reminded of this fact.[54]

In retrospect it can be seen that Schlieffen's letter of 13 March 1901 formed a turning point in the formulation of the operations plan against the United States — despite Diederichs's continued efforts on behalf of the direct invasion project. It marked a return to sober military planning and a turning away from what can only be termed the reckless offensive-oriented thinking that had characterized Admiralty Staff planning ever since Mantey's first *Winterarbeit* of 1898. It further constituted a return to Admiral von Tirpitz's *Stützpunktpolitik* — the policy of acquiring a system of naval bases girdling the globe — which, as shall be seen later, found its most distinct expression in the work of Vice Admiral Wilhelm

Büchsel.[55] And finally, the letter lucidly demonstrates that a German-American conflict was a very real problem, that serious operational planning was under way among Germany's highest naval as well as military leaders, and that in line with the expansionist theories of the navalism and imperialism of the period, the Germans did not shrink from contemplating and planning a war three and a half thousand miles from their shores, for stakes (Samoa, the Philippines, West Indies, and the like) that can at best be described as mediocre and which were out of all proportion to the risks involved.

German-American relations underwent further deterioration in 1901 through publication of a book pointing out the feasibility of German naval and military operations against the United States. The author, Baron Franz von Edelsheim, was a first lieutenant in the elite Second Uhlan cavalry and at the time of publication attached to the General Staff. In *Operations Upon the Sea: A Study*, Edelsheim clearly foresaw a successful landing on the eastern seaboard of the United States. The navy's role would be limited primarily to hit-and-run attacks against the major seaports while the army would fight the decisive battles on land. The baron espied victory for Germany in the sorry state of the American army, calculating that of its 65,000 troops only some 20,000 could be deployed against the invading German forces. About 10,000 men would have to be kept out West to guard against an Indian uprising. The American militia was dismissed as worthless. Edelsheim realized that operations into the interior of the country would be hopeless, but he believed that the seizure of large parts of the east coast as "pledges" would suffice to make the United States come to terms with Germany.[56] Schlieffen was extremely upset over this untimely publication, officially denying that it had any connection whatsoever with the General Staff.[57] The Foreign Office and Naval Office quickly added their denials.

However, Germany's semiofficial military journal *Militärwochenblatt* immediately reviewed the book. Twice. One reviewer expressed the conviction that Germany was now sufficiently armed at sea to risk an encounter with the United States Navy, while a second added that Edelsheim had achieved his purpose "of making broad circles receptive to the idea" of a German-American war. The first reviewer closed by asking how this invading armada would be supplied for an extensive period in American waters. It was a fair question and one that defied explanation not only by Edelsheim but also by the Admiralty Staff.[58]

The impact of Edelsheim's work upon German-American relations was utterly ruinous. Although they obviously could not know that the book very closely paralleled official planning, American leaders were now certain that Germany harbored hostile intentions in the Western Hemisphere. On 19 November 1901 Jules Cambon, the French ambassador in Washington, could report to Foreign Minister Théophile Delcassé that German-American relations:

> . . . are worse. . . . One is jealous, one knows that one fights on either side for the commercial supremacy of the world; there is no agreement possible in this field, and it suffices that some guard-lieutenant at Berlin occupies his leisure in organizing on paper an invasion of American territory by German troops to give new strength of actuality to Admiral Dewey's saying that the first war of the United States would be with Germany.[59]

Cambon hit the nail on the head. Two weeks after General von Schlieffen's celebrated communication to Diederichs on the most likely landing site for a German invasion of the United States, Senator Henry Cabot Lodge of Massachusetts informed Vice-President Theodore Roosevelt* that he considered a German landing in Boston — his constituency —"well within the range of possibilities." The United States must constantly be on guard. "The German Emperor has moments when he is wild enough to do anything." However, Lodge considered a German landing in South America (Brazil), as propounded by the German economist Gustav Schmoller, a more likely prospect. Roosevelt, in turn, informed Lodge that Germany was indeed the real menace to the United States, emphasizing that the Germans "count with absolute confidence upon our inability to assemble an army of thirty thousand men which would in any way be a match for a German army of the same size."[60] Moreover, American naval officers returning from the German autumn maneuvers in 1900 were "greatly impressed with the evident intention of the German military classes to take a fall out of us when the opportunity offers."[61] The book by Edelsheim showed Americans where the danger lay. Perhaps the only American official still oblivious to the anti-American sentiment in Germany was the naval attaché in Berlin, William H. Beehler, who continued to laud the "remarkably competent Emperor" and the merits of "one Commanding Officer endowed with supreme authority to successfully conduct combined operations."[62]

Naval planners in Berlin were provided by various sources with further reports on German-American relations during 1901. Ambassador Holleben was becoming more pessimistic every day. Whereas earlier he had recommended a German-American rapprochement, in August 1901 he advised gloomily that only a temporary "*modus vivendi*" on the basis

* Roosevelt had been governor of New York from 1898 to 1900; in January 1901 he became vice-president and in September of that year assumed the presidency after the assassination of William McKinley.

of Frederick the Great's motto, "*Toujours en vedette*" (Always on guard), could be attained. On the economic front, Germany and the United States were presently under an "armistice" with both sides preparing for the final showdown. McKinley, the ambassador predicted, would try to avoid war. Roosevelt favored war with Germany, as did Lodge. Holleben reported that navy as well as army officers in the United States were convinced that "sooner or later there will be war between the United States and Germany." American naval planners especially favored a war and hoped to provoke it "à la Manila." It was a cruel dilemma and there existed only one possible solution: Germany, as Europe's major economic power, "must accept battle with America." Moreover, the day would soon come when Germany and the United States could no longer avoid the question of "German naval bases in South America." The ambassador apparently was aware of German preparation of a contingency war plan against the United States because he cautioned Berlin not to overestimate the importance of capturing New York, Boston, or other cities along the eastern seaboard in the event of war. It was true that Puerto Rico could easily be seized and used as a German base, but there was no ready antidote against America's vast resources. In the final analysis, Holleben argued that only rapprochement with Great Britain could protect Germany from the American "danger."[63]*

The first secretary of the German legation in Washington, Count Albert von Quadt, in October 1901 submitted a rather curious report of conditions in the United States to the new chancellor, Count Bernhard von Bülow. It foreshadowed many of the views concerning America's moral decay that were later to be associated with the National Socialist regime. Quadt reported that New York and Philadelphia were veritable moral sewers. The pool halls stood under police protection, the thousand houses of ill repute received police support in "recruiting"— especially underage girls—and organized crime worked in unison with the law. Bribery ran rampant and reigned supreme: in government contract awards, customs inspections, legal decisions, and congressional votes. No less than one-third of Philadelphia's thirty-million-dollar budget ended up in the pockets of the mayor and his city council each year. Most important, this corruption would soon affect the officer corps. In a country where soldiering was "a business like any other" rather than a matter of "class privilege," the armed forces would inevitably be undermined and rendered less effective by such civilian corruption. The Kaiser

* A similar prognosis was received by the Naval Office from Professor Ernst von Halle of Marburg University on 1 August 1901. Halle often acted as economic adviser to Tirpitz on naval appropriations. Foreign Office Archives, Bonn, West Germany, Vereinigte Staaten von Amerika No. 1, vol. 12.

was so impressed by the report that he circulated it to the Prussian minister of the interior, the minister of finance, and the police president of Berlin.[64] And when Quadt sent a *Washington Post* article of 20 October 1901 in which Senator Joseph B. Foraker of Ohio stressed America's dire need for markets in the Orient, Wilhelm ostentatiously predicted: "There is where we will probably collide."[65]

In the meantime, in Berlin both Admiralty Staff and General Staff continued their efforts toward discovering a mutually acceptable landing site. Schlieffen informed Diederichs of the drawbacks of Provincetown and Rockport, pointing out that intelligence sources available to him — in the form of an article by Captain Charles Train — suggested that the United States was expecting a German landing in the Boston area.[66] Holleben cabled Bülow that Admiral Dewey had long ago concluded that a German attack would be directed against the islands of St. Thomas and St. John in the West Indies.[67] These two reports, though conflicting in their estimates of possible landing sites, clearly showed that the United States was alive to the problem of a German invasion and that its planners had recognized the most likely German approach routes. Diederichs thereupon abandoned all previous calculations, and on 6 January 1902 requested information from Rebeur-Paschwitz in Washington regarding the defense works of Long Island. Diederichs was especially interested in Great Gull, Gardiner, Fisher, and Plum Islands. He further wanted to know if Block Island was fortified and if it was in the "American defense network." The admiral bluntly asked the naval envoy for his opinion about a possible landing in Gardiner's Bay, followed by a land attack on Brooklyn.[68]

The immediate outcome of this correspondence was an Admiralty Staff *Denkschrift* on 15 January 1902 recommending an assault on Puerto Rico, followed by a blockade of American Atlantic and Gulf of Mexico seaports and eventual operations against the major trade centers in the northeast, especially Boston and New York. "Most effective would be a landing on Long Island (for example, in Gardiner's Bay) and a joint advance by land and sea against Brooklyn and New York." In case the German invading armada met defeat, it could easily withdraw to "San Juan de Portorico" or even to Germany.[69] Still another memorandum from that year gave the first pronouncement concerning Germany's political aims in the Caribbean. "Once in possession of Portorico we will never return it."[70]

This renewed interest in combined army-navy operations against New York was reflected in the assignment of *Winterarbeiten* in 1901–1902. Diederichs ordered an evaluation of "the strategic and tactical value" of the United States Navy and the "military geography" of the United

States, the West Indies, and South America. On 21 April 1902 Lieutenant Magnus von Levetzow, attached to the Naval Academy and destined to become Admiral Reinhard Scheer's chief of staff in 1918,* submitted his analysis of the most suitable invasion route for Germany in case of war with the United States. Levetzow recommended a direct assault on New York, culminating in the conquest of Fishers Island and Fort Wright. The study must have found favor with the Admiralty Staff, because during September and October of that year Levetzow boarded S.M.S. *Vineta* to inspect Haiti, Port-au-Prince, and Puerto Cabello as possible *Stützpunkte*. His reports (2 October to the Kaiser; 26 September and 14 October to the Admiralty Staff) reiterated an old theme: "The operations against the east coast of North America probably will have to be of short duration." Therefore, he suggested hit-and-run bombardments of the coastal stretch between Portland, Maine, and Cape Cod (à la Edelsheim). But when Levetzow suggested that operations against the United States take the form of cruiser warfare to interrupt American shipping and communications, he was immediately relieved of his assignment — a clear indication of the fate awaiting anyone who even indirectly came into opposition with Tirpitz's battle fleet concept.[71]

Early in 1902 the Admiralty Staff underwent another change in command. Rivalry between Tirpitz and Diederichs finally forced the Kaiser to choose between the two. As successor to Diederichs the choice fell on Vice Admiral Wilhelm Büchsel, until then chief of the General Department of the Naval Office and thus a close aide of Tirpitz. But Büchsel was not given time to continue Diederichs's work on the operations plan against the United States. For hardly had he taken over his new position when events in Venezuela once again raised the prospect of a German-American conflict to the front pages of the world's press.

* In the sea battle at Skagerrak (Jutland) on 31 May 1916 Levetzow was chief of the Operational Division of the High Sea Fleet; from August to November 1918 he was Scheer's chief of staff.

THREE

# The Way West (1901–1906)

We will do whatever is necessary for our navy, even if it displeases the Yankees. Never fear!

— WILHELM II *to Ambassador Holleben February 1902*

IT IS NO SIMPLE TASK TO EVALUATE GERMAN POLICY ON THE ACQUISITION OF territory in the Western Hemisphere. American leaders were certain that such was the German objective, the Kaiser and his advisers later denied it, and documents hint at but do not substantiate it. There can be little doubt that German naval planners coveted a base *somewhere* in the Western Hemisphere at *some* time and *some* place. For without it, Tirpitz's entire *Stützpunktpolitik* would be scuttled. And it is self-evident that certain segments of German finance and industry likewise harbored ambitions in Latin America. A Naval Office estimate of June 1900 gives some insight into officially known investments on this continent: 100 million marks in Colombia; 200 million each in Mexico, Venezuela, and the West Indies; 250 million in Central America; 270 to 300 million in Chile; 350 million in Brazil; and almost 600 million in Argentina. In all, over 1.5 billion marks were invested in South America, with an additional one-half billion in Central America and two billion in the United States.[1]

While this in no way forces one to conclude that Germany would be willing to back this capital investment with force, it nevertheless partly accounts for her keen interest in political developments in this area. If one further keeps in mind the aforementioned desire of certain German economists to establish a German colony in Latin America to absorb her excess population, it becomes readily clear that this region was a critical factor in the deliberations of Germany's political leaders, economists, industrialists, financiers, and, last but not least, naval planners.

Americans were well aware of German economic and financial interests in Latin America and they carefully recorded the numerous boasts and predictions of the Kaiser and his entourage regarding German ambitions there. This situation was further compounded by Germany's unwillingness to recognize officially the Monroe Doctrine, and exacerbated by her participation in a blockade of Venezuelan ports in 1902. Thus before concluding our analysis of German contingency planning against the United States between 1901 and 1906, it is profitable to explore the international tension engendered by actual — as well as alleged — German aims in the Western Hemisphere. Did Germany really plan to seize a base in the West Indies? In Brazil? In Mexico? Why did she not recognize the Monroe Doctrine? What were her motives in extending a naval blockade against the Venezuelan harbors? These are some of the questions designed to shed further light on German naval planning at the turn of the century and, as we shall see later, concurrently on the considerations of the United States Navy concerning the possibility of war with Germany in the Atlantic.

## German Bases in Latin America?

By 1900, Germany had shifted the theater of her most acute rivalry with the United States from the Philippines to South America. The Atlantic replaced the Pacific as the most likely point of confrontation, much to the delight of the British. When Wilhelm II confided to his uncle King Edward VII that "German naval construction is directed not against England but America," this was quickly passed on to Andrew Carnegie and, through him, to Theodore Roosevelt.[2] And the Kaiser's celebrated marginalia once more reveal ample justification for Roosevelt's fears of Germany's hostile intentions in the Western Hemisphere. When the German ambassador to Mexico wired in January 1900 that a German colony in Latin America was of greater value than all of Africa, Wilhelm noted: "Correct! That is why *we* must be the 'paramount power' there!" The following month Ambassador Holleben cautioned from Washington that Americans still feared a German landing in the Western Hemisphere, but that perhaps an agreement for a coaling station might be negotiated after President McKinley's reelection through Andrew White, Whitelaw Reid, and others. The prospect did not appeal to the Kaiser. "That is irrelevant! South America is no concern of the Yankees!" In May 1900 Holleben once more warned that the United States was carefully watching German activity in Latin America. Again Wilhelm grew irritated.

"Once we have a decent fleet this, to a certain degree, becomes immaterial. South America simply is no concern of the Yankees." Perhaps the most representative statement of Wilhelm's attitude toward Latin America was written on yet another cautionary communication from Holleben: "Fleet, fleet, fleet."[3]

The Kaiser's customary braggadocio was supplemented over the years by several acts of armed intervention in Latin American waters that greatly irritated the already apprehensive Americans. As early as 1893, Wilhelm had dispatched two warships to Rio de Janeiro "to protect Germans" during that nation's civil war.[4] Four years later, after Emil Lüders, a German subject and onetime officer in the elite Berlin Guard-Cuirassiers, was arrested in Haiti for resisting the local police, two German naval vessels appeared off Port-au-Prince, Haiti's capital, and shelled it on 6 December 1897 — the very day that the German parliament began debate on the First Navy Bill. The Wilhelmstrasse managed at the last moment to avert possible disaster when Wilhelm wished to pursue this interference in Haitian domestic affairs: "I refuse to accept the verdict of a board of arbitration when I can obtain my rights [*sic*] with cannon."[5] And reported German activities in Mexico had traditionally been a point of contention between the Reich and the United States. Ever since Emperor Maximilian's brief reign in Mexico in the 1860s, the United States had been on guard against European aspirations in the nations south of the Rio Grande, specifically against Germany's alleged desire for a coaling station in Magdalena Bay (Baja California). Even the cautious Holleben believed that Germany required a naval station in Mexico, and he was certain that the day would come when Germany and the United States "would openly have to settle this issue."[6]

However, the most active approach to Latin America was adopted by German naval leaders. They could be certain of the Kaiser's support. In 1902, at the outset of the Venezuelan crisis, Wilhelm made this perfectly clear after a warning from Holleben that "realization of our navy's plans" in Latin America could lead to war with the United States: "We will do whatever is necessary for our navy, even if it displeases the Yankees. Never fear!"[7] These sentiments were passed on to the ambassador with orders to burn them immediately.

During the Spanish-American War, German admirals had coveted a naval base in the West Indies. The Admiralty had recommended acquisition of coaling stations in the Western Hemisphere and Admiral von Tirpitz, basing his information on Mahan's article "The Isthmus and Sea Power" in the *Atlantic Monthly* of September 1893, demanded that the Foreign Office prepare the way for the seizure of St. Thomas and Curaçao in the wake of the general peace settlement of the former

Spanish Empire.[8] Germany's special military envoy in Washington, Count Götzen, cabled support. Germany must always maintain warships in the Caribbean, he argued, in order to protect her citizens and property against "the moods of half-civilized authorities" in "states that are constantly in revolution." Especially the proposed isthmian canal necessitated German naval presence in these waters.[9]

The argument did not fall on deaf ears. Tirpitz was aware of the strategic significance of the future canal: American control would confront Germany with the choice of one day having to wage war over it or of relying upon other, longer and more difficult seaways such as the Suez Canal and Cape Horn. Moreover, the canal would allow the United States Navy to move its forces freely from one coast to the other and, conversely, prevent Germany from combining her home fleet with her Pacific cruiser squadron in the event of war with the United States. Bedazzled with grandiose naval dreams, Tirpitz even envisaged that the day might come when the states south of the Rio Grande would throw off the yoke of American domination, organize a joint Latin American navy, and join the German fleet in battle against the United States Navy.[10] Thus the canal might yet come under German control, the Monroe Doctrine be revoked, and Latin America opened up to German economic exploitation.

Such surrealistic speculation ended abruptly in 1901 when the German Foreign Office informed Tirpitz that Germany possessed absolutely no legal rights for even a share of the proposed isthmian canal. Thus thwarted in his effort to gain a share of the canal, Tirpitz turned to an enfilading plan of attack. An island in the West Indies, he argued, would give Germany a high degree of control over at least the eastern terminus of the canal. Naval planners in Berlin now vied with one another to recommend suitable targets in the Caribbean; most frequently mentioned were the Dutch islands of Curaçao and St. Eustatius as well as Dutch Guiana. This activity, in turn, elucidates Tirpitz's earlier statement to Count Anton Monts, chief of the Admiralty, that his attention had already in 1898 been "directed towards Holland."[11]

But other areas were also open to speculation. Especially popular was the notion that private brokers might purchase an island somewhere off the coast of Latin America and, after a reasonable number of years, turn it over to the German government. Attention now centered especially on Port Otway near Cape Tres Montes, a small island in Brazil's Rio Bay, Magdalena Bay in Baja California, and Fonseca Bay on the west coast of Honduras.[12] Albert Ballin of the Hamburg-America Line, initially an avid supporter of Tirpitz's naval plans, lent his company's name to these attempts to purchase a foothold in the West Indies. By the turn of the century, Ballin agreed to purchase as much land as possible on St. Thomas and transfer it to the Reich at a later date, hoping thereby to throw the United States off the track. As Ballin put it, "behind every German [merchant] vessel abroad must stand the German battleship!" He and Tirpitz later turned their eyes to Kingston, Jamaica, and even initiated negotiations toward forming a German consortium to finance a canal across the Panamanian isthmus. But these proposals were too adventurous and potentially explosive for even the Kaiser.[13]

German naval officers recognized from the start that their principal adversary was Theodore Roosevelt, whom they regarded as the "Kaiser of America" as well as the "American Tirpitz." Germany's naval attaché in Washington, Rebeur-Paschwitz, became obsessed with the likelihood of a German-American clash over Latin America, flooding Berlin with reports of Mahan's writings concerning German aspirations there as well as in the West Indies.[14] Rebeur-Paschwitz sadly noted that the United States had appointed herself as "referee" in the Western Hemisphere. "And herein, provided that we are not willing simply to subordinate ourselves to this referee, I see the danger of a collision which we cannot dismiss, but for which we must prepare ourselves militarily."[15] Specifically, the attaché lamented that Germany did not emulate the American policy of sending warships into South American waters and rivers, such as the Amazon and the Orinoco, under the guise of business or scientific expeditions.[16] Above all, Rebeur-Paschwitz urged his government to prepare for a future confrontation with the United States; war could not be avoided. In January 1902 he prodded Berlin "to seize *every* possible opportunity . . . to acquire a strategically indispensable military base" in Latin America. Only the navy, he argued, was in a position to judge what territory to take. The press, while encouraging Germans to think more in terms of colonial expansion, would have to desist from naming specific objectives. In case of war with the United States, Germany would simply have to adopt a tough strategic stance in the West Indies, "which, as far as I know, is contemplated in leading circles." The envoy favored seizure of a base in the Caribbean, to be followed by an assault upon one of the major trade centers in the northeast, "preferably Boston." Whatever the case, he admonished naval leaders in Berlin time and again to step up planning for the approaching conflict.[17]

American suspicions and fears concerning German intentions in the Western Hemisphere were acutely aroused in September 1902 when the German gunboat *Panther* intervened in yet another Haitian civil war. Haitian revolutionaries had seized the government's gunboat *Crête-à-Pierrot* and stopped a German vessel, taking from it arms and munitions destined for the government. Berlin ordered reprisals, and on 7 September the gunboat *Panther*, stationed in the West Indies with the German East American squadron, captured and destroyed the *Crête-à-Pierrot.* The Kaiser added fuel to the flames by wiring the ship's commandant: "Bravo, *Panther!*"[18] The overall political climate created by such overt incidents — trivial in themselves — was perhaps best expressed by the Mexican government newspaper *El Imparcial* in 1903. It depicted the German-American rivalry as a historical parallel to the wars between Carthage (the United States) and Rome (Germany). The prize was not Sicily but Latin America. The paper compared the two giants to electric batteries being charged; soon they would explode "and ignite a world-wide fire." "Heated sentiments dominate on the shores of the Elbe as well as the Mississippi." In the end, either Berlin or Washington would trigger the confrontation in the style of the elder Cato: *Ceterum censeo Carthaginem esse delendam* (It is my opinion, despite all else, that Carthage must be destroyed).[19]

## The Monroe Doctrine

The Monroe Doctrine, enunciated in 1823 to protect the American continents against European intervention or invasion, was widely ignored by European states, many of which saw it merely as a cloak for United States domination of Latin America. The German Foreign Office, until around 1900, insisted on referring to the Washington government as the "United States of North America" in all its official documents as an indirect protest against the Monroe Doctrine. And even the British did not recognize Monroe's dictum until the first decade of the twentieth century. European statesmen were especially concerned that the United States might attempt to extend the doctrine beyond the American continents. In 1887 the Iron Chancellor's son, Herbert von Bismarck, who was then secretary of state for foreign affairs, claimed that American interests in Samoa foreshadowed an extension of the Monroe Doctrine to the Pacific Ocean, transforming that body into "an American lake." His father, in May 1898, shortly before his death, described the Monroe Doctrine as "a species of arrogance peculiarly American and inexcusable," as an "insolent dogma."[20] Wilhelm II agreed with his former chancellor. He regretted that Europe had not taken advantage of the Civil War to intervene in American affairs, specifically to support the South against the North — a notion not unique to the Kaiser. Moreover, it was Wilhelm's belief that American involvement in the Philippines in 1898 had ushered in a new age of imperialism for the United States, and that as a result she would have to give up the Monroe Doctrine.[21]

By the turn of the century the Monroe Doctrine seemed most threatened by Germany in Brazil. Although the German population in southern Brazil was only 350,000 out of a total Brazilian population of eighteen million, there were signs that Germany took special interest in Rio Grande do Sul (200,000 Germans). Apart from the aforementioned ambitions of German economists in this region, Berlin was active in preserving and furthering German traditions here: the Reich financed German schools and churches, the Colonial Society recruited financiers for investment, the navy periodically sent warships into Brazilian waters to "show the flag," and no less than nine German consuls toured southern Brazil, often incognito. The Spanish-American War seemed to many to offer a splendid opportunity to establish a German colony here after the Kiaochow model. The United States could hardly protest at a time when it was seizing territory in the Far East. The Pan-German publication *Alldeutsche Blätter* rallied to the side of the Pan-Germans, who complained that "Uncle Sam was subjugating Brazil with Monroe Doctrine and lard, [with] gunboats and Methodist preachers."[22] A German-Brazil Union was founded in 1899 to encourage German trade and emigration to Brazil. And in April 1900 Admiral von Tirpitz bluntly informed the Reichstag's budget committee that in the future Germany would have to establish a heavily armed and manned naval station in East Asia "as well as on the coast of Brazil."[23] This point was vociferously supported by German naval commanders in Latin American waters, one of whom informed an American colleague: "So far as we Germans are concerned, you can have Amazonas but we intend to take Rio Grande do Sul."[24] It argues little for the economic, or Marxist, analysis of colonialism and imperialism that this German-American confrontation over Brazil reached its apex at a time when American investment in Brazil was virtually nonexistent. It also occurred when German-American trade rivalry was at a low ebb as a result of the European economic depression of 1900–1901, and when hostile clashes took place in Brazil only between rival Protestant missionaries.

Germany's dilemma over whether to recognize the Monroe Doctrine as well as the underlying problem of relations with the United States with regard to Latin America became acute in 1902 when the Kaiser's brother, Admiral Prince Henry of Prussia, visited the United States. On the surface his trip in February and March was a diplomatic triumph. Prince Henry had received explicit instructions not to mention the Boer War (now in its bitter final stages), at all times to denounce alleged German aspirations in Latin America as "absurd figments of the imagination," and the Wilhelmstrasse had even supplied him with an "official" version of the events in Manila in 1898.[25] At Harvard University's Sanders Theater, during an academic meeting convened to bestow an honorary Doctor of Laws degree upon the Kaiser's brother, the prince led three cheers for Theodore Roosevelt, and the audience replied by singing "Die Wacht am Rhein." Chancellor von Bülow hailed the visit as an expression of the historic friendship between the two powers.[26]

But this aura of good feeling belied the facts. The prince's journey had caused a diplomatic furor in Berlin prior to his departure. Victor Wiegand had cautioned Prince Henry early in 1902 against discussing the alleged "injustice of the Spanish-American War."[27] And soon word reached Baron von Holstein in the Foreign Office that the prince had expressed his desire "to bring something concrete back from this trip." Holstein soon learned from intimate sources — Prince Henry's court chamberlain, Vice Admiral Baron Albert von Seckendorff, and the Prussian ambassador to Hamburg, Heinrich von Tschirschky — that Prince Henry planned to demand from Roosevelt a "German sphere of influence in South America." Holstein at once surmised that Admiral von Tirpitz and the navy stood behind this proposal. Moreover, Prince Henry had adopted the curious position that as a naval officer he was not bound to observe the usual customs and limits of diplomatic acumen and tact. Finally, he had expressed his intention to discuss the Manila incident and especially Dewey's role therein. Holstein, by his own account, managed to prevent such embarrassing talks only after threatening to obtain an imperial injunction forbidding the prince to raise these sensitive issues.[28]

Admiral Georg Alexander von Müller, chief of the Naval Cabinet, accompanied Prince Henry to the United States. Müller was a man who had been accused of harboring "liberal" tendencies and of possessing a relative who had fought on the "wrong" side of the barricades in the Revolutions of 1848, which adds interest to his observations and impressions of American life, politics, and the military establishment. He was impressed by the physical appearance of American congressmen, but he suspected that there were many "labor foremen" among them, and that it was not the "first social class" of the land that was represented in the Lower House. On the other hand, at the White House and among the "Captains of Industry and Commerce" Müller found what he termed "the political aristocracy of the land." With regard to the officer corps of the armed forces, Müller believed that the Annapolis midshipmen stood socially above the West Point cadets;* however, both corps were below the "social niveau" of the German officer corps because their

* President Roosevelt consented to his daughter's christening the Kaiser's yacht; Wilhelm, in turn, renamed torpedo boat "D2" the *Alice Roosevelt*. Foreign Office Archives, Bonn, West Germany, Deutschland No. 138, vol. 21, Wilhelm II to Foreign Office, 1 January 1902; Roosevelt to Wilhelm II, 22 March 1902.

applicants were supported by state subsidies and thus often came from "craftsmen" backgrounds.[29]

A German naval officer who visited Newport News that same year left for the Kaiser a different, perhaps more representative impression. The commander of the cruiser *Vineta* (Stiege) found Americans dominated by "boundless vanity and arrogance." The traditions and restraint of the Old World were entirely absent. "The 'upstart' is present in all of them to varying degrees, and the beast of prey often lurks just under the surface."[30]* Given such simplistic preconceptions of American society, it is surprising that the prince's visit came off as well as it did and that the topic of Latin America was not raised during the two weeks that he was in the United States.

The issue of Germany's official position regarding the Monroe Doctrine threatened to come to a head in parliament in 1903. As a result of the Venezuelan blockade (see pages 76–85), Great Britain had officially recognized the Monroe Doctrine. The Pan-German press posed the rhetorical question whether the Berlin government should follow this "dishonorable" act. Such a course, the *Alldeutsche Blätter* ominously suggested, would not only "check German acquisition of territory in South or Central America," but also "create new domestic opposition" for Chancellor von Bülow at home. On the other hand, the chancellor could be certain that failure to recognize the doctrine at this point would provide further proof to Americans that Germany did, indeed, cherish secret territorial ambitions in the Western Hemisphere.

Bülow turned to Tirpitz. The admiral suggested that the government refuse to discuss the matter, or, should that prove impossible, simply give vague, evasive explanations of German intentions.[31] Bülow was rescued by the fact that the matter never came up in parliament. Holleben's successor in Washington, Baron Speck von Sternburg, later verbally assured Presidet Roosevelt that Germany respected the Monroe Doctrine. But when German-born Harvard Professor Hugo Münsterberg suggested that the day might come when the United States would annex Canada, and Germany in turn take a colony in Latin America, Wilhelm II was ready: "All right."[32]

The German popular press continued to keep the question of territorial aggrandizement in the Western Hemisphere in circulation. The

* See also the report from envoy Speck von Sternburg to Bülow, 30 June 1903, claiming that "nigger burnings and lynchings" had numbered 3,200 in twenty years. Walther Wever, the German consul in Chicago, informed Bülow on 26 May 1903 that there existed widespread fear in the United States of an increased influx of Jewish immigrants. "The position of the English-Americans toward the Jews is as deprecatory as I have seen it in no other land." Foreign Office Archives, Bonn, Vereinigte Staaten von Amerika No. 1, vol. 14.

*Grenzboten* clamored for a colony under the German flag in Brazil, and the U.S. State Department was informed by its envoy in Santiago that the 120,000 Germans in Chile had not been assimilated and remained loyal to the Reich.[33] The *Tägliche Rundschau*, in speaking of the Monroe Doctrine, asserted that "the insolence of the United States . . . is . . . simply unbearable," while the Bismarckian *Hamburger Nachrichten* called it "a piece of incredible impertinence."[34] Moreover, German warships continued to cruise in Latin American waters, therewith providing Germanophobes and naval enthusiasts in the United States with sufficient fresh material to keep the flames of anti-German sentiment burning. The *Panther* especially became for Americans a veritable "red rag."[35]

Above all, the Kaiser never undertook the one official act that might have eased German-American tensions — recognition of the Monroe Doctrine. He steadfastly insisted upon the right of European nations to interfere directly south of the Rio Grande should European rights and interests there be violated. At times he hoped that the Latin American states would join together against the United States in a fashion similar to that by which Europe had united against the "yellow peril"— an oblique reference to the suppression of the Boxer rebellion in China during 1900–1901 (in which Japan had also participated). But in the end Wilhelm rejected Roosevelt's dictum that the United States alone possessed the right to exercise "police powers" in Latin America. "I can never agree with such an interpretation of the Monroe Doctrine."[36]

Perhaps the closest one can come to summarizing Germany's policy on the Monroe Doctrine is through Tirpitz's axiom that "naval construction and gaining time" were Germany's primary objectives around 1900. In other words, she would maintain a low profile, avoid open confrontations with the United States in Latin America, and make a basic policy decision in this matter only at a future date, when she could support her stance with thirty-eight first-class battleships. But Tirpitz was not granted the requisite period of peace and tranquility. In Venezuela the Monroe Doctrine was put to the acid test almost two decades before the Tirpitz fleet was scheduled to be completed.

## Venezuelan Blockade (1902–1903)

Venezuela's default on numerous European loans in 1901 caused Germany to join with Great Britain and Italy in establishing a blockade of that nation's major port facilities.* Germany's participation in the

* The German Foreign Office estimated that Germany's investment in Venezuela lay between 150 and 180 million marks, far surpassing that of any other foreign

blockade probably comes closest to fitting the Marxist stereotyped theory of aggressive capitalism and imperialism, of the government's armed might in the service of private capital.[37] Berlin estimated that by 1901 German business and finance had invested between 150 and 180 million marks in Venezuela, much of it in the Greater Venezuelan Railroad Company. The concession for this so-called "Baghdad Railway of South America" had been awarded to Friedrich Krupp Company in 1887 and the railway was financed primarily by the Berlin Diskonto and the Hamburg Norddeutsche Bank.[38] Obviously, some concern also had to be paid to the safety of the approximately one thousand German nationals living in Venezuela. But the question of German prestige and honor soon dominated all others with the Kaiser. Encouraged by Roosevelt's decision that the Monroe Doctrine did not aim at protecting a Latin American state "that misconducts itself," provided "that punishment does not take the form of the acquisition of territory by any one European power," Wilhelm II adopted a swaggering tone in November 1901 when it was reported that personnel from the cruiser *Vineta* had brawled with Venezuelan police. "Government absolutely must ask for our forgiveness and perhaps salute our flag with twenty-one shots, or else I will order bombardment."[39] The *Deutsche Zeitung* reminded its readers that three hundred and fifty years earlier, the medieval German house of Welser had in the service of Emperor Charles V marched through Venezuela with drums beating.[40] This argument was to be repeated some thirty years later by Adolf Hitler.

German measures against Venezuela proceeded slowly. In the summer of 1901 the Italians had expressed their desire to join any action designed to force Venezuela to fulfill her financial obligations, and in January 1902 the British were asked about their position on this matter. But above all, the Kaiser did not wish to take action in Latin America while Prince Henry was in the United States on a goodwill tour.[41] Furthermore, the German navy calculated that it could not make ready the requisite shallow-draft warships until the autumn of 1902, a season when the rigors of the tropical climate would be at their lowest. In fact, naval planners in Berlin, totally captivated by Mahan's battle fleet concept, realized that they lacked sufficient blockade ships, and that as a result effective action could only be undertaken in conjunction with the

---

nation. An initial loan of 44 million marks for railroad construction in 1894 had been guaranteed by the Venezuelan government at 7 percent interest; that interest had never been paid. As a result, in 1896 a new credit of 26 million marks was extended to Venezuela, this time at an annual interest rate of 5 percent. Once again the interest payments never came. In January 1901 President Cipriano Castro's government officially refused to recognize all loans negotiated before he had come to power (May 1899). Bundesarchiv-Militärarchiv, Freiburg im Breisgau, West Germany, F 5175, vol. 1, 39–50, Bülow to Wilhelm II, 30 December 1901.

British Royal Navy. Points of international law also remained to be ironed out.[42]

The German Admiralty Staff noted as early as August 1901 that a blockade of Venezuela would have to be carefully prepared in order not to arouse unnecessarily American suspicions of German intentions in the Western Hemisphere. To this end, they agreed from the start to deploy only light cruisers and no battleships.[43] To complicate matters, the British had rejected the notion of a "peaceful" blockade as "unjustifiable in international law," and the Kaiser on 7 January 1902 had ruled out a formal declaration of war against Venezuela.

These delays, in turn, infuriated the German press. The *Tägliche Rundschau* and the *Berliner Tageblatt* attacked the alleged "weakness" of the German government in dealing with Venezuela, and the agrarian *Deutsche Tageszeitung* chided Bülow's fear of "Onkel Sam." The semi-official *Kreuzzeitung* trumpeted that it was "preposterous" to regard American military might as sufficient to "prevent German expansion in the New World if that were to assume a territorial aspect."[44] General Waldersee, now Wilhelm's adjutant general, quickly joined this attack on the Bülow government, agreeing that the chancellor grossly overestimated possible American reaction.[45] In any event, Roosevelt's vigor and dynamism in defending the Western Hemisphere against possible German encroachments were nowhere better displayed than in 1902–1903 during the Anglo-German-Italian blockade of Venezuela. The President was a veritable whirlwind of activity: he attempted to purchase the Virgin Islands, Culebra was transferred to the Navy Department for development as a naval base "in case of sudden war," a naval officer was dispatched to Venezuela to keep an eye on German naval operations, Congress was requested to grant funds for naval maneuvers at Culebra, possible landing sites for both German and American troops along the Venezuelan coast were secretly scouted, the fleet was mobilized at Culebra with Admiral Dewey in command, and a naval envoy was sent to Caracas to help prepare the Venezuelan defense against a European invasion.[46]

Ironically, Admiral von Tirpitz seems to have been dead set against the Venezuelan blockade. Perhaps because he was at that moment actively pursuing a policy of reconciliation with Great Britain, but more probably because he was afraid of any armed conflict during this "risk" period of naval construction, he opposed the adventurous undertaking and earned for himself the slight: "Tirpitz has no stomach for a fight . . . Tirpitz has shown similar lack of nerve on other occasions."[47] In fact, Tirpitz was probably guided by more sober calculations: the navy's budget was severely strained, the proposed blockade would cost almost five million marks, and additional funds could be obtained only by involving parliament[48] — a most undesirable turn of events.

On 9 December 1902 a small Anglo-German naval armada finally began a "peaceful" blockade of Venezuelan ports, destroying one enemy warship and seizing three of the remaining four. Chancellor von Bülow had recommended the blockade "in order to uphold Germany's prestige and [to] protect her interests in South and Central America."[49] The British blockaded La Guaira, Carenero, Guanta, Cumaná, Carúpano, and the Orinoco delta; Germany patrolled Puerto Cabello and Maracaibo; and the Italians supported the action with two warships on 16 December 1902.[50] On 13 December the British cruiser *Charybdis* and her German counterpart *Vineta* shelled two Venezuelan forts, Libertador and Vigía, into submission. President Cipriano Castro thereupon transmitted to Washington his willingness to accept international arbitration; London concurred on the seventeenth and Berlin followed suit two days later. On 20 December 1902 the "peaceful" blockade was transformed into an official "wartime" blockade until the Hague Court settled the dispute.

Unfortunately this did not end the Venezuelan affair as far as German-American relations were concerned. For on 17 January 1903 the gunboat *Panther* was fired upon and repelled by Fort San Carlos as it attempted to enter the Straits of Maracaibo. The *Vineta* responded four days later by leveling the fort. Commodore Georg Scheder cabled Wilhelm II that he had been motivated to do so by the "swaggering, provocative manner in which the Venezuelans had celebrated their triumph" over the *Panther* on the seventeenth.[51] In other words, to uphold German honor and prestige. The Kaiser censured the *Panther*'s action and reprimanded her captain, but commended Scheder for protecting German honor by immediately attacking Fort San Carlos.[52]

The latter act was widely denounced in the United States. In vain did Speck von Sternburg, then the new chargé in Washington, assure Roosevelt that the Kaiser "would no more think of violating that [Monroe] doctrine than he would of colonizing the moon." At least Wilhelm could not reach the latter. The Kaiser also tried to soothe American feelings by lending official support to Sternburg's denials concerning alleged German hostile intentions in the Western Hemisphere. But whatever benefit this might have reaped was quickly dissipated when Wilhelm formally complained about Admiral Dewey's "extremely foolish" pronouncement that American naval officers regarded Germany as "their next enemy."[53]

Germany's willingness to submit the Venezuelan dispute to the Hague Court provided little satisfaction to her statesmen and sailors. Dewey's overpowering naval presence in the Caribbean had aroused bitter resentment and frustration. Ambassador von Holleben, about to leave his post in Washington, caustically commented that the Americans were building a mammoth fleet "in the same manner that rich parvenus like to maintain a stable of race horses." The diplomat noted that the British had been reduced in American deliberations to a "negligible quantity" while Germany had been promoted to the unenviable spot, formerly reserved for the British, of most probable enemy. Holleben's parting gesture was to remind Berlin that Uncle Sam understood only naked power; all attempts to "win America's favor" were doomed to failure.[54]

The Kaiser felt particularly frustrated by the Venezuelan matter. He was most resentful that the British had managed through skillful propaganda to depict Germany as the real aggressor in Venezuela, and he toyed with the idea of seeking more cordial relations with the United States in order to isolate Great Britain.[55]* Yet at the same time that his hatred of "perfidious Albion" seemed to dictate a rapprochement with the United States, he realized that the latter's friendship could be purchased only by recognition of the Monroe Doctrine and general relaxation of colonial rivalry — at Germany's expense. It was a dilemma and one that Germany managed to resolve eventually only by adopting Tirpitz's formula that the two Anglo-Saxon maritime powers were, in fact, one economic and political bloc dedicated to keeping Germany contained on the European continent.

In the end, the Venezuelan episode most benefited the United States Navy. Though Congress in 1902–1903 agreed to construct an additional five battleships, the navy's greatest gains were not material but in terms of national prestige. The relatively small European naval force consisting

* The Anglo-German cooperation was denounced by Rudyard Kipling in "The Rowers," published in *The Times* on 22 December 1902. Kipling wrote of the victorious British troops returning from South Africa only to be ordered to sail to Venezuela:

> There was never a shame in Christendie
> They laid not to our door —
> And you say we must take the winter sea
> And sail with them once more?
>
> Look South! The gale is scarce o'erpast
> That stripped and laid us down,
> When we stood forth but they stood fast
> And prayed to see us drown.

Kipling concluded:

> In sight of peace — from the Narrow Seas
> O'er half the world to run —
> With a cheated crew, to league anew
> With the Goth and the shameless Hun!

*The Times* defended it as "a sentiment which unquestionably prevails far and wide throughout the nation." O. J. Hale *Publicity and Diplomacy with Special Reference to England and Germany 1890–1914* (London 1940), 259–60.

of fourteen ships (Great Britain 28,750 tons, Italy 14,800 tons, and Germany 11,147 tons) blockading Venezuela was overshadowed by Dewey's Caribbean fleet of fifty-four warships (129,822 tons) and, in fact, proved to be a threat neither to American security nor to the Monroe Doctrine.[56] Admiral Dewey, by combining near Puerto Rico the United States North Atlantic, South Atlantic, European, and Caribbean naval squadrons, accomplished his primary objective of flaunting American naval might. A historian of the Venezuelan affair has noted: "Never before had a full American admiral commanded a fleet at sea; never before had such a powerful concentration of American naval force been assembled." Moreover, the second highest senior naval officer, Rear Admiral Henry C. Taylor, accompanied Dewey, so that the latter could well crow that "Germany could not possibly get a fleet over here that could fight such an aggregation."[57] But the German action had been well exploited: America was once more made aware of the supposed German threat in the Western Hemisphere. The United States Navy, after its fall maneuvers in November 1902, concluded that the German planned blockade of Venezuela made war "most probable" and that the United States must "at all times . . . be in a better state of preparation for war than Germany is, and her every move must be met by a corresponding preparatory action on our part."[58]

The United States Navy at this time (summer of 1902) also turned to the need to protect the Panama Canal with bases on the perimeter of the Caribbean Sea, often referred to as the "American Mediterranean" in United States naval circles. Admiral Dewey wished to acquire or expand — and at worst prevent from falling into European hands — the following bases: Guantánamo Bay in Cuba, the Danish West Indies, Culebra along with the Virgin Islands, Almirante Bay and Chiriquí Lagoon on the Caribbean side of the Isthmus (from Colombia), and Bahia in Brazil. Nor did Dewey ignore the Pacific coast of South America. Here he sought the Pearl Islands or Port Elena in Central America, Chimbote (Ferrol and Samanco bays) on the Peruvian coast, and Ecuador's Pacific island group (the Galápagos Islands).[59]

To assure a continuous "better state of preparation," American naval enthusiasts united to emulate the German Navy League. Public pressure for an increase in the fleet had been steadily mounting in the United States. Nurtured by retired naval officers, prominent financiers, industrialists, and corporation lawyers, this as yet unorganized propaganda helped the United States Navy obtain Congressional approval for the construction between 1902 and 1905 of ten battleships, four armored cruisers and seventeen light cruisers. The program called for annual expenditures of from 85 to 118 million dollars, and Roosevelt longed for further matériel increases in order by 1920 to possess a fleet of forty capital ships.[60] There were in the United States, as in Germany, certain influential circles that spearheaded the new wave of navalism:

Shipowners, exporters, producers of goods entering largely into foreign commerce, and citizens anxious to enhance the power and prestige of the United States, all had favored increasing the Navy. The same was true of shipbuilders, the metallurgical industries, and others who participated directly or indirectly in the profits of naval construction. Then there were the professional members of the Service who had a perfectly natural desire to see their institution grow and prosper. And finally, there were the politicians, for some of whom . . . liberal naval appropriations served as a means of political advancement at the polls.[61]

In 1903 the United States Navy League was founded with the support of J. P. Morgan, Seth Low, George Westinghouse, and Charles M. Schwab, among others. Its main function under Admiral A. S. Barker was to publish a monthly journal dealing with naval affairs of public interest (from 1903 to 1906 entitled the *Navy League Journal*, and from 1907 to 1916 *The Navy*).[62] In June 1903 the *Navy League Journal* described its German model and counterpart, "whose astounding results we shall strive to emulate," as "the fourth sea-power in the world."[63]

The United States fleet had made significant strides since the Spanish-American War, when it had possessed only four first-class and two second-class battleships as well as two armored cruisers (compared with seven battleships and six coast-defense armored ships for Germany). By 1907, after Roosevelt's hectic construction pace, the United States had a fleet of sixteen battleships and six armored cruisers, while Germany possessed twenty-three battleships, eight coastal defense ships and eleven large cruisers. Moreover, the United States Navy decided in September 1905 to commence construction of the *Dreadnought* class superbattleships. Though there was a small vociferous minority that fought the naval program as "imperialistic, militaristic, grossly expensive, a menace to our peaceful relations, and calculated to impoverish the country," it could not stem the tide of navalism and imperialism that was sweeping the land.* However, Wall Street's *New York Evening Post*, the bible of

* Some of the leaders of the minority were Representatives Claude Kitchin (North Carolina), T. E. Burton (Ohio), J. G. Cannon (Illinois), chairman of the Committee on Appropriations, and Senator Eugene Hale (Maine), chairman of the Senate Naval Committee. Roosevelt was especially irritated by Hale's opposition and he confided to Sternburg: "I wish it were possible to make Senator Hale learn his [Tirpitz's] speech [on behalf of battleship construction] by heart! It might do him good." Foreign Office Archives, Bonn, Vereinigte Staaten von Amerika No. 5a, vol. 22, Roosevelt to Sternburg, 3 March 1905.

capitalism for many Marxists, deplored the development. "This game of getting more ships for our officers, and then more officers for our ships, has been worked long enough."[64]* But the specter of German naval operations in the Western Hemisphere served to provide backing for the naval increases.

German naval planners quickly recognized and accepted this fact of life. The Admiralty Staff on 4 May 1903 agreed that alleged German intentions to seize a base in the Western Hemisphere had been exploited successfully by American naval supporters.[65] The Admiralty might have added that the Venezuelan blockade had the same effect upon American fleet expansion as the Boer War had exercised on similar German increases five years earlier. And Sternburg reminded Berlin "that it is undeniable, that a relatively acute animosity has existed between the American and German navies ever since the Manila incident."[66]

The shelling of the Venezuelan forts by German warships whipped anti-German sentiment in the United States to fever pitch. President Roosevelt expressed his shock and horror to the German chargé Speck von Sternburg: "Are people in Berlin crazy? Don't they know that they are inflaming public opinion more and more here? Don't they know that they will be left alone without England?"[67] Roosevelt undoubtedly vastly overrated the possibility of war with Germany as a result of the Venezuelan crisis in his famous "posterity letters,"† but there can be no doubt that the issue was on everyone's lips and widely considered to be a distinct possibility in the not too distant future. Secretary of the Navy William H. Moody informed Sternburg that Germany had replaced Great Britain as the yardstick for American naval expansion, and that the United States Navy would soon steam into European waters in order to counteract the European presence off Venezuela.[68] The army commander in California, General Arthur MacArthur, pleaded that National Guard units be sent to Hawaii because he suspected that Germany would next test the Monroe Doctrine in that Pacific region.[69] And the *Army and Navy Journal* was most concerned that Germany planned to create a "Pacific American Squadron" to supplement its "Atlantic American Squadron." The journal was certain that the Kaiser planned to seize a base in the West Indies and denounced his policy as "one of opportunism, pure and simple." The slightest indication of American retreat

* The *Post* had traditionally been close to Carl Schurz and had stood for economic cooperation with the Reich. Moreover, it feared that vast naval expenditures would seriously jeopardize American finances at this time.

† It should be pointed out that Ambassador von Holleben was absent from Washington between 14 and 26 December, and did not call at the White House between 6 and 31 December 1902.

"from our advanced position in support of the Monroe Doctrine" would prompt the Germans to set foot in Latin America. "He is, indeed, a short-sighted observer who does not see in these powerful German squadrons, patrolling the American continent on the East and on the West, the possible foretoken of momentous eventualities in the affairs of the world."[70]

The Kaiser, in turn, lamented that the Venezuelan action had generally upheld America's right to play the role of the policeman south of the Rio Grande. "This would have been impossible were we now sufficiently strong at sea."[71] There could be no clearer elucidation of Germany's long-range policy toward Latin America. The monarch demanded an immediate increase in the size of the German navy, but shipyards were already fully occupied with the Navy Bill of 1900.

Finally, it is interesting to note that the Venezuelan affair in no way relaxed American apprehensions concerning a direct invasion of the American mainland by Germany. Captain C. D. Sigsbee, head of the Naval Intelligence Office, informed Secretary of the Navy Moody on 21 January 1903 of his certainty that any German attack would be directed against Washington rather than Boston or New York, with Annapolis serving as the German base of operations. "No other objective in the United States is now so inviting for attack as the city of Washington." Reminding the secretary of the British and Canadian route in 1814, Sigsbee pointed out the obvious advantages of a German assault on this city. The national gun shop, the gold and silver of the Treasury, the government archives, and national prestige all precluded a German attack elsewhere. Captain Sigsbee disagreed with Admiral Dewey's belief in a German invasion of the West Indies:

> In order to clearly perceive of the exposed condition of the National Capital, it is only necessary to conceive the United States fleet as having been sent to the West Indies through a feint in the latter region by a strong naval power.[72]

This point of view accurately reflected German thinking in the winter of 1898; since then German planners had abandoned historic-bureaucratic-demographic factors. Sigsbee was further concerned with possible German espionage and infiltration. On 11 March 1903 he officially recommended a survey to discover whether American sailors with German names were:

> . . . native born or naturalized; how long in the service before naturalization; how long in this country; how long in the navy; whether their tattoo marks are emblematic of patriotism to Germany or to this country, etc.

He believed that Germany "has a spy system on board our ships, a system most easy of accomplishment," and he worried whether artillery officers with German names would purposely fire off the mark in the event of war with Germany.[73] In Berlin the month of March witnessed equal fervor, though along more serious lines.

## Operations Plan III (1903–1906)

On 21 March 1903, in the wake of the Venezuelan action, Vice Admiral Wilhelm Büchsel, chief of the Admiralty Staff, attended his first Imperial audience on the state of naval planning against the United States:

There can be only *one* objective for Germany's war strategy: direct pressure on the American east coast and its most populous areas, especially New York; that is, a merciless offensive designed to confront the American people with an *unbearable* situation through the dissemination of terror and through damaging enemy trade and property.

Germany still maintained numerical superiority in warships and thus "the *advantage of the offensive*" lay solely with her. But she could not endure a war of attrition, and Büchsel therefore favored immediately forcing a decisive naval encounter with the United States Navy. Culebra and Puerto Rico were singled out as the best *Stützpunkte*, especially since they would give Germany control over the eastern terminus of the Panama Canal when it was completed. Such a plan would compel the American fleet to do battle in the Caribbean and would, in any case, provide good "pawns for the final reckoning."[74] The Imperial audience was unique in one respect; for the first time Admiralty planners concerned themselves with the overall political situation:

*Necessary prerequisite* for a German war against the United States is a *political constellation in Europe* which accords the German Reich a totally free hand in foreign affairs. Any uncertainty in Europe would preclude a successful war against the United States. Thus we do not seek such a war, but it can be forced on us.[75]

It is indicative of the spirit of the age that the United States in 1913, as we shall see later on, counted on precisely such a political alignment in Europe.

Büchsel's realization that politics and diplomacy were, of necessity, integral parts of naval planning resulted in the first formulation of German maritime war aims. The permanent possession of Culebra and Puerto Rico would give Germany a "valuable strategic position" for the final peace settlement, thereby assuring her a role for the future in this area. "Permanent possession" of these islands "for us represents a dike against the effrontery of the Monroe Doctrine." In short, the Reich's aims were: "Secure position in the West Indies. Free hand in South America. Revocation of the Monroe Doctrine." To achieve these goals, Büchsel ruled out a direct assault on New York City as too risky; "on the other hand, a landing on and occupation of Long Island with a resulting threat to New York from the west end of this island seems feasible." This time the older ships of the *Baden* and *Siegfried* classes could be left behind because sufficient new constructions were available. Artillery and troops would be taken along to secure Culebra and Puerto Rico. The Kaiser agreed to the occupation of Culebra and asked both Admiralty Staff and General Staff to finalize plans for the occupation of Puerto Rico.[76]

In many ways Büchsel's *Immediatvortrag* marked the apex of all the planning that went into the contingency war plan against the United States. Here, before the Supreme War Lord, he gave practical expression to the aggregate thoughts of a generation of German proponents of *Weltpolitik*. The hopes and aims of the "fleet professors," and especially of Gustav Schmoller, were to reach fruition in the German "free hand in South America." With "revocation of the Monroe Doctrine" German industry could, with impunity, exploit economic concessions in Venezuela, Brazil, Argentina, and other Latin American states. And "secure position in the West Indies," to be realized through permanent possession of Culebra and Puerto Rico, marked the return of Admiralty Staff thinking to Tirpitz's *Stützpunktpolitik* (acquisition of naval stations girdling the globe). Büchsel once and for all abandoned the offensive-oriented strategy of Vice Admiral von Diederichs in favor of a more cautious *Etappenoffensive* — a step-by-step offensive. Yet, whereas Diederichs had directed his efforts primarily toward the goal of forcing the United States to enter peace negotiations, Büchsel now committed Germany to a naval offensive designed to destroy the Monroe Doctrine and with it America's dominant position in the Western Hemisphere. The fulcrum of German naval planning had thus shifted from an offensive military to an offensive military-political campaign.

By 1903 there remained little doubt among Germany's political as well as military leaders that the United States had become the most probable future opponent. In February of that year Sternburg reported that he had been informed by his Austrian colleague Hengervár von

Hengelmüller that people "spoke openly of an impending war with Germany" in Washington and "even in New York's conservative clubs." The following month the new German naval attaché, Lieutenant Erwin Schaefer, cabled that the ambassador from the Netherlands had been told by Dewey that war with Germany lay just around the corner and that the Americans looked forward to the coming conflict.[77]

Such ominous communications were not taken lightly in Berlin. In November the Naval Office informed the Kaiser that additional naval appropriations would have to be obtained by 1907 because Germany had "first and foremost to be ready for the collision with England or America." Both Anglo-Saxon powers were expanding their fleets at an alarming rate and the German people were not yet sufficiently prepared psychologically to keep up the pace. "A large portion of the German populace is still unenthusiastic about our overseas policies; the notion of *Weltpolitik* is not popular." The navy suggested that headway might best be made by basing future naval increases on mounting "severe North American encroachments" on European affairs.[78]

In light of this, the final calculations for the operations plan against the United States rapidly approached completion. On 25 April 1903 Büchsel informed General von Schlieffen that the navy could provide the necessary troops for the occupation of Culebra. Once the United States Navy had been defeated, the requisite land forces would be transported to Puerto Rico by the ocean liners of the Norddeutsche Lloyd and Hamburg-America lines.[79] On 14 May Schlieffen answered that the army required 12,000 men, 3,700 horses, and 671 mechanized vehicles for the occupation of Puerto Rico, which maintained a 6,600-man garrison. The chief of the General Staff did not foresee any difficulty in transporting this quantity of men and horses: "The China Expedition proved the capacity of the two large steamship lines, the North German Lloyd and the Hamburg-America Line, which were able without straining to transport about 14,000 men and 3,700 horses along with their requisite supplies."[80]* Schlieffen did not think that any further work was needed on the plan. By 27 November 1903 it was officially referred to as Opera-

* The force was to be modeled on the expeditionary corps sent to China in 1900. In addition to various railroad, telegraph, and sapper crews, among others, there would be:

| | |
|---|---|
| 12 battalions of 750 men | 9,000 men |
| 1 regiment cavalry | 660 |
| 1 regiment field artillery | 1,100 |
| 1 Royal heavy howitzer unit | 528 |
| 1 battalion pioneers, three companies | 650 |
| TOTAL [approximately] | 12,000 men |

Bundesarchiv-Militärarchiv, Freiburg im Breisgau, West Germany, F 5174b, I, 190–91.

tions Plan III (O.P. III).[81]* An Admiralty Staff study that same day optimistically prophesied: "We will be met at the entrance to the Caribbean Sea . . . only by the [U.S.] Atlantic Squadron, reinforced at most by 2 capital ships." Public opinion in the United States, the naval planners argued, would force the American admirals to leave part of their fleet at home in order to protect major seaports along the eastern seaboard.[82]

During the next two years Operations Plan III underwent only minor alterations and clarifications. In the winter of 1904–1905 the problem of supplying the initial invasion forces, both naval and military, was detailed in fourteen separate studies.[83] The central problem of supplying these forces over an extended period in American waters simply was avoided; the Admiralty Staff concerned itself even at this advanced stage of planning only with the initial phases of the operation. It was calculated that the German armada would now be ready to leave Germany not before the fortieth day of mobilization and reach Puerto Rico twenty days later.[84] Tirpitz's Naval Office lent support to these plans, informing the Admiralty Staff on 25 March 1905 that it could provide coal for a journey of 10,000 nautical miles. Its studies further revealed that at any given time at least thirty freighters totaling 100,000 tons, for the supply train, could be located and requisitioned in Germany's North Sea ports alone.[85]† On the same day the General Staff informed Büchsel that an inquiry by Major Erich Ludendorff had revealed the harbor of Ponce as the best landing site on Puerto Rico.[86]‡ The navy now estimated that it would need 1,750 sailors for the occupation of Culebra. Schlieffen's calculations for Puerto Rico also climbed to 793 officers, 14,780 soldiers, and 894 mechanized vehicles.[87]

A final point of interest is the German estimate regarding the caliber of the armed forces of the United States.§ Throughout the early period,

* On 18 September 1899 the chief of the Admiralty Staff, Rear Admiral Felix Bendemann, had ordered the following operations plans drawn up: "I. (war against France); II. (war against France and Russia); III. (war against England); IV. (war against North America)." Bundesarchiv-Militärarchiv, Freiburg im Breisgau, West Germany, F 5174b, I, 43. It is likely that the Franco-Russian rapprochement, which ultimately led to the Entente (1904), caused the Admiralty Staff to discard its Operations Plan I (war against France), thereby advancing the other plans a case higher. Unfortunately, it is not possible to document this assertion; the naval records contain only sparing information on the priority and numerical classification of the various plans.

† This communication from the Naval Office to the Admiralty Staff on 25 March 1905 also did not raise the key issue of supplying this force after the initial crossing. Did they plan to live entirely off the land?

‡ Schlieffen had earlier mentioned Mayagüez Bay, Aguadilla Bay, and Port Guánica as possible landing sites on Puerto Rico.

§ After the First World War, Tirpitz wrote: "The American navy . . . was as little a dangerous opponent as was the French navy; it observed with a certain jealousy two constant themes dominated German evaluations of American naval personnel: the detrimental "fusion of the executive with the engineer officer corps" and the "repeated jumps in seniority."[88]* On 1 May 1906 a most comprehensive report on American naval personnel was drafted. The old themes were once again aired, but with a new emphasis:

> The tremendous increase in personnel has led to an extremely acute officer shortage. . . . Apart from increasing the number of cadets, they have even been forced to reduce the training at the Naval Academy from the already shortened period of 3½ (instead of 4) to approximately 3 years as well as to expel inferior elements from the naval school . . . only with great reluctance.

Moreover, it was calculated that active American naval officers were generally well advanced in age — flag officers between fifty-nine and sixty-two years old, while in Germany they were between fifty-one and fifty-six; captains between fifty-five and sixty-one, and in Germany between forty-two and fifty-two. "The spirit of the naval officer corps is judged to be good, even if nepotism and patronage are not infrequent." A major obstacle to reform was that "one does not like to go back on the creator of the present system, the erstwhile Under Secretary of the Navy, Roosevelt." The sailors of the American fleet "are not the best elements" of society "and only seldom do fervent desire or enthusiasm drive young people to serve the flag." The high rate of desertion (10.7 percent, or 3227 men in 1905) brought with it "unreliability in a large portion of the remaining personnel." Further, of the 6600 discharges annually, excluding desertions, only about one-half were due to normal circumstances, the rest due to "moral or physical disabilities." Of the enlisted men, 83.7 percent were American born, 6.8 percent naturalized citizens, and 9.5 percent foreigners. Among the noncommissioned officers, 74.8 percent were natives, 20.9 percent naturalized, and 4.3 percent aliens. It is interesting to note that the study did not mention the possibility of espionage — much less sabotage — by German-born sailors serving in the United States Navy, as Captain Sigsbee had feared.[89]

There was an element of truth in this criticism. The United States Navy, as well as its British and German counterparts, throughout this period suffered from a shortage of qualified naval officers. "The personnel shortage bore directly on the problem of efficiency. With officers and crews overworked, training and discipline inevitably suffered." Above

---

the higher war potential of the German navy, even though the latter had been built for billions [*sic*] less." A. von Tirpitz *Erinnerungen* (Leipzig 1920), 160, fn. 2.

* It might be remembered that the Organizational Regulations of the Imperial German Navy from 26 June 1899 had ordered advancement strictly upon the basis of seniority (*Anciennität*), thereby excluding the possibility of rapid advancement beyond and ahead of one's classmates. See *Untersuchungen zur Geschichte des Offizierkorps. Anciennität und Beförderung nach Leistung* (Stuttgart 1962), 126ff.

all, naval gunnery was at a dismal level. Practice was unpopular and often left to the discretion of the commanding officer. And the Navy Department remained indifferent to the introduction of precise instruments for range finding, gun sighting, and gun pointing. It was only through the special efforts of President Roosevelt and Lieutenant William S. Sims, destined to head the American naval staff in London during the First World War, that the United States Navy corrected this deficiency. By December 1906 Roosevelt could inform Congress that the fleet's firing accuracy had improved fully 100 percent.[90]*

The year 1906 also brought changes in German naval strategy. The political alignment in Europe had shifted to Germany's decided disadvantage by the summer of that year. This is reflected in the Admiralty Staff's revision of Operations Plan III (1903), entitled "March to the West" and worked out by Captain Georg Hebbinghaus: "A German declaration of war against the United States is only possible if we are allied with England and [if] our flank is protected against France by Austria, Italy, and possibly also Russia." Under such a political constellation, German forces would be landed in Canada and commence land operations against the United States. However, Hebbinghaus realized that in 1906 Great Britain could not be counted upon to show only "ill-will" and since French neutrality was hardly likely, all Germany could do in case of war with the United States was to gain control of the major maritime lanes "and acquire pawn objects far distant from the American mainland."[91] Such fantastic preconditions could not justify the existence of a potentially explosive contingency war plan, and on 9 May 1906 Vice Admiral Büchsel ruled: "O.P. III is no longer directed specifically against the United States." Instead, it was transformed into a theoretical exercise because of the increase in the American fleet and especially because of the political situation in Europe.[92]†

What is surprising is not that the plan was discarded after barely three years, but that it should ever have been formulated and have lasted that long. In 1904 Germany had already suffered the twin blows of the Anglo-French Entente Cordiale and the Russian refusal of a

* Vice Admiral Büchsel felt that this lack of training and preparation might "dampen war fever in the United States," but he reminded his fellow officers that it was their "duty" to prepare for a struggle with the United States, which remained "a distinct possibility." Bundesarchiv-Militärarchiv, Freiburg im Breisgau, West Germany, F 2017/PG 65962, 211, memorandum for an Imperial audience, 4 May 1903.

† By 1908 the United States Navy was second only to the British in first-class battleships and third in the world in total tonnage built and building. Harold and Margaret Sprout *The Rise of American Naval Power* (Princeton 1943), 272ff. The following year the United States Navy had twenty-seven battleships in commission or building. Finally, it is interesting to note that Operations Plan III ended up as a German blueprint for gaining a foothold in Brazil.

military alliance. The First Moroccan Crisis in 1905, though resulting in the dismissal of French Foreign Minister Delcassé, revealed Italian and American opposition to German expansion. The naïve Björkö agreement of 1905 between Wilhelm II and Nicholas II, which called for a Russo-German offensive and defensive alliance (with the possible later admission of France) and was rejected by the respective governments, further compounded Germany's isolation in Europe. Only Austria-Hungary remained solidly in the German camp.

From 1904 to 1906, the central theme of Germany's foreign policy had been the forging of a continental bloc, headed by Germany, against Great Britain. By 1905 this policy had failed. The "New Course" of Bülow and Tirpitz had suffered shipwreck. The navy had not increased Germany's appeal as an ally but rather had brought France and Great Britain closer together. And with Russia making overtures to the Entente partners, Germany's *Weltpolitik* was effectively checkmated. In addition, the British dreadnought program of 1905–1906 undermined Tirpitz's entire naval policy.* In light of this, even the most militant and anti-American officials of the Reich could not fail to recognize the frivolity of a contingency war plan that called for full-scale operations on the east coast of the United States, to be followed by land operations against several major cities.

The obituary for the "New Course," that was to lead Germany "toward glorious times," was delivered by the Prussian General Staff. For it was precisely at this juncture, in December 1905 and January 1906, that General von Schlieffen drafted the famous memoranda that bear his name.[93]† With the realization that Germany was now firmly committed

* Volker R. Berghahn, in "Zu den Zielen des deutschen Flottenbaus unter Wilhelm II," *Historische Zeitschrift*, vol. 210, 86ff., asserts that the British dreadnought program destroyed "the entire calculations and projections of the Naval Office." Tirpitz, according to Berghahn, had estimated that the British would not be able to keep pace with German battleship construction and naval concentration in the North Sea, and that German personnel training and technical innovations would grant her fleet a real chance of success against even a numerically superior opponent. The dreadnought program crossed these calculations by placing naval construction on an equal footing. Moreover, it was the Germans, and not the British, who ran into financial difficulties as a result of dreadnought construction (ibid., 90ff). Berghahn has expanded his arguments in *Der Tirpitz-Plan. Genesis und Verfall einer innenpolitischen Krisenstrategie unter Wilhelm II* (Düsseldorf 1971).

† The "Schlieffen Plan," with which Germany entered the First World War eight years after the general's retirement, stipulated that because Germany was surrounded on all sides by enemies who, jointly, were stronger than herself, the only salvation lay in opposing the enemy with better communications (France) with superior force while only holding the other (Russia) at bay; thereafter, Germany's superior railroad network would allow her to hurl her armies against the other enemy in the east.

to wage a two-front campaign in any future European war, Operations Plan III must have seemed more and more a vision from a far-distant past.* Unfortunately, American leaders could not possibly have been aware of this turn of events.

* Leading army officers had long viewed the navy with mounting suspicion. In 1896 Count Waldersee stated: "The Kaiser seems to be totally obsessed with naval increases." Two years later the general commented bitterly: "The navy more and more cultivates the notion that future wars will be decided at sea. But what does the navy propose to do if the army is defeated, be it in the West or in the East? The honorable gentlemen obviously do not like to think that far ahead." Cited in J. Meyer *Die Propaganda der deutschen Flottenbewegung 1897–1900* (Bern 1967), 189. Such a situation was to arise precisely in October 1918.

FOUR

# Contingency War Planning: Washington (1900–1913)

> [W]hen conditions at home are no longer bearable and Germany is strong enough, Germany will insist upon the occupation of Western Hemisphere territory under the German flag, and the United States will then have to defend her policy by force, or acquiesce in the occupation.
>
> —*Black War Plan, Summer 1913*

IT HAS BECOME ABUNDANTLY CLEAR IN THE PRECEDING CHAPTERS THAT American political and naval leaders were concerned with the possibility of a German invasion of the Western Hemisphere, either in the West Indies or along the eastern seaboard of the United States. To varying degrees, American statesmen and sailors proclaimed the nation's need to build a mammoth fleet against the alleged German menace. Indeed, by the turn of the century Germany was widely regarded as the only possible opponent. The United States had little to fear from her continental neighbors, Canada and Mexico. France was regarded as a traditional "friendly," and Russia had ceased to be a world power after her defeats by Japan in 1904–1905. Great Britain, deeply embroiled in the struggle for South Africa's gold, was anxious to foster cordial relations with Roosevelt's America, as witnessed by her compliant behavior in the Venezuelan blockade in 1902 and in the Alaska boundary settlement in 1903. Germany, then, was the most formidable foe as well as the most dangerous rival. For only the Reich managed in the first decade of the twentieth century to keep pace with American production and commerce. Her iron and steel industry was second only to that of the United States by 1910, and she was more than a match in related fields such as chemical production, electrical innovations and developments, machine tools, and heavy armaments and armor plate production. Moreover, her almost instant rise to major naval power status, commencing in 1898 and expected after further naval expansion in 1906, 1908 and 1912 to reach fruition in 1920 with sixty capital ships, accorded her the requisite armed might with which to protect her trading rights and acquire new concessions at various points of the globe. Finally, as we have seen, Wilhelmian Germany had not hesitated to confront and challenge American expansion in Samoa, the Philippines, and the West Indies. America's leaders needed no clearer portents of coming conflicts and confrontations.

The State Department, especially, was panicked by the German "threat" to the United States. The Kaiser's personality played no small part in this. Ambassador Bartlett Tripp in Vienna cabled Secretary of State Richard Olney in 1896: "What will the Emperor do next? — is on everyone's lips. He may always be counted upon to do the unexpected thing and to do it without any apparent necessity for so doing."[1] Such "pathological suspicion of Germany," as William L. Langer called it, was also to be found with St. Loe Strachey, Henry White, Brooks Adams, Henry Cabot Lodge, and John Hay. The latter, as ambassador to the Court of St. James's in 1898 shared his Germanophobe outlook with Lodge:

> The jealousy and animosity felt towards us in Germany . . . can hardly be exaggerated. . . . The Vaterland is all on fire with greed, and terror of us. They want the Philippines, the Carolines, the Samoas — they want to get into our markets and keep us out of theirs. . . . There is to the German mind, something monstrous in the thought that a war should take place anywhere and they not profit by it.[2]

Senator Henry Cabot Lodge, partly through his close association with President Roosevelt, became an influential spokesman of anti-German sentiment in the United States. He frequently lectured about the German "threat" in the West Indies, and in Brazil, arguing that "only a strong and well equipped navy" could protect the Western Hemisphere against German violation of its territories.[3] In May 1900 Lodge publicly aired his views in the *Congressional Register*, warning that Germany might seize the Dutch islands in the West Indies, an act that could only be equated with a declaration of war. He continued:

> I am by no means convinced that some European power, perhaps one of those whose navy is just now receiving such a rapid increase, may [not] want to test that [Monroe] doctrine and that we may find ourselves called upon to protect Brazil or some other South American State from invasion. . . . I am not conjuring up imaginary dangers. I think that they exist and are very real.[4]

Above all, Wilhelm II was too volatile. "He is unstable, crazy for notoriety — not to be trusted. Not a man to rely on at all — with a saving sense of the danger of war and a strong inclination to bully up to the verge of war."[5] It is fruitless to continue citing countless similar utterances; suffice it to say that the senator could never rest on this matter, being convinced that "the German Emperor has moments when he is wild enough to do anything."[6]

Of course, the man most obsessed with the possibility that Germany might set foot in the Western Hemisphere was Theodore Roosevelt. Because of this, he even advocated supporting Great Britain in Europe against Germany. Roosevelt, as governor of New York, made this abundantly clear to Secretary of War Elihu Root in January 1900: "If disaster came to the British Empire, we might face abandoning the Monroe Doctrine and submitting to the acquisition of American territory by some great European military power, or going to war."[7] Roosevelt's speeches in defense of the principles of 1823 are almost legendary and certainly legion. In February 1900 he had informed John Hay, now secretary of state, of his stand on the doctrine in conjunction with the proposed isthmian canal:

> If we invite foreign powers to a joint ownership, a joint guarantee, of what so vitally concerns us but a little way from our borders, how can we possibly object to similar joint action say in Southern Brazil or Argentina, where our interests are so much less evident? If Germany has the same right that we have in the canal across Central America, why not in the partition of any part of Southern America?

Roosevelt concluded that the United States should resist all attempts by European powers "to control, in any shape, any territory in the Western Hemisphere which they do not already hold."[8] In later years he never wavered significantly from this point of view, despite some ambiguous rhetoric for the benefit of German leaders.* Roosevelt was absolutely certain that Germany was "the only power with which there is any reasonable likelihood or possibility of our clashing within the future." He depicted her as "a great growing power" with "ambitions in extra-European matters . . . so great, that she may clash with us."[9]

That "clash," according to Roosevelt, was most likely to be over

* Roosevelt claimed that he informed the German consul general in New York, Karl Bünz, that he was "delighted to see South America kept open commercially to Germany" and that he would not "object" if "a German-speaking community in a South American state . . . set up for itself." However, the discussion ended with a stern warning that the United States would never condone the seizure, by Germany or any other European power, of "a foot of soil in any shape or way in South America," or the establishment of "a protectorate under any guise over any South American country." *Selections from the Correspondence of Theodore Roosevelt and Henry Cabot Lodge 1884–1918* (New York 1925), I, 494, Roosevelt to Lodge 19 June 1901.

some territory in the Caribbean Sea, particularly the Dutch and Danish islands there. The Rough Rider described these spots as "constant temptations to Germany unless, or until, we take them away. The way to deliver Germany from the temptation is to keep on with the upbuilding of our navy."[10] He was adamant on this point: only a "first-class navy" rather than international controls or courts (The Hague) could protect American rights in the Western Hemisphere.[11] In 1905 he worried that the Kaiser might "hanker" after a coaling station in the West Indies, possibly under the guise of "commercial purposes."

It is the thin end of the wedge and I do not like the move at all. A coaling station is what Germany most lacks in our waters and the Kaiser could use this commercial station for warships. He is restless and tricky and this ought to be looked after. It is and always has been a danger point.[12]

The President was acutely aware of the economic threat that Germany posed for the United States, and alive to the danger that economic factors might possibly compel continental Europe to unite and even to declare war against the United States. But in the final analysis, partly due to the influence of Mahan, he gave primary importance not to economic but to strategic-military factors. "Modern Germany is alert, aggressive, military and industrial. . . . It respects the United States only in so far as it believes that our navy is efficient and that if sufficiently wronged or insulted we would fight." He was pursuing his policy of speaking softly but carrying a big stick. Roosevelt, like Holleben on the German side, believed that only force could deter aggression and command respect. More than any other American leader, he had closely monitored German activities in Samoa, the Philippines, the West Indies, Latin America, and Hawaii — not to mention China and Africa. Indeed, Roosevelt had favored war with Germany in 1889 over Samoa, and in 1897 he described the Reich anew as "the Power with which we may very possibly have ultimately to come into hostile contact."[13] He continued to tout Germany as America's most probable future enemy, and he trumpeted alleged German military superiority: "They are counting upon their ability to trounce us."[14]

The American President at times felt a certain empathy towards the German emperor. When Wilhelm praised him, Roosevelt commented: "He's really thoughtful, isn't he?" And when the Kaiser presented the President with a picture of the two leaders shaking hands, upon which Wilhelm had written, "When we shake hands, we shake the world," the American leader mused that his Imperial friend possessed "a real sense of humor." Nevertheless, Roosevelt, like Lodge, feared Wilhelm II's volatile and unpredictable nature. "If the Kaiser ever causes trouble it will be from jumpiness and not because of thought-out and deliberate purpose." At various times Roosevelt deplored the Kaiser's "pipe dreams," his "brain storms," his "sudden vagaries," and his "wholly irrational zigzags." In classic understatement, Roosevelt once commented: "Bill is a thought jumpy."[15] The President certainly would have appreciated the evaluation of the Kaiser rendered at this time by Sir Edward Grey, the British foreign secretary: "The German Emperor is ageing me; he is like a battleship with steam up and screws going, but with no rudder, and he will run into something some day and cause a catastrophe."[16] And with uncanny insight the President rightly discerned the base root of the Anglo-German naval rivalry that threatened to catch the United States in the middle:

> The Kaiser sincerely believes that the English are planning to attack him and smash his fleet, and perhaps join with France in a war to the death against him. As a matter of fact the English harbor no such intentions, but are themselves in a condition of panic terror lest the Kaiser secretly intend to destroy their fleet and blot out the British Empire from the map! It is as funny a case as I have ever seen of mutual distrust and fear bringing two peoples to the verge of war.[17]

A decade later the "funny case" turned deadly serious.

Roosevelt, in his fear of a German invasion of Western Hemisphere territory, could always count upon the support of the popular jingo press as well as the so-called "respectable" newspapers. The *New York Herald*, *New York World*, *New York American*, *Norfolk Virginian Pilot*, *Boston Journal*, *Baltimore American*, and *Chicago Inter-Ocean* could generally be relied upon to demand armed maintenance of the Monroe Doctrine.[18] Specific accusations were heaped upon Germany with alarming regularity: in 1899 the *New York Herald* inquired, HAS BRAZIL SOLD LAND?; the following year the *New York Sun* proclaimed, GERMANY IS THREATENING. SIGNS THAT THE KAISER IS ABOUT TO SQUEEZE VENEZUELA; in 1901 the *New York Herald* announced that the Hamburg-America Line was purchasing a base in Colombia for the German navy; and in 1902 it again warned, FOREIGN HANDS OFF HAYTI![19]

It should, however, be pointed out that Colonel Henry Watterson's *Louisville Courier-Journal* proved to be a healthy exception. The paper deplored the possibility of a German-American war over Latin America in defense of American honor. "For what? For a riffraff of Latins who hate us and of mongrels in almost abject ignorance and degradation, and a territory we shall never be able to acquire, and not worth the acquiring if we should be able." Watterson recommended that the United States seize the territory required for the isthmian canal, allow Germany a base in Latin America, and put an end to "wanton, senseless, hypocritical jingoism."[20] But the public would not endorse such a course. Especially the United States Navy continued with egotistical relish to beat the drums of anti-German sentiment.

It should be pointed out that American naval planners, like their German counterparts, were fully committed to the concept of offensive naval operations *à outrance*, of a Cannae at sea. Some found war "delightful"; others "superhuman." Captain Bradley Fiske, the officer responsible for the development of war plans in the administration of President William Howard Taft, saw it as "the acme of the endeavor of man." Admiral Mahan cherished "warlike habits" and decreed that "an occasional beating" was "good for men and nations."[21] Admiral Tirpitz would certainly have seconded Mahan's stance on war: "War, once declared, must be waged offensively. The enemy must not be fended off, but smitten down."[22] To this end, in 1890 a committee composed of six American naval officers had recommended that although the chance of war at the time appeared to be "at a minimum," the United States would have to launch a massive naval construction program encompassing no less than two hundred warships of all classes. The six planners reasoned that the world was on the brink of "commercial competition" which, in due course, was "certain to reach out and obstruct the interests of foreign nations." Specifically, the United States needed capital ships capable of attacking "points across the Atlantic."[23] Such speculation, which was also prevalent in German Admiralty Staff thinking, was reinforced by the events in Samoa in 1889 and 1898, the Philippines in 1898, and Venezuela in 1902. As we have seen, shortly after the confrontation with the Germans at Manila, Dewey had asserted that in fifteen years Germany would probably have successfully challenged both Great Britain and France in Europe. This, in turn, would be followed by an attack upon the United States, culminating in the occupation of New York and Washington. Thereupon the United States would be forced to revoke the Monroe Doctrine and pay a huge indemnity to Germany.[24] More mundanely, Dewey crowed at the time of the Venezuelan blockade that his fleet maneuvers at Culebra had provided "an object lesson to the Kaiser, more than to any other person."[25]

Two cardinal points emerged in the United States Navy's deliberations at the turn of the century: belief in Germany's hostile intention to set foot in the Western Hemisphere, and in her challenge to the United States for control of the world's major markets. Both points forced upon the Reich the role of America's most probable future opponent. Whenever German warships appeared in Latin American waters, there arose in the public press in the United States a swarm of articles accusing Germany of the most dastardly intentions in that region. Scientific expeditions, hydrographic surveys, commercial ventures, steamship sailings, and cordial diplomatic visits were all viewed with a skeptic eye. Technological developments such as increased cruising radius resulting from expanded coal bunker facilities served only to revise strategic considerations, not devalue them. Thus the threat of future German coaling stations in the Caribbean receded in American planning only to be replaced by the fear of direct invasion.

The actual planning of operations in the event of war with Germany rested with the Navy's General Board, founded in March 1900 after the Spanish-American War. Its function was to prepare strategic and operational war plans, and to recommend size, composition and distribution of the fleet — in short, a combination of Germany's Naval Office and Admiralty Staff. Although the board's relation with other naval organizations was not clearly defined and its role under the civilian secretary one of advising and not ordering, Admiral Dewey's seventeen-year tenure as presiding officer (until his death in January 1917) gave it a strong voice in naval policy. The admiral was joined on the board by the president of the Naval War College, the chief of the Bureau of Navigation, and the chief of the Office of Naval Intelligence as ex-officio members; especially talented officers were placed on the board as their services were required. Some of the more prominent among the latter were Admiral Royal B. Bradford, Captain A. S. Crowninshield, Admiral Bradley A. Fiske, Captain Nathan Sargent, Admiral Charles Sperry, Admiral Henry C. Taylor, Admiral Richard Wainwright, and Captain Asa Walker. And when the General Board in October 1903 called for a naval construction program by 1919 consisting of forty-eight battleships and twenty-four armored cruisers — compared with Germany's planned total in 1920 of thirty-eight battleships and twenty-two battle cruisers — no one doubted that this fleet was designed primarily to provide the United States Navy with a safe margin of superiority over Germany.[26]

Naval construction and commercial competition were inseparable components for men such as Roosevelt, Lodge, and Dewey. Captain Sigsbee of Naval Intelligence in December 1902 expressed this view: "Since the United States, Great Britain and Germany are competing for world trade, it is natural to compare our Navy with the Navies of those nations." The problem was that Great Britain's Royal Navy could not be matched for decades to come; Germany, on the other hand, offered "a fair comparison."[27] Partly from "active fear" and partly from "lack of confidence," American naval officers constantly eulogized the fighting power and efficiency of the German navy. In March 1902 Captain

Sigsbee had estimated that the built German naval strength was fully 50 percent greater than that of the United States Navy.[28] And Commander William H. Beehler, naval attaché in Berlin, spoke publicly of "thirty first-class battleships" that made Tirpitz's fleet "three times as strong as the United States Navy," an observation that drew a start from the Kaiser: "I say! Damn it, those I would like to see!"[29]

But there were also those who viewed already greater horizons. Captain Richmond Hobson, a widely known veteran of the Spanish-American War, bluntly stated in 1902 that the United States would have to possess by 1930 a fleet equal in size to that of all the other navies of the world combined.[30] Captain Sigsbee also had illusions of naval grandeur: "I do not understand why Germany should be used to fix the limit. We should be at least twice as strong. Double Germany in sea power, for Germany is an inland country of Europe."[31] The thought would have moved Tirpitz to the point of panic. And when Ambassador Count Paul von Metternich cabled from London that President Roosevelt desired a navy "not the biggest, but as efficient as any," Wilhelm II disagreed: "No! He did *mean* the biggest!"[32]

The General Board's planning against Germany proceeded slowly because numerous obstacles had to be overcome. In the first place, the United States Navy simply did not possess officers with sufficient academic training or the staff experience required for systematic planning. Until 1913 it had been content to muddle through on a day to day basis. "War plans," Professor Warner R. Schilling suggests, were "miscellaneous collections of information about foreign nations" and "suggestions for the fleet commanders." No systematic planning guided naval policy. "Ten years passed between the time the General Board defined American naval needs to be a fleet equal or superior to Germany's and the time when the Board made a systematic study of the problem of a German-American war."[33] Secondly, the board constantly complained that the navy did not receive its proper share of federal funds and favor. In February 1913 it expressed its feelings on this matter to Secretary of the Navy Josephus Daniels: "The fleet as it exists . . . is the growth of an inadequately expressed public opinion . . . and has followed the laws of expediency and of the temporary passing passion of non-understanding political parties."[34] Finally, the fleet of forty-eight capital ships created on paper in 1903 had not materialized rapidly enough to justify far-reaching planning by the General Board. The board was disappointed even in its highest and most enthusiastic patron, President Roosevelt. The latter, as we have seen, in December 1901 had received Congressional approval for the construction of thirty-one warships, and in December 1905 he decided that the navy could get by adequately with the twenty-eight battleships and twelve armored cruisers then either in commission or under construction. Although this figure fell far short of the board's demand of October 1903 for forty-eight battleships and twenty-four armored cruisers, the President remained adamant in his belief that "at least in the immediate future" no further new construction "beyond the present number of units" was required. The forty armored ships would place the United States Navy second only to France and Great Britain, and approximately equal to Germany.[35] Moreover, the board's decision in September 1905 to construct the new dreadnought battleships merely aggravated the acute budgetary difficulties that the navy constantly faced in both houses of Congress.

That the Navy General Board still deemed it necessary to draw up a war plan against Germany when most of these hurdles had been overcome by 1913 shows the very seriousness with which the possibility of war with Germany was treated in Washington. It seems to indicate that the American contingency war plan was not merely the result of "routine considerations"— words that the German naval historian Walther Hubatsch adopted to defuse Germany's Operations Plan III.[36]* A "routine plan" would have been comprehensible at the time of the Samoan tangle; by 1913, after fifteen years of confrontation and suspicion, such reasoning simply does not suffice.

In fact, the period from about 1900 to 1913 was filled with growing anxiety of German intentions in the Western Hemisphere and corresponding strategic planning. Germany's increasing isolation in Europe and her decision by 1906 to cancel Operations Plan III, of which the United States Navy could hardly be aware, did not in the least relax American apprehensions and fears of German operations in American waters. The high priest of navalism, Alfred Thayer Mahan, expanded on this point in 1906, at the very moment when Admiral Büchsel transformed the German contingency plan into a theoretical exercise:

> Germany is desirous of extending her colonial possessions. Especially is it thought that she is desirous of obtaining a foothold in the Western Hemi-

* Moreover, Hubatsch incorrectly claimed that the study by Mantey "never matured into an operations plan" and that it remained a "*Unikum*." German naval officers have criticized my use of the term "operations plan" to describe Operations Plan III, adding that Gerhard Ritter also failed to appreciate the meaning of the term "operations plan" when he applied this label to the famous Schlieffen Plan. I do not object to being thus categorized and maintain my right to define as an official "operations plan" a contingency war plan developed by Admirals Diederichs, Büchsel and Tirpitz, supplemented by the calculations of General von Schlieffen, and officially accepted during Imperial audience by Kaiser Wilhelm II, who possessed exclusive powers to determine German foreign as well as military policies. To argue that Operations Plan III is "only" on a level with the famous Schlieffen Plan, is, in my opinion, according it too much weight; hardly the opposite.

sphere, and many things indicate that she has her eyes on localities in the West Indies, on the shores of the Caribbean, and in parts of South America. It is believed in many quarters that she is planning to test the Monroe Doctrine by the annexation or by the establishment of a protectorate over a portion of South America, even going to the extent of war with the U.S. when her fleet is ready.[37]

Concrete expression of this residual fear had been rendered by the Naval War College in the summer of 1903, when it studied the possibility of a German-American war in the Far East. American officers opted for a concentration of their fleet in the Atlantic rather than the Pacific, denoting the former as the more sensitive danger point. Even a war over possession of the Philippines would necessitate a recall of American capital ships to the Atlantic Ocean. These findings were seconded that same year by the Naval War Game Society of Portsmouth, Great Britain, and clearly reveal the American fear of a German invasion of the Western Hemisphere. Moreover, when civil disturbances in Panama erupted against Colombian rule in 1903, the United States Navy immediately directed its envoy in Berlin to maintain a close scrutiny of German naval movements; it feared that Germany might seize this opportunity to make her move in the West Indies.[38]

The General Board shared this stance. In June 1904 it joined with army leaders in studying the likelihood of attack by a European naval power if the United States should be tied down in Latin America. "Most probable cause of war would be some act or purpose undertaken by a European power which conflicted with the policy enunciated by President Monroe." By December 1905 Admiral Dewey had made the basic strategic decision to concentrate American battleships in the Atlantic, a clear indication that Germany rather than Japan ranked as the most probable future opponent. The following year the board once more ruled that Germany posed the greatest threat to the United States. American planners were absolutely certain that the Reich planned to seize territory in the Western Hemisphere the moment her fleet was ready. And in 1909 the board yet again depicted Germany as its "most formidable" enemy, pointing out that she had replaced the United States as second among the world's naval powers.[39]

Incredibly, the United States Navy appears not to have given any credence to diplomatic events in Europe between 1897 and 1913. If in 1906 her planners had counted on "passive, if not active assistance" from Great Britain in the event of a German attack on the Monroe Doctrine,[40] by 1913 the General Board viewed the situation much more pessimistically, deciding to rely solely upon its own strength and resources. In all probability the turbulence of international events since 1897—the Spanish-American War of 1898, the Boer War (1899–1902), the intervention in China (1900–1901) to put down the so-called Boxer rebellion, the Russo-Japanese War (1904–1905), the First Moroccan Crisis (1905), the Anglo-French-Russian Entente (1907), the Second Moroccan Crisis (1911), and the First Balkan War (1913)—obfuscated the German dilemma in Europe and encouraged American planners not to rely on any aid or forces other than their own. Otherwise their deliberations between 1910 and 1913, culminating in the Black War Plan, make little sense.

In 1910 the General Board reviewed the various factors that pointed to Germany as America's primary adversary. The Reich's population was increasing at an alarming annual rate of 900,000. Therefore, she would soon have "outgrown her borders." The only available areas of territorial expansion lay in the temperate zones of Latin America. But the Monroe Doctrine blocked her path in this direction. Thus Germany, the "uneasy state of Europe," and the United States were of necessity on a collision course. The board could see no other possible adversaries in Europe. Russia was totally ignored. France was regarded as being "unusually friendly." And Great Britain possessed sufficient naval bases and sea power and was most vulnerable to American might in Canada.[41]

Captain Fiske reminded his fellow board members that "wealth and power" were the prizes at stake. Like his German counterparts, he was utterly convinced that economic competition would eventually lead to war. "There is no rivalry more bitter than trade rivalry. There is nothing more dangerous to peace. There is nothing for which men will fight more savagely than for money."[42]

Other portents also loomed. Mahan pointed out in 1909 that the fuel capacity of German capital ships was constantly being increased, thus indicating operations outside European waters. The Office of Naval Intelligence reported that in 1911 Germany would possess ten dreadnoughts while the United States had only four in service, and that Tirpitz's four new battle cruisers were without equal in the United States Navy. The *Army and Navy Register* in 1912 drew the conclusion that German naval superiority would make "European defiance of our tradition [Monroe Doctrine] complete and effective." Commander William S. Sims, an outspoken advocate of Anglo-Saxon solidarity, saw only one solution. In 1910, during a speech in London's Guildhall, he advocated an Anglo-American alliance by promising the British every man, every ship, and every dollar of the United States if that island empire were threatened seriously by Germany.[43] But naval planners in Washington preferred their own solution: a contingency war plan designed to meet a German invasion of the Western Hemisphere. In fact, there were published around this time several books that were clearly anti-German in content: Lewis Einstein *American Foreign Policy* (1909), Herbert Croly *The Promise of American Life* (1909), Homer Lea *The Day of the Saxon* (1912), Roland G. Usher *Pan-Germanism* (1913), and Admiral Dewey's *Autobiography* (1913). Franklin D. Roosevelt, upon becoming assistant secretary of the navy in 1913, quickly found that "the Power that we were building to guard against was Germany."[44]

In Germany, Vice Admiral von Diederichs had played a major role in the formulation of Operations Plan III against the United States; in 1913 Admiral Dewey presided over the General Board that developed the Black War Plan* against Germany. Thus the "men of Manila" carried out their antagonisms and animosities on the drawing boards of the naval staffs. The American planners believed that Great Britain would look upon a German attack on the Monroe Doctrine with sympathy and offer passive support because she stood to gain the most from a clash between her two main commercial rivals. Britain, the United States Navy officers calculated, would "effectually provide against the interference of other interested European powers," leaving Germany free to make war "with the certainty that her rear is safe from attack."[45] There appeared no prospect of succor from any European power:

> The United States has already differences with Russia; the French criticise our methods freely and are in sympathy with British European policy; it is too soon after the Spanish-American war to expect sympathy from Spain; Italy is in accord with France and England upon certain international issues, and Austria with Germany.

The planners' horizon was a deep black. "The United States is therefore isolated and can count upon no active friend in Europe whose interests coincide with hers." Admiral C. E. Vreeland of the General Board cautioned the House Naval Affairs Committee that no reliance could be placed on existing diplomatic alignments because they could change within the year.[46] Hence, despite the turn of events in Europe since 1897, American naval leaders still thought in 1913 in terms of an isolated German-American war.

The key to this seemingly incredible belief lies in the deep-rooted economic Darwinism that the board's planners had inherited from Mahan:

> History shows that the trade rivalry brought about the successive humiliation of Holland, France and Spain by Great Britain. The three great competitors

* The board used color codes for its first two war plans: black for Germany and orange for Japan (1911).

for the world's trade are now the United States, Great Britain and Germany. Following the teachings of history, two of these must in the sequel be practically subordinated to the third.

"Trade competition," along with a burgeoning population and the need for protected overseas markets, would force Germany at some future point to violate the Monroe Doctrine. "A battle is on throughout the world for commercial supremacy wherever German and American goods are brought into competition." Surely the Kaiser would strike the minute that his mammoth fleet was ready. The United States could not avoid a collision with Germany:

> The steady increase of Germany's population; harder conditions of life as the home population becomes denser; the steady expansion of German home industries which must find a *protected* market abroad; the desire of the Imperial Government for colonial expansion to satisfy imperial needs; and the pronounced distaste of the Imperialists for the absorption of German immigrants by other nations; — these factors in the situation all lead to the conclusion that when conditions at home are no longer considered bearable and Germany is strong enough, Germany will insist upon the occupation of Western Hemisphere territory under the German flag, and the United States will then have to defend her policy by force, or acquiesce in the occupation.

These documents must appear surrealistic to the reader in the eighth decade of the twentieth century: a German invasion of the Western Hemisphere precipitated by economic rivalry and supported by Great Britain, with Europe remaining neutral owing to past differences with the United States or to fear of Great Britain.

But there were also strategic calculations at work. The General Board defined the "well established national policies" of the United States as: "No entangling alliances; The Monroe Doctrine; The Open Door in the Far East; Asiatic Exclusion; Exclusive military control of the Panama Canal and its contiguous waters."[47] It expected the German thrust to be directed against "The Monroe Doctrine," and noted the ability of her navy to deliver "a crippling blow in a matter of hours." With the increased cruising radius of German warships, the Atlantic "moat" had been vastly reduced as an effective deterrent. "The width even of the Atlantic Ocean does not give us safety, but merely complicates the question of supply and communications, and affords the nation attacked a few days of grace before the blow falls." And, as we have seen, "the question of supply and communications" had hardly troubled German naval planners in formulating Operations Plan III.

Dewey and his aides from the start ruled out even a temporary landing in Germany because of the distance between the two nations and the strength as well as quality of the German standing army. "There can be no permanently successful occupation of *home* territory by either of the belligerents." Nevertheless, it was estimated that Germany possessed enough cargo space to transport a military force of 200,000 (!) men in addition to her fleet.[48] This would enlist 80 percent of her entire shipping just for fueling the initial crossing. Thereafter, approximately 40 percent of her maritime tonnage would be required for further fuel supplies. The difficulty of providing such additional necessities as fresh water, food, medical supplies, ammunition, reinforcements, and the like for an extended stay in American waters was not even raised by the General Board. In fact, American naval planners did not expect Germany to embark on such a bold project, since the time required to ship a force of more than 25,000 men across the Atlantic would give the United States ample time to mobilize its forces, both at sea and on land.

The Black War Plan ruled out the possibility of a direct German "descent in force . . . a raid on the United States Atlantic coast." Such a maritime gamble was dismissed outright as having no possible chance of success. At best, if the American fleet were divided between the Atlantic, where Dewey had concentrated his entire battle fleet, and the Pacific stations on the first day of mobilization, Germany could seize most of the Caribbean area. If the fleet were stationed on the Atlantic coast in its entirety, Germany might at best occupy an island or two in the West Indies. It is necessary to keep in mind that the General Board thought only in terms of capital ships; small cruisers and other light craft could remain in the Pacific in the event of war with Germany. The planners did not for a moment consider leaving part of their fleet behind to defend Boston or New York, as had been suggested by Captain Sigsbee of Naval Intelligence and envisaged by the German Admiralty Staff in its memorandum of 27 November 1903.

The General Board expected a German armada of 25,000 men to pass the English Channel on the seventh day after mobilization.* It was estimated that this convoy would recoal either at the Azores or the Cape Verde Islands and then proceed to Margarita Island off the coast of Venezuela. Upon defeating the American fleet — according to the German plan — the armada would head either for Samaná Bay or Culebra. The latter could be reached twenty-seven days after a declaration of war. To meet such a threat, Dewey and his planners proposed to assemble all available capital ships in lower Chesapeake Bay by the fourteenth day of mobilization, proceeding to Culebra twenty-four hours later. The United

* Here, as in all their calculations, the American planners had left themselves a sufficient margin of error. Compare this estimate with Schlieffen's calculations of 14 May 1903 calling for 12,000 (subsequently 14,000) men.

States Navy would take up battle formation and await the arrival of the German forces at Culebra, attacking the approaching enemy well to the east of this island. The General Board expected a German force consisting of nineteen battleships, four battle cruisers, and eighteen predreadnoughts.* Numerically the American fleet would be 18 percent weaker in capital ships and almost 50 percent in dreadnoughts. Yet the board felt confident that its fleet was enough of a "risk" to deter a German invasion of the Western Hemisphere:

> It would be suicidal for Germany, with a fleet only approximately equal to that of the United States, and in addition handicapped by the presence of the heavy train necessary for such distant operations, to attempt a descent upon American possessions in the Caribbean in the presence of the full American fleet at Culebra with a moderate train, protected by the advance base armament, and with ample supplies in fortified ports nearby.[49]

The Black War Plan concluded with an ancient adage: "Thus will readiness for war serve to prevent war."

A comparison of these two war plans, Operations Plan III and the Black War Plan, at once contrasts the offensive spirit of the German planners with the strategic defensive recommended from the start by their American counterparts. The seven-year difference in time of formulation is not crucial in explaining this contrast. German naval plans steered away from an offensive strategy not because of any doubts regarding the capability of their battleship fleet, but only because deteriorating political and diplomatic conditions in Europe required after 1905 a military policy (the Schlieffen Plan) that committed German land forces to lightning strikes first west and then east; in short, to a plan that robbed the navy of all initiative. The massing of American naval power at Culebra, the very spot chosen by Admiralty Staff, General Staff, and the Kaiser as the most suitable German *point d'appui*, well in advance of the planned arrival of the German forces, almost certainly points to a naval disaster for Germany. The United States Navy was prepared to meet a German invasion flotilla by the twenty-seventh mobilization day. In fact, the cumbersome mobilization envisaged in Operations Plan III foresaw a landing on Culebra at the earliest between the thirty-ninth and

* There is an evident error in the American calculations of German naval strength: the Reich in 1913 possessed not nineteen but seventeen battleships. In all probability, the General Board mistook two German battle cruisers for battleships. The selection of Culebra appears to have been the result of expert guessing; the documents make no mention of a possible intelligence leak.

the forty-fourth mobilization day (the March 1899 study). Later German revisions called for a still later arrival at Culèbra. Under such conditions, the United States Navy could, in all probability, have even brought its Pacific units to the Caribbean theater in time for the decisive naval engagement, a course that Dewey did not deem necessary.

There was also manifest in the German deliberations a general lack of respect for American land as well as sea power, except for the highest-ranking officers. Insufficient discipline, morale, training, technical-industrial capacity, naval construction know-how, and Congress's niggardly allotment of funds all had been reported as undermining the effectiveness of the United States armed forces. Eberhard von Mantey even detected in the democratic principle of free speech a curb on American naval development. Such sentiments were not expressed on the American side. The Kaiser might frequently be singled out for ridicule; his armed forces were accorded the highest respect.

A common element in the thinking of German as well as American planners was the obsession with economic competition as the probable cause of an impending war. The officers of the General Board were so steeped in Mahan's teachings that they feared that a German attack against only Panama or the Monroe Doctrine, and not against the continental United States, would, as in 1812, result in a division of opinion at home. "The fear of financial loss by the influential wealthy classes in the United States . . . will tend to force a peace after early successes, and before the United States can be placed upon an adequate war footing."[50]

Final comment must surely direct attention to the dangers inherent in such planning. It no longer suffices, as has all too often been the case, simply to dismiss these plans as the labor of junior staff officers eager for promotion and anxious for recognition. In Germany the Kaiser, General Staff, and Admiralty Staff — men such as Wilhelm II, Schlieffen, Tirpitz, Diederichs, Büchsel, Ludendorff — and in the United States men such as Roosevelt, Dewey, Lodge, and Daniels all contributed to the formulation of war plans. Moreover, it is all too easy to lay the blame solely on the professional soldiers:

> Blind to the power in the earth, as exemplified by trench warfare, and neglecting the whole spirit of the defensive, comparatively, while embracing the theory of the offensive *à l'outrance*, these officers, naval and military, made preparations, on training grounds and in the plans of General Staffs, which were based on gross misconceptions of the actuality presented by modern war on land and sea.[51]

For where were the wiser counsels of the political leaders? Of the intellectuals? And of the public press? They were all too often at the side, or even ahead, of the Roosevelts, Lodges, Bülows, Tirpitzes, as well as at the meetings of the respective navy leagues. We are once again left with Bismarck's warning that by painting the devil on the wall one makes him at last appear. There can be no doubt that this "devil" did, in fact, appear and that he contributed in no small way to the deterioration of international relations which ultimately led to the catastrophe of 1914–1918.

# II

# The Great War
# (1914–1918)

FIVE

# Germany and the United States at War (1917–1918)

> We struggled unconsciously for world dominion before we had secured our continental position. This of course, I can say only in the most intimate circles, but anyone who looks at the issue relatively clearly and historically cannot remain doubtful of it.
>
> — GENERAL WILHELM GROENER *before Prussian Army Officers 19 May 1919*

MUCH OF THE PRECEDING SECTION HAS DEALT WITH THE THREAT, BOTH REAL and alleged, of a German-American confrontation at the turn of the century — that is, with the possibility that trade rivalries might lead to armed conflict between these two late arrivals on the colonial scene. It has been noted how events in far distant places such as Samoa, the Philippines and South America deeply affected German-American relations, and finally prompted both navies to draft contingency war plans against each other. But war never came. This section, on the other hand, deals with war itself: the German-American conflagration between 1917 and 1918. It is necessary to determine its causes, its logic, and above all its place in the larger framework of German-American relations between 1888 and 1941. Why did Germany opt for war with the United States in 1917? What benefits did she hope to reap from such a course? Was she aware of the military and industrial strength of her new adversary? To what extent did experiences from the earlier period determine the decision to go to war? And finally, how did American admirals react to the German naval initiative?

Kaiser Wilhelm II had lamented Germany's lack of sea power during initial contacts with Americans at Samoa and in the Philippines. By 1917, however, the ratio of German to American dreadnoughts was in Germany's favor (19:14); Admiral von Tirpitz hoped to be able by 1920 to meet not only the United States Navy but especially the British Royal Navy in a major encounter on the high seas.

Between 1898 and 1912 Tirpitz had wrung from the Reichstag a series of naval bills and supplements (*Novellen*) for creation of a fleet including thirty-eight battleships and twenty-two battle cruisers to be completed by 1920 at the earliest.[1] He had been careful not to reveal any specific tasks for this force. The admiral had hinted that such an aim could "really not be put in writing." He calculated that "future power shifts" in Asia and South America would seriously weaken the British Empire; in order to capitalize on this development, Germany would have to build a strong fleet "as soon as possible." Failure to do so would reduce her to the status of "a poor farming country."[2] In short, Tirpitz believed that Germany should not be content to sit back and consolidate the gains of 1871, but would have to make the transition from a strong European to a major world power. The established might of Great Britain with her empire, as well as the growing strength and influence of Russia, the United States and Japan, meant that the Reich could not afford to waste time; she had to lay the foundations for her world status now if she hoped to compete in the future with these giants.

Here Tirpitz found himself in conflict with army leaders. While the latter continued to think and act in traditional Prussian terms, naval leaders developed aims and programs that constituted a direct break with Bismarckian politics. The army saw Germany still as a continental land force (*Landmacht*) and remained continental in its primary objectives; the navy's view was of an aspiring world power (*Weltmacht*). The army aspired to territorial gains in eastern Europe, while the Navy represented the imperialism of the "wider world" outside continental limits. This basic policy difference was first revealed during the Samoan conflict in 1888–1889 discussed in the preceding section; it hampered strategic planning during the First World War and, as we shall see, had fateful consequences during the Second World War.

The possibility of war divided generals and admirals in 1914. The army was prepared for combat; in fact, it desired it before France and Russia especially, both undergoing vast armaments programs, could catch up with German land strength. The navy, on the other hand, desired peace. War now would be premature; only sixteen capital ships were available in 1914, and the rest of the battle fleet of sixty heavy units would not be ready for at least five years. Admiral von Tirpitz attempted until the last moment to prevent a German declaration of war, brushing aside the empty claims of Wilhelm II and Gottlieb von Jagow, state secretary of the Foreign Office, that the British would not become involved in a general European land war. Moreover, Tirpitz feared that the chancellor, Theobald von Bethmann Hollweg, might seize this opportunity to arrange an eleventh-hour naval agreement with "perfidious Albion." Nor did he accept the advice of his closest aide, Admiral Eduard von Capelle, that while "many swords will be rattled and much poisonous ink spilled, Europe will not tear itself to pieces over Serbia." For Tirpitz knew full well that London could not stand by and allow a repetition of 1870–1871. Such a course would enable the Reich to acquire strategic naval bases on the Channel coast and perhaps on France's Atlantic shore, thereby jeopardizing Britain's control of Atlantic shipping lanes. The state secretary's last-minute pleas for peace with Russia — if war with Britain became inevitable — were also ignored by the Kaiser and the chief of the General Staff, General Helmuth von Moltke; neither found advantage in Tirpitz's desire to "set the whale against the bear."[3] Above all, the admiral feared that a general European war would be fought by Germany not for her "place in the sun" but for the defense of the Bismarckian borders of 1871.

Yet in the end he had to bow to army pressure. On 26 July Tirpitz with a heavy heart recalled the fleet from its maneuvers off Norway. By 4 August 1914 Germany found herself embroiled in a major land war against Russia, France, Great Britain, and Serbia. Her only ally was Austria-Hungary, as Italy preferred not to honor her Triple Alliance commitments to Berlin and Vienna. Admiral Georg Alexander von Müller, chief of the Naval Cabinet, had believed all along that war with London was "unavoidable," and he was delighted that the Wilhelmstrasse had managed to make Germany appear as the nation attacked — "The mood is brilliant." Wilhelm II returned his insignia as Admiral of the Fleet and Field Marshal to King George V: "This was the thanks for Waterloo." Sir Edward Grey, more realistically, had stood at the windows of Whitehall in London on the evening of 3 August and prophesied: "The lamps are going out all over Europe. We shall not see them lit again in our lifetime." The "lamps" had also been extinguished for Admiral von Tirpitz.[4]

As is well known, the German land onslaught (Schlieffen Plan) failed to crush France in the fall of 1914, and Europe settled into a siege struggle that deployed some three million men in a long slit of trenches stretching from the Channel almost to the Swiss border to the south. And the war at sea also stagnated. The "Tirpitz fleet" was not sufficiently strong to challenge Britain's Grand Fleet in the naval Armageddon that Tirpitz, a staunch disciple of Mahan, had preached since coming to the Naval Office. Admiral Sir John Jellicoe, for his part, would not risk his Grand Fleet needlessly. The British government and Foreign Office imposed a long-distance blockade strategy upon the fleet: by November 1914 the Dover Straits had been closed and all neutrals were required to undergo search in the Downs; and the route round northern Scotland was patrolled by elderly armored cruisers and armed merchant cruisers, with a maritime contraband station at Kirkwall subjecting all neutrals to search. While this blockade embittered especially the United States, which attempted to uphold the doctrine of "freedom of the seas," it nevertheless transformed the North Sea into a "dead" sea and denied all maritime succor to Germany. The First Sea Lord, Admiral Sir Henry Jackson, agreed that this "anemic" blockade was a poor substitute for a possible "second Trafalgar," but he was adamant in its importance: "This war will make history and we need not be too particular about precedents."[5] The single naval engagement on 31 May 1916 at Jutland, though technically a German victory, did not alter this impasse one iota. The British in their northern anchorages at Scapa Flow, Cromarty and Rosyth could not lose the war, and Germany conversely could not win it, so long as a major naval encounter was avoided. It was a cruel situation for Tirpitz.* The only discernible solution appeared to rest with a submarine *guerre de course*, a *jeune école* strategy that was anathema to the "German Mahan."

A number of European states entered the titanic struggle on the Continent between 1914 and 1916 according to wherever they gauged advantage. The Central Powers (Germany and Austria-Hungary) were reinforced in November 1914 by Turkey, and in October 1915 by Bulgaria; the Anglo-French-Russian Entente received additional support in May 1915 when Italy canceled the Triple Alliance and declared war against Austria-Hungary, while Romania came over in August 1916. Japan, Greece, Portugal, and Montenegro also rallied to the Entente. The United States, however, had played no significant role in Germany's decision to go to war, and with all the armies initially expecting a quick war ending by Christmas 1914 at the latest, there seemed little likelihood that the American republic would become directly involved in European affairs.

## The Calculated Risk (9 January 1917)

The German naval leadership prior to 1917 was primarily concerned with the British Grand Fleet stationed in Scapa Flow, and with the merchant shipping that kept the British war effort supplied and uninterrupted. To interdict the latter, the Germans on 22 February 1915 decided

* The heavy ships of the world's second largest navy spent most of the war swinging at anchor in the sanctuary of the Jade River and Elbe River anchorages. Zeebrugge and Ostend in occupied Belgium were used only by destroyers and submarines.

to establish a war zone around the British Isles within which every commercial vessel would be sunk without warning.

Already, at this early juncture in what was eventually to become a long, bitter struggle, a basic rift was revealed between German civilian and naval experts. While Imperial Chancellor Bethmann Hollweg fully expected that a special conference would be convened to discuss the creation of the war zone, the navy opted for a more direct approach. On 3 February 1915 the Kaiser toured the Wilhelmshaven naval station, and Admiral Hugo von Pohl, chief of the Admiralty Staff and recently designated next chief of the High Sea Fleet, lured the monarch away from his civilian entourage, escorted him on a personal inspection of the port, and quickly convinced his Supreme War Lord of the need to instigate an unrestricted undersea offensive against all commercial shipping bound for the British Isles. Moreover, Pohl at once informed the semiofficial Wolff news agency of the Kaiser's decision, thereby presenting civilian leaders with a *fait accompli*.[6]

The Admiralty Staff had not expected any adverse reaction from neutral powers and was therefore taken aback when the United States announced that it would "hold the Imperial Government to a strict accountability" for any destruction of American ships or lives, and that it would "take any steps it might be necessary to take to safeguard American lives and property and to secure to American citizens the full enjoyment of their acknowledged rights on the high seas."[7] Here, in a nutshell, was the American position on unrestricted submarine warfare. The United States, for its part, would not be bullied into surrendering its trade with Great Britain and would, if necessary, defend that right with force. Germany, in turn, hoped sincerely to keep the United States from joining the Entente powers, but not at the cost of surrendering unrestricted submarine warfare. These diametrically opposed positions brought over the next two years constant tensions between German naval and political leaders — which are beyond the scope of this study — as well as between German and American diplomats.

The widening rift between Berlin and Washington was centered on so-called "incidents" at sea. The most famous of these "incidents" on the high seas occurred on 7 May 1915 when a German submarine torpedoed the British liner *Lusitania*, resulting in the loss of 128 American lives. A sharp American protest was heeded by Germany, especially since Italy joined the Entente on 23 May, and because the German army was anxious not to have the other neutrals (Bulgaria, Romania and the Netherlands) follow the Italian example. The *Lusitania* sinking clearly pointed out where future German-American friction might arise.

Germany's vacillating attitude toward the United States during this period can best be seen in the conflicting confusion that characterized her diplomatic reports. The Reich's ambassador in Washington, Count Johann Heinrich Bernstorff, urged his government to cease unrestricted submarine warfare and instead join President Woodrow Wilson in his efforts to maintain the "freedom of the seas" and, if possible, rescind the illegal British naval blockade of Germany. On the other hand the German consul general in New York, Erich Hossenfelder, the economic expert attached to the German embassy in Washington, H. F. Albert, and the Chamber of German-American Commerce in New York steadfastly advised Berlin that the United States would stay out of the war at all costs, and that Germany could therefore "kindly but forcefully" reject Wilson's protests concerning the loss of American lives and property on the high seas.[8] This group received support from the state secretary of the Naval Office, Admiral von Tirpitz, and from the chief of the Admiralty Staff, Admiral Gustav Bachmann; Bernstorff's sole supporter in the government was the deputy chancellor, Karl Helfferich.

German-American relations were further strained on 19 August 1915 when the British liner *Arabic* was torpedoed and three American lives lost. The Kaiser headed off a new crisis on 30 August by ordering that no liners be sunk without previous warning. Admiral Bachmann resigned. Tirpitz's request for dismissal was rejected by the Kaiser. The new chief of the Admiralty Staff, Admiral Henning von Holtzendorff, reaffirmed on 18 September the Imperial order against sinking liners without warning, thereby temporarily laying to rest this whole bitter question.

But American arms and munition deliveries to the Entente continued unabated. German suspicions of American duplicity and deception mounted. In September 1915 the German military and naval attachés (Franz von Papen and Karl Boy-Ed) were declared *personae non grata* for their part in amateur spy and sabotage operations (see pages 154–155). Worse yet, on 7 November 1915 the Italian passenger ship *Ancona* was attacked by U-boats, resulting in twenty American casualties. Although the Austro-Hungarian government accepted full blame for this incident, the Germans bore the brunt of American rancor and hate.

Early in 1916 Germany's military leaders began once more to push for unrestricted submarine warfare. General Erich von Falkenhayn, chief of the General Staff, argued that since Bulgaria had become an ally of the Central Powers and Serbia had been militarily defeated, the time was ripe for a new naval offensive designed to deprive the Entente of American succor.

Admiral von Holtzendorff fully agreed. On 7 January 1916 he informed Chancellor Bethmann Hollweg that the advantages to be gained by ending the war in six months through an all-out submarine offensive were so great that an American declaration of war against Germany could easily be taken into the bargain. Twenty days later the admiral asked the Foreign Office to do all it could to avoid a break with the United States, but said that unrestricted submarine warfare would have to come — even if Wilson would thereby be prompted to declare war.[9] Tirpitz shared this view and assured the chancellor that a break with the United States need not be feared because the entry of the latter into the war would not greatly affect the military situation in Europe. The United States, according to Tirpitz, would not be able to build new merchant tonnage at a rate sufficiently high to offset that being destroyed by German submarines.[10]

When this communication did not have the desired effect of converting Bethmann Hollweg to the undersea offensive, Tirpitz penned a lengthy memorandum to the chancellor in which he outlined the basic issue at stake in this war. The United States, he argued, had been hostile toward Germany from the start, and would ultimately side with Great Britain because of "common racial ties," especially between the ruling elites, and above all because of the "ever growing trustification of English and American finance capital." Tirpitz depicted the United States, still a neutral, as "a directly involved enemy of Germany," and he even predicted that one day Great Britain and the United States would combine to defeat Japan. It was therefore of the utmost importance that the Imperial government realize that the United States was "directly interested in the fate of the English economy and thus, along with England, in the defeat of Germany."[11]

This turned out to be one of Tirpitz's last official acts as state secretary of the Naval Office. He was not invited to attend important military discussions and his counsel on naval affairs was seldom sought. As a result he resubmitted his resignation, which the Kaiser accepted on 10 March 1916. Ironically, three days later the German government decided to resume unrestricted submarine warfare.

No sooner did Germany reopen the hunting season on commercial maritime traffic than another "incident" further poisoned German-American relations. On 24 March 1916 the French liner *Sussex* was torpedoed without warning, and again American blood was shed. Though President Wilson protested energetically, Admiral Tirpitz from retirement roundly argued that concessions to the United States were incompatible with Germany's national prestige. In fact, Tirpitz was now willing to commit Germany to an all-out naval strategy. Only a victorious outcome of the war, he argued, could clear the way for *Weltpolitik;* a compromise settlement in effect meant defeat for Germany. "His Majesty consoles himself and is consoled by the chancellor with the thought about the Second Punic War against Carthage. . . . I do not believe in the Second Punic War." The admiral opposed this interpretation because it would mean accepting a less than final judgment in *this* war, and because it would deny Germany annexation of Antwerp and Flanders. Such a course, he feared, would result in "economic and military defeat" at the hands of the British, causing Germany "to sink down to [the level of] a declining European continental state." He found consolation in the conviction that the present war was "the beginning of the end of England's status as a world power."[12] No longer hampered by the responsibility of office, Tirpitz was beginning to reveal publicly some of his innermost thoughts.

American protests over the sinking of the *Sussex* once again prompted German leaders to cancel unrestricted submarine warfare on 24 April 1916. But, as with the previous cancellation, the issue remained alive, and throughout the summer of 1916 was debated both in official government circles and in public. Crown Prince Wilhelm vociferously endorsed the naval offensive, convinced that war with the United States was of little consequence compared to the need to destroy Great Britain's "vital strength." The heir to the throne boldly asserted that "America is not a serious military opponent. Its million-man army exists only on paper, [and] the creation and deployment of this [army] on the Continent are only military flights of fantasy accepted by the Anglo-American press alone."[13]

Admiral von Holtzendorff had come to the conclusion by August 1916 that only unrestricted submarine warfare could prevent a German catastrophe. Tirpitz's successor, Admiral von Capelle, agreed. And through junior officers, Captains Adolf von Trotha and Fritz von Bülow, the fleet made its views on this matter known to the new army commanders, Field Marshal Paul von Hindenburg and General Erich Ludendorff. Bülow stressed especially past "American inability militarily to organize their forces against Spain and Mexico." Hindenburg concurred, regarding the Americans militarily to be a negligible quantity.[14]

A German diplomat close to the Imperial court, General Karl von Treutler, took up the issue of unrestricted submarine warfare with Hindenburg in October 1916. The field marshal informed Treutler that naval experts had assured him that the United States would "draw no serious consequences" from such a step. Moreover, according to Hindenburg, these same naval experts had guaranteed that an American entry into the war would harbor "absolutely no ill effects in the military realm"—"no tactical entity of the American armed forces could ever set foot on European soil" because of the U-boats. At this point in the conversation, Treutler recorded, Hindenburg turned to Ludendorff and asked: "What is your opinion?" The First Quartermaster-General of the army reportedly replied: "I do not give a damn about America [*Ich pfeife auf Amerika*]."[15]

Events on the high seas once more made these debates acute. On 28 October 1916 a German submarine attacked the British merchant ship *Marina*, resulting in nine American casualties. And on 6 November 1916 another German U-boat torpedoed the British passenger ship *Arabia;* this time there were no American casualties, but many Americans were aboard the vessel. German U-boat commanders now countered American protests over these sinkings without warning; they claimed that because of the British policy of arming merchant as well as passenger ships, conduct of the undersea offensive according to the rules of cruiser warfare was no longer tenable.

In fact, the British Admiralty had begun early in 1915 to arm merchant ships with two 4.7-inch guns because it calculated that German submarines carried relatively few (usually six) torpedoes and hence nearly half the time used their 8.8-centimeter deck guns to destroy their prey. By April 1916 about 1,100 freighters had been armed and results were quickly discernible: between January 1916 and January 1917, 68 percent of unarmed ships were destroyed by U-boat gunfire and only 22 percent escaped, while 3.9 percent of armed ships were sent to the bottom by gunfire and 76 percent escaped. A number of small "special service ships"— the so-called "Q" ships — were also fitted with guns and designed to lure the unsuspecting submarine to the surface in order not to waste a precious torpedo on such small craft.*

In December 1916 Admiral von Holtzendorff seized the initiative in order to resolve the troublesome issue of unrestricted submarine warfare. He informed Hindenburg on 22 December that although "war with America is such a serious matter that everything must be done in order to avoid it," nothing should prevent the Reich from deploying the weapon "that will bring us victory at the right moment." The United States, Holtzendorff counseled, would not be able to reinforce the Entente effectively because its shipping would be destroyed by the U-boats. Moreover, American troops could not be sent to Europe because the Atlantic

* In his book *Lusitania* (1973), Colin Simpson claimed that the ship was more heavily armed than cruisers of the British *Cressy* (or *Bacchante*) class (two 9.2-inch and twelve 6-inch guns). However, this claim is not substantiated to any degree, and certainly impossible with reference to the *Cressy*. Moreover, Simpson did not — as he claimed — work in the Freiburg military archives (Bundesarchiv-Militärarchiv). Nor did he order photostatic copies of the documents from that depository. And finally, Simpson's claim to the war log of the submarine U-20, which torpedoed the *Lusitania*, is also fictitious, as the U-boat's log ends in January 1915 — more than three months before the *Lusitania* was hit.

would become unsafe for transports, and American loans could not compensate for lack of access to the European battlefields. The admiral concluded that unrestricted submarine warfare should therefore commence by 1 February 1917 in order to force peace by 1 August, "even if it brings America into the war, since we have no other choice."[16] Two days later Hindenburg cabled his full agreement to Holtzendorff.

Certain mathematical calculations lay at the base of Holtzendorff's decision. He estimated that Great Britain possessed approximately eleven million tons of shipping, including neutral vessels. If German submarines could sink an average of 600,000 tons per month for six months, and if about 1.2 million of the available 3 million tons of neutral shipping could be frightened off the seas, Great Britain would lose almost 40 percent of her shipping, a "final and irreplaceable loss."[17]

The decision to resume unrestricted submarine warfare was reached on 9 January 1917 at Imperial military headquarters in Pless. The previous day Hindenburg had bluntly put forth the army's position: "We fully expect war with America and have made all preparations for it. The situation cannot get any worse." Holtzendorff met with the Kaiser shortly hereafter and once more stated the navy's position:

> America under Wilson's leadership is not friendly toward us. . . . Her entry into the war will not bring her any advantages and only extremely limited, and in no way decisive, advantages for the Allies. Money as well as words will be hurled at us; military developments will come either not at all or too late to have effect. American military succor cannot delay England's demise as a result of unrestricted submarine warfare. And if England sues for peace, who will fight on?

The admiral then posed the rhetorical question whether a German decision to forego unrestricted submarine warfare would bring the United States into the anti-British camp. "No, because she will pursue her own interests which are closely bound to England."[18] Captain von Levetzow, chief of the Operational Branch of the High Sea Fleet, also paid a visit to the chancellor that same day. As an official spokesman for the fleet, he assured Bethmann Hollweg that the U-boats could destroy 500,000 tons of shipping per month. "*This* I could guarantee . . . with good conscience for the fleet, *and thus I did so*." Levetzow also informed the chancellor that the fleet expected an American declaration of war as a result of the undersea offensive because the U-boats had become "a question of prestige" in the United States. "It is of no importance to the *fleet* whether America enters into the war."[19]

The Crown Council in Pless on 9 January 1917 brought together

Wilhelm II, Hindenburg, Ludendorff, Bethmann Hollweg, and Holtzendorff, among others. In little more than one hour it was decided to resume unrestricted submarine warfare on 1 February 1917. Admiral von Holtzendorff took the lead in the deliberations. "England would be defeated within six months, at the most, before a single American had set foot on the Continent. The American danger did not frighten him." Hindenburg stressed that the naval initiative would curtail American munitions deliveries, and he discounted Wilson's latest peace initiative, arguing that peace negotiated by the American president would not give Germany what she needed.[20] Bethmann Hollweg, although deeply concerned over the consequences of the decision, promised to do what was possible to avoid American belligerency, but he made it perfectly clear that "it was necessary for us to anticipate . . . the entry of America into the war."[21]

The Kaiser was of one mind with his military commanders. He informed Admiral von Müller that same day that he "fully expected America's entry into the war" as a result of the naval offensive. And when Ambassador Bernstorff cabled the monarch on 16 January that war with the United States was certain if that country's ships were attacked without warning, Wilhelm noted "that is irrelevant" in the margin.[22]

The bold naval initiative pleased German military experts. General Ludendorff felt confident that the submarine war would interdict the enemy's supply of ammunition and thus spare Germany a second battle of the Marne.[23] Count Bernstorff in Washington strongly opposed the decision, certain that it would cause a break with the United States.[24] But Bethmann Hollweg sharply rebuked him: "I am well aware that with this step we are running in danger of bringing about a break and possibly war with the United States. We are decided to accept this risk."[25] The Kaiser stood firm and supported the naval policy. "In case a break with America is unavoidable, it cannot be changed! We will proceed."[26]

The German Foreign Office now entered the scene. On 17 January 1917 British naval intelligence intercepted a coded telegram from the German foreign minister, Arthur Zimmermann, to the German minister in Mexico, Heinrich von Eckardt. This document, handed over to the Americans, contained instructions that if the United States were to go to war with Germany as a result of unrestricted submarine warfare, Mexico should be offered an alliance with Germany on the basis of: "Joint war strategy. Joint peace negotiations. Abundant financial support and approval on our part that Mexico reconquers former territory lost in Texas, New Mexico [and] Arizona." Eckardt was asked to call on the Mexican president and to invite the latter to ask the Japanese to join this constellation.[27] The "Zimmermann telegram," coupled with unrestricted submarine warfare, squarely placed Germany on a collision course with the American republic.

Zimmermann informed the United States ambassador in Berlin, James Gerard, on 31 January 1917 of the Reich's decision to resume the undersea offensive *à outrance*. The foreign minister claimed that "the military and naval people had forced this [act] and said that America could do nothing." Gerard felt that Zimmermann was aware of the magnitude and consequences of the decision, but that "Germany had this weapon and must use it no matter what the consequences were." The ambassador informed his government of Germany's reasoning in this matter and concluded that it partly stemmed from Germany's "contempt and hatred for America" as "a fat, rich race without sense of humor and ready to stand for anything in order to keep out of the war."[28]

Whatever the case, Germany's decision to resume unrestricted submarine warfare on 1 February 1917 reflected the counsel of a naval pressure group headed by Admiral von Holtzendorff. It carried along an eager Kaiser, a willing General Staff, a reluctant chancellor, and a reticent Foreign Office. Germany's leaders thus rejected a negotiated peace in favor of a victor's peace. They opted for a massive undersea attack on commerce to end the war before the United States could intervene with sufficient force to affect the outcome decisively. And there can be little doubt that the decision was taken with the full realization that it would lead at least to a diplomatic break and most likely war with the United States.

The vast majority of German naval officers supported the resumption of unrestricted submarine warfare. When it became apparent to Vice Admiral Franz Ritter von Hipper, chief of Scouting Forces, by 4 February 1917 that the United States would join Germany's opponents as a result of the undersea offensive, he caustically noted that the United States "could not possibly work any harder against us in the future than it has already done to date. . . . The U-boats will now have the last word."[29] Vice Admiral Wilhelm Souchon, the German naval commander in the Mediterranean, reflected the thoughts of many of his colleagues when he stated that war with the United States would merely clear the air. "Now . . . we have finally been given a free hand against the Yankees."[30] The admiral felt confident that any expansion of American armed forces would be undertaken "not for the Entente" but "for a future confrontation with Japan and Mexico."[31]

Admiral von Tirpitz was quite pleased with the decision of 9 January 1917. Already, as state secretary of the Naval Office, in August 1915 he had assured Bethmann Hollweg that the United States was solely motivated by "business interests" and therefore German goodwill in the form of cessation of U-boat warfare would have absolutely no material effect.[32] Now in retirement, he could be more specific. The masses in the United States, Tirpitz calculated, desired peace, but especially the "trust magnates" wanted war for its accompanying profits. Germany had little to fear from an American declaration of war. "The Yankee fleet is of no consequence to us." German submarines would destroy troop transports en route to Europe. "Convoying of merchant ships is worthless in the face of U-boat attacks."[33]

General Ludendorff concurred with these naval experts. He had informed the industrialist Hugo Stinnes in 1916: "The United States does not bother me . . . in the least; I look upon a declaration of war by the United States with indifference."[34] The general was confident that the submarines would intercept any American transports on the high seas, and thereby preclude American participation in the land war in France.

To be sure, there were isolated voices of dissent, especially during the early war years, and at one point in 1915 the Kaiser even entertained the notion of uniting all neutrals, including the United States, to rally to Germany's side in defense of the principle of freedom of the seas. However, as with so many of his spur of the moment ideas, this one was short-lived.[35] Captain Karl Boy-Ed, now in the Admiralty press section, reported in 1916 that the German public, while thirsting for action at sea, opposed "conflict with the United States."[36]

Perhaps the most ardent opponent of unrestricted submarine warfare was Lieutenant Commander Ernst von Weizsäcker, destined to become state secretary in 1938 and Adolf Hitler's ambassador to the Holy See in 1943. In February 1916 Weizsäcker described as "reckless" the overall attitude among naval officers with regard to the submarine offensive. "No one expects any military support for the foreign army fronts by the United States. Financially, the latter is already our enemy; at sea, matters could not possibly get worse; the question of submarine warfare could thus be solved with one blow." In September Weizsäcker objected when the Admiralty Staff proposed to send two U-boats to the American east coast to attack British convoy escorts, warning that such a step could bring the United States into the war. The Admiralty Staff spokesman retorted: "That is precisely what we want. The stone must somehow finally be set in motion."[37] The chief of the High Sea Fleet, Admiral Reinhard Scheer, opposed this particular course, but the matter left little doubt where the officer corps stood on this issue.

Bethmann Hollweg's son-in-law, Count Julius von Zech von Burckersroda, a military adjutant, was among the earliest opponents of the submarine gamble. He informed his friend General Treutler on 14

January 1917: "May God grant that the 9th of January will not have marked the death of the German Empire." The chancellor's *intimus,* Kurt Riezler, was likewise most concerned about the undersea offensive. His diary throughout January reveals constant references to the "terrible fate" that lay in store for Germany "despite all vows [for success] by the navy"; it was simply "a leap in the dark." Nagging doubts concerning unrestricted submarine warfare could not be laid to rest: "One cannot believe the navy, but one can also not deny it faith." And on 1 April 1917, Riezler lamented that most of continental Europe would be brought to the verge of starvation through the British long-distance blockade by 1918, while Britain with American aid would triumph in 1918 despite the U-boats.[38] It proved to be a good guess.

But the die was cast. Germany was irrevocably committed to an all-out undersea offensive against all commercial shipping on the high seas.[39] Her leaders opted for this course in the belief that it constituted the Reich's last chance for winning the war, and in the hope that Great Britain could be forced to sue for peace before the intervention of the United States could turn the tide of war against Germany. The German-American conflagration, so often talked about since the first meeting in Samoa in 1888, was now close to reality.

## The War at Sea (1917)

German leaders on 1 February 1917 gambled the Reich's future on an incredibly small force. Just over one hundred U-boats were operative, which meant that about thirty were in battle positions at any given time. Captain Andreas Michelsen, commander of U-boats, later claimed that only thirty-six submarines were available for sea duty on 1 February, when the offensive was to start. In addition, the available forces were broadly distributed among the various fronts: forty-eight in German ports on or near the North Sea, twenty-three in captured Belgian harbors, nineteen in the Mediterranean, and ten in the Baltic. These boats were organized in five flotillas attached to the High Sea Fleet at Wilhelmshaven, two flotillas stationed at Bremerhaven and Zeebrugge, two flotillas at Pola and Cattaro in the Adriatic, and one at Libau (Liepaja) in the Baltic. A group of U-cruisers, converted merchant submarines of the *Deutschland* class, was based on Kiel.[40]

Incredibly, the U-boat force never expanded appreciably during the remainder of the war. A British naval historian has shown that the 133 boats on hand on 1 January 1917 increased only to 144 by 1 January 1918. In the interim 87 had been built and 78 destroyed.[41] Part of the reason lies in the realm of finances. Admiral Büchsel estimated in March 1916 that the cost of constructing large U-boats (800 tons) had increased some 23 percent since 1914 — from 2.3 milllon marks to 2.823 million per unit.[42] Moreover, construction costs in 1917–1918 were to soar to 4.4 million marks per unit (U-96), while submarine cruisers (U-139–141) cost 10.8 million marks. But long-cherished naval prejudices and traditions also played a major role. Tirpitz's successor, Admiral von Capelle, was acutely aware that the submarine offensive, popularly referred to as "the war of ensigns and lieutenants," was causing a rift between junior and senior officers. U-boat service was draining the fleet of its best junior officers at an alarming rate, with the result that senior officers began to fear for the future of capital ships and balanced fleets. Speaking at Hamburg in January 1917, Capelle went so far as to suggest that the Imperial German Navy after the war would have to create "a special cemetery for our existing submarines" in order to placate disgruntled flag officers.[43] In fact, the High Sea Fleet after 1 February was primarily concerned with securing German sea lanes in the Baltic Sea for vital Swedish iron ore deliveries, and with protecting the egress and return of submarines in the North Sea. As a result, three squadrons of the High Sea Fleet were deactivated during 1917–1918.[44] Thus clashes with American surface vessels on the Atlantic were highly unlikely.

Initial German successes at sea surpassed all expectations. In February some 540,000 tons were torpedoed, an increase of about 170,000 tons over January. In March the Allied losses were set at 600,000 tons.[45] The military was exultant. Admiral von Holtzendorff informed Foreign Minister Zimmermann that Hindenburg would overrule the Foreign Office whenever he felt that the diplomats were not providing the Admiralty Staff with wholehearted support. After all, he reminded Zimmermann, war was merely an extension of diplomacy by other means.[46] Intelligence sources available to Holtzendorff suggested that Great Britain would be able to withstand the U-boat onslaught for only a few months before the lack of raw materials and foodstuffs would force her to sue for peace.[47] Ludendorff was delighted with this news and boldly predicted that "we can expect that a total success of U-boat warfare can be reached in the 5–6 month period suggested by the Admiralty."[48] And with regard to the United States, the general was not unduly alarmed: "America will probably declare war on us in the near future. But . . . she will not take an active part in the military conflict in Europe in the near future. Reason: unwillingness of large circles in America to do so." However, Ludendorff warned against provoking the United States unnecessarily, especially by sending U-boats into American waters.[49]

At first German naval leaders clung to the slender hope that the

United States might avoid war. Captain Boy-Ed of the Admiralty Staff, who had spent several years in Washington as the German naval attaché, informed Admiral Prince Henry, the Kaiser's brother, in March 1917 "that the Americans will not declare war" for fear of losing the war profits already harvested. Boy-Ed also argued that one should not overlook the strong pacifist movement headed by William Jennings Bryan and supported especially by American women, the lack of available merchant tonnage, the "lack of military preparedness" of the navy and particularly the army, and the possible domestic problems that a declaration of war might unleash among the German, Austrian and Irish groups in the United States. Prince Henry was relieved. "In other words, business as usual!"[50]

The influential Industrial Club in Düsseldorf was also apprised by the Admiralty Staff that Germany had nothing to fear from an American declaration of war because the United States could not possibly train a large army in a relatively short period of time. Nor did it possess the ships to send such an army to Europe. Furthermore, the American economy could not possibly expand its production of war goods, and here also the combination of insufficient merchant tonnage and submarine warfare would prevent an increase in deliveries to the Allies.[51]

Unfortunately for Germany, the American response was quite different: on 6 April 1917 the United States declared war on Germany as a direct response to the unrestricted submarine offensive. German naval officers at first wanted to respond by expanding undersea operations to the eastern seaboard of the United States, but the Kaiser vetoed such speculation. Wilhelm II did not want to arouse what he considered to be the less militant regions of the American republic, the Midwest and the West. And while the Admiralty felt that sinkings off the eastern seaboard of the United States might inhibit arms shipments to Great Britain, the Foreign Office deplored what it considered to be any unnecessary provocation of the United States.[52] The Germans incredibly tried to maintain the fiction that they were not at war with the United States, and it was not until 22 May 1917 that the Admiralty Staff authorized attacks on American shipping within the war zone around the British Isles.[53]

In the weeks immediately following the American declaration of war, German naval commanders continued to counsel both the general public and civilian leaders not to fear American military or economic power. The Naval Office held a special news conference on 10 April 1917, during which it took note of "fantastic rumors" concerning American mobilization "of millions of combatants and an unbelievable number of submarine chasers" that were under construction and which would soon arrive in European waters. Editors were asked to suppress such wild tales. The Naval Office reassured the German press "that the American navy cannot possibly play a decisive role as far as we are concerned, either in the near future, or perhaps for the entire course of the war."[54] One week later Captain Boy-Ed informed Rear Admiral Ludolf von Usslar that "in the foreseeable future there can be no talk whatsoever of American military aid to the Entente. This applies fully also to the American navy."[55]

Admiral von Holtzendorff continued to stress the effectiveness of the submarine offensive. On 21 April 1917 he circulated a memorandum to all senior naval commanders informing them that "the United States will not be able militarily to intervene in Europe before October," and that given the present success of the U-boats, Great Britain, France and Italy would have lost their "ability to conduct warfare" by October.[56] The chief of the Admiralty Staff would not relinquish the hope that German submarines might yet operate in American waters. He refused in April 1917 to deny British newspaper reports that German submarines were operating off the United States east coast, arguing that it would "do no harm at all if the Americans were scared and believed that U-boats were already stationed in their waters."[57]*

Admiral Georg Hebbinghaus shared this optimism. He informed Admiral von Holtzendorff's brother Arndt, a lobbyist in Berlin for Albert Ballin's Hamburg-America Line, that the United States could not effectively assist the British. The United States, Hebbinghaus stated, would never be able to bring significant land forces to Europe. If President Wilson attempted to conscript a large army, he would deplete the American labor force and thus curtail arms production. America, "a poorly populated country," could not sustain both industrial and military expansion. Moreover, she lacked the necessary tonnage to transport an army to Europe, and her sailors were known to be "the worst random conglomeration of riffraff that one could possibly imagine."[58]

This optimism, however, was no longer dominant in army circles by the summer of 1917; Hindenburg's staff was beginning to show concern. The antisubmarine tactics of the Allied and Associated Powers, especially the policy of convoying large numbers of merchant ships across the Atlantic under the protection of escort destroyers and cruisers, was rapidly decreasing the effectiveness of the U-boats. Hindenburg now regretted that the Admiralty Staff had announced a specific deadline (October) for the submarine victory over Great Britain, and while he remained confident that the U-boats would eventually succeed, he feared adverse public reaction if the time limit should be extended.[59] Bethmann

* Albert Ballin of the Hamburg-America Line saw this as proof of "how totally unpolitical these men in blue are." Bundesarchiv, Koblenz, West Germany, Berichte von Holtzendorff, R1/vol. 12, Ballin to Arndt von Holtzendorff, 21 April 1917.

Hollweg was also becoming more pessimistic, perhaps realizing his mistake in not opposing more vigorously the decision of 9 January 1917; he feared that Austria-Hungary might not last out the year and that the British would not yield by the fall of 1917. Only in the east was there some flicker of hope for a quick end to the war: General Alexei Brusilov's offensives against the Austro-Hungarians in June 1916 had been blunted by German counterattacks and cost Russia over a million soldiers, leading in March 1917 to the overthrow of Czar Nicholas II and the establishment of a provisional government. The latter, outwardly led by Alexander Kerensky, in July 1917 placed its political life in Brusilov's hands, but the general's renewed offensive against the Austro-Hungarians was once more halted by a German counterattack. Total casualties for Russia now approached nine million, and the German armies took Riga and mounted a relentless drive deep into the Ukraine and Caucasus as well as against Petersburg. Yet even this monstrous Russian debacle did not, according to the German chancellor, sufficiently offset the Reich's inability to break the military impasse in the west; and the French would probably hang on as long as American succor was assured.[60]

Reports from the front brought little cheer. Sinkings in May dropped to 600,000 tons from the April high of 900,000 tons. And while the June total rose to 700,000 tons, that for July fell to 550,000 tons. From this point on, monthly sinkings rarely topped the 350,000 mark. The undersea war also took its toll of German submarines and crews. Whereas only twenty boats were destroyed in the first half of 1917, forty-three went to the bottom in the second half of that year.[61] The United States Navy Department's input into the antisubmarine campaign was hardly staggering: only one division of six destroyers was dispatched to Queenstown (Ireland) during May of 1917, while early in June an additional eighteen units arrived in Europe. The United States destroyer force in European waters had by September 1917 still reached only thirty-six ships. Admiral William S. Benson, chief of Naval Operations, continued to fear a German naval assault against the east coast of the United States or the Caribbean Sea, and he accordingly refused to disrupt his fleet organization in home waters. The realization that the submarine posed a serious threat indeed to Britain's vital maritime lifeline across the Atlantic came only slowly in Washington, where planners at first seemed content to make available to the Admiralty primarily American merchant shipping.

The growing disenchantment in official circles with the naval initiative was compounded by the first signs of civilian discontent. Matthias Erzberger of the Center Party proclaimed that military victory was no longer within reach, and that only on the basis of a negotiated peace could the Reich survive.[62] Walther Rathenau, the organizer of the German war economy, pointed out to Ludendorff that the United States and Great Britain together could replace with new construction all the merchant shipping that Germany destroyed.[63] Ludendorff attempted to blunt these attacks by pointing out to parliamentary representatives on 13 July 1917 that only the U-boats could interdict the steady flow of American supplies and men to Europe, and so destroy the war economies of the Entente powers by denying them the necessary raw materials. He admitted that he had from the start calculated that the Americans would enter the war against the Reich, but this risk had to be incurred in order to stem the steady stream of supplies, especially to Great Britain.[64]

Given this disillusionment with unrestricted submarine warfare, it is not surprising that on 14 July 1917 Hindenburg's headquarters ordered that the undersea offensive should not be extended to American waters until a "continuous" effort could be mounted. Isolated actions could only affect public opinion adversely, and possibly bring other neutrals into the Allied camp.[65]

The Kaiser, having to all intents and purposes surrendered command to the duumvirate of Hindenburg and Ludendorff, gravitated ever closer to a world of fiction and fantasy. In April 1917 he supported the navy's demand that upon successful conclusion of the present war, Germany would demand from the United States reparations in the amount of thirty billion dollars.[66] At a Bellevue (Berlin) Crown Council in September, Wilhelm — according to Foreign Minister Zimmermann — sought to temper the growing disappointment of his "boys in blue" by "engaging in utterly fantastic expositions." Specifically, the Kaiser asked that a German victory be followed by a naval display of power in South American waters designed to extort huge reparation payments from nations such as Cuba and Brazil. State Secretary of the Foreign Office Richard Kühlmann begged that this utopian proposal be struck from the conference records.[67] Earlier, in a private talk with Admiral von Holtzendorff in July 1917, Wilhelm had sought to overthrow in one bold stroke all existing alliances and alignments and to seek a bond with Russia, Japan and Mexico, "designed as a sort of pincer and counterweight to the Anglo-American alliance." The Kaiser ended this conversation by informing Holtzendorff that the leaders of the Allied and Associated Powers were seeking a solution to the world conflagration "not with a lantern, but by strolling past the lantern [post] from which they will soon hang."[68] Yet, not surprisingly, when the German Foreign Office reported in August 1917 that war fever in the United States had subsided appreciably, Wilhelm was quick to take the credit: "That is because I forbade naval units to attack America."[69] Obviously, Germany could expect little leadership from this source.

One might well ask, given these early signs that the U-boat offensive was being blunted by Allied countermeasures, why the Germans chose to continue along present lines. The answer lies in the political sphere. In the United States Woodrow Wilson, Josephus Daniels and Admiral William Sims had jointly infused the Navy Department with a spirit of activity; in Great Britain, David Lloyd George had forced the Admiralty to take measures to provide escorts for merchant shipping when that body failed to respond to the German submarine threat. In Germany such a course was not open, even if Chancellor Bethmann Hollweg had been willing to pursue it. No Imperial chancellor could challenge successfully the impregnable position of Hindenburg and Ludendorff with both the Kaiser and the home populace. And General Ludendorff stubbornly clung to a military policy that he could not abandon without conceding defeat to civilian critics. In this dilemma, the military felt compelled to support the submarine offensive in public and to press privately for improvements in its effectiveness.[70]

Late in 1917 the German naval command turned to a number of experimental tactics to counteract the antisubmarine activities of the Allied and Associated Powers. Sinkings continued to decline overall: in September 1917 the tonnage torpedoed was 352,000; in October 460,000, in November 290,000, and in December 400,000. Something had to be done. Navy leaders rejected a plan to hunt convoys with packs of submarines because there were not enough boats available to cover all the major trade routes. The U-boats attempted to pool their information of merchant ship sightings and they also tried to intercept the convoys nearer to shore, where the larger escorts left the ships.[71] In addition, the war zones, especially around the British Isles, were expanded in order to force the enemy to disperse his escort forces.[72]

The High Sea Fleet also attempted to alleviate the plight of the U-boats. Several surface raids into the North Sea were conducted in yet another attempt to force the Allies to scatter their antisubmarine craft. In October 1917 the German light cruisers *Brummer* and *Bremse* intercepted an Allied convoy and destroyed ten freighters and two destroyers on the route between Great Britain and Norway. In December four destroyers and a light cruiser managed to destroy one escort destroyer and six freighters during another surface raid in the North Sea. The Admiralty Staff hoped that these surface attacks might be implemented on a regular basis, but the Allies counteracted them by assigning heavier naval units as escorts to the North Sea convoys. The Germans thereupon refrained from committing their capital ships against convoys and instead concentrated on naval operations in the Baltic Sea designed to assist army operations in the Baltic states.[73] But these tactics did not basically alter the tide in the undersea offensive on the high seas.

The German naval effort was also seriously impaired by continued disorganization and renewed dissension. The Admiralty Staff (Holtzendorff) and the High Sea Fleet (Scheer) commanded submarine flotillas independently, so that the Kaiser was forced in October 1917 to mediate conflicts between these two.[74] Command over the few available submarine cruisers brought further rancor between Holtzendorff and Scheer. This command tangle was partially resolved in December 1917 by the appointment of Vice Admiral Ritter von Mann-Tiechler to head a newly created U-Boat Office.[75] Mann-Tiechler at once tried to increase the production of submarines, but his efforts came to naught when General Ludendorff refused to transfer to the navy the requisite labor force.[76]

The discontent of a few "hawks" notwithstanding, the Admiralty Staff refused to order submarine operations off the east coast of the United States. By September 1917 Berlin finally dropped its pretense that it was not officially at war with the United States. Yet there was still no official German declaration of war against the United States, and to maintain this fiction German admirals declined to send U-boats to American stations. In October Germany enlarged the blockade zones in the Atlantic Ocean, but carefully avoided including American territorial waters in the new war zone. Commerce of nonbelligerents moving to the United States was regarded as neutral shipping until December 1917, by which time it had become ludicrous to maintain the fiction of "no war."[77] In fact, German and American troops now faced one another in France: the first contingent of doughboys arrived in Europe in June 1917, and their strength at the front increased that year from 12,000 in July to 129,000 in December.

The year 1917 ended without Great Britain suing for peace as a result of unrestricted submarine warfare. Yet another year of combat faced the Reich, and with the growing suffering in terms of human lives and the staggering costs of the war, Germany's naval commanders turned their attention to the problem of the future peace, especially to the issue of war aims. It may therefore be useful to interrupt this account of the war at sea to analyze what German naval leaders expected to reap from a successful outcome of the present war.

## German War Aims and the United States

The United States, as previously stated, played no strategic role in Germany's decision to go to war in August 1914. Yet as the war dragged on and as the prospect of unrestricted submarine warfare raised the possibility of a German-American confrontation on the high seas, a few naval planners in Berlin turned their attention to the issue of war aims. When Captain Magnus von Levetzow became chief of the Operational Branch of the High Sea Fleet in January 1916, he inherited a memorandum, "Discourses upon Our Maritime Situation," from his predecessor, Commander Wolfgang Wegener. This document contained some interesting considerations:

> We still do not know how this war will unfold and who will remain as our final opponent. We can fight the war against England with U-boats; a war with America, for example, only with capital ships, and none of us today can predict when the fleet will assemble . . . on the Atlantic for the battle for world supremacy.[78]

Wegener's study not only foreshadowed the future unrestricted submarine warfare against Great Britain, but also alluded to a future struggle against the United States on the high seas for control of the western maritime arteries. And perhaps with such reasoning in mind, Rear Admiral Karl Hollweg of Tirpitz's Naval Office drafted a prognosis entitled "Further Development of the Navy After This War" in which he called for the construction of a German fleet of forty battleships, forty small cruisers and two hundred submarines.[79]

Such considerations led senior German naval officers between 1914 and 1917 to define a general program of war aims. Two points need to be made, however, before briefly discussing this subject. First, these were only *ad hoc* aims for a war that in the view of most naval officers had come five years too early. And second, these aims were designed to prepare the Reich for a future conflagration with the Anglo-Saxon maritime powers. Admiral von Tirpitz, in sharp contrast to German army leaders, from the start desired a separate peace in the east with both Russia and Japan in order to gain a free hand against the western naval powers, thereby laying the foundations for Germany's future *Weltpolitik*.

On 26 November and 24 December 1916, at the request of the chancellor, Admiral von Holtzendorff drafted the navy's first comprehensive war aims program for the government. It left no doubt that Holtzendorff regarded the present conflict as the prelude to a major showdown on the Atlantic Ocean. The chief of the Admiralty Staff defined five major areas in which he hoped to improve Germany's naval position. In the European theater he sought to annex the Belgian coast with the harbors of Bruges, Ostend and Zeebrugge,* the Courland coast with Libau (Liepaja) and Windau (Ventspils), and the Baltic islands Moon and Oesel. In addition, he coveted the Danish Faeroe Islands, 160 nautical miles west of the Shetland Islands, which would "open up the way to the free ocean for us [and] *form the first breach in England's dominant maritime geographic situation*" (italics in the original).[80]

In the Atlantic sphere, Holtzendorff cherished naval bases at either Dakar or the Cape Verde Islands, and at the Azores. These new German possessions would be necessary to disrupt enemy sea trade in future wars, to protect Germany's maritime commerce, and for use as supply bases for the forward bastions of her Central African colonial empire, which was eventually to be established.

In the Far East, the admiral planned to retain Germany's existing bases in New Guinea, the Bismarck Archipelago, Yap, and Kiaochow. He hoped to acquire Tahiti in order to interrupt American trade between the Panama Canal and the Orient in future wars. In the West Indian Ocean, he wanted Madagascar along with the great harbors of East Africa, as both would be vital for Germany's future colonial empire in Central Africa. In the East Indian Ocean, Holtzendorff planned to purchase one of the large Dutch islands. And finally, in the Mediterranean area he desired the harbor of Valona on the Albanian coast as a naval base, along with a land connection to the Austro-Hungarian Empire.[81]

All these territorial claims expressed the navy's strategic concept of getting direct access to the Atlantic Ocean and ultimately control of its major commerce lanes. Field Marshal von Hindenburg incorporated these aims into his own war aims program, which was basically endorsed by the Kaiser and the chancellor. Captain von Trotha recommended them to General Ludendorff, and tactfully assured the latter that neither German victories over Russia and France nor the possession of Serbia, Romania and Montenegro were of primary importance. "A peace which does not secure our maritime power is not a *German* peace."[82]

Holtzendorff's program was supplemented in July 1917 by Captain von Trotha's analysis of what territories he thought were necessary for future German world power. The key, according to Trotha, was Africa. In East Africa, Germany would require control of the entire central coast on the Indian Ocean, partly to secure a base for German expansion in the

* Tirpitz, in his Stettin *Denkschrift* of 27 April 1916, called German possession of Belgium "the cornerstone on which one can build a German world power equal to that of the Anglo-Saxons and the Russians." See Holger H. Herwig "Admirals versus Generals: The War Aims of the Imperial German Navy 1914–1918," *Central European History*, vol. 5 (September 1972), 215.

direction of Mesopotamia. The "central coastline of western Africa," which Trotha declined to define precisely, was likewise to be annexed in order to allow German control of the South Atlantic, including the approaches to both southern capes.[83] Such was the blueprint for German naval aspirations in the Indian and South Atlantic oceans. What clearly emerged once again was the desire to acquire bases on the eastern shores of the Atlantic — be it at the Faeroe Islands or Africa — in order to challenge what German naval officers regarded as an Anglo-Saxon monopoly of western maritime trade routes.

These war aims considerations were widely disseminated by naval commanders in order to rally public support behind them. Only a few prominent retired officers such as Vice Admiral Karl Galster and Captain Lothar Persius raised objections; they pictured a German occupation of Belgium as a permanent thorn in Great Britain's side and thus a source of future wars. Both these officers denied the military value of this advanced base in the English Channel because it would not provide Germany with free access to the Atlantic.[84]

But these men stood alone. Holtzendorff refined his 1916 war aims program and presented it to the Kaiser on 14 February 1918; yet again he found the monarch in complete agreement with the navy's stance on this matter.[85] Admiral von Tirpitz, in his official capacity as head of the mammoth Fatherland Party,* continued to rally large segments of the German populace behind the navy's war aims program. While he was now convinced that a final military decision in Europe lay in the distant future, he nevertheless predicted that intense economic warfare would continue unabated even after a compromise peace. The western naval powers, he argued, were striving for financial "world monopoly." Compromise with either Great Britain or the United States would spell the end of Germany as a free power and would bring about her "economic demise." The admiral never flagged in his insistence that the Reich was struggling against Anglo-Saxon capitalist monopoly, and that military defeat in the present war would deliver Germany into the clutches of this Anglo-Saxon "conspiracy."[86]

This "Tirpitzean" thinking had permeated the German naval officer corps. Vice Admiral Albert Hopman, the German naval commander at Odessa on the Black Sea, in May 1918 drafted a letter on future German naval policy that found its way to the Kaiser and to Ludendorff. Hopman bluntly stated "that our goals lie, now as before, in the West and along the [Atlantic] Ocean rather than in the East and the Black Sea."

* The Fatherland Party was an allegedly nonpartisan pressure group of one and a quarter million members which crusaded for a war of annexations and indemnities; in short, for a victor's peace.

He thereby seconded Tirpitz's plea for a separate peace with Russia in order to intensify the war at sea in the west. Certain long-range considerations guided Hopman in reaching this conclusion:

> We must have an ally for future decisions of global dimensions. This can never be England or America, hence it can only be . . . Russia, politically, militarily and economically chained to us. Japan will sooner or later have to join this [alignment] in the East as the left wing of the alliance. Only in this way can we prevent world domination by the Anglo-Saxons.[87]

The letter greatly irritated Ludendorff, but it clearly defined the navy's stance on where the true fulcrum of the present struggle lay. Moreover, Ludendorff's opposition, combined with the failure of the undersea offensive, forced Holtzendorff's retirement in August 1918. A new Navy Supreme Command under Admiral Reinhard Scheer and Captain von Levetzow on 1 August replaced Holtzendorff and the Admiralty Staff.

However, shortly before Holtzendorff's departure the Admiralty Staff once more reiterated its war aims program. It confirmed its earlier Atlantic program, including the retention of Flanders and a naval base in either Finland or Murmansk — both designed to outflank the British Isles and provide Germany with that cherished access to the Atlantic Ocean. The naval planners were willing to renounce their demands for the Atlantic islands, such as the Azores, provided they could obtain instead a number of suitable naval bases from French and Portuguese colonies in West Africa. The Mediterranean program still centered around a naval base at Valona, but now included also the Albanian hinterland, Constantinople with the Dardanelles, and a naval station in the Gulf of Alexandretta. These, the Admiralty Staff planners declared, were minimum goals, vital to the preservation of Germany's present status. Further acquisitions would have to be made in the near future if Germany was to pursue an effective *Weltpolitik*.[88]

Captain von Levetzow, Scheer's chief of staff, in September 1918 incorporated most of Holtzendorff's aims in the Supreme Command's war aims program. He informed General Paul von Bartenwerffer, chief of the Political Division of the General Staff, that while Germany might not be able to retain the Flanders coast, it must at all costs possess the Murmansk coast. Furthermore, Levetzow wanted Germany to acquire Constantinople as a *Stützpunkt* for "all future wars." He also insisted on either Valona or Cattaro as a naval base in the Adriatic Sea, and echoed Holtzendorff's plea for a German naval station at Alexandretta as the terminal for a German oil pipeline from northern Mesopotamia, which, Levetzow stressed, would have to remain in German hands. Finally, he wanted Bengasi in North Africa as the first step toward a future German colonial empire in Central Africa.[89] Although these war aims had become utterly unrealistic by late September 1918, they nevertheless demonstrated that the naval leadership never abandoned Tirpitz's basic foreign policy concept.

It cannot be overstated that Admiral von Tirpitz enjoyed the support of the vast majority of German naval officers in his private endeavors to delineate the Reich's war aims program. Tirpitz urged naval commanders to work for a separate peace in the east with Russia and Japan, military victory over France in the west, major maritime successes against Great Britain and, subsequently, the United States. The war, he argued, must be concluded with Germany's position in Europe secured, and with sufficient naval bases around the globe for a successful pursuit of *Weltpolitik* in the future. This basic concept, generally supported by Admirals von Holtzendorff, Scheer, von Trotha, and Captain von Levetzow, was to be taken up thirty years later by officers who served, primarily as lieutenants, under these men in 1918. But in 1918 the program hung on the slender thread of submarine successes against Allied shipping on the high seas.

## The War at Sea (1918)

German naval intelligence estimated quite correctly at the end of 1917 what the United States Navy had stationed in European waters: six battleships and thirty-six destroyers in Ireland (Queenstown), twenty cruisers and destroyers in England (Plymouth), twenty-two destroyers in France (Brest and St. Nazaire), as well as other escort craft scattered over various ports such as Sheerness, Portsmouth, and the Orkney Islands.[90] Within a few months the Admiralty Staff reported that some two hundred thousand American troops had been landed in France and Great Britain since April 1917, and that the United States Navy had stationed additional battleships and heavy cruisers in the Firth of Forth.[91]

Holtzendorff's sources were fairly accurate. American landings in January 1918 raised the American Expeditionary Force to 176,000, by June to 722,000 and by August to 1,293,000 troops in France. The supplies necessary to equip and outfit the growing American military presence on the western front increased from 12,000 tons in July 1917 to 536,000 tons in July 1918. Four United States superbattleships—*Florida*, *Wyoming*, *New York* and *Texas*—were dispatched to the

British Grand Fleet in Scapa Flow by January 1918 under Rear Admiral Hugh Rodman; a fifth, the *Arkansas*, joined the fleet in July 1918. These were the pride of the United States Navy, and alone in weight of broadside fired they possessed 64 percent superiority over the most modern German dreadnoughts (*König* class). Before the year ended, Admiral Benson had sent virtually his entire destroyer force (sixty-eight units), five cruisers, nine submarines, and 121 so-called subchasers — in all, 354 vessels — to assist the British against the submarine menace.[92]

Despite these reports of American assistance to the Entente, German naval leaders continued to regard the United States Navy as a negligible quantity. Admiral von Holtzendorff informed the Kaiser accordingly during an Imperial audience on 30 January 1918. "The military *support of the United States* — since war began the only [*sic*] new support for our enemies — cannot have a decisive effect owing to lack of merchant tonnage." He believed that the Americans faced an alternative, "*either an army, or material aid*," since they would be forced by unrestricted submarine warfare and the resulting shortage of commercial shipping to make a choice between supplying the Entente powers with war materials or recruiting, training and supplying an army for deployment on the western front. If the Americans should choose the latter course, Holtzendorff predicted, they could at best provide the Entente with one division per month, or 300,000 men by the end of 1918.[93] Here he proved less accurate: by November 1918 the United States maintained an army of 1.97 million men in France.

Admiral von Tirpitz continued to press for an all-out naval effort against the Anglo-Saxon maritime powers. In February 1918 he argued that France would never agree to a separate peace because she could not resist American and British pressure to pursue the war. And whereas he had earlier rejected the notion that the present struggle was a parallel to the Second Punic War between Rome (Germany) and Carthage (Great Britain), the admiral now conceded that the comparison was valid because the United States had taken up the fight against Germany for economic motives and in order to gain a free hand in East Asia. Tirpitz tirelessly reiterated his conviction that "the English-speaking world forms one bloc despite internal strife. It demands world hegemony." There could be no compromise. Failure to defeat the Anglo-Saxon world in the present war would reduce Germany to a second-rate world power.[94]

General Ludendorff, during 1917–1918 the virtual dictator of Germany, also refused to admit defeat in the undersea offensive early in 1918. Events in Russia buoyed his optimism: V. I. Lenin had, in the wake of General Brusilov's military disaster, seized power in Petersburg (Petrograd) in November 1917, and during the following month opened peace talks with the Germans. Ludendorff therefore stubbornly clung to the position that if the U-boats could sink sufficient tonnage to prevent a rapid reinforcement of American troops, the German army might force the issue on the western front in a planned all-out massive offensive in the spring (Operation Michael).[95] On 22 January 1918 he reassured the Foreign Office: "The effects of submarine warfare are undoubtedly very noticeable in England. Our immediate purpose is to bring England to her knees unswervingly and with all our energy."[96]

Developments on the eastern front once more came into play. On 10 February 1918 Russo-German peace negotiations were broken off by Leon Trotsky at Brest-Litovsk with his famous "no war, no peace" declaration. Wilhelm II, in turn, demanded that the Bolsheviks be "beaten to death," and on 18 February Generals Max Hoffmann and Rüdiger von der Goltz launched Operation Faustschlag. The Germans, having already recognized an independent Finland and an independent Ukraine, rapidly advanced against the disorganized Russian resistance and occupied Narva, Pskov and Kiev. Lenin agreed to terms on 23 February in order to stave off German occupation of the "cradle of the revolution" (Petrograd), and on 3 March the Bolsheviks signed the German treaty at Brest-Litovsk whereby Russia lost Poland, Courland and Lithuania. Estonia and Livonia nominally remained under Russian rule, but in fact were subjected to "German police power."

This turn of events greatly pleased Wilhelm: "The Balticum is one and I will become its master and [will] tolerate no opposition. I have conquered it and no lawyers can take it from me! . . . Balticum is a whole, in personal union under Prussia's king, who has conquered it! Just as under Frederick the Great!"[97] Victory in the east, combined with the greatest hopes for Ludendorff's planned assault with sixty divisions in March 1918 against the Allied line Arras–St. Quentin–La Fère, produced a military panacea and expectations of great land gains in the west as well. However, not all military commanders shared this belief. General Wilhelm Groener, destined to replace Ludendorff as first quartermaster-general, was far more prophetic in his diary: "Since we must count more and more on the arrival of American troops despite Tirpitz and the U-boats, the offensive becomes a last attempt to speed an end to the war."[98]

Admiral von Holtzendorff, perhaps in an attempt to dispel such mounting pessimism, informed the Foreign Office on 26 February that the submarines could destroy enough Allied shipping to offset new construction and still bring the war to a successful conclusion. He calculated that the U-boats could send some 650,000 tons of merchant shipping to the bottom per month; shipwrecks and other natural calamities would account for an additional monthly loss of 45,000 tons. He estimated that the Allied and Associated Powers could construct about 345,000 tons of shipping per month; therefore the net reduction would reach about 350,000 tons. On the basis of this mathematical calculation one could project that by the middle of 1918 Germany's enemies would have at their disposal only approximately 10.5 million tons of merchant shipping to transport some sixty million tons of supplies as well as American troops and their gear to Europe.[99]

At this late date (February 1918) General Ludendorff finally agreed to release skilled labor from munitions plants to naval shipyards in order to increase the output of U-boats, which now received first priority. But the measure came too late and construction facilities were inadequate: during the first ten months of 1918 only seventy-four new submarines were delivered — barely enough to keep pace with combat losses.[100] Thus instead of depriving the western coalition of about 650,000 tons per month (not counting new construction), the U-boats managed to bag only about half that. In January 1918 the submarines destroyed 357,000 tons of merchant shipping; it was to be the highest monthly quota in 1918. In April some 279,000 tons went to the bottom, and by September the figure had slipped to about 188,000 tons.

By the end of February 1918 more than 200,000 United States troops had landed in Europe despite the navy's boast that it could never be done.[101] American ships sailed to Europe on sea lanes far removed from the normal hunting grounds of the German undersea raiders. Moreover, ships used for troop transports were fast, camouflaged with dazzle paint, and well protected by armed escorts. Their routes were kept secret and zigzag evasive tactics were developed to give the U-boats the slip.[102] The combination of these various novel antisubmarine tactics brought immediate results: not a single troop transport was torpedoed en route to Europe. A few statistics underline the vast dimension of the German Admiralty Staff's miscalculation in this area. Between March and October 1918 the United States landed 1,759,000 troops in Europe, and accounted for 75 percent of the 5,197,000 tons of supplies unloaded in France in 1918. And whereas in July 1917 the United States had been able to send only 94,000 tons of supplies to Europe, by July 1918 the figure had climbed to 1,753,000 tons. The assurances of German naval experts notwithstanding, the submarine offensive had clearly failed to stem the tide of supplies from the United States to her European allies.[103]

The state secretary of the Naval Office, Admiral von Capelle, facing mounting civilian and parliamentary criticism of the unrestricted submarine campaign, attempted to present a strong front. He informed Reichstag leaders in April 1918 that "the American submarine chasers, about which we have heard much ballyhoo, have failed." Capelle further told the deputies that with regard to American military performance, her troops and her aircraft had only had minimal effect. He concluded with the astounding statement: "All in all, one can discern that the economic difficulties confronting our opponents have only increased as a result of America's entry into the war."[104]

That naval authorities privately were of different opinions can be witnessed by their continued efforts to overcome the throttling effects of the Allied antisubmarine tactics. In April 1918, in an effort further to disperse the enemy's heavy naval units and to relieve the submarines, the High Sea Fleet — as the cruisers *Brummer* and *Bremse* the year before — was sent on a surface raid into the North Sea. But this attempt to intercept convoys sailing from Bergen (Norway) to Scotland encountered not a single enemy ship and was highlighted only by the mechanical breakdown of the battle cruiser *Moltke*, which snapped a propeller shaft and had to be towed home down the length of the Jutland peninsula. The High Sea Fleet hereafter remained in its anchorages in the Jade and Elbe estuaries and never sallied forth again.[105] The Grand Fleet, strengthened by the addition of the American dreadnoughts, maintained the relentless distant blockade from the two holes of the North Sea, Dover and Scotland.

A more promising enterprise seemed to be a revival of plans to extend the submarine war zones to the American east coast. As early as 28 February 1918 Holtzendorff pleaded with the Kaiser to commence unrestricted submarine warfare in American waters by mid-May, when the navy would be able to release two submarine cruisers of the *Deutschland* class for duty there. Similar reasoning in 1941 produced Operation Paukenschlag (see pages 240–241), but then as now not much was gained. Germany possessed only six of the converted merchant submarine cruisers, and they were slow and clumsy. To be sure, German naval engineers had developed a new submarine cruiser capable of fifteen knots and specifically designed for commerce raiding on the high seas. But certain technical difficulties could not be corrected in time, and only two of these new U-cruisers ever saw active service. To add insult to injury, though the U-cruisers were placed under the command of the U-Boat Office, they were operated from Berlin as independent entities, thereby precluding their use as motherships to coordinate "wolf pack" tactics on Allied shipping.[106]

But Holtzendorff continued to call throughout the spring of 1918 for submarine activity on the eastern seaboard of the United States. On 3 March he informed the state secretary of the Foreign Office, Richard Kühlmann, that improved submarine tactics allowed an expansion of the war zones. "The military necessity of scattering as much as possible the antisubmarine forces of our enemies makes it necessary to increase the area of the blockade zones." Specifically, studies recently undertaken revealed that "the best chance of success lies in an increase of unrestricted submarine warfare to the east coast of the United States" because commercial traffic could be interdicted more easily at well-known assembly points than at unknown destinations. "Up to now political considerations and the lack of development in the effectiveness of the U-boats have prevented us from expanding the spheres of operation to the American coast. The technical objects . . . are no longer with us. In my opinion, political considerations no longer exist."[107]

Kühlmann did not agree. He quickly advised Holtzendorff from Bucharest, where he was negotiating a peace treaty with Romania, that political considerations did indeed exist. He argued that hostile actions in American waters would inflame public opinion, especially in those regions where war fever was relatively low. Such naval operations might also interrupt Chancellor Count Georg von Hertling's hopes for peace in the wake of President Woodrow Wilson's announcement of the Fourteen Points.[108] Hertling, in turn, supported Kühlmann, arguing that the navy's policy would bring the remaining neutrals into the war against Germany and that the navy did not possess sufficient U-cruisers to get the job done.[109]

Now, as in January 1917, army leaders once more entered the discussions. General Ludendorff strongly favored submarine warfare in American waters and informed Kühlmann of the crucial need to intercept American troop transports to France. "Political considerations must be dismissed owing to the serious commitment of the United States to the war and to the impotence of the antiwar elements [in the United States] before the dictates of military necessity."[110] Field Marshal von Hindenburg also joined the lists, informing the Kaiser that "the American leaders are moving ever growing numbers of troops to the western front, so that every day takes on greater meaning."[111] He was especially anxious to commence attacks on American troop transports.

Diplomats as well as military and naval leaders turned to Wilhelm II to resolve this issue. The Kaiser, ever true to form, equivocated and postponed the decision as long as possible. On 1 April 1918 he "basically approved" Holtzendorff's plan to extend the war zone to the east coast of the United States by mid-May.[112] Yet delays ensued. On 23 June Wilhelm counseled postponement.[113] Five days later he refused to allow submarine attacks in American waters, arguing that Germany lacked sufficient vessels to make a success of the effort. "One should not repeat the error of the spring of 1915."[114] On 2 July the Kaiser had a final confrontation with

Hindenburg and Ludendorff on this matter. This time Wilhelm not only reiterated his argument that Germany lacked sufficient submarines, but further announced that such a course of action would adversely affect the German position in South America. "So far opinion in Argentina and Chile is not at all unfavorable. We must prevent their disposing of our ships under pressure from Wilson" (German merchant ships interned in Latin American ports were being sought by the United States). Chancellor Hertling stood firm in his opposition to the naval effort. The matter was ended abruptly after another plea by naval officers when the Kaiser decided against the proposal. "I am of different opinion and it will remain with that."[115] According to the chancellor, Wilhelm was extremely annoyed by this naval pressure and he dismissed "the gentlemen of the navy rather rudely."[116] Further efforts were made in July to change the monarch's mind, but for once he stood firm against his soldiers and sailors. And when Admiral Scheer, about to assume supreme command of the navy, opposed Holtzendorff on this matter, it receded from view.[117]

Civilian leaders were equally divided over this issue. Those who favored unrestricted submarine warfare in American waters were encouraged by naval leaders and frequently provided with technical material to buttress their arguments. Gustav Stresemann of the National Liberal Party was informed in June 1918 by retired Admiral Karl Dick that U-cruisers would be dispatched to the American east coast by 1 July. "Each U-cruiser carries a small metal airplane that can be dismantled and stored on board."[118] Somewhat more realistic was the reaction of Walther Rathenau, the economic planner, who echoed the mounting disappointment with naval and military leaders who had promised earlier that no American army would ever set foot in Europe. Instead, about one million American soldiers were deployed in France by July 1918, and more were arriving every day.[119]

Some of the submarine cruisers did operate in American waters, observing the rules of cruiser warfare. Their primary purpose was to create diversions and to cause the Allied and Associated Powers to disperse their antisubmarine craft over a greater area in the Atlantic. Admiral von Holtzendorff also hoped that some of the United States troop transports might be destroyed off the major east coast ports, an act which would cause widespread civilian fear and force Washington to curtail its mounting matériel and manpower assistance to the Allies. As previously stated, Germany possessed only two new U-cruisers (armed with fourteen torpedoes and one 15-centimeter [6-inch] gun) in addition to the seven merchant submarines. Therefore, at any given time only one of the U-cruisers and two merchant submarines could operate in American waters off (chiefly) Boston, New York and the Chesapeake Bay, and the time required to reach the United States and to return to Germany greatly limited their stay in this theater of the war. In all, seven raids by German undersea craft occurred between 7 June 1918 and the end of the war, but their accomplishments were minimal. Approximately 110,000 tons of merchant shipping were destroyed during these forays, but not a single eastbound troop transport was attacked — much less destroyed.[120]

The Germans also attempted to enhance unrestricted submarine warfare in September 1918 by increasing U-boat production. Already in the summer of that year all construction on surface vessels had been suspended; the army now agreed to provide the requisite skilled labor. The resulting Scheer Program, designed to parallel the famous Hindenburg Program for the army, which in 1916 had proposed to double munitions output and to triple that of machine guns and artillery, called for an increased monthly production of U-boats from 12.7 in October 1918 to thirty-six by the fourth quarter of 1919. In all, the navy ordered the construction of 450 submarines as well as two battleships and fifteen cruisers. Scheer agreed to a gala public announcement of the program named in his honor "in order to diminish the ugly mood in many circles" of the populace and to impress the Reich's enemies with her determination to carry on the war. Yet the admiral realized that the program was primarily a psychological ploy and that it stood little chance of realization. In fact, Scheer termed it "a twelfth-hour attempt to save everything."[121]

The Scheer Program, or at least the ballyhoo that accompanied it, temporarily lifted the spirits of German military, naval and civilian leaders. Commander Dietrich Meyer, a fleet staff officer, reported to Admiral Franz Ritter von Hipper, the new chief of the High Sea Fleet, that army headquarters remained fairly optimistic regarding the outcome of the war. The Allied and Associated Powers, Meyer stated, desperately needed significant military successes to offset mounting domestic problems. The French were "at the end of their strength"; the British were most concerned because "their trade was slowly falling into the hands of the Americans"; and the Americans were finally beginning to feel the enormous financial burdens of the war as well as the increasing difficulty of supplying their troops in France.[122]

Others, however, no longer accepted naval prognoses at face value. Conrad Haussmann of the Progressive People's Party complained to fellow Reichstag members that the navy was causing "great damage" by allowing the U-boats to operate in American waters at all.[123] And Stresemann, an ardent supporter of submarine warfare from the start, now also began to waver in his support. He ruefully wrote to a colleague, Dr.

Georg Zöphel, that Admiral von Capelle had initially assured parliamentary leaders "that the significance of American aid was equal to nil," a proclamation based on the calculation that for every soldier the United States would require five tons of merchant shipping. Moreover, Capelle had given his word that the United States would never be able to transport 500,000 men across the Atlantic to France. Nor could Uncle Sam, according to the admiral, in two years construct sufficient tonnage to supply the Allies in Europe. Bitter and disillusioned, Stresemann now laid even the blame for the failure of Ludendorff's spring offensive squarely at the feet of naval leaders.[124]

Similar feelings were being aired by certain army officers. In August 1918 General Karl von Einem recalled being informed by General Ludendorff in January 1917 of the resumption of unrestricted submarine warfare. Einem's first query had been "And America?," to which Ludendorff had replied: "What can she do? She cannot come over here!" Now the game was over and Einem was becoming aware of the magnitude of that gamble in January 1917. "This was a great mistake, brought about by the navy which really believed that it could bring England to her knees in half a year. And how many believed them! Even I was a believer."[125]

Germany's military situation grew increasingly worse during the summer and fall of 1918. Ludendorff's Michael offensive, launched in the west on 21 March, reached the Marne salient by the end of May, but Marshal Ferdinand Foch managed to halt the German advance in mid-July around Rheims. General John "Black Jack" Pershing had finally wisely allowed his eighteen oversized American divisions to be deployed by the French commander, and they played a decisive role in blunting the assault of the two hundred divisions at Ludendorff's command. Moreover, Americans were now arriving at the rate of 300,000 per month, and Foch was emboldened by this to launch a long-prepared stroke against the German Marne salient. It was completely successful, and on 8 August French and Canadian troops broke through the German lines at the Somme and British tanks completed what Ludendorff termed "the black day of the German army in the history of the war." By the first week of September, the Germans had been driven back to their positions before the Michael offensive, to the so-called Hindenburg line. Furthermore, on 29 September Bulgaria withdrew from the war and the Turkish armies in Palestine were trapped and rounded up by an Anglo-French force under Field Marshal Edmund Allenby. Germany's major ally, Austria-Hungary, was also on the verge of collapse. The German victory over the Italians at Caporetto in November 1917, which had inflicted upon Italy almost 500,000 casualties and the capture of 250,000 men, had not sufficed to end the war in the south, and the collapse of Bulgaria opened the way to an Allied advance on Austria-Hungary's rear through Serbia. On 29 September German military leaders lost their nerve and counseled the Kaiser to seek an armistice. Ludendorff repeated this call for an end to the war on 1 October, and two days later Prince Max von Baden became the new chancellor. He at once appealed to President Wilson for an armistice, and unrestricted submarine warfare came to an end on 16 October in accordance with the terms of Wilson's second note. By 26 October Ludendorff was forced to resign. Austria-Hungary asked for an armistice on 30 October, and Turkey capitulated that same day.

German naval leaders proved surprisingly willing to cease the undersea offensive. A new bold, grand design had entered their heads: the fleet could be sent against the combined British and American surface vessels stationed in the North Sea. Admiral von Hipper concluded that "an honorable fleet engagement, even if it should become a death struggle," was preferable to an inglorious and inactive end to the fleet.[126] Rear Admiral von Trotha, Hipper's chief of staff, was equally adamant on this matter, arguing that a fleet engagement was needed "in order to go down with honor."[127] And Scheer was not the man to stand in the way of such an adventurous undertaking. "It is impossible that the fleet . . . remain idle. It must be deployed." As chief of the Seekriegsleitung he also counseled that the "honor and existence of the navy" demanded the use of the High Sea Fleet even if "the course of events cannot thereby be significantly altered."[128] On 24 October 1918 the naval command formally adopted Operations Plan No. 19 (O-Befehl Nr. 19). Neither the Kaiser nor the chancellor was informed of this development, despite the fact that at one point Germany's admirals considered asking Wilhelm to come aboard for the final naval assault. Scheer did not think it "opportune" to inform them, especially the chancellor, of his intentions.[129] Execution for the operation was set for 30 October 1918.

Operations Plan No. 19 called for one destroyer group to be sent to the Flanders coast and another to the mouth of the Thames River, while the High Sea Fleet took battle station in the Hoofden (the North Sea between Holland and Great Britain). The British Grand Fleet, according to the German plan, would leave its anchorage in Scapa Flow to meet the two "baits," which thereupon would draw the British Grand Fleet to Terschelling, a Dutch island in the North Sea, where the naval Armageddon would take place. Twenty-five submarines were in position to intercept the advance of the British and American naval units. It was hoped that a spectacular German naval victory would offset the recent defeats on land.

The German plan took account only of the British battle fleet. They failed to appreciate the fact that there was another major power involved in the struggle. It was quite in keeping with the consistent claims of German executive officers that American naval forces as a whole were not worthy of their consideration. Thus no thought was given to the United States Navy units stationed either at home or in Europe. Yet there were five American battleships attached to the Grand Fleet in Scapa Flow, and another three in Ireland. Five American large cruisers and almost seventy escort destroyers were operating in European waters.[130] And finally, the overall American capital ship strength was now thirty-nine, far surpassing that of Germany.[131]

But the test of strength failed to materialize. By the night of 29 October 1918 the fleet was in open rebellion because sailors had overheard their officers discussing the upcoming "death ride." Dreams of battle and honor quickly faded. Operations Plan No. 19 died in Wilhelmshaven harbor on 29–30 October when stokers refused to get up steam. German hopes of altering the course of the war by use of sea power thus ended ingloriously. The crews of destroyers and submarines alone remained loyal to the Kaiser, and when Hipper attempted to mobilize the fleet on 1 November he discovered that approximately four hundred to five hundred men on each of the battleships *Friedrich der Grosse*, *Thüringen* and *Helgoland* were in open rebellion. The naval command's attempt to isolate and disperse the rebellious elements failed utterly; the sailors sent to other ports, such as Cuxhaven, Hamburg and Kiel, merely raised the banner of revolt there. By 9 November all major German cities were in open revolution against the Imperial government in Berlin, and many areas threatened to secede from the Bismarckian Reich. The ghost of Bolshevik revolution loomed on the horizon.

The Kaiser's naval officer corps suffered surprisingly few casualties. It appears that only three officers died as a result of revolutionary violence in Kiel, and about an equal number were wounded. A typical attitude among naval officers was that of Hipper, who on 9 November, when the sailors of his flagship raised the red emblem, quietly packed his bags and unmolested went ashore. Grand Admiral Prince Henry of Prussia, Wilhelm's brother, had already on 5 November fled Kiel, wearing a red armband and driving a truck that flew the red flag. The Kaiser was most perturbed by the naval collapse. When Admiral Scheer informed him on 9 November that the navy could no longer be relied upon, Wilhelm replied sarcastically: "My dear admiral, the navy has deserted me very nicely!" It was the last time that he saw his admirals, whom he dismissed with the words: "I no longer have a navy."[132] On 10 November 1918, after General Groener had informed him that the army also could no longer be relied upon, Wilhelm II boarded the splendid cream and gold Imperial train for the last time and passed in the darkness of night into exile across the Dutch border. The last of the Hohenzollerns thereby closed out more than five centuries of his family's rule in north Germany.

The end now came quickly. On 6 November German delegates left Berlin to seek an armistice with the victorious Allied and Associated Powers, and three days later Prince Max von Baden resigned and turned over the reins of power to the Social Democrat Friedrich Ebert. At 5 A.M. on 11 November Germany signed the terms of the armistice in Foch's railway carriage in the Forest of Compiègne; six hours later the First World War came to an end.

The victors at Paris decided on 13 November that all German submarines (176) were to be surrendered in English ports, and that ten battleships, six battle cruisers, eight light cruisers, and fifty destroyers were to be interned also in British anchorages because no neutral countries would allow the High Sea Fleet to be interned in their ports (as originally specified in the terms of the armistice). German naval commanders at first thought about scuttling the submarines, but this notion was quickly dropped when Foch made it well known that he would occupy Heligoland if the Germans destroyed their U-boats.[133]

On 19 November 1918 the pride of Admiral von Tirpitz's navy—eleven battleships, five battle cruisers, eight light cruisers, and fifty destroyers—left Wilhelmshaven for the last time. The British commander, Admiral Sir David Beatty, accompanied by Rear Admiral Rodman and three hundred and seventy warships, met the Germans and escorted them into the Grand Fleet's anchorage at Scapa Flow. Here the ships remained for six months under trying weather and morale conditions while the Allied and Associated Powers hammered out the various peace treaties in Paris—Versailles for Germany, Neuilly for Bulgaria, Sèvres for Turkey, St. Germain for Austria, and Trianon for Hungary.

When the final naval provisions of the Versailles Treaty became known, including surrender of the ships at the Scottish moorage and dismantling of those in German ports, Vice Admiral Ludwig Reuter, the commander in Scapa Flow, took decisive action. At 1 P.M. on 21 June 1919 he scuttled the ships under his command. The British managed to save only one battleship, three light cruisers, and eighteen destroyers. It was an unprecedented spectacle in the annals of naval history: approximately 500,000 tons of warships, estimated at $203,783,000, slipped beneath the waves in Scapa Flow. Outraged and obviously humiliated, the British harbor patrol panicked and opened fire on the German sailors in their lifeboats, resulting in thirty casualties. For this act of defiance, the Germans had to deliver five additional cruisers and about 400,000 tons of dry docks, tugs, floating cranes, dredges, and the like.[134] With this, the "Tirpitz" fleet ceased to exist.

## Epilogue

Despite all the braggadocio in January 1917 when unrestricted submarine warfare was adopted, Germany's admirals had not especially favored war with the United States either at that time or under such an alignment of powers. At the turn of the century, when the Reich felt free to challenge the United States at sea, she had not possessed sufficient sea power to do so. In 1917 she could claim numerical superiority in capital ships over the United States, but she was not free to challenge the latter because of the British blockade of the North Sea. The decision to resume unrestricted submarine warfare was directed not so much against the United States as against Great Britain. The hope was to force "perfidious Albion" to her knees by cutting off her supply of munitions and foodstuffs from across the Atlantic Ocean. That such a policy might bring the United States into the war and thereby expand it was taken into the bargain because Germany felt that the U-boats were her last means by which to break an apparent stalemate in the land war. Moreover, German naval leaders pursued this course partly because of their general belief that the United States Navy was a negligible quantity — based on its performance in the Spanish-American War — and partly because they had been taught by Tirpitz ever since 1898 that the two Anglo-Saxon maritime powers were one inseparable bloc, united by common language and common desire to keep Germany off the world's markets. This aspect of the issue cannot be stressed sufficiently. It explains the eagerness with which German admirals, in 1917 and again twenty years later, urged their government to treat Great Britain and the United States as one indivisible enemy. It helps us to understand the lighthearted manner in which Admirals von Holtzendorff, von Tirpitz, von Trotha, and Scheer accepted war with the United States without so much as bothering to undertake careful studies of their new opponent's industrial and military capability. And it explains the failure of German leaders at any time to court the favor of the United States and possibly to take advantage of Anglo-American tensions and rivalries in order to drive a wedge between these two economic competitors.

The preoccupation of German naval experts with the parallel between the First World War and the Second Punic War between Rome and Carthage is also revealing. Tirpitz had initially rejected this comparison because it meant that Germany could not totally destroy Great Britain's world power in this war; once the United States had entered the conflict, he reversed his stance and accepted the historical parallel. Tirpitz thereby admitted that the war could only weaken — not conquer — Great Britain; she would have to succumb in a "Third Punic War." In such a future war German naval commanders placed all their hopes. Then the United States would be the main rival for the spoils of the British Empire. Rear Admiral von Trotha clearly expressed this in July 1918: "If England is broken, then the present world system will change; in any case, we cannot prevent America from benefiting thereby. England will never be broken by our struggle against America; that can only remain a peripheral theater of the war."[135]

Vice Admiral von Trotha, in March 1919 appointed head of the newly created Admiralty, supervised the liquidation of the "Tirpitz" navy. The Versailles Treaty, signed in the Hall of Mirrors on 28 June 1919, restricted the German navy to six elderly battleships, six cruisers, and twenty-four destroyers; all submarines were denied her (Article 181). Naval personnel was to be limited to 15,000 men (Article 183), all naval fortifications were to be dismantled, all colonies ceded to the major Allied and Associated Powers (Article 119), all naval air matériel destroyed, and the Kiel Canal was in effect internationalized (Article 380). Given these dire circumstances, Trotha could only attempt to lay the foundations for a distant, brighter future. "I want to preserve the smallest seed so that when the time comes, a useful tree will grow from it."[136] The "seed" collected and preserved were junior naval officers named Carls, Ciliax, Dönitz, Lütjens, and Raeder, among others, and the "tree" that grew from the seeds twenty years later was the Kriegsmarine of Adolf Hitler's Grossdeutsches Reich.

Lieutenant Commander von Weizsäcker placed the issue in broad perspective on 5 October 1918 when he blamed the German defeat on "the premature parvenu-like attempt by Germany to play a decisive role in the world against England's opposition before the young Reich had been secured on the Continent."[137] Ludendorff's successor, General Wilhelm Groener, seconded this analysis on 19 May 1919 when he informed Prussian army officers: "We struggled unconsciously for world dominion before we had secured our continental position."[138] The lesson to be drawn for the future was that Germany needed to establish hegemony in Europe before challenging the Anglo-Saxon maritime powers for control of the Atlantic. The third section of this study will explore to what degree Adolf Hitler and his naval commanders heeded this lesson, but before proceeding to this, it is necessary to study the reaction of American admirals to the German naval challenge in 1917.

SIX

# United States Strategy (1917–1918)

> The possible combinations, of powers and circumstances, are too numerous and too pregnant with possibilities adverse to our interests to permit us to consider any plan other than one which will permit us to exercise eventually the full naval and military strength of the United States in the defense of our interests.
>
> — ADMIRAL WILLIAM S. BENSON
> *February 1917*

AMERICAN ADMIRALS WERE HARDLY SURPRISED BY THE OUTBREAK OF WAR in Europe in August 1914. Except for Admiral Mahan, who urged that the United States should enter the war on the side of the British, there was little activity in Washington. Yet Germany's dominant role in the Central Powers, coupled with her past interference in the Western Hemisphere, convinced the same naval planners that there could be no permanently neutral stance for the United States. The chief of Naval Operations, Admiral William S. Benson, later stated:

> It was my firm conviction that sooner or later the United States would be drawn into war with Germany, whether it was with the Allies, or after the war with the Allies was completed. . . . In fact, I felt that conviction before the war started in 1914.[1]

To be sure, Benson here took full advantage of historical hindsight, and his comments do not square with his stance during 1914–1917.

The General Board of the Navy, headed by Admiral George Dewey, was not unduly alarmed by the prospect of war. Nor was it blind to the possibility of a future confrontation with Germany. On 1 August 1914 the board informed Secretary of the Navy Josephus Daniels of future strategic alternatives:

> If Great Britain is drawn into the war, the German fleet will be neutralized as far as any danger from it to our interests in the immediate future is concerned. If she is not, and if the end of the war should find Germany stronger

than ever in her European position and with her fleet practically unimpaired, the temptation will be great to seize the opportunity for obtaining the position she covets on this side of the ocean. We should prepare now for the situation which would thus be created.[2]

The board herewith reiterated not only the fears and obsessions of Roosevelt, Lodge, Dewey, and others that Germany was determined to seize territory in the Western Hemisphere at the earliest convenient moment, but also the Black War Plan hypothesis that an undefeated Great Britain would assume a neutral stance in any future German-American war.

Admiral Fiske, on the other hand, expressed more alarm. The German march into France, he argued, threatened "the very existence of the United States."[3] Moreover, naval organization was insufficient to meet the requirements of modern warfare, and he asked Congress to authorize the creation of a "general staff" for the navy in order to make it as efficient as that of Germany. But Secretary Daniels managed to scuttle the plan, denouncing it as a blatant attempt to "Prussianize the American Navy."[4]* Thus the war in Europe caused little initial activity in the United States Navy. For the most part, it adopted a wait-and-see attitude.

After war was declared on August 4, President Woodrow Wilson proclaimed the United States neutral and ordered all aliens under American jurisdiction to "remain at peace with the belligerents and maintain a strict and impartial neutrality." From the start Germany failed to adhere to this principle. In November 1914 the German Foreign Office entertained a quixotic plan by a Dr. Wirth from Munich to incite some 250,000 German-Americans and 300,000 Irish-Americans against Canada. This lunatic scheme, to be financed with one hundred million marks from secret funds in the Prussian War Ministry, envisaged a crossing into Canada at some twenty to thirty points by these 550,000 plus an additional 100,000 German reservists then estimated to be in the United States or Canada, who were to be camouflaged in cowboy garb. There were, in fact, about 8 million German and 4.5 million Irish residents in the United States, which at this time (1910 census) had a population of 92 million, and most of these desired the United States to remain neutral in the European war. Only a minority of Germans (who in 1915 ostenta-

* Ironically, the Imperial German Navy suffered from a lack of centralized, unified command because Admiral von Tirpitz feared that a rival might emerge and supplant him. Tirpitz hoped that in time of war the Kaiser would simply appoint him to head the various naval commands. See Walther Hubatsch *Der Admiralstab und die Obersten Marinebehörden in Deutschland 1848–1945* (Frankfurt 1958) for the lack of a German naval "general staff."

tiously celebrated St. Patrick's Day) and Irish (who drank toasts to Bismarck) hoped that the British North Sea naval blockade would prompt the United States to side with the Central Powers. The idea of mobilizing the Germans and Irish in the United States against Canada had been suggested as early as 1911 by General Friedrich von Bernhardi, but proved to be as "realistic" in 1914 as it had been then.[5]*

Somewhat more realistically, in December 1914 the German Foreign Office, the General Staff, Ambassador Count Johann Bernstorff and Military Attaché Captain Franz von Papen in Washington considered the possibility that Japanese troops might be channeled to the European front via the Canadian Pacific Railroad. It was quickly agreed that Papen should direct sabotage operations against the railroad in the Canadian West; the General Staff in Berlin agreed to finance these activities. In addition to intercepting Japanese military transports along the Canadian Pacific Railroad by dynamiting the bridges over the MacLeod River east of Banff Bow as well as the Sawback and Claster tunnels in the Rockies, Papen on 18 December 1914 informed the General Staff that he intended to recruit and train Canadian Indians in the use of explosives for similar projects. The General Staff in Berlin on 19 January 1915 cabled its consent to this utterly utopian undertaking, but events in eastern Canada prevented Papen from traveling west to supervise the project. The German military attaché had simultaneously planned to sever the Canadian land supply routes to Halifax, Nova Scotia, and St. John, New Brunswick, but unfortunately for Papen, one of his agents, Werner Horn, was captured on American soil after an unsuccessful attempt to blow up the railroad bridge over the St. Croix River near Vanceboro, Maine. The *New York Times* reported the incident on 3 February 1915. Undaunted, Papen continued to organize small groups of fifty to one hundred former German reservists in Chicago, St. Paul, Seattle, Detroit, and San Francisco for future sabotage.[6]*

American Secret Service counterespionage details kept the German embassy in Washington — and both Bernstorff and Papen — under close surveillance. A major breakthrough was scored on 24 July 1915 when agent Frank Burke intercepted a briefcase belonging to Dr. Heinrich Albert, a German privy councillor attached to the Washington embassy

* Bernhardi's opus *Der kommende Krieg* (Berlin 1911) was designed to update Karl von Clausewitz's monumental *Vom Kriege*, and it constituted a then unheard of critique of Schlieffen's master plan of 1905–1906. In 1912 Bernhardi published his most famous tract, *Deutschland und der nächste Krieg* (*Germany and the Next War*).

* Both Papen and Bernstorff are strangely silent on this aspect of their careers: Franz von Papen *Die Wahrheit eine Gasse* (Munich 1952), 57, and J.-H. Graf Bernstorff *Deutschland und Amerika* (Berlin 1920), 107.

as commercial attaché. The captured material clearly pointed to major German espionage activities against the neutral United States: Albert and Papen apparently dispensed about two million dollars a week to interrupt industrial production, to encourage strikes, especially of dock and munitions workers, to purchase an American airplane company and its patents, to corner the market in liquid chlorine used for poison gas, and to interdict the flow of raw cotton to Great Britain. Most sensational and shocking was a document outlining a German plan to invade the United States — after war had been declared — somewhere along the isolated stretches of the New Jersey coast. An initial force of a hundred thousand men, after being reinforced, was to cut New York off from the rest of the country and thereby starve it to death, ultimately forcing the United States government to sue for peace.[7] These documents were leaked to the *New York World*, which published them. The impact can scarcely be overrated; here was written proof of German intentions to violate territory in the Western Hemisphere. Roosevelt, Lodge, Dewey, and others had seemingly been right all along. The German journalist George Sylvester Viereck, a relative of Kaiser Wilhelm II, later commented: "A veritable nest of intrigue, conspiracy and propaganda reposed placidly in the portfolio. Its loss was like the loss of the Marne."[8]* Of special interest here is that these documents lent credibility and strength to the deliberations that lay behind the American Black War Plan of 1913.

By 1915, with the major European powers involved in the war, the General Board finally conceded that its Black War Plan was in need of some revision. It now calculated that Germany was in no position to threaten the Western Hemisphere; her burgeoning population was no longer a cause for overseas expansion because that population was "now being decimated by war"; and the struggle for world markets and trade was laid to rest because German trade was "for the moment nonexistent."[9] Moreover, the board could discern no immediate cause for war. With the German High Sea Fleet bottled up in the North Sea, there appeared little likelihood of "incidents" on the high seas. Nor did the board fear that American arms shipments to the Allies would prompt Germany to seek retaliatory measures. The only danger, the planners felt, might result from German or Austrian mistreatment of American citizens residing in those countries. And finally, the board saw no areas in which the United States could assist the Allied war effort: the absence of the German fleet from the Atlantic rendered the United States fleet superfluous, and fifty thousand American expeditionary troops would

* The briefcase also contained the cipher to a secret German code that later helped the Americans break the Zimmermann telegram.

be of little concern to a German army already fighting some three million Allied troops.[10] The board concluded by reasserting its 1913 Black War Plan strategy: the fleet was to be kept in the Atlantic, recruitment spurred, coastal defenses built up, intelligence services coordinated, and merchant ships armed. On the outside chance that Germany might risk an armed clash, the fleet would, as before, be mobilized in lower Chesapeake Bay, proceeding to the Caribbean Sea on the fifteenth mobilization day in order to meet the German invasion armada off Culebra.[11]

Such sober calculations did not, however, preclude independent prognoses designed to inflame public opinion against Germany. In the spring of 1915 the Navy Department, primarily at the insistence of Admiral Fiske and Assistant Secretary Franklin D. Roosevelt, received Secretary Daniels's consent to stage mock war games along the eastern seaboard of the United States. On 22 May the department announced the result of the games: the invader, relying heavily upon armored cruisers (Germany possessed four), which sliced through American armed scouts while avoiding battleships, had established a base in the Chesapeake Bay region. Although the "German" invading forces were considerably smaller than those foreseen in the Black War Plan, the games had the desired effect of alarming Americans to the potential threat of foreign invasion.[12] In fact, none of the Naval War College studies conducted between 1901 and 1913 had accorded such a German plan any measure of success. And lest there be any doubt as to the identification of the "enemy," J. Bernard Walker of the *Scientific American* pointed the finger directly at Germany in his lurid diatribe *Fallen America! The Sequel to the European War.*[13]*

In addition to these fears of the German "danger," there was manifest in American naval deliberations prior to 1917 also an ancient bias against Great Britain; namely, traditional Anglo-American differences concerning the doctrine of "freedom of the seas."† Admiral French E. Chadwick, a former president of the Naval War College, in August 1914 defined immediate and practical problems in case of a British victory in Europe:

* Walker's tangled mind depicted a defeated Germany which, forced to pay an indemnity of fifteen billion dollars to the Allies in Europe, invaded the United States instead and had occupied the east coast before a refugee government in Cincinnati sued for peace.

† Admiral Benson stated the traditional American view on this matter in November 1917 during an inter-Allied discussion of merchant shipping: "In order that the various countries of the world may carry on their trade and may be of real assistance to each other, there must be free communication, and that communication can only be carried on through the freedom of the seas." Holger H. Herwig and David F. Trask "The Failure of Imperial Germany's Undersea Offensive Against World Shipping February 1917 – October 1918," *Historian*, vol. 33 (August 1971), 623.

> Destroy Germany, and you will then see how much England's good will toward the United States amounts to. . . . Nothing could have been more cordial than Anglo-German feeling until Germany began to be a great industrial power and a great sea carrier as well as a sea power. We are also a great industrial power and have a fleet. But — if England is once in a position to deal with us as she may be able to deal with Germany, the British Empire will turn on us as it has turned upon Germany. The *World* balance of power thus demands that Germany shall not be crushed.[14]

Admiral Mahan had warned American political and naval leaders for decades about the German menace in the Western Hemisphere; now Admiral Chadwick (retired, like Mahan, in 1915) suggested that Great Britain, if victorious in Europe, would pose no less a threat to the future of the United States. In February 1915 Captain Harry P. Huse, chief of staff to the Atlantic Fleet, synthesized both fears in a report to Secretary Daniels:

> A victorious Germany means a great army and a great navy flushed with success and animated by the spirit of Bernhardi.* With such tools at his command the Kaiser is not likely to stay his hand until he has practically attained the dominion of the world. . . .
>
> On the other hand should the Allies be successful, it is difficult to see what would restrain England in her ambition to retain and extend the commercial supremacy on the seas she has held for two centuries.

Huse was a prime exponent of the social Darwinistic thinking that had characterized Black War Plan calculations over the past decade:

> The United States . . . is ambitiously turning its eyes to the sea and bids fair to at least make an attempt to extend her commerce. England fought Spain and France and Holland for this reason and was quite ready when a legitimate excuse offered to meet Germany in the present war. There is no reason to believe that the United States as a commercial rival would receive any different treatment.

There was no escape from future complications and conflicts: "In either case then, the United States is sure to come in conflict with one or the other sooner or later."[15] For Captain Huse there existed only one solution to the problem: increased naval construction and war preparedness.

This ambivalence in American naval planning was reflected in the major construction program of 1915–1916. In October 1915 President

* General Friedrich von Bernhardi, then on the eastern front; author of *Germany and the Next War* (*Deutschland und der nächste Krieg*), 1912. See also the Bernhardi note on page 154.

Wilson and Secretary Daniels requested from Congress funds for a five-year naval construction program; Congress on 29 August 1916 authorized the President in the Naval Appropriation Act to construct by 1 July 1919 about 156 ships costing 91.2 million dollars. The act included ten battleships, six battle cruisers, sixty destroyers and torpedo boats, and sixty-seven submarines. The three-year building program was expressly designed to give the United States a navy second to none. It is interesting to note that it called for the construction of an additional sixteen capital ships, eventually giving the United States Navy twenty-nine battleships and six battle cruisers, rather than hundreds of destroyers designed to sweep the seas clear of German submarines. Thus long-range American capital ship requirements were given priority over immediate Allied antisubmarine needs despite the recent losses of American lives on the Atlantic in the sinking of the *Lusitania* (7 May 1915), *Arabic* (19 August) and *Ancona* (7 November).[16]

While Admirals Benson and Fiske were convinced that the United States would eventually have to fight Germany, neither man anticipated and much less desired American participation in an Allied coalition against the Reich. In fact, both naval leaders believed that Germany would emerge victorious from the present war and that, while Great Britain would not be crushed in the process, they should nevertheless prepare for a future German-American war. Obviously, two years of European warfare had not shaken their Black War Plan mentality; in 1915 as in 1913, Great Britain was expected to remain neutral in a German-American war.

The pivotal position of the chief of Naval Operations deserves some elucidation. Admiral Benson was the chief link between the government and the navy and, as such, strategically placed to influence both the Navy Department and, through the secretary of the navy, the President. Benson attempted to steer an independent course, convinced that in the long run Great Britain posed no less a threat than Germany to the development of American naval and commercial expansion. On 2 February 1917, the day after Germany resumed unrestricted submarine warfare, Secretary Daniels reported to Wilson on a sounding of Benson's views: "He had the same abhorrence of becoming enlisted with either side of combatants that you expressed. His view is that if we lose our equipoise, the world will be in darkness. He expressed the hope that you would find a way to avert the calamity."[17] Certainly Benson could hardly have chosen words better designed to appeal to the President's idealism.

The same month Admiral Benson prepared his own memorandum on the naval situation. Of paramount importance was the need "to secure guarantees for the future," and not to become captivated by temporary tactical necessities. Regardless of the outcome, the European war threatened to confront the United States with future dangers:

> The possible combinations, of powers and circumstances, are too numerous and too pregnant with possibilities adverse to our interests to permit us to consider any plan other than one which will permit us to exercise eventually the full naval and military strength of the United States in the defense of our interests.

Benson was especially concerned that the United States might "eventually have to act alone"—to face a victorious Germany without allies or friends, as the Black War Plan had postulated. While he agreed that antisubmarine craft "may have a deciding influence on the present war" and should therefore "be built quickly," he nevertheless counseled "that vessels should be built not only to meet present conditions but conditions that may come after the present phase of the world war." Benson thus cemented his firm belief that the United States should continue to build a "balanced fleet" designed, if necessary, to "dispute the freedom of the seas with potential enemies." The future was uncertain and full of pitfalls. "We may expect the future to give us more potential enemies than potential friends so that our safety must lie in our own resources."[18] Great Britain was thus alluded to as a potential opponent no less dangerous than Germany.

Admiral Benson illustrated this point of view again in March 1917, when Rear Admiral William S. Sims, commandant of the Naval War College, was secretly sent to London to prepare for possible future Anglo-American naval collaboration. According to Sims's testimony in 1920 before a committee of the Congress investigating the conduct of the war, Benson allegedly enjoined him not to "let the British pull the wool over your eyes. It is none of our business pulling their chestnuts out of the fire. We would as soon fight the British as the Germans." Benson defended himself rather lamely: "Well, I might put it this way. I thought that there were certain things going on that we ought to be prepared for in an emergency. . . . I never had any idea that we would have to fight any other country; no."[19]

Whatever the case, the mounting menace posed by German U-boats in the Atlantic forced the United States Navy early in 1917 once more to redefine its strategy. The 1915 supplement to the Black War Plan had espied no need for either American naval units or large armies to be sent to Europe; it remained firmly wedded to the original go-it-alone strategy of the Black War Plan. In addition, American naval planners once more shied away from any plans detailing a coalition war against

Germany. On 4 February 1917 the General Board finally recognized the immediate danger of submarine warfare, but it agreed to detach American destroyers and other patrol craft for service only in American waters. Once again in line with the Black War Plan, the board decided to assemble the fleet in lower Chesapeake Bay in order to counter a possible German thrust into the Caribbean area.[20] Thus postwar security, represented by capital ship strength, once more precluded all-out attention to antisubmarine warfare.

On 5 April 1917, the day before the United States Congress declared war against Imperial Germany, the General Board prepared a lengthy summary of its strategic position for Secretary Daniels. While it was prepared to enter into negotiations with Allied governments concerning joint naval operations, the board nevertheless reminded Daniels "that should peace be made by the powers now at war we must also be prepared to meet our enemies single-handed. We should not depend upon the defensive but prepare for and conduct a vigorous offensive." And in line with Mahan's teachings that the battle fleet formed the locus of American naval power, the board stressed once more the need to maintain at optimum levels the "strength of the fighting line, large as well as small vessels."[21] It was a complete triumph for Mahan's "balanced fleet" concept. The board also shared Benson's belief that Germany was likely to emerge victorious from the war, and rejected — simply by omission — Sims's conviction that Great Britain would come to the aid of the United States in any future conflict.

The entry of the United States into the war on 6 April 1917 finally forced Benson to adopt a more cooperative and less nationalistic view towards the war at sea. The Black War Plan mentality slowly began to wane in the face of German submarine successes in the Atlantic. Benson now agreed to provide American patrol craft to the British for antisubmarine warfare, but he maintained sufficient destroyers in American waters to protect capital ships against possible German attacks. He did so convinced that the Allies might be defeated in the summer of 1917, and that as a result the United States would be left to fend for itself against the Kaiser's fleet. And Germany possessed a favorable strength advantage:* nineteen dreadnought battleships and five battle cruisers built and building against fourteen American dreadnought battleships built and building.[22] Benson later explained:

* Admiral Benson's figures were not entirely accurate. Germany in 1917 possessed twenty dreadnoughts and five battle cruisers in the North Sea, while the United States had seventeen dreadnoughts, twenty-five elderly battleships, no battle cruisers, twenty-five cruisers, and seventy-four destroyers. The Reich also had available twenty pre-dreadnought armored ships, mostly in the Baltic Sea.

. . . my first thought . . . was to see first that our coasts and our own vessels and our own interests were safeguarded. . . . We might have sent more destroyers — a few more; but I doubt if I would have sent more destroyers, because I felt very strongly the necessity of safeguarding the battleships . . . I felt that I had to look after them.

Rear Admiral Charles J. Badger, a member of the General Board, concurred. He likewise stressed that prospects for the Allies appeared extremely bleak in April and May 1917, and that there was "no telling" how the United States "might become involved with Germany." Thus he seconded Benson's position that "we should look out for ourselves and our own fleet until we could see about it."[23] Moreover, the Navy Department also worried about the possibility that Germany might develop bases to support submarines in the western Pacific by occupying unfrequented bays and harbors in the Western Hemisphere.

The apparent ambivalence in American naval planning between national long-term capital ship policies and immediate coalition needs to combat the German submarine danger exasperated Allied naval officers. Admiral R. A. Grasset, the French commander in the Caribbean, did not hide his sentiments. He was appalled by the American lack of preparedness:

I have been constantly surprised that the American Navy, of which we have a high opinion in France, has prepared neither a plan of war nor acquired a clear conception of modifications caused in all naval branches by the actual war.

The United States Navy also seemed to lack the requisite dynamic leadership:

I have been not less astonished by the lack of scope that American officers with whom I have been in contact have seemed to present to me. Admiral Benson is very little informed on the questions treated by the general staff; his spirit is slow and he does not seem possessed of the moral authority that comports with his rank and functions; he is . . . a bureaucrat who arrived at the grade of admiral by political changes happening in the ministry.[24]

It was partly to answer such criticism that Admiral Sims in the summer of 1917 turned his attention to several measures designed to increase and improve the American antisubmarine effort. On 14 April 1917 he cabled from his headquarters in London that the United States was grossly misinformed concerning the danger of the German underwater offensive, the general military plight of the Allies, and the war potential of the Russians. As to the U-boat menace, Sims discounted the possibility that the Germans would send boats to the east coast of the United States and argued instead that an all-out effort should be mounted against the submarines in the Atlantic. The Allies had lost approximately 500,000 tons of merchant shipping in February and March; during the first ten days of April an additional 200,000 tons of shipping had been torpedoed. Here was the issue upon which the outcome of the war seemed to turn. "The issue is and must inevitably be decided at the locus of all lines of communications in the Eastern Atlantic." Sims recommended that American destroyers be dispatched immediately to Queenstown.[25]

Two days later Secretary Daniels asked Sims why the British did not simply blockade the German coast in order to inhibit the egress and return of U-boats. Sims agreed with the British Admiralty that a close blockade was "quite unfeasible." The following day Sims explained to Admiral Benson why merchant ships had not been convoyed across the Atlantic: "The area is too large; the necessary vessels are not available."[26] Above all, only American succor could assist the British in the monumental task of convoying thousands of merchant ships traveling at different speeds, originating from numerous ports, heading for diverse harbors, and commanded by officers and owners speaking various languages.

Help shortly arrived from two sources. On 24 April the United States Navy dispatched a flotilla of six destroyers to Queenstown,[27] and over the next month some twenty-four destroyers arrived on station in Europe.[28] Most important of all, by the end of April the British had reached the crucial decision to convoy merchant shipping. Led by David Lloyd George and Rear Admiral Alexander L. Duff, the Royal Navy wisely accepted this tactical innovation; the First Sea Lord, Admiral John Jellicoe, grudgingly lent his support to the measure when faced by the prime minister's resolute stance on the matter.

The convoy system proved markedly more successful in preventing losses of merchantmen than the old system of isolated sailings. It entailed the use of cruisers or armed merchantmen as escorts for merchant shipping on the high seas away from the principal danger zones. In those waters close to European ports where submarines lurked in wait, fast and maneuverable destroyers assumed the responsibilities of escort. The system immediately achieved notable success.[29]

The decision to convoy was greeted with approval in Washington. Some American leaders had long shared Lloyd George's belief that the British Admiralty had not exercised sufficient imagination in coping with the submarines. As early as 25 February 1917 President Wilson had expressed the view that the British "ought to convoy,"[30] and in May suggested to Secretary Daniels that convoys add to their deceptiveness by "changing courses and ports."[31] Wilson did not want to interfere unduly in naval affairs, but he maintained an interest in them and he nursed growing suspicions of British competence.[32]

However, several policies recommended by Washington aggravated Sims and severely strained not only his relations with the United States Navy Department but also his effectiveness as American liaison officer with the Royal Navy. Sims opposed the Navy Department's decision to arm merchant ships, arguing that such a diversion of men and material would hamper the antisubmarine war. The ships were slow and the guns would not preclude attack without warning. In fact, Sims informed Daniels that in six weeks some thirty armed ships had been torpedoed without ever sighting a U-boat. There remained only one course of attack: "The mission of the Allies must be to force submarines to give battle."[33]

Sims also rejected the notion of close-in mining of all German ports. There were not enough mines available for total effectiveness, he argued, and the Germans could sweep the mines away as long as their fleet controlled these waters. "The presence of our [destroyer] flotillas on this side is of more value than five hundred thousand mines four months from now."[34] For similar reasons Sims also turned down a proposal to mine the North Sea and to create a barrage stretching from Scotland to Norway, even though Washington later forced the latter proposal through against Sims's objections.[35]*

Finally, Sims turned his attention to the possibility that Germany might attempt to deploy large submarine cruisers of close to two thousand tons originally designed as commerce carriers (the *Deutschland* class) on the American coast. Benson had feared such German actions since April 1917. These underwater vessels could mount two guns and carry about thirty torpedoes, but they were slow and devoid of maneuverability. Sims discounted the submarine cruisers, arguing that reserve battleships could be used as escort vessels in the middle passage until relieved by destroyers in the dangerous waters close to Great Britain.[36]

* Earlier opposition, aside from lack of patrol craft, was based primarily on the lack of efficient mines, but the United States had developed an "antenna" model that was both safe and effective and could produce it in sufficient numbers (100,000) for a massive barrage. Sims's objection that the barrage would violate Norwegian waters had been dissipated by the violence of the war. Moreover, the General Board decided that it was "the only big thing the combined navies could do." See E. David Cronon, ed. *The Cabinet Diaries of Josephus Daniels, 1913–1921* (Lincoln, Nebraska, 1963), 221–22, 228, 229. Daniels diary for 16–17 October, 29 October, and 30 October, 1917.

Yet even at this critical juncture in the summer of 1917, when the German submarine offensive reached its apex, the General Board could not easily shed long-cherished strategic concepts. Destroyer construction would seriously curtail capital ship construction and thereby threaten the entire "balanced fleet" concept, which, the board argued, was necessary if the United States hoped to "meet a possible new alignment of powers at the end of the present war or the German fleet if it succeeded in taking the offensive."[37]

In the final analysis, the General Board was caught between the Scylla of the immediate German submarine threat and the Charybdis of executive authority. Admiral Sims had on 3 July 1917 bitterly complained of Admiral Benson's cautionary approach to the war at sea to his friend Captain William V. Pratt:

> It would be very funny, if it were not so tragic, the spectacle of many dozens of ships, destroyers, yachts and so forth parading up and down the American coast three thousand miles away from where the vital battle of the war was going on. How is it that they cannot see that this is as wrong as it possibly can be from a military point of view.[38]

Sims's pleas were soon answered — albeit too late for the ardent Anglophile. On 6 July a special board on antisubmarine devices headed by Captain Pratt recommended that the United States build two hundred destroyers beyond those already authorized (sixty in August 1916).[39] Benson was lukewarm, but President Wilson and Secretary Daniels supported destroyer construction and agreed to build the additional escort craft under the 1916 Naval Appropriation Act. Both the General Board and Admiral Benson bowed and now agreed to concentrate their efforts primarily upon antisubmarine warfare for the duration of the war — at the risk of endangering long-term capital ship construction programs.

The United States was also called upon to counteract the German U-boat menace by increasing her merchant tonnage. The British foreign secretary, Arthur James Balfour, acting upon Prime Minister David Lloyd George's plea to Woodrow Wilson in September 1917 to create "some kind of Allied Joint Council, with permanent military and probably naval and economic staffs attached to work out the plans for the Allies," invited Colonel Edward M. House in October to attend meetings of the War Cabinet as commissioned special United States representative. House, accompanied by Admiral Benson, among others, arrived in London on 7 November. Balfour indicated at once that the western coalition would have to construct some eight million tons of shipping that year, and that the American share would amount to no less than six million tons.[40] The Germans had projected that sinkings of 900,000 tons a month would reduce British shipping by 35 percent on 1 July and 50 percent on 1 October.[41] In fact, the Germans did not approach this figure in the summer of 1917: 558,000 tons were destroyed in July, 512,000 tons in August, and 352,000 tons in September.

Nevertheless, Imperial Germany's undersea offensive against world shipping continued to occupy Allied diplomats and naval leaders. In September 1917 Ambassador Walter Hines Page in London ominously cabled Secretary Daniels:

> Our army in France had bought coal in England, but it can't get ships to carry it. The French and Italians will again suffer for coal this winter — not enough ships. Practically every problem of the war turns on ships. If the Allies had the ships that have gone down, they could pretty quickly end the war. The Germans are able to continue only because of their submarines.[42]

Yet even the attempt to reach a basic agreement to produce jointly the necessary merchant shipping was not devoid of inter-Allied wrangling. Each country suspected the other of developing its wartime shipping with an eye not only to the exigencies of the war but also to international trade competition after the conclusion of hostilities. The British envoy in Washington, the crotchety Sir Cecil Spring Rice, perhaps put it best when he stated that in the United States there was "an undercurrent of feeling that, by the end of the war, America will have all the ships and all the gold in the world, and that the hegemony probably of the world, and certainly of the Anglo-Saxon race, will pass across the Atlantic."[43] An inter-Allied discussion of merchant shipping, attended by both House and Benson in November 1917, brought only general consensus to build more; specific proposals, such as that put forth by Balfour, were torpedoed by mutual distrust and postwar considerations.

Approximately eight months after the American declaration of war against Germany, Admiral Benson provided Great Britain with much needed naval succor. In November 1917 he dispatched four coal-burning dreadnoughts to Europe.[44] Moreover, he now outlined an American blueprint for victory over the German submarine menace in the coming year: a division of battleships would be attached to the British Grand Fleet; the entire American battle fleet could be sent to European waters in the spring of 1918 if conditions warranted this step; the distant barrage in the North Sea was to be laid; the Straits of Dover were to be mined; a Planning Section in London would be created; naval relations with the various Allied governments were to be improved; and finally, an Allied Naval Council would be founded in order to coordinate naval policy. In practical terms Benson agreed to provide the British with more patrol craft, to spur development of naval aviation, and to improve port facilities in Europe, especially along the French coast.[45]

The United States was now obviously prepared to increase her assistance to the western coalition. But the new year hardly seemed inviting, given the strong likelihood that in the wake of the disasters to Russia and Italy which had taken place late in 1917 (see pages 130, 146), Germany would launch offensives on the western front designed to bring the war to a close. Furthermore, there also existed the possibility that the Reich might escalate the war at sea either by intensified submarine activity or by sorties into the North Sea by the High Sea Fleet.

In January 1918 Sims's newly created Planning Section in London prepared a broad-ranging estimate of the naval war. It began with a prediction of German intentions. The enemy would mount the "maximum possible sustained attack on the sea communications of the Allies." Unrestricted submarine warfare would continue, with its field of activity enlarged to counteract improved antisubmarine measures. Large submarine cruisers would be deployed in foreign waters to force dispersion of antisubmarine forces. The Allied barrage operations in the North Sea and the Straits of Dover could expect enemy raids. And the German High Sea Fleet would continue to avoid a confrontation with the British Royal Navy — reinforced by segments of the American battle fleet — and remain a "fleet in being" in the truest sense of the term. The Planning Section was aware that German submarine cruisers of the *Deutschland* class might undertake diversionary raids in American waters if the convoy system foreclosed available targets in European waters. For the Allies, only the offensive promised success. "The ultimate solution to the submarine menace is tactical and not strategic."[46]

When it became apparent early in 1918 that the corner had been turned in the war against the German submarines, the Planning Section reverted once again to earlier Mahan thinking. Now that the Germans had apparently failed in their attempt to force Great Britain to the peace table, temporary construction policies were matched against future needs. In May 1918 Sims's planners in London charted a course for future American maritime building. The document, signed by three naval captains as well as a marine colonel, returned in spirit to the 1913 Black War Plan. Economic competition was singled out yet again as the primary mover in international politics. "War is the ultimate form of economic competition . . . and the intensified economic struggle of the past fifty years has led to the present war." The "necessity for markets" and population pressure were the major reasons for "those fundamental policies assuming an aggressive aspect." Even diplomacy was judged, in reversed Clausewitzean reasoning, to be "itself a kind of war," and its weapons likewise were not "words and logic," but the "naval, economic, and military forces that are in readiness to support the attitude of the diplomatist." Such *Realpolitik* views suggested that the United States would face the likelihood of "sudden war" for decades to come.

The Planning Section singled out three "aggressive Powers" that merited special attention: Great Britain, Germany and Japan. The latter two were bent on "forcible expansion" because "their racial characteristics are virile and militaristic, and their form of government autocratic." With regard to Germany, the United States had already been forced to go to war in order to protect her "commercial rights upon the sea." A German victory in Europe could only result in future violation of the Monroe Doctrine through a German attempt to tap "the undeveloped riches of Mexico, Central America and South America." Postwar trade rivalry would furthermore result in German efforts to impose "unacceptable conditions upon our sea trade." On the other hand, Sims's subordinates foresaw danger also in a British victory in Europe:

> No matter how mild or pacific our attitude, the mere fact that we seek to keep our tonnage profitably employed will bring us into commercial competition with other nations. Competition in itself is a kind of war, by which we seek to win what otherwise might belong to our rivals. In the future, as in the past, we must expect commercial competition to be the most frequent cause of war. We therefore must, more than ever before, expect to excite the jealousy of other sea-going powers.[47]

The most striking feature of this study, as Warner R. Schilling has pointed out, was the belief that the present war would not "improve American security vis-à-vis Germany." Despite its being written when the United States had been at war with Germany for slightly over a year, the memorandum closely paralleled the Black War Plan analysis of 1913. Like the General Board, Sims's officers foresaw no allies in the event of war with Germany in the future. In fact, unlike the 1913 plan, it was now assumed that Germany would possess allies — at least Austria-Hungary. Thus American planners finally gave recognition to the increasing importance since 1913 of international relations, even if only those detrimental to the special interests of the United States. Sims's Planning Section in London, in a subsequent memorandum to Admiral Benson in June 1918, warned that the United States might one day be confronted by "an alliance of those powers whose form of Government are similar," that is, Germany, Japan, Austria, Turkey, and Russia. Sims's staff had closed its May 1918 synopsis accordingly with a request that the United States lay down twenty-one new dreadnoughts and ten battle cruisers.[48]

In the face of such dire predictions from London, the General Board in Washington in June 1918 turned its attention to naval construction and in September drafted its own postwar naval construction program. It recommended the addition of twenty-eight capital ships (twelve battleships and sixteen battle cruisers) to the 1915–1916 building program (which had authorized a fleet of twenty-nine battleships and six battle cruisers). The General Board herewith sought to provide the United States with a battle fleet of over sixty capital ships, including thirty-nine battleships. It is obvious that American naval planners in September 1918 no longer had in mind one isolated opponent, but future naval combinations. Professor Schilling suggests that the board's standard was the combined Anglo-Japanese fleet (sixty-two capital ships built and building), although "preoccupation of wartime naval planners with postwar German-American relations would suggest that a German-based combination was the standard."[49] In fact, Germany and Austria-Hungary in 1918 possessed approximately sixty capital ships between them, and Admiral von Tirpitz's master plan (of 1898–1912) to create by 1920 a German fleet consisting of sixty capital ships, to be replaced automatically every twenty years, alone comes dangerously close to the General Board's recommendations.

It is interesting to note that during the summer of 1918, Germany finally decided to extend submarine warfare to the eastern seaboard of the United States — as Admiral Benson had feared all along. However, the Reich did not possess sufficient ocean-going craft (U-cruisers and U-merchant cruisers) to mount a major offensive, and Sims's earlier predictions that such a move would be only a minor distraction was proved to have been correct. Only six raids were undertaken by U-boats in 1918, commencing with the arrival of *U-151*, which between May and July managed to destroy twenty-three coastwise and fishing vessels of 59,000 tons off the coast between New York and Cape Hatteras. *U-156* in July caught a tug and four barges off Cape Cod before she was destroyed in the Great Northern Barrage in the waters between Scotland and Norway — which the United States Navy was closing with about 100,000 of its new "antenna" mines. Subsequent patrols by *U-140*, *U-117* and *U-155* in August and September brought little result: the German raiders were frequently driven away from their prey by gunfire from the armed merchant ships or their escort vessels. The most spectacular success of the U-boats in American waters came on 19 July 1918, when mines laid by German submarines off Fire Island destroyed the armored cruiser *San Diego*.[50]

As the plight of the Central Powers became apparent in September

1918, Admiral Sims in London took note of British concern over the possibility of a final desperate sortie by the German High Sea Fleet. He himself doubted that Germany would risk an all-out engagement with the Grand Fleet — buttressed by Rear Admiral Hugh Rodman's six superdreadnoughts — in order to reverse the trend of events on land. Others shared his view: "I have found nobody in the Admiralty or outside of it that believes in the probability of the High Sea Fleet giving battle."[51] No one in London apparently quite understood the desperate spirit of Germany's naval leadership, which, as we have seen, prompted Admirals Scheer and Hipper, among others, in October 1918 to plan a final sortie against the Allied naval forces stationed at Scapa Flow, Cromarty and Rosyth. The refusal of German sailors to participate in what they considered to be a final, glorious "death ride," designed to salvage the honor of the Imperial German naval officer corps at the eleventh hour, ultimately led to revolution in Germany and the scuttling of the High Sea Fleet in Scapa Flow in June 1919.

Germany's military demise in October 1918 released the United States Navy from further strategic deliberations for the war in Europe. The American naval effort had been significant: the United States Navy had transported about 45 percent (900,000 men) of the American troops sent to Europe; it had provided 27 percent of the convoy escorts and 12 percent of the battleship strength of the British Grand Fleet; laid 80 percent of the North Sea mine barrage; and maintained twenty-three naval stations in Europe. Moreover, it had committed 368 ships, including 128 submarine chasers, to the war in Europe, with some 70,000 men and 5,000 officers.[52] And while the United States Navy did not provide the backbone of the Allied naval effort, there can be little doubt that its naval units, both in Europe and in reserve in American waters, provided the requisite lever for cracking the U-boat menace and, ultimately, the overall German war effort.

As to final disposition of the German fleet and German colonies, naval leaders in Washington were agreed that the Kiel Canal should be internationalized and that Germany should have none of her former colonial possessions. However, since the admirals had been critical of Napoleon Bonaparte's attempts to limit by law the size of the Prussian army in 1806, they declined to rule on the future of the High Sea Fleet, which was to be temporarily interned in Scapa Flow.[53] The Planning Section in London suggested another, more realistic reason for this curiously moderate stance:

> Viewing the situation from a strictly American point of view, if the German fleet were destroyed, Great Britain would be at liberty to do with our new merchant marine as she thought fit, since her naval power would so far out-

balance our own as to make it practically impossible for us to oppose her, no matter how arbitrary her methods might be. It is not for a moment suggested that the German Fleet should ever be an ally of the American Fleet against Great Britain, but it is suggested that the presence in Europe of the German Fleet is a balance wheel governing any undue or arbitrary ambition on the part of those who may temporarily be in power in Great Britain.[54]

Such Bensonian and Black War Plan thinking must have irritated Admiral Sims, and it is hardly surprising that he neither approved the study nor sent it on to the Navy Department in Washington.

In the end, American "war aims" turned out to be extremely moderate and rational. Rejecting the British premise that "even the most unpromising detached ocean rock will, if kept long enough, develop some useful purpose," American naval leaders were content to let others (Japan, Australia and New Zealand) acquire German islands in the Pacific, provided that they remained unfortified. The General Board's proposal to take advantage of Great Britain's war indebtedness to purchase Bermuda, Jamaica and the Bahamas was dismissed by political leaders. It remained for another global confrontation to allow American admirals to gain at least naval bases on these islands. Nor did they realize their desire to occupy or to control other strategic bases from Mole St. Nicholas and Samaná Bay to the Danish West Indies and the Corn Islands off Nicaragua.[55]

With Germany safely out of the way, there remained the nagging problem of Anglo-American trade rivalry. Captain Pratt, an ardent advocate of Anglo-American naval cooperation during the recent war, already in August 1918 informed his friend Admiral Sims that while it was desirable for the two Anglo-Saxon maritime powers to "police" the world, trade competition might threaten the "very close relations" between the two. Pratt was especially concerned about the "element" in the United States Navy that though willing to fight Germany, "nevertheless has no love for England." Was he thinking of his chief, Admiral Benson? "The Hun," Pratt feared, might attempt to exploit mounting trade rivalry between the United States and Great Britain once the war was over. To counteract this, Pratt suggested that the two nations lay "the cards on the table" and divide the world's markets on a "fifty-fifty basis."[56] Nothing could better have substantiated Admiral von Tirpitz's longstanding claim that the two Anglo-Saxon maritime powers had, indeed, pursued such a course since at least the mid-1890s.

However, this contention of an Anglo-American "conspiracy" against Germany can be defused by taking one final glance at the strategic deliberations that guided the London Planning Section in November

1918. Sims's staff gave expression to doubts and fears that had troubled American naval planners for the past three decades:

> Four great Powers have arisen in the world to compete with Great Britain for commercial supremacy on the seas — Spain, Holland, France, Germany. Each of these Powers in succession have been defeated by Great Britain and her fugitive Allies. A fifth commercial Power, the greatest one yet, is now arising to compete for at least commercial equality with Great Britain. Already the signs of jealousy are visible. Historical precedent warns us to watch closely the moves we make or permit to be made.[57]

Thus the circle was once again squared: American admirals had returned to the go-it-alone strategy of the Black War Plan. But this time, in November 1918, the United States Navy possessed a mighty fleet of forty battleships, thirty-two cruisers, sixty-eight submarines, and 125 destroyers. Finally, the failure of Germany's naval leaders to recognize and, if possible, to exploit such American fears or jealousies concerning Great Britain's commercial and sea power was not the least of their contributions to the debacle of October 1918.

# III

---

# The Third Reich and the United States (1933–1941)

SEVEN

# Background: Hitler, Raeder, and the United States

It is irresponsible to believe that this struggle between Europe and America will only be economic in nature.

— ADOLF HITLER
*1928*

IN THE WAKE OF THE ARMISTICE ON 11 NOVEMBER 1918, GERMANY AND THE United States both retreated from international power politics. The United States Congress failed to ratify the Treaty of Versailles and, in effect, left France and Great Britain to oversee the application of the various Paris treaties to the vanquished powers (Germany, Austria, Hungary, Bulgaria, and Turkey). America's primary concern in Europe was the issue of reparations (the Dawes Plan of 1924 and the Young Plan of 1930); initial estimates of German payments to the Allied and Associated Powers ranged upwards of 33 billion dollars. Germany, for her part, ceased to be an active factor in European grand strategy. By provision of the Versailles Treaty, her army was reduced to one hundred thousand and her navy to fifteen thousand men, and she was not allowed to maintain an air force. In material terms, the Reich was forbidden to build tanks, aircraft for military purposes, heavy guns, submarines, or surface ships displacing more than 10,000 tons. An Allied Control Commission toured the land to ensure enforcement of these conditions. In addition, Germany was not allowed to enter the League of Nations until 1926, and all her erstwhile colonies (14 million people based on 1.2 million square miles) were divided among France, Great Britain, Japan, Australia, and New Zealand according to a complicated mandate system supervised by the League of Nations from Geneva. Germany also suffered territorial losses in Europe: Eupen-Malmédy to Belgium; Alsace-Lorraine as well as the coal-rich Saar basin for fifteen years to France; North Schleswig to neutral Denmark; and West Prussia, Posen, Memel, and parts of Upper

Silesia to Poland and Lithuania. In all, the lost territories deprived her of 65 percent of her iron ore deposits and 45 percent of her coal. It became an article of faith with virtually all German political parties under the Weimar Republic — with the exception of the Communists (KPD) and the Social Democrats (SPD) — to work for the retrieval of these 25,000 square miles and 6 million people. Finally, the Reich's major waterways were internationalized, with the result that the navy was deprived of control over the Kiel Canal, the vital link between the North Sea and the Baltic Sea requisite for any future two-front conflict.[1]

On the international front, Germany remained, along with the Soviet Union, the outcast of Europe. Not surprisingly, these two nations drew together for lack of viable alternatives in 1922 at Rapallo and in 1926 at Berlin. The resulting treaties, ostensibly trade agreements, nevertheless in secret accords established the so-called "Black Reichswehr," an arrangement whereby German officers trained their Russian counterparts in the Red Army while the Reich was allowed to test in Russia those weapons prohibited under the Versailles Treaty. The navy, for its part, sent a few elderly capital ships and cruisers on good-will and training missions — especially to South America — and continued to bide its time in the hope that the future might allow once again the development of a mighty battle fleet as in the days of Tirpitz.

It was, in short, a time of wait and see. The Weimar Republic, which continued to fly the Bismarckian black-white-red tricolor alongside the democratic black-red-gold, was a house divided among itself, and one that was heavily burdened with the peace settlement of 28 June 1919. While the coalition Social Democratic, Democratic and Catholic Center parties attempted to make a go of Germany's first experiment in democracy under presidents Friedrich Ebert (to 1925) and Paul von Hindenburg, there were too many factions that desired to see its downfall: the Communists, who wanted to establish a soviet-style workers' and soldiers' state; the separatists in the Rhineland and Bavaria; the monarchists who longed to recall Kaiser Wilhelm II to the throne from his self-imposed exile at Doorn in the Netherlands; other monarchists who wanted possibly a Bavarian Wittelsbach dynasty; and the growing number of groups on the lunatic right that were either individually or all at once Pan-German, anti-Semitic, *Völkisch,* monarchist, militant, fascist, and so on. Much to their delight, the Weimar Republic continued to call itself a *Reich,* or empire, with a *Reichs*wehr for an army and a *Reichs*marine for a navy. Under these chaotic conditions, there could be no talk of a German foreign policy with regard to the United States.

This situation changed abruptly on 30 January 1933 with the appointment of Adolf Hitler as chancellor of the German Reich. Hitler immediately set out to revise the Versailles settlement. He canceled all reparations payments and took Germany out of the League of Nations (1933); the Saar basin, after a plebiscite as stipulated in the 1919 treaty, was restored to Germany (1935); universal male conscription was renewed (1935); the Rhineland was occupied and remilitarized (1936); Austria was occupied and incorporated into the Greater German Reich (1938); Czechoslovakia was dismembered (1938–1939); and Memel was annexed (1939). In addition, Hitler in March 1935 also announced to the world the establishment of a German air force — which already then possessed 1,888 aircraft and 20,000 officers and men — as well as a modern navy.* The Luftwaffe, under Air Marshal Hermann Göring, became involved in European affairs within a month of its official founding date when, in August 1936, it dispatched twenty-six transport planes to shuttle about ten thousand troops of General Francisco Franco from Spanish Morocco to the Spanish mainland to launch an attack on the Spanish government. For much of the three ensuing years of internecine struggle, Germany maintained in Spain some two hundred aircraft of the Kondor Legion, including fifty modern "Junkers 52" bombers under General Hugo Sperrle.[2] Hitler had permitted the German intervention in Spain partly with an eye towards bases for future expansion (Central Africa, Atlantic Islands, United States), but primarily in order to test reaction — especially British — to German military involvement in European affairs. He received his answer, of course, in the form of the Anglo-French declaration of nonintervention in the Spanish Civil War.

The growth of the German navy, on the other hand, was hardly so spectacular. The Reichsmarine of the Weimar Republic, headed since 1928 by Admiral Erich Raeder, was on 1 June 1935 transformed into the Kriegsmarine (War Navy) of Adolf Hitler. Raeder's position as chief of the Naval Command was changed to commander-in-chief of the navy, and the Naval Command became the Supreme Command of the War Navy (OKM). The navy in September 1939 was headed by Grand Admiral Raeder, who in his dual capacity as chief of the Naval War Staff (Seekriegsleitung) possessed a group of naval planners headed by Rear Admiral Otto Schniewind (chief of staff of the Naval War Staff) and Captain Kurt Fricke (chief of the Operations Division of the Naval War Staff), who as vice admiral was to succeed Schniewind in the summer of 1941. Rear Admiral Karl Dönitz was initially "leader" of U-boats, but on 17 October 1939 was promoted to "commander" of U-boats with status equal to that of the fleet chief. The latter post belonged in the fall

* The Luftwaffe in September 1939 entered the war with 1,170 level and 335 dive bombers as well as 1,320 fighters.

of 1939 to Admiral Hermann Boehm, who was responsible for his actions to the chief of the Naval War Staff (Raeder) and who had under him the various front commanders, including those of Scouting Forces and Armored Ships. Raeder's planners had also drafted for use in 1944–1945 plans to create two special heads of Naval Group West and Naval Group East, each to command a battle fleet; the navy in September 1941 further splintered its command structure by establishing these posts for Admirals Alfred Saalwächter (West) and Conrad Albrecht (East).[3] Naval construction programs came under the auspices of the Seekriegsleitung and will be taken up in the latter part of this chapter.

Adolf Hitler also entered into formal relations with Italy and Japan at the time of the Spanish Civil War. Joachim von Ribbentrop, the Führer's special adviser on foreign policy, in November 1936 concocted the so-called Anti-Comintern Pact between Germany and Japan; Benito Mussolini's Italy joined it in November 1937 after the Duce had already the year before spoken of an "Axis Rome-Berlin." The pact, often referred to as an alliance "without backbone," was primarily a propaganda device, and established only "benevolent neutrality" in the event that one or more of the signatories was drawn into war. The timing of the pact was excellent, as it coincided roughly with Joseph Stalin's decision to intervene in the Spanish Civil War on the Loyalist side as well as with the first of the famous "show trials" during Stalin's barbarous purge of Soviet civilian and army leaders. But whereas Ribbentrop saw the anti-Comintern agreement as the cornerstone of his policy of keeping Russia intact and perhaps using her in Persia and India as a common opponent of Great Britain — the "real" enemy — the Führer regarded it as only a temporary expedient to display to the world the newfound solidarity among the major authoritarian powers. This prestige effect was increased in March 1939 when Franco joined the German-Japanese-Italian combination against the Communist International.

Of far greater import for subsequent European history was the stunning news on 23 August 1939 that Germany and Russia had concluded the so-called Nazi-Soviet Nonaggression Pact, which shocked both Mussolini and Franco. Stalin and Ribbentrop (who was hailed upon his return from Moscow as a "second Bismarck") in a secret protocol agreed "in the event of a territorial and political transformation," to divide eastern Europe along a line running from the northern border of Lithuania, south along the Narew-Vistula-San Rivers. Both dictators cynically decided to leave open the question of whether "the maintenance of an independent Polish State appears desirable."[4] Hitler, who had received in September 1938 at Munich from Great Britain only a free hand to dismember Czechoslovakia, and not — as he desired — all of Europe in return for "guaranteeing" the security of the British Empire, was now triumphant. A "fourth partition" of Poland was imminent—without incurring the risk of a two-front war in 1939.

The United States, not a signatory to the June 1919 settlement, was not directly involved in these measures. And when she took an active interest in European affairs, especially after Hitler tore up the Munich agreement by establishing so-called protectorates over Bohemia and Moravia early in 1939, she was sharply rebuked by Hitler.[5] For the United States played a role, albeit distant, in Hitler's thoughts and deliberations. She was not an immediate political or military threat to Germany, nor did she constitute a potential outlet (*Lebensraum*) for German expansion. But she could not be ignored. She stood, at least in theory, behind Great Britain and France and was in control of the vital Atlantic maritime arteries that led from Europe to Africa and to South America. If Hitler yearned for more than hegemony in Europe, if he was indeed more than just another "traditional European statesman," he would have to come to grips sometime with the future relationship of Germany and the United States.

How did Adolf Hitler view the United States as a factor in German strategy—especially in the light of our analyses of the periods 1889–1906 and 1917–1918? To what degree was he a prisoner of his past? What elements in his "program" were new? What were his aspirations with regard to overseas colonies? What role would sea power play in his ambitions? What were the hopes and aspirations of Germany's naval leaders? Did they cling to strategic concepts developed by Admiral von Tirpitz according to Mahan's doctrine that the battle fleet formed the locus of sea power? Or did they draw the lesson from the First World War that only *jeune école* warfare—especially in the form of an unrestricted undersea offensive against commerce moving to Britain on the high seas—could overcome Germany's disadvantageous geographical situation in the southeastern corner of the North Sea, and Britain's overwhelming superiority in surface vessels? And on what strategic points was there agreement between the Führer and his admirals? It is my hope that the answers to some of these questions will provide background for the later discussion of the role that the United States assumed in the global considerations of Adolf Hitler and Admirals Erich Raeder, Otto Schniewind, Kurt Fricke, Rolf Carls, Otto Groos, and Gerhard Wagner.

## Hitler's View of the United States

Hitler's views on the United States prior to 1939 were a mixture of ignorance and bias. Of all the major powers ultimately involved in the Second World War, he probably knew least about the United States.

Hitler's *Mein Kampf* (1925) contained only scant references to the United States, but his *Second Book* (1928) gave written form to his misconceptions and biases regarding that country. He lamented that Europe was allowing its best "blood" to emigrate to the United States, with the probable result that Europe would eventually be reduced to a continent of "degenerate, animalistic" pleasure seekers. The rapidly expanding economy of the United States threatened Europe with American "world hegemony," and the fertile soil of the American plains would make that country, rather than the Soviet Union, a future world power. But Hitler rejected the Wilhelmian notion of a pan-European tariff league directed against the United States. The "fundamental, basic error" of this scheme was that it attempted "to replace human quality with human quantity." A general European economic union would lead only to "racial chaos and confusion," and ultimately to a "bastardization and niggerization of cultured humanity." The solution lay elsewhere. Only a state which preserved its racial purity could hope successfully to challenge the United States. "It is the mission of the National Socialist movement to prepare and to strengthen our fatherland to the utmost degree for this task." Hitler also pointed out in his *Second Book* that Great Britain would soon find its primary adversary no longer in Europe but in the United States. A showdown between Europe and the United States could not be avoided. "It is irresponsible to believe that this struggle between Europe and America will only be economic in nature."[6]

As chancellor, and in keeping with his general refusal to abandon in adult life preconceptions and fallacies from earlier times, Hitler made no serious effort to acquaint himself with conditions prevailing in the United States. Preferring to judge situations in terms of social and racial rather than economic and military factors, he developed his stereotyped picture of the United States. As a capitalist democracy with a free press and the majority rule principle, it was *ipso facto* on a lower level than the centrally organized Reich. Hitler confided to a close friend that he regarded the United States as merely one isolated part of the greater *Judenproblem* (Jewish problem); both Wall Street and the federal government in Washington were, he contended, in the clutches of the Jews.[7]

Hitler's initial evaluation of President Franklin D. Roosevelt was somewhat more flexible. He frequently lauded Roosevelt's New Deal politics. But he also set guidelines for the press concerning the President's foreign policy: "Second Wilson. . . . First agitator, then apostle of peace. Wants to give the world his blessings after he has generated an unprecedented war psychosis."[8] The war, of course, rapidly altered this earlier stance. Hitler climaxed his speech in the Reichstag on 11 December 1941, declaring war on the United States, with the following comparison:

Roosevelt was rich and I was poor. Roosevelt transacted business deals, I shed my blood. Roosevelt speculated and raked in millions, I lay in a military hospital. Roosevelt supported himself with the power of a capitalist party, I led a popular movement.[9]

And as the tide of Hitler's fortunes ebbed drastically in 1942, his personal tirades against Roosevelt increased both in frequency and in tone — the American leader's paralysis was now attributed not to polio but to syphilis.[10] Ernst Hanfstaengl was perhaps closest to the truth when he stated that the United States was simply beyond Hitler's scope and comprehension. During the last days in the bunker Hitler admitted as much: "The war with America was a tragedy, senseless and devoid of any basic reality."[11] Yet it was only the timing, not the principle, of the war against the United States that bothered Hitler.

Hitler left little written material concerning his views on the United States and never visited that country, but he did have sources of information. Before his term in office as chancellor he derived his knowledge about the United States primarily from three contemporaries: his fellow party functionary Kurt Lüdecke, his Munich acquaintance Ernst "Putzi" Hanfstaengl, and the journalist Colin Ross.

Hanfstaengl has left a detailed account of his conversations with Hitler on this topic in the 1920s. Hitler, it appears, developed an interest only in Henry Ford, mainly because of the latter's anti-Semitic stance, his mass production of automobiles (which Hitler planned to copy with the Volkswagen), and his possible role as a political backer. Hitler compared the Ku Klux Klan to his own National Socialist German Worker's Party (NSDAP) and wished through it to spread his ideas at least into the southern United States. He met few Americans during these years, according to Hanfstaengl, and even the rare occasions on which he did proved to be of little value. In 1923, for example, Hitler contacted Wilhelmina Scharrer, a daughter of the Busch brewing family in St. Louis, in an unsuccessful attempt to raise financial support.[12] There were, however, a few aspects of Americana that found favor with Hitler: the separation of church and state, the immigration restrictions of 1924 (which he regarded as an attempt to protect the "Nordic race" in the United States), and the sheer vastness of the land.[13] Hitler had derived his image of American *Lebensraum* as a boy from the western novels of Karl May, a writer who had never set foot in the United States. But the negative side of the ledger, also vividly sketched in by Hanfstaengl, far outweighed the positive. Hitler basically viewed the United States as a land in which "gangsters, corrupt politicians and Jews" controlled the government and where "kidnapping, stock fiascos, and millions of unemployed" were only outward symptoms of a society in decline and decay. "America. That is nothing but millionaires, beauty queens, gangsters, and ridiculous records."[14] But he was positively stirred by the applause, the marching bands, and the general hoopla associated with Harvard football games. When Hanfstaengl, a former Harvard student, first described this American autumnal ritual with its rhythmic chants of "Harvard, Harvard, Harvard — rah, rah, rah!," the Führer reportedly jumped to his feet and began to march up and down simulating a drum major. "Magnificent, Hanfstaengl, that is precisely what we need for our movement!" Thus, according to Hanfstaengl, "Harvard, Harvard, Harvard — rah, rah, rah!" became "Sieg Heil, Sieg Heil, Sieg Heil."[15] Finally, the man who later styled himself "the world's greatest military commander" flippantly dismissed the United States Navy as a negligible quantity: "One simply blows up the Panama Canal and the American fleet will not be able to play a decisive role on either side" of the isthmian canal.[16]

Hermann Rauschning also broached the subject of the United States several times during his talks with Hitler in 1932–1934.* He claimed that Hitler in 1933 assured him that the United States would never again become involved in a general European war, and that it was "on the brink of revolution" from which only he, the Führer, could save it. Hitler reiterated all his standard racist clichés: the United States was in the hands of "Jewish adventurers and financial magnates"; its policy in 1933 revealed "the last death pangs of an antiquated, corrupt system." Moreover, a "financial clique" ruled the land "under the fiction of democracy," and only the "healthy" middle classes and the farmers resisted the corruptive influence of the Jews and the Negroes. The United States, according to Hitler, had begun its long decline following the tragic triumph of the North in the Civil War. With that turn of events, the United States ceased to be a nation and became instead a "conglomeration of disparate elements." Hitler assured Rauschning that the American "is no soldier." And Joseph Goebbels hastily added that the United States "will never become dangerous for us."[17] In fact, the famous doctor repeated this conviction in 1939 when asked what goals Germany would pursue after she had defeated France and Great Britain. "You must know whose turn it will then be — the United States."[18]†

Especially in the critical period between 1938 and 1941, little sober counsel came to Hitler from Germany's diplomatic and military repre-

* A number of historians today persist in discounting Rauschning's book *Gespräche mit Hitler* (New York 1940) as a historical source, but its accuracy and historical value are analyzed and substantiated by Theodor Schieder in *Hermann Rauschnings 'Gespräche mit Hitler' als Geschichtsquelle* (Opladen 1972), 60ff.

† Goebbels shared Hitler's belief that the collapse of the United States would come through "internal" decay.

sentatives abroad. The German ambassador in Washington, Hans Dieckhoff, warned in vain that any conflict with Great Britain would eventually bring the United States into the war on the British side.[19] Dieckhoff's reports displeased the Führer and he was soon removed from a position of influence. Instead, Hitler read "with great interest" a tract by Baron B. G. von Rechenberg entitled *Roosevelt America — A Danger!* wherein the aristocrat derisively denounced Roosevelt's "Jewish advisers." Rechenberg did not for a moment doubt that "a freemason of the 32nd order" (Roosevelt) would support the "Jewish plans for world dominion." The American President, according to the baron, thought inevitable "the coming of a world state under the leadership of the chosen people and the transformation of the human race into one hodge-podge of humanity." Freemasons, communists, and especially Jews controlled the United States. Hitler kept a copy of Rechenberg's work with him and ordered the Foreign Office and the Propaganda Ministry to familiarize themselves with it and make use of it in their work.[20]

Rechenberg's political star rose meteorically. He was soon advanced to the rank of major and "SS Obersturmbannführer," asked to head the National Socialist War Veterans' Union, and to take over the foreign section of the Nazi press agency. Hitler was so impressed by Rechenberg's revelations — undoubtedly because they confirmed his own misconceptions — that they were soon classified as confidential documents and handled secretly. The Führer forbade any mention of his interest in them. And in 1941 Rechenberg again cautioned his Führer in a new brochure about the American danger. "US-America is today the largest Jewish nation in the world, and New York the largest Jewish city in the world." The baron estimated that almost ten million Jews had in the past "fled like rats" to the United States, where they refused to do manual work, leaving this to the "Nordic races," the Negroes, mulattoes, and desperadoes. Instead, some twenty thousand sons of Israel had infiltrated the Roosevelt administration and the federal reserve system. Even the cabinet was not immune: Morgenthau (finance) was a Jew, Perkins (labor) was a Jew, Ickes (interior) was a "suspected Jew," Hull (foreign affairs) was married to a Jew; moreover, each cabinet member had attached to his staff at least one Jewish adviser "to keep him in line." Rechenberg again denounced Roosevelt as a communist, a freemason, and a man of Jewish blood, pursuing the goals of "his Jewish employers: the destruction of Germany."[21]

Colin Ross proved no better as a harbinger of truth. He depicted Roosevelt to Hitler in 1941 as a dictator who tried to veil his ruthless rule by denouncing the fascist leaders as "tyrants," and as a man who had bought votes with nine billion dollars spent on public welfare under the New Deal. Roosevelt, according to Ross, hated Hitler as well as

Mussolini because deep down he was a "frustrated fascist."[22] And the reports of Germany's military representatives in Washington likewise were designed to please the Führer rather than to report accurately on conditions in the United States. General Friedrich von Boetticher, Germany's military attaché in Washington, informed the Foreign Office in March 1941 of Roosevelt's arrogance and of the country's lack of preparedness for war. Roosevelt, "influenced by Jews and Englishmen," would declare war on Germany only because of Jewish pressure. The United States Air Force was antiquated. Her fleet was no match for that of Japan. And only her "vassals," China and Great Britain, were making a show of it.[23]

Assisted by these reports, Goebbels in November 1941 produced a fifteen-minute film entitled *A Stroll Through America.* Its premiere was reserved for Hitler and Ernst von Weizsäcker, state secretary of the Foreign Office. The film began with an aerial view of the Statue of Liberty, and then zoomed in on Roosevelt and his "Jewish henchmen" addressing Congress. Shots of Eleanor Roosevelt were next, followed by reports of strikes "suppressed brutally with gun and gas." Then came frames dealing with industrial sabotage, hunger protests, ghetto housing, cynical newspaper accounts of suicides, "grotesque Negro dances (jazz and jitterbug)," and "brutal, nauseating boxing matches." Unfortunately, the closing segment of the film dealing with the murder of Charles Lindbergh's child had to be deleted because the murderer was German. The film was judged to be "juicy and effective propaganda for domestic consumption."[24] This, then, was the official image of the United States that the German government presented to its people one month prior to declaring war upon the United States.

## National Socialist Foreign and Colonial Policies

"Germany will either become a world power or will cease to exist."[25] This declaration, italicized in Adolf Hitler's *Mein Kampf*, was not idle phraseology. It formed the basis of Germany's foreign policy from 1933 until 1945. The realization of Germany's status as a world power remained for Hitler his life's mission. Nothing better demonstrates this point of view than his "Nero" order of 19 March 1945,* his

* The "Nero" or "Scorched Earth" directive ordered the retreating German armies to destroy all industrial and supply depots and installations in Germany so that they would not fall into enemy hands. Andreas Hillgruber and Gerhard Hümmelchen *Chronik des Zweiten Weltkrieges* (Frankfurt 1966), 149.

hastily composed "Political Testament" on the last day of his life, or these words uttered in the winter of 1941: "I am also as cold as ice in this: if the German people are not willing to take an active part in their self-preservation, good: then they shall cease to exist."[26] Hitler's final judgment of the German people was already contained in these words. Germany had failed in its historic mission to become a truly great *world* power; it had failed to establish its hegemony over continental Europe; and therefore it had shown itself unworthy of the even greater tasks set down by the Führer. And these had aimed at nothing less than world dominion (*Weltherrschaft*). Albert Speer gave expression to this objective in architectural terms. Berlin was to become the "capital of the world," and here in a specially constructed assembly hall, topped by a gigantic dome 250 meters in diameter, Hitler would receive the tributes and accolades of his subjects. The monstrous hall was initially to be crowned with an eagle clutching a swastika in its claws 290 meters above ground level; however, Hitler later changed the swastika to a globe, "which Hitler did not desire to possess merely as a symbol." Speer also claims that the inner circle around the Führer never doubted that the war was being waged for "world hegemony."[27]

Adolf Hitler's overall program has been aptly summarized as "the complete superimposition and penetration of originally vulgar Machiavellian foreign policy concepts [and] aims with the most radical form of universal, racist-ideological anti-Semitism."[28] The natural prerequisite for its fulfillment was consolidation of absolute internal power, to be followed by establishment of German rule over central Europe. This preparatory part of the program, to be completed by 1940, would be achieved first by peaceful revision of the Versailles *Diktat* and thereafter by localized military campaigns, each one to be conducted against only one isolated opponent. The first major phase of the program was to be reached approximately by 1943–1945 with the creation of a German continental imperium stretching to the Ural Mountains, and it would be a period, according to Hitler, of a "policy of bold risks." This phase was clearly reflected in Hitler's armaments program, which stressed quality rather than quantity, as well as in the accompanying blitzkrieg concept. A general war, especially one involving Great Britain, was to be avoided at all costs until the completion of the first major phase, which would end with the creation of a German colonial empire in Central Africa, a strong surface fleet designed already for the coming conflict with the United States, and a chain of advanced German naval bases (*Stützpunkte*) on the Atlantic islands. This part of the program Hitler would personally supervise; the second part was reserved for the next generation. For the final test the Führer would leave behind a "Super

Germany" stretching from the Urals to the Pyrenees, with France and the Soviet Union eliminated as powers, to be supplied with raw materials from its colonial empire in Central Africa, and ready to assume the struggle from its advanced bases in the Atlantic. Of the four remaining world powers, Japan was far removed and for the moment absent in German plans, and hence the major outstanding issue would be whether Great Britain would join Germany for the final reckoning with the United States. If so, the war would "come to America" in the fullest sense of the term.[29]

A central tenet of National Socialist ideology was the overriding importance of struggle, survival, battle, war, *Kampf*. Hitler had stressed the necessity of human struggle in *Mein Kampf* as well as in his *Second Book*. Hermann Rauschning had noted no change in attitude in Chancellor Hitler in 1933: "War is the most natural, most everyday" occurrence. "War is eternal, war is everywhere. There is no beginning, there is no peace settlement. War is life. War is every struggle. War is an ancient way of life."[30] And the Führer did not ease up on this thesis during the Second World War. In his famous "table talks" he stated: "For the good of the German people we must desire war every fifteen or twenty years." Even after the tide of battle had turned against him, Hitler recorded for posterity his belief that a nation, like an individual, needed a "little bloodletting" in every generation.[31] And while the principal "bloodletting" would take place in Europe, there would also be limited action on the Continent's periphery.

Adolf Hitler began to raise the "colonial question" with increasing frequency in the late 1930s, especially at the famous Nuremberg party rallies. In 1936 he stressed the economic value of colonies for Germany; a year later the thronged masses were again harangued on this subject; and in 1939 he announced at Nuremberg that his one and only demand of Great Britain was the return of Germany's former colonies. And Hitler encouraged the National Socialist Colonial Union, founded in 1936 after the dissolution of the old Wilhelmian Colonial Society, to drum up enthusiasm for colonial acquisitions among the German people. The Führer likewise did not fail to drive the point home to his more august followers. In November 1937 and September 1938 he lectured army generals concerning Germany's need for colonies.[32] Hitler first demanded the return of Germany's former African colonies on 7 March 1936, and in his Reichstag speech on 6 October 1939 he expanded this demand to include all former colonies. But specific projects for regaining former colonies or obtaining new ones did not get under way until the summer of 1940.

In fact, any attempt to define Adolf Hitler's colonial policy is a most tortuous undertaking. In both *Mein Kampf* and *Second Book*, Hitler rejected the colonial policy of Kaiser Wilhelm II because it had been a composite of strategic, emotional, prestige, and economic determinants. Gerhard Weinberg suggests that colonialism to Hitler meant "the acquisition of territories suitable for German settlement after the expulsion, extermination, or enslavement of the local population."[33] Yet the Führer did, at times, put forth rather traditional arguments in favor of colonies.

The most comprehensive account of Hitler's views on this subject, as expressed on the few occasions when he chose to speak about it during his early tenure as chancellor, comes once more from the pen of Hermann Rauschning. Moreover, Rauschning is the only source for Hitler's plans concerning German settlements in South America, an issue that directly affected German-American relations. Klaus Hildebrand, in his massive compilation of National Socialist colonial policy, does not once deal with South America.[34] Rauschning, on the other hand, insists that Hitler confided to him in 1933 that he would "create a new Germany" in Brazil, a notion that had been dear to the hearts of Gustav Schmoller and other German economists of the Wilhelmian period. Germany, according to Hitler, would provide Latin America with capital, a spirit of enterprise, and a *Weltanschauung*. "Our youth will learn to colonize." The Führer did not envision military conquest of South America — he rejected for himself "the role of William the Conqueror"— but instead sought to gain this area with the help of resident Germans, local "upper social classes," and a "revolutionary fifth column" composed of Indios. German medieval families such as the Fugger and the Welser, Hitler argued, had once invested heavily on this continent, and thus the Third Reich could lay claim to a historical precedent upon which to build. One year later, at the urging of Sir Henry Deterding, an official of Royal Dutch Shell, Hitler called for German control of Mexico, believing that this nation was endowed with unlimited natural resources which he could tap to finance his policy of conquest in Europe. Perhaps boyhood dreams of Spanish empire were manifest in this notion. In any case, in addition to South America, Hitler expressed to Rauschning an interest in regaining Germany's South Sea colonies and in creating "a German dominion in Central Africa."[35]

Once in office, the Führer encouraged the propagation of such ideas by appointing Ernst Wilhelm Bohle, formerly of South Africa, head of the National Socialist Workers' Party foreign affairs branch. The organization grew from three thousand members in 1933 to twenty-eight thousand in 1937. It established over five hundred cells in foreign countries. Alfred Rosenberg was given command of yet another organization dedicated to furthering the welfare and interests of Germans overseas, the foreign political office of NSDAP. In the United States these organizations made contact with the Friends of the Hitler Movement, later renamed Friends of the New Germany, and still later the German-American Bund. Under the leadership of Fritz Kuhn it mustered some three to five thousand supporters. A national branch of NSDAP was founded in Paraguay in 1931, and soon another sprang up in South Africa. But nowhere did these movements attract large numbers of adherents. In Argentina the local National Socialist Party barely embraced 5 percent of the population; in Brazil 2.5 percent; in Chile it scored perhaps its greatest achievement with 9 percent.[36]* If Germany was to play an active role in the Western Hemisphere, she would need a sizable fleet capable of establishing and defending her interests, primarily against the Monroe Doctrine and the United States Navy.

## Hitler, Raeder, and Sea Power

Adolf Hitler was not familiar with the sea. In 1928 he wrote: "On land I am a hero, at sea a coward."[37] Certainly the latter part of the statement is accurate. He never learned to swim, displayed a "panicky fear" of sailing even on tranquil Bavarian lakes, and generally maintained an aversion to water throughout his life.[38] Most German naval officers — and historians — have been eager to attribute Germany's naval disasters between 1939 and 1945 to the land-oriented mentality of the Austrian Hitler. As early as March 1933 Admiral Erich Raeder, head of the German navy, laid the foundations for this convenient apologia: "It is, of course, readily understandable that, being a native of Austria who has spent the greater part of his life in South Germany, naval matters are somewhat strange to him."[39] And Raeder as well as his successor, Grand Admiral Karl Dönitz, energetically pursued this line of argument at the Nuremberg International Military Tribunal.

Yet this view is too simplistic. Deeper issues than environmental differences divided Hitler and his naval leaders. The latter were steeped in the Tirpitz school of thought, regarding the United States and Great Britain as one "nation," as one "race," united rather than divided by Atlantic maritime arteries. And against this *Angelsachsentum* (Anglo-Saxon alliance) Germany was forced to declare economic and military warfare if it wanted to assert itself as an independent world power.[40]

* L. de Jong, in *Die deutsche Fünfte Kolonne im Zweiten Weltkrieg* (Stuttgart 1959), emphatically denies that the "fifth column" movements achieved any prominence.

Here, and not to the east, naval leaders uncovered the "real" enemy. Hitler's admirals, like their predecessors and erstwhile superiors in 1914–1918, once again desired an understanding with their eastern neighbors in order to struggle for *Weltpolitik* with their western rivals. Hitler was of a different opinion. He regarded Tirpitz's High Sea Fleet as a "romantic plaything" and as a "parade piece." The old Wilhelmian naval slogan, "Our future lies with the sea," he judged to be a major strategic error.[41] The scuttling of the German fleet at Scapa Flow in June 1919 was not, as the navy repeatedly claimed, an "act of honor." For Hitler, the very act of internment already constituted "dishonor."[42] In January 1943 an irate Führer vented the full measure of his displeasure over naval developments in Germany:

> The role of the High Sea Fleet during the [First] World War was meaningless. The excuse that the Kaiser did not want to deploy it does not hold water. We lacked men willing to deploy it even without the Kaiser's permission. A great deal of military potential thus lay idle while the army continually fought heavy engagements. The revolution and the scuttling in Scapa Flow are not annals of honor for the navy.[43]

And better than his admirals Hitler realized that Germany's unrestricted submarine offensive had been a major cause for defeat in the First World War; by bringing the United States into the war it had broken the deadlock of 1916.

Yet in one respect Hitler did share the precepts of his naval advisers: the overriding importance of a single decisive naval engagement, a Cannae at sea. He was strengthened in this belief by Rear Admiral Magnus von Levetzow, Scheer's last chief of staff and Hitler's first police president of Berlin. But Hitler and his admirals differed over the timing of such an encounter. While the latter wished to engage the British Royal Navy at the very outset of a general European war (in 1944–1945) in order to grant Germany control of the seas, Hitler would hear of it only after he had established German hegemony over continental Europe. Hitler made this perfectly clear in 1931 during an interview with the journalist Richard Breiting: "At the moment we do not need a High Sea Fleet. . . . Only when we have secured our *Lebensraum* in Europe can we demand equality on the seas."[44] In short, Hitler drew the same lessons from the debacle of 1918 that General Wilhelm Groener had presented to German army officers in May 1919.

Admiral Raeder seems to have been particularly slow in realizing that Hitler's ambitions would involve Germany in a clash with Great Britain long before the first major phase of the Führer's overall program was completed. In fact, Raeder took at face value Hitler's statement in *Mein Kampf* that Germany needed Great Britain as an ally. In November 1933 the admiral informed the British naval attaché in Berlin, Captain G. C. Muirhead-Gould, that Germany would not build a fleet directed against Great Britain. Raeder proclaimed rather pompously — and incorrectly — that "concepts from the Tirpitz era have no place in present-day Germany." Most important of all, he offered Great Britain "one squadron of battleships," which could be "of great importance" in erasing the parity "between the English and the American fleets." This German contingent, the admiral added, would be a "political plus" for Great Britain in her "inevitable" conflict with the United States.[45]

Raeder here echoed Hitler's proclamations from the previous decade. Already in *Mein Kampf* Hitler had suggested that the United States would replace Great Britain as "ruler of the waves."[46] In the *Second Book* he repeated this notion, and further suggested that in return for British neutrality while Germany achieved hegemony on the European Continent, he would support Great Britain in the future war with the United States. Naturally, Great Britain would be a "junior partner" in this arrangement.[47] Yet once again there surfaced a major point of contention between Führer and admiral: while Hitler regarded the "understanding" with Great Britain as a prerequisite to the final struggle between German-dominated Europe and the United States, Raeder was certain that it was impossible to drive a wedge between the two Anglo-Saxon naval powers. In this, the admiral was a true product of his early environment. Years of close contact with Admirals von Tirpitz and von Hipper had cemented his unbending devotion to the concept that war with Great Britain automatically meant war with the United States. And to this end, Raeder desired a balanced fleet à la Mahan with an emphasis on battleships.

The Anglo-German naval agreement of 18 June 1935 permitted Germany to construct a surface fleet up to 35 percent of the British fleet and an undersea fleet up to 45 percent of British submarines; three years later Germany negotiated parity with Great Britain concerning the latter. However, German shipyards were not sufficiently developed to build up to the limits allowed under the treaty before September 1939, and hence Raeder and his staff — who calculated that they would reach 35 percent of the British surface fleet only by September 1942 — found their energies absorbed entirely by ship construction. Matters of politics and strategy were shelved for the time being. But the fateful year 1938 forced many, Raeder among them, to reevaluate past beliefs and misconceptions concerning Hitler's overall program.

During May 1938, following the appointment of Joachim von Ribbentrop as foreign minister on 4 February and the *Anschluss* of Austria on 13 March, Hitler informed Raeder not only that he intended to dismember Czechoslovakia, but also that he expected the navy to complete construction of ten "superbattleships" by 1944. By this date, the Führer announced, the Soviet Union would have been crushed by the Wehrmacht. The war at sea against either Great Britain or the United States, or both, could then begin.[48] Hitler informed his military paladins early in 1938 (January 22) that it was the duty of the 110 million Germans in central Europe "to own the world one day." The Führer now hinted that the war with the Soviet Union was not his "life's goal," but merely a vital step towards preparing Europe for the inevitable clash with the two Anglo-Saxon powers.[49] But as time went by, Hitler became ever more convinced that Great Britain and her empire were growing weak, and that by waging warfare against Germany, Great Britain would lose her status as a world power. He thus posed for Britain "the option between the USA and the rising world power Germany."[50] But before then, Great Britain might "foolishly" become involved with Germany in a localized European conflict. Raeder became alarmed. Had he not been assured time and again by Hitler that the navy could count on peaceful expansion until 1944–1945?

Hitler's directive of 30 May 1938 for "Case Green" (war with Czechoslovakia) made it abundantly clear to the navy that war with the western European powers was considerably nearer than they had up to now let themselves believe. The Seekriegsleitung (Commander Hellmuth Heye) in July 1938 prepared a memorandum on the German-Czechoslovakian situation for the Führer, in which it equated war in 1938 with France and Great Britain with the end of the Reich. The chief of staff of the Naval War Staff, Vice Admiral Günther Guse, recommended that Raeder contact army leaders and attempt to dissuade Hitler from war before Germany was sufficiently armed.[51] As is well known, war was avoided at the last moment on 30 September 1938 in Munich, where Prime Minister Neville Chamberlain gave in to Hitler's demand for German acquisition of the Czechoslovak Sudetenland in order to avoid a "quarrel in a far away country between people of whom we know nothing." The Munich agreement was welcome news indeed for the German navy, insofar as it apparently offered the prospect of several more years of peace in which to build capital ships.

Any lingering doubts that Admiral Raeder may have had regarding the magnitude of Hitler's goals must have been erased in September 1938 when he asked Admiral Rolf Carls, his fleet chief, to translate the Führer's overall program into cold, hard naval language. Carls argued that if Hitler was really serious in his desire to make Germany a truly *world* power —

and who could doubt that? — it would entail "conquest of colonies, *secure maritime arteries*, and *safe, free access to the oceans*" (italics in the original). Such a course would encompass a confrontation with the Royal Navy, which in turn would mean war with Great Britain and the empire, with France, probably with the Soviet Union, and with "a number of overseas states; thus against one-half to two-thirds of the world." Carls did not bother to mention the United States specifically: German naval leaders automatically included her in their references to a war against Great Britain.[52] But just to make certain that there existed absolutely no doubt in this matter, Carls proposed to station two naval groups, each consisting of one battle cruiser, one heavy cruiser, one aircraft carrier, four auxiliary cruisers, and five submarines, in waters adjacent to the east and the west coasts of the United States.[53] At least Admiral Carls perceived a clear notion of what Hitler's program meant in terms of naval strategy and deployment.

Vice Admiral Guse on 25 October 1938 drafted what eventually became the basic document for any future European war. The so-called "England Memorandum" belongs, according to Michael Salewski, among "the most decisive and historically most important documents" of the German navy "before the war."[54] The navy reiterated its firm belief that it would not be called upon to shoulder its share of the burden before 1944–1945, but estimated for then an enemy constellation much as it appeared in September 1939. The primary antagonist would once more be Great Britain, which had won the First World War without risking its superior surface fleet in battle (other than at Jutland). Raeder's staff thus concluded that the destruction of commerce bound for the island kingdom was of paramount importance, much more significant than damages inflicted upon Britannia's battle fleet. In fact, the German navy was fully aware that it could not risk a decisive surface engagement in the North Sea; such a course would provide "slender" chances of success even between equal fleets, and "none" at all against a superior British force. Moreover, the naval staff — as it had in 1936 — once more rejected unrestricted submarine warfare as a solution to Germany's naval strategy. "*We must not expect very substantial successes from an offensive naval strategy with U-boats only*" (italics in the original). It was argued in Berlin that submarine warfare would have to be conducted according to prize rules (that is, by first warning ships to be destroyed); and British antisubmarine defenses (convoy, depth charges, hydrophones, nets, and the like) were sufficiently developed after the experiences of 1914–1918 to blunt any German undersea offensive from the start.

However, the Seekriegsleitung also possessed a further reason why it did not favor emphasis upon submarine strategy: a U-boat fleet could never accord the Reich a future *Weltpolitik*. Surface ships alone could provide control of the world's vital sea lanes, and the naval staff desired a special type of ship that would be faster than Britain's heavy units, but with better armor and ordnance than British cruisers. The answer was sought in the famous "pocket" battleships (fast battleships, or super battle cruisers). A fleet of these special craft could interrupt Britain's maritime lifeline and, in good Tirpitzean logic, make her more readily compliant with German demands for equality upon the seas. This new "risk theory" would also — according to German plans — prompt London to work for the return of Germany's lost colonies, and here Hitler and Raeder found themselves once more on the same track. "*Every naval strategy is* dependent *upon bases*" (italics in the original).

These deliberations were in 1938 highly speculative, as the Reich possessed only three pocket battleships (*Admiral Graf Spee*, *Admiral Scheer* and *Deutschland*), the elderly battleships *Schlesien* and *Schleswig-Holstein*, the heavy cruiser *Admiral Hipper*, the battle cruisers *Gneisenau* and *Scharnhorst*, the light cruisers *Emden*, *Königsberg*, *Köln*, *Leipzig*, and *Nürnberg*, thirty-four destroyers, and fifty-seven submarines (of which only twenty-three were fit for service in the Atlantic). Still under construction were the battleships *Bismarck* and *Tirpitz* (laid down in 1939), the aircraft carrier *Graf Zeppelin* (1938), the heavy cruisers *Blücher*, *Prinz Eugen*, *Seydlitz*, and *Lützow* (1937–1939), and the light cruiser *Karlsruhe* (1939). The British navy, by contrast, in late 1938 consisted of fifteen battleships, seven aircraft carriers, fifteen heavy and forty-nine light cruisers, 183 destroyers, and fifty-seven submarines; the French navy (under Admiral François Darlan) of nine battleships, three aircraft carriers, nineteen cruisers (seven heavy), seventy-two destroyers, and eighty-six submarines.[55]

It was against this possible western coalition that Admiral Raeder's planners in 1938–1939 began to develop their naval construction program. On 27 January 1939 the German navy finally developed the "Z" or "Ziel" program. It called for the construction, by 1948 at the very latest, of a balanced modern navy: ten battleships, fifteen pocket battleships, four aircraft carriers, five heavy cruisers, forty-four light cruisers, sixty-eight destroyers, ninety torpedo boats, twenty-seven ocean-going submarines, and 222 U-boats.[56] This force, staffed with officers carefully screened and chosen by Admiral Raeder and imbued with fervent National Socialist spirit, was designed with the United States in mind. It was not intended simply for a conflict with Great Britain.[57]* The "Z-Plan" was by no means meant to define the ultimate strength of the German navy. Yet

* Both historians Andreas Hillgruber and Jost Dülffer (see note 57) concede that Raeder was probably unaware of this fact because Hitler allowed the admiral insight into only his "immediate next step" of the program. Michael Salewski (see note 57) sees the Z-Plan directed against Great Britain alone.

it was the basic blueprint for German victory at sea. It was amended and expanded, as will be seen later, in the summer of 1940 to make it more specifically adapted for warfare against the United States.

The final peacetime strategic deliberations of the Kriegsmarine developed the basic "double-pole" concept. Admiral Hermann Boehm, fleet chief, in May 1939 defined Germany's strategy in a war against Great Britain on the basis of the winter maneuvers of 1938–1939 as "the *attack against* Great Britain's *oceanic maritime lanes and operations* against the English fleet in the North Sea." These "*two poles*" (all italics in the original) mentioned by Boehm lay at the heart of all future deliberations for the war at sea. That same month, as Hitler began to step up preparations for "Case White" (the war against Poland), the navy drafted contingency operations orders. These stated that the Reich "already today finds itself in a prewar situation" and that the future conflict would probably find Germany allied in Europe with Italy, Hungary and Spain as well as Japan overseas, while her opponents would consist of Great Britain and France, closely tied to Poland and Turkey. The United States was considered to be a "benevolent neutral" vis-à-vis Great Britain; Russia's disposition was stated as being "unclear"; and the Netherlands, Belgium and the Scandinavian countries were considered steadfast neutrals. Given this constellation of powers cleanly divided into two major camps, the Seekriegsleitung concluded that any war in Europe would rapidly take on global dimensions and that Germany would have to prepare a fleet capable of taking on such a challenge. Her immediate policy would consist of conducting submarine warfare off the enemy's coast, dispatching commerce raiders into the Atlantic Ocean (which in all likelihood would not be able to return), and undertaking surface sorties into the northern North Sea in order to prevent the opponent (Great Britain) from establishing a tight blockade as in 1914–1918. But Raeder's planners warned yet again that war in 1939 "would confront the navy with tasks for which its present state of readiness is not adequate."[58]

Finally, there existed on the eve of war in Europe a division of opinion between Hitler and his admirals with regard to the personality and policies of President Roosevelt. We have already seen Hitler's evaluation of the American leader. His admirals were more rigid; they regarded Roosevelt as a most dangerous leader, highly rated and highly feared. Germany's naval planners were convinced that Roosevelt was "irrevocably pursuing his course of annihilating Germany," a point of view that goes far to explain the eagerness with which they pressed Hitler for an early declaration of war against the United States.[59] The United States thus once more loomed on the horizon as a potentially decisive factor in any future European conflagration.

## *Background: Hitler, Raeder, and the United States*

Admiral Raeder must have realized early in 1939 that war was imminent. He would not have until 1944–1945 to prepare for the expected clash with the Royal Navy. Instead, Germany would once again have to confront Great Britain at sea before her fleet was ready for the task. And once again the prospect arose that a general European war would spill over into the Atlantic and raise the specter of American involvement in the war. Both Hitler and Raeder were aware in September 1939 of the possible uncomfortable parallel between this war and the 1914–1918 conflict. Then both men had been mere cogs in Germany's military machine; now they were the directors of that instrument of destruction.

EIGHT

# Once More World War (1939–1941)

> I will not live to see it, but I am happy for the German *Volk* that it will one day witness how Germany and England united will line up against America.
>
> — ADOLF HITLER *September 1941*

THE KEY TO THE SUCCESSFUL COMPLETION OF THE FIRST PHASE OF HITLER'S overall program lay in his ability to avoid Great Britain's involvement in his localized *Blitzkriege*. Here was a remnant of Wilhelmian thinking: in return for British acceptance of German hegemony on the Continent and return of Germany's lost African colonies, Hitler would "guarantee" the security of the British Empire (especially against the American rival), as well as let Great Britain partake in the future division of the French colonial empire.[1] This was the "generous offer" that Hitler was to extend to Great Britain until well into 1942. Yet the British guarantee of Poland's independence, though not of her borders, on 31 March 1939 raised the first serious doubts in Hitler's mind. By the end of August 1939 the Führer found himself in a corner, from which he escaped only by accepting the certainty of Great Britain's immediate involvement in the war. Germany found herself in a position similar to that of July and August 1914, and once again her leaders opted for a "flight to the front" (*Flucht nach vorn*). For Hitler was convinced that time was running against him. His military forces were prepared for a localized military campaign against Poland; the western democracies were ill prepared for any kind of armed conflict. If he was to realize the first phase of the program in his own lifetime, Hitler would have to act now and accept the war with Great Britain for the time being. "From the morning of 3 September 1939 Hitler found himself in a large war which he had planned neither for this time nor in this alignment of powers."[2]

## Hitler and Raeder at War (1939–1940)

This turn of events hit Admiral Raeder hard. Hitler's gamble — to invade Poland and accept the danger of a war with Great Britain — shattered the relative tranquility that the admiral had enjoyed since 1933. His bitterness and disappointment with the Führer's course of action came out most strongly in a memorandum which he prepared on 3 September, but which he did not include in the navy's official war diary. The Führer had promised all along, Raeder lamented, that the German navy could count on peace with Great Britain until approximately 1944–1945. Thus the war came five years too early once again; the German navy once more was not equipped to meet the British Royal Navy in combat. Raeder admitted that he could not risk a decisive naval engagement in the North Sea, and he further questioned the likelihood of successful "tip-and-run" operations against the island empire. However, he quickly decided that this time the German fleet would not remain idle and confined in port. It would understand "how to die gallantly"— a notion that it had accepted in the First World War only in the fall of 1918. Only by "dying gallantly," Raeder suggested, could the navy hope for eventual rebirth and expansion in future generations.[3] Here was a further notion that lucidly demonstrated that Admiral Raeder was ever conscious of the fact that the navy had precipitated the downfall of the Reich and the outbreak of revolution in October 1918. He was determined never to let that happen again, regardless of the cost.

The United States had not figured as a vital factor in Hitler's decision to invade Poland on 1 September 1939. The Führer had been warned by Ambassador Dieckhoff, General Ludwig Beck, and General Georg Thomas[4] that the United States would not stand aside and allow Germany to conquer Europe, but the Führer discounted this advice. German naval planners, on the other hand, calculated from the start that war with Great Britain would ultimately bring the United States into the conflict. Raeder pressed Hitler on 10 October 1939 for unrestricted submarine warfare against *all* maritime commerce moving to Great Britain, regardless of the political repercussions of such a policy:

> All objections *must* be rejected. Threats of America's entry into the war, which appears certain with the continuance of the war, must also *not* lead to limitations [of the submarine offensive]. The sooner [it] begins and the more brutal, the earlier the effects and the shorter the war. All limitations prolong the war.

The admiral noted that both the Führer and General Wilhelm Keitel, head of the army, "*fully* agreed with this" (all italics in the original).[5]

Yet Hitler better remembered the lessons of the First World War. He constantly warned his admirals to exercise the utmost caution concerning American interests at sea. In 1917–1918 German naval leaders had unsuccessfully urged the government to declare unrestricted submarine warfare in American waters; now they again advanced this bold and provocative measure. But Hitler raised no objections on 2 October 1939 when American states proclaimed a pan-American "safety belt" around the Americas south of Canada, defining a three-hundred-mile to thousand-mile zone in which belligerents were warned to refrain from naval action. Moreover, on 23 February 1940 the Führer vetoed Admiral Raeder's proposal to send two submarines to Halifax, Nova Scotia, "owing to psychological effect on America."[6]* Three months later he further refused Raeder's request to shell the French-occupied island of Aruba (Lesser Antilles), because "oil centers belong to Standard Oil, thus American corporation."[7] On 3 May 1940 he informed Italian dictator Benito Mussolini that President Roosevelt's latent hostility would encourage him "to end this war as quickly as possible."[8] And when the German navy established a war zone around the British Isles on 17 August 1940, Hitler made certain that it corresponded precisely to the area into which the United States had forbidden its citizens and ships to sail.[9] Above all, Hitler opposed an all-out submarine offensive against Great Britain because it directly opposed his political policy of an "understanding" with that power. Thus Hitler and his admirals from the very beginning found themselves committed to diametrically opposed concepts of the war in the west.

Adolf Hitler had good reason to counsel restraint. The embryonic German fleet was far inferior in strength to the British fleet: in battleships 2 to 15; aircraft carriers 0 to 6; "pocket" battleships 3 to 0; heavy cruisers 2 to 15; light cruisers 6 to 49; destroyers and torpedo boats 34 to 183; and submarines 57 to 57.[10]† It was hardly a match for the combined British and American fleets.‡ Hence it was tactically desirable to

* Raeder even hoped to solicit the support of the Foreign Office for this naval initiative. Precisely the same arguments had been put forth by the German foreign ministers Arthur Zimmermann and Richard Kühlmann in the autumn of 1917 and the summer of 1918 against the demands of Admiral Henning von Holtzendorff, chief of the Admiralty Staff, for unrestricted submarine warfare to be extended into American waters.

† The German navy in September 1939 possessed two old battleships, two battle cruisers, three pocket battleships, eight cruisers, and twenty-two destroyers; two battleships and one cruiser were completed during the war. F. H. Hinsley *Hitler's Strategy* (Cambridge 1951), 1.

‡ The United States had the following forces in the autumn of 1941 (numbers in parentheses represent vessels under construction): 15 (8) battleships, 5 (3) aircraft

deemphasize the naval war, to avoid provoking the United States through careless torpedoing of its ships, and to concentrate instead on the construction of the fleet that would be required after 1945, following the final victory over the Soviet Union. Germany's immediate task lay primarily in establishing her hegemony over continental Europe, thereby creating the requisite base for later expansion and conquest.

In all fairness to the German navy it should be pointed out that in 1939, as in 1917, there were a number of naval officers who sharply disagreed with the policy of adventurous submarine warfare *à outrance*. Perhaps the most outspoken critic was Vice Admiral Kurt Assmann. On 15 October 1939, the very day on which Raeder once again demanded unrestricted submarine warfare against *all* commerce bound for Great Britain, Assmann cautioned against repeating the error of 1 February 1917. He rejected Admiral Raeder's assumption that the United States would automatically enter any general war against Germany, flatly calling it a misconception resting upon "superficial examination and false analysis of American politics" during the First World War. Assmann warned that Raeder's course was "incredibly dangerous" because it could easily lead Germany once more to declare "economic-military warfare" against the United States without the proper means and resources for such an effort. "We came to the conclusion on 9 January 1917 that our means were sufficient for this task — and we deceived ourselves!" But the German naval leadership in 1939, as in 1917, was not about to entertain sober estimates of the military situation. Raeder noted on Assmann's report that Germany was well on the way in 1917 to throttling Great Britain's imports "and would have succeeded under stronger political leadership."[11] Certainly Raeder could be sure of "stronger political leadership" in 1939. But would that automatically guarantee military success? Or had this argument in 1917 served to cover up military failures and shortcomings?

On 23 November 1939, after the rapid defeat of the Polish armed forces, Hitler informed his military leaders of his next objective: defeat of France and Great Britain. Only by clearing his western flank, the Führer suggested, could he gain the necessary security to attack the Soviet Union. "We can only attack Russia if we are free in the west." He then cited the factors that had contributed to the brilliant success of German arms in the east, concluding: "As a final factor I must, in all modesty, name myself: indispensable." Hitler now viewed himself in the

carriers, 18 (4) heavy cruisers, 19 (21) light cruisers, 200 (98) destroyers, and 111 (37) submarines (Friedrich Ruge *Der Seekrieg 1939–1945* [Stuttgart 1956], 185). By the time Germany declared war on the United States, she had lost the pocket battleship *Graf Spee* (17 December 1939), the heavy cruiser *Blücher* (10 April 1940), and the battleship *Bismarck* (27 May 1941).

position of Frederick the Great in 1740 and Otto von Bismarck in 1866 and 1870. "No compromises." The issue was clear cut: "Victory or defeat!" Europe was the prize at stake.[12]

But before the attack in the west was launched, the German navy was given an opportunity to show its mettle. Close on the heels of defeat in 1918 many German naval officers, and especially Rear Admiral Wolfgang Wegener, had pointed out that there were only two possible solutions to Germany's disadvantageous strategic position in the North Sea: possession of Channel and Atlantic seaports on the French coast or control of the waters between the Shetland Islands and Norway. Either would provide Germany with access to the Atlantic Ocean.

There appeared after 1 September 1939 little opportunity to acquire bases in the west, as only eighteen U-boats and the pocket battleships *Admiral Graf Spee* and *Deutschland* could be released for *guerre de course* warfare in the Atlantic; the battle cruisers *Gneisenau* and *Scharnhorst* were still undergoing final sea trials, and the cruisers had to be maintained in the Baltic Sea against Poland. Yet Admiral Raeder yearned for action — partly to overcome the "psychological effect" of idleness "upon the crews"— and, remembering the fleet's unrest in 1917 and 1918, decreed "that the moment had arrived when the Armored Ships *must* be dispatched for an energetic sortie against enemy trade." The initial results of the war at sea had been most meager: *Deutschland* on 15 November returned to Gdingen (Gdynia) in the Baltic Sea after netting two ships of 6,962 tons, and *Admiral Graf Spee* had scored only slightly better by the beginning of December with nine ships of 50,089 tons in the Indian and Atlantic oceans. As a result, Captain Hans Langsdorff was told in November 1939 to plan his return home in January or February 1940 during the new moon period. Raeder ordered the *Deutschland* renamed *Lützow*, not only to confuse the enemy and thereby assist the *Admiral Graf Spee*, whose whereabouts were now known, but also because Hitler feared that loss of a ship carrying the country's name could have "highly undesirable psychological repercussions for the navy and the entire German *Volk*."[13]

Admiral Wilhelm Marschall, fleet chief, on 21 November took the *Gneisenau* and *Scharnhorst* out to sea for the first major sortie against commerce bound for the British Isles in the area between the Shetland Islands and the Danish Faeroe Islands. Although Marschall found precious little in the way of merchant shipping, he did partly realize the other aim of the "double-pole" strategy when he destroyed the British auxiliary cruiser *Rawalpindi*. Yet after only six days at sea, Marschall returned home for fear of being caught by either the superior British or French fleet. Rear Admiral Schniewind was utterly disenchanted with what he considered to be timid fleet leadership, and decreed that German ships be sent into action "with ruthless determination." This order was not enforced because on 17 December 1939 the pocket battleship *Admiral Graf Spee* was destroyed by her crew in Montevideo (River Plate) after an ill-led encounter with the British warships *Ajax, Achilles* and *Exeter.* The Führer, according to General Alfred Jodl, army chief of staff, was "very upset" over the loss of the ship, and Raeder, sensing the navy's displeasure that the *Spee* had not gone down in fleet action, ruled: "The German warship fights with full deployment of its crew until the last shell, until it is victorious or until it goes under with flag flying."[14]

The navy's highest officer quickly sought to overcome the negative reaction to the loss of the pocket battleship by planning a new fleet operation not as a strategic diversion (as in November), but for the "destruction of enemy forces." On 18 February 1940, *Gneisenau, Scharnhorst,* the heavy cruiser *Admiral Hipper,* eight destroyers and ten U-boats under Admiral Marschall steamed north to raid the Norway-Shetland sea traffic and to lure British surface units into submarine traps. But Operation Nordmark was canceled after only two days with little success, and two similar sorties (operations Wikinger and Schleswig) planned for that same month were also blown off. Schniewind thereupon informed Raeder that the navy would have "to convince" Germany's leaders of its strategic and tactical value if it wished to receive future support and funds.[15]

Admiral Raeder hardly needed encouragement, and on 9 April 1940 launched Operation Weserübung, the invasion of Norway.* Vice Admiral Günther Lütjens deployed almost the entire German surface fleet for the undertaking, which was designed both to gain the strategic bases requisite for outflanking Britain in the northeast and to display the fighting power and morale of the German navy. The operation was a success, but the price was high. Three cruisers, including the heavy cruiser *Blücher,* ten destroyers, and four submarines were lost.[16] Nonetheless, the British were now outflanked according to Wegener's doctrine and the way to the open ocean was free to Germany — as it had never been during the First World War. To secure for Raeder also a position outflanking Great Britain in the southwest (Brest) remained a task for the Wehrmacht.

The so-called phony war in the west ended abruptly on 10 May 1940. Almost fifty German divisions invaded Luxembourg, Belgium and

* The following fleet units were involved in Operation Weserübung: battle cruisers *Scharnhorst* and *Gneisenau;* heavy cruisers *Admiral Hipper* and *Blücher;* pocket battleship *Lützow* (ex *Deutschland*); and light cruisers *Köln, Königsberg, Karlsruhe,* and *Emden.*

the Netherlands that morning, but the main strike came with General Karl von Rundstedt's Army Group Ardennes, composed of forty-four divisions and with an armored column over one hundred miles long and stretching fifty miles to the other side of the Rhine. Hitler's aims were threefold: to take France out of the war, neutralizing her fleet and colonial empire and acquiring her Channel and Atlantic ports through a dictated peace settlement; to force Great Britain into an agreement with Germany in terms of *Weltpolitik* now that France was out of the war; and to keep the United States out of the conflict through the twin blows of quick military victory over France and rapprochement with Great Britain. These measures, in turn, would free the Führer to pursue his main objective of establishing German rule over European Russia. Only in the first of these aims was Hitler successful. On 22 June, France capitulated in the wake of the Dutch (15 May) and Belgian (28 May) surrenders. A victorious Germany was joined on 29 May by Romania and on 10 June by Italy.[17]

The armistice signed by France on 22 June in the forest of Compiègne, in the very same railroad car in which Germany had been humbled in 1918, stipulated that the country was to be occupied north of a line running west and north of Geneva – Dôle – Tours – Mont de Marsan – Spanish border; that her army (as that of Germany in 1919) was to be limited to 100,000 men; and that a French government was to be created in the southern unoccupied regions. The latter was realized on 9–10 July 1940 when Marshal Henri Pétain and Pierre Laval established at Vichy a formal government which was quickly recognized by all the major neutral powers, including the United States. The naval clauses of the armistice turned out to be most moderate: the French Mediterranean fleet, consisting of three battleships, two battle cruisers, fourteen heavy and light cruisers, thirty-eight destroyers, and forty-two submarines, was to be "assembled and disarmed in ports to be specified," and the Reich "solemnly declared" that it had "no intention of utilizing the French men-of-war for its own use" either at the present or "at the conclusion of peace." In fact, the French navy was disposed of in a quite different manner. On 3 July 1940 a British squadron (Force H) under Admiral Sir James Somerville destroyed or crippled three French battleships and one cruiser at Mers-el-Kebir, near Oran, after Admiral Marcel Gensoul had declined a British ultimatum either to turn his ships over to the British or to join them in the war against Germany and Italy. This action, which constituted the first Anglo-French battle since Waterloo one hundred twenty-five years before, was followed by the seizure of two French battleships and other smaller craft stationed since the fall of France in Plymouth and Portsmouth.[18]

The German navy had hardly played a role in the war against France. Hermann Göring triumphantly proclaimed that his air force would now "smash" Great Britain. And the navy? It continued to press for an escalation of the war at sea against Great Britain. On 21 May 1940 Hitler decided, in response to an inquiry from Admiral Raeder, that the navy should not concentrate all its submarine forces against Great Britain but instead employ its resources to develop a comprehensive U-boat construction and officer training program. "After the conclusion of major operations against France he [Hitler] will place primary emphasis on the submarine and Ju 88 programs."[19]* Work on the "Z-Plan" had virtually been suspended since the beginning of the land war. The navy was anxious to assume its role in the present war. Hitler agreed in principle. On 4 June 1940 he again stated that victory over France would be followed by emphasis on airplane and submarine construction and by reduction of the army.[20] But he was, of course, merely soothing the nerves of his restless naval leaders.

On 4 June 1940 the navy launched Operation Juno, designed as a strike by *Gneisenau*, *Scharnhorst*, *Admiral Hipper*, and six destroyers from Wilhelmshaven into the northern North Sea in an attempt to bring "relief" to the German army in France as well as to interdict commerce bound for Great Britain. The force steamed as far north as the Narvik-Harstad line, and managed to destroy the British aircraft carrier *Glorious*. The Naval War Staff was ecstatic. "Especially the *capital ships* must acquire recognition through such a success" (italics in the original). But Raeder's plans to initiate more surface raids were quickly dampened when the *Scharnhorst* was immobilized by a torpedo hit. The squadron returned to Trondheim in Norway, and a bitter Naval War Staff blamed fleet chief Admiral Marschall for recklessly having exposed his ships to undersea attack, and now spoke of the sinking of the *Glorious* as a "decided stroke of luck." A subsequent operation by *Gneisenau* and *Hipper* on 10 June lasted only two days and brought no sizable results. Marschall was sacked as fleet chief and as commander of the Naval Group West and replaced with Vice Admiral Günther Lütjens, the officer who had been in charge of Operation Weserübung in April 1940. On 14 June Raeder ordered an "active, offensive advance" against the enemy as soon

* The Ju 88 program was a first priority project for the development of a twin-engine dive bomber. By the fall of 1941, however, it had to be cut back to one-third production capacity owing to lack of fuel supplies (Albert Speer *Erinnerungen*, Frankfurt 1969, 197–98). German aircraft production rose from 2,518 (737 bombers) in 1939 to 10,247 (2,852 bombers) in 1940, but the workhorse remained the He 111, which could carry 4,400 pounds of bombs and had a range of 760 miles. General Walther Wever's cherished "Ural" bombers (Ju 89 with a range of 1,240 miles, and Do 19 with a range of 1,800 miles) were not built in significant numbers in 1940.

as possible, but Lütjens's sortie on 20 June ended on a bitter note when the British submarine *Clyde* torpedoed and badly damaged *Gneisenau.* Raeder was livid and ordered that further fleet operations were to be conducted with *Admiral Hipper* alone, but cooler heads prevailed and the navy had to be content to rest until its only two capital ships were in commission again.[21]

Operation Juno had been a classic example of the "double-pole" strategy, and further designed to show the Führer the value of the newly gained bases in Norway (à la Wegener). But when the army took the French Channel and Atlantic ports in May and June 1940, the navy was unable to take advantage of this strategic blessing because of the temporary loss of the two capital ships. Instead, work continued on transforming Trondheim into a first-rate naval base while Brest, Cherbourg, St. Nazaire, and Bordeaux were only later exploited as strategic bases. The "problem Norway"— according to Michael Salewski — had begun to be removed from all "sober, strategic analyses"; if for the navy Norway became primarily the memory of "*the feat of arms of this war*" (italics in the original), for Hitler it had become already the "decisive zone of this war," which had to be protected at all costs.[22]

Although the Führer had on 21 May promised that after the campaign in France armaments priority would go to the air force and the navy, and had followed this up three days later with his Führer Directive No. 13 for intensification of the maritime struggle in British waters, German admirals were greatly disappointed in the settlement concluded with France. Admiral Alfred Saalwächter of Naval Group West denounced what he termed the "far-reaching moderation" of the armistice and the "renunciation" of "justified demands by the victor," meaning in all probability German acquisition of France's colonies in Africa and the Middle East as well as of her fleet. But the navy, which had not exactly turned the tide against France in May and June 1940, could not afford a confrontation with Hitler on this matter. It remained only to incorporate the new territories in the overall naval structure: Vice Admiral Arnauld de la Perrière became special Coastal Commander "Southwest," and new command posts were established as "Holland" and "Belgium/North French Coast"; later Admiral Karl-Georg Schuster was appointed "Commanding Admiral France" under Saalwächter. The British response to these various German moves was to declare a blockade of the European coast on 27 June 1940.[23]

The fall of France presented Hitler with a host of possible follow-up operations and considerations. On 21 May, as his armies were mopping up the remnants of the French army, Hitler informed his military staff: "We are looking for contacts with England on the basis of a division of the world." On 2 June he had again expressed his conviction that Great Britain was now ready to conclude a "sensible peace" which would "finally free his hands" for the "great and real task: the settling of accounts with Bolshevism."[24] And on 13 June Hitler had used an interview with Hearst European correspondent Karl von Wiegand to renew his "generous offer" to Great Britain. "It was never my intention or goal . . . to annihilate the British Empire." Hitler reiterated his past offers to Great Britain whereby in return for guaranteeing the British Empire, Germany would receive a free hand in the east, British protection of her coastline in the event of war, and return of her former colonies. The interview also contained a veiled warning to the United States: "America for Americans, Europe for Europeans." The Führer took it upon himself to interpret the Monroe Doctrine for Roosevelt. "The purpose of the Monroe Doctrine was not to prevent European powers from interfering in American affairs . . . but *to prevent America from interfering in European affairs*" (italics in the original).[25]

The question comes to mind, was Hitler really serious in his attempt to come to an "understanding" with Great Britain? Albert Speer is of this opinion. He records what torment this problem brought to Hitler as early as the fall of 1935:

> I really do not know what to do. It is too grave a decision. I would fondly like to join with England. But the English have often in history shown themselves to be unreliable. If I go with them, then it is over forever between Italy and us. The English then drop me and we are left sitting between two chairs.

On the other hand, Speer recalled that "Hitler spoke, as he was to do often later on, of his willingness to guarantee the Empire in return for a global arrangement." And again: "His regret at not having been able to come together with England ran like a red thread throughout the period of his rule."[26] West German historian Andreas Hillgruber maintains that Hitler sought an "understanding" with Great Britain as late as the Ardennes offensive in December 1944.[27] Whatever the case, this "understanding," which ran counter to the plans of his naval planners and his foreign minister, Joachim von Ribbentrop, was severely endangered by the unrestricted submarine warfare as well as by Germany's European conquests. Great Britain was now isolated from the Continent and, as Admiral Wegener had suggested in the 1920s, strategically flanked by German naval bases in the northeast (Norway) and in the southwest (Brest). In fact, it was from this position of strength that Hitler hoped to dictate an "understanding" to Great Britain on his own terms. This created the apparent paradox of Hitler's repeated claims concerning the desirability of an Anglo-German "understanding" and the fact that throughout the Hitler period virtually every approach to Germany from London was rejected in Berlin.

Hitler's successful campaign against France and his public announcements in June 1940 forced Raeder, at least temporarily, to consider the possibility of a German rapprochement with Great Britain. In January 1940 his staff had boasted that the German victory in Poland was making the world "dangerous also for America." German naval officers accused Roosevelt of desiring war with Germany and of preparing the American people for such an event "with the help of freemasons and Jews."[28] The navy announced in May that the American President was abandoning neutrality in order to enter a conflict which German naval leaders interpreted as the "greatest economic struggle of all times."[29] National Socialist racism, a vulgar Marxism, and anti-American feelings ran rampant in the navy's official war diary in the spring of 1940. But after the Wiegand interview of June 13 Raeder acknowledged, during a discussion with Colonel Walter Warlimont, chief of the Home Defense Division of the OKW (army), that Hitler did not intend to destroy the British Empire because this would weaken the white race. The admiral repeated the Führer's suggestion that Germany and Great Britain come to an "understanding": Britain would share in dividing up the French empire while Germany would be given back her former colonies and a free hand in continental Europe.[30] Yet at the very moment that Admiral Raeder was paying at least lip service to Hitler's plans for an Anglo-German rapprochement, his naval staff was compiling a list of war aims and a fleet construction program that left no doubt that Germany intended to replace Great Britain as the major European maritime power and to challenge the United States for control of the Atlantic.

Raeder had personally set the ball rolling on 26 May 1940 when he asked his principal advisers, Rear Admiral Otto Schniewind and Captain Kurt Fricke, to draw up such a list of war aims as well as a blueprint for future German naval expansion to supplement the "Z-Plan." Flushed with success against Norway and further intoxicated by the heady wine of military victory over France and the Low Countries and possession of Atlantic seaports, Raeder's aides drafted several proposals in response to their chief's request. Fricke, assisted by Rear Admiral Gerhard Wagner, later on chief of the Operations Division, submitted his proposal on 3 June 1940, while Schniewind followed suit on 6 July. Both reports were synthesized for Hitler on 11 July by Raeder. For the sake of simplicity and clarity, the following analysis will present the major themes central to all three reports.

Amidst the serenity of the wooded Alpine slopes at the Obersalzberg, high above Berchtesgaden, far removed from the realities of the war at sea, Admiral Raeder dangled before the Führer's eyes the navy's plan to realize the elusive dreams of 1914–1918. The admiral presented what a recent West German historian terms "the colorful dreams of a prisoner in solitary confinement."[31] Raeder and his staff estimated that upon successful completion of the present war Germany would control northern, western, and southeastern Europe. Specifically, the navy would hold a chain of strategic bases and harbors stretching from the northern tip of Norway to the Pyrenees. Norway, Denmark, the Netherlands, Belgium, and northern France would furnish Germany's naval bastions. These continental possessions would be supplemented by a German colonial empire in Central Africa. Admiral Fricke's surgical knife carved out for Germany generous slices there: the Belgian Congo, French Equatorial Africa, all French holdings south of the Senegal estuary (including Dakar, French Guinea, the Ivory Coast, large areas of the French Sudan, and Dahomey), Angola, Northern Rhodesia, Nyasaland, and parts of Mozambique. In addition, the African Atlantic islands would likewise pass into German hands.[32] These aims, presented to the German Foreign Office on 27 July 1940, closely paralleled those expounded by Rear Admiral Adolf von Trotha in 1917.

Fricke did not hesitate to name the United States as Germany's logical future opponent. The present war, he suggested, would end with the military defeat of the Soviet Union, and British withdrawal because of the strangling effect of the submarine war. Germany, in control of the North Sea, the Mediterranean, the Black Sea, and the Baltic Sea, self-sufficient and immune to attack on the Continent, and with a reservoir of raw materials in Central Africa, would have to prepare for the unavoidable clash with the two Anglo-Saxon maritime powers. The main enemy would then be the "American fleet strengthened by the tradition, war experience, and surviving matériel of the British fleet." And because the United States could not be defeated by cutting off its supplies of imports, the German fleet "would have to be able to seek and destroy the opponent's fleet." A defensive naval strategy did not cross Fricke's mind for one moment. "We must recognize that in every war against an opponent *outside Europe*, we can go after him only if we have first wrested control of the sea from him in battle" (italics in the original). Control of the Atlantic sea lanes could only be gained by engaging and defeating the United States Navy off the coast of America. "Defensive [strategy] can never win a war." Here was the complete return to Operations Plan III of 1903–1906!

But Fricke and his staff already envisaged even greater global confrontations. In this euphoria of victory and future conquest, Germany's naval planners conjured up the prospect of a German-Japanese conflict. Fricke and Wagner warned that if Japan were used to help defeat Great Britain in the present struggle, she might decide to establish her own "world empire" in the Far East in the coming "years or decades." "Hence here, also, the possibility exists that a new opponent will arise whom we can only oppose with sea power."[33]

Such Herculean tasks demanded a home fleet of sixty to eighty battleships, fifteen to twenty aircraft carriers, 100 cruisers, and 500 submarines — supported by a commerce-raiding fleet of 115 cruisers, 250 destroyers, and some 1,200 supporting craft. But even Fricke realized in July 1940 that it would be utterly impossible for Germany to create this monstrous naval armada in the near future. He therefore called for the construction in ten to fifteen years of a first stage of naval building: twenty-five battleships, eight aircraft carriers, fifty cruisers, and 400 submarines for the home fleet; sixty-five cruisers, 150 destroyers, and 500 supporting craft for the commerce-raiding fleet.[34]

Fricke's naval construction program revealed the fateful addiction of Hitler's admirals to the concepts of Mahan and Tirpitz. The future fleet was to find its strength mainly in the heavy classical units such as battleships and cruisers, which were overrated at the expense of modern naval arms such as aircraft carriers, submarines, and naval air power. Nevertheless, Rear Admiral Schniewind, Raeder's chief of staff, supported Fricke and Wagner in their evaluation of the future war at sea. Schniewind pointed out that Great Britain would seek and receive assistance from the United States:

> . . . which, in turn, takes great interest in a strong European England, whereby the United States of America will become of necessity an enemy of Germany. The two Anglo-Saxon powers will maintain their enormous sea power in order to protect their world empires, in some cases to rebuild them, and will become that opponent of Germany with whom we have to reckon in the near future.

Schniewind flatly predicted that Germany would become "an oceanic naval power of first magnitude." This program, he announced, would bring to fruition the frustrated naval hopes and aspirations of centuries.[35]

Admiral Rolf Carls was also anxious to be heard. He wanted Germany to annex outright all of eastern France and to create German satellites in Norway, Denmark, and the Netherlands; the remainder of France and Belgium would have to be "smashed after the Czechoslovakian model." Carls demanded that Germany occupy and hold the Suez Canal, and he planned to solve the navy's oil supply problems by taking over all foreign oil concessions in Persia. He planned to station the German fleet at Trondheim and to use Spitzbergen, the Faeroe Islands, the Shetland Islands, Iceland, and Greenland as a sort of naval dagger pointed at the United States. The Channel Islands and Brittany (both taken in June 1940) would protect Germany from naval attack; Casablanca and Morocco would secure the approaches to Germany's Central African colonial empire. Needless to say, Carls endorsed all claims put forth by Fricke and Wagner or Schniewind that were not specifically mentioned in his own scheme. Not even Madagascar, Mauritius, or North Borneo escaped his scrutiny. And while he admitted that his aims might appear to be somewhat "fantastic," he nonetheless informed his fellow officers that they were all "justified" if Germany wanted to assume "her share of the world's territories."[36]

How receptive was Hitler to these naval proposals? Gerhard Weinberg has shown that in the summer of 1940 Hitler pursued similar goals at least with regard to Central Africa. The Führer desired a solid belt of German holdings stretching from the Cameroons to the coast of East Africa, the return to Germany of South-West Africa, large areas of Morocco, and control of the Atlantic islands;[37] he was not one to be modest when it came to territorial acquisitions. But, in the first place, Hitler still hoped that Great Britain would join Germany as a "junior partner" against the United States — General Franz Halder observed on 13 July 1940 Hitler's so-called "reluctance" to force the British to the peace table because this might destroy the empire, and not Germany but Japan and the United States would be the principal beneficiaries.[38] And secondly, Hitler wanted to avoid a confrontation with the United States at this particular juncture. His eyes were riveted elsewhere: the Soviet Union.

The "Russian question" was central to Hitler's racial and military policies: the war in the east would rid the world of the breeding ground of Jewish, internationalist, Bolshevist germs,* and provide Germany with the requisite source of raw materials and foodstuffs for future struggles. In addition, Hitler now viewed quick military victory against

* Hitler informed his generals on 30 March 1941: "Communism is antisocial criminality. . . . We are talking about a war of annihilation. If we do not regard it as such, we will defeat the enemy, but in thirty years we will again face a communist enemy. . . . Commissars and secret police are criminals and must be treated as such." On 21 July he declared: "The Jews are the scourge of humanity. . . . Hence Russia has become the hearth of pestilence." He would not tolerate the survival of "even one Jewish family." Ten days later Göring instructed Reinhard Heydrich to launch the "final solution" of the Jewish "problem." Cited in Andreas Hillgruber *Deutschlands Rolle in der Vorgeschichte der beiden Weltkriege* (Göttingen 1967), 114, 116.

the Soviet Union as the best means of releasing him from the diplomatic and military impasse in the west:

> Britain's hope lies with Russia and with the United States. If Russia drops out of the picture, America, too, is lost for Britain, because elimination of Russia would tremendously enhance Japan's power in the Far East.[39]

By defeating the Soviet Union, Hitler calculated, Germany would finally force the main issue in the west. In particular, if Germany followed up her victory over the Soviet Union with a drive in the direction of India via Iran and Iraq, and if Japan became active in Southeast Asia, now that German victory cleared its back against the Soviet Union, then the United States would have to become actively involved in the Far East. This, in turn, would leave Great Britain isolated against the *Weltmacht* Germany. Under such a constellation, Britain could either side with Germany against the United States or perish as a world power.

However, during the summer and fall of 1940, while his generals were busily plotting the invasion of the Soviet Union, Hitler proved willing to toy with the fancies of his admirals. He took an active interest in selecting future Atlantic bases, preferring Iceland, the Azores, the Cape Verdes, and the Canaries. On 20 June 1940 he considered obtaining French Madagascar "for the settlement of Jews under French responsibility,"[40] but on 11 July Admiral Raeder successfully advised the Führer against this step "because Atlantic remains the main theater of the war." Hitler thereupon decided to trade French Morocco to Spain for one of the Canary Islands, and he instructed the navy to ascertain which of the islands, apart from the two largest, would be most suitable as a German naval base.[41]

German plans for the seizure of the Atlantic islands were accelerated by the Anglo-American agreement of 2 September 1940, whereby Great Britain received fifty destroyers in return for granting the United States ninety-nine-year leases on naval bases in Newfoundland, Jamaica, Trinidad, British Guiana, St. Lucia, Bermuda, and the Bahamas. This turn of events came as no surprise to Raeder's staff. German naval planners judged it to be "an openly hostile act by the United States against Germany." Moreover, the destroyers-for-bases deal foreshadowed "imminent closest cooperation between USA and Great Britain." The navy's official war diary once more reveals an old article of faith from the Wilhelmian period:

> The empire will, of course, undergo great alterations, but according to all foresight will probably realize its resurrection in an *Anglo-Saxon world em-*

*pire.* Prerequisite for this: understanding between USA and England concerning Canada. *This understanding has now been reached.* [Italics in the original.][42]

Admiral Raeder conferred with Hitler on 6 September 1940 in Berlin to work out a joint answer to this Anglo-American initiative. In fact, the meeting soon assumed far greater significance, for Raeder suggested not only a change in the war against Great Britain but also a sweeping reappraisal of Germany's grand strategy on land and at sea. He had decided by the fall of 1940 that Great Britain could not be defeated militarily. The submarine offensive had been blunted by American aid to Great Britain, and the halfhearted invasion plans for Great Britain (Operation Seelöwe) had been shelved at least until the spring of 1941.* And there appeared to be no alternative strategy in the Atlantic. Raeder rejected Hitler's plans for the occupation of Iceland (Operation Ikarus),[43]† and he likewise ruled out the Führer's scheme to invade southern Ireland.[44]‡ The admiral did, however, come up with what he felt was a viable alternative: he would strike at Great Britain indirectly by way of a strategic diversion in the Mediterranean, perhaps thereby creating a German "land bridge" to India.[45] This was the grandiose objective of the Mittelmeer concept that Admiral Raeder presented to Hitler and army leaders in Berlin on 6 September 1940.

This strategy, though not yet officially presented as a "genuine alternative to the strategic offensive in the East," proposed to counter the destroyers-for-bases deal with a major naval initiative by Germany and Italy in the Mediterranean Sea designed to gain control of the Suez Canal, Gibraltar, the Atlantic islands, and the French holdings in northwest Africa.[46]§ Raeder was most concerned that the United States would seize the Atlantic islands and northwest Africa before Germany could

* The navy had first brought up Operation Seelöwe (Sea Lion) on 21 May 1940. Hitler at first showed no interest in the scheme, but on 16 July recommended it in a personal directive. Acrimonious debates between the two services delayed planning; the army opted for landings on a broad front from Ramsgate to Lyme Bay, while the navy wanted to concentrate landings in a small zone in the Straits of Dover. The Führer postponed Seelöwe on 12 October 1940 because of deteriorating weather conditions. However, it is doubtful that he ever intended to proceed with it. See F. H. Hinsley *Hitler's Strategy*, Cambridge, England, 1951, 64–78.

† Raeder vetoed the plan on 20 June 1940 because Germany lacked the forces necessary for the invasion.

‡ The navy's war diary stated on 27 November 1940: "Operation must be rejected by SKL as being totally hopeless." Bundesarchiv-Militärarchiv, Freiburg im Breisgau, West Germany, PG 32035 Case 115, p. 354. Raeder informed the Führer of this conclusion on 3 December 1940.

§ It is interesting that the Commander of U-boats, Rear Admiral Karl Dönitz, opposed the Mittelmeer concept, arguing that only the war against commerce bound for Great Britain could force that nation into submission.

get there, and he proposed to block such a move with Operation Felix: the projected occupation of Gibraltar, the Canaries, the Cape Verdes, and the Azores.* This scheme would not only preclude American landings in North Africa, but would also secure the whole continent for future German exploitation as envisaged by the navy in its memoranda of June and July 1940. Raeder stressed that Felix would not be an operation of "secondary importance," but "one of the main blows against Britain." It was imperative that it be carried out "before the USA steps in."

The admiral then laid down his estimate of future developments in the Atlantic. He foresaw what he termed the "creation of a corporation USA/England." The destroyers-for-bases deal was a natural "preliminary phase of future development." Raeder did not believe that the United States would enter the war at the present time: "In the interest of [its] own power, [we] need hardly reckon with decisive material and manpower support for the British motherland." But there remained the nagging problem of the Atlantic islands. The United States might decide to occupy the Azores and the Canary Islands in case Spain or Portugal entered the war on the side of the Axis powers. "Therefore Führer considers occupation of Canary Islands through air force necessary and possible." Raeder assured Hitler that he could supply the islands with oil through tankers originating from Spain.[47]†

For a brief moment Adolf Hitler became interested in this vast naval enterprise. On 26 September 1940 he decided that in order to secure his Central African colonial empire as well as his maritime flank against the United States, "England-USA must be thrown out of northwest Africa." In case Spain came over to the Axis side, as Hitler still hoped and believed, "Canaries, possibly also Azores and Cape Verdes, must be secured previously through air force." Admiral Raeder concurred. He reminded Hitler yet again "that the foreseeable further development of the war — entry of the United States into the war — necessitates that Germany expand her fleet already now to optimum strength." A strong surface fleet was the vital prerequisite for "the further advance across the ocean

* Operation Felix was first approved by Hitler on 24 August 1940. Detailed plans were completed on 27 November 1940. See Walther Hubatsch, ed. *Hitlers Weisungen für die Kriegführung 1939–1945. Dokumente des Oberkommandos der Wehrmacht* (Frankfurt 1962), 72–75. The operation was postponed, though not canceled, early in January 1941 because of British successes against the Italian army in North Africa.

† The German chargé d'affaires in the United States, Hans Thomsen, wired on 14 September that the destroyers-for-bases agreement merely revealed that "the Jews have suddenly abandoned pacifism in favor of world [power] politics." Bundesarchiv, Koblenz, West Germany, Büro des Staatssekretärs, USA, vol. 3, Thomsen to Foreign Office, 14 September 1940.

(for example, question Canaries, Cape Verdes, Azores, Dakar, Iceland, etc.)." This line of argument appealed to the Führer. On 14 October he returned to the subject, asking Raeder if the navy could transport sufficient troops and supplies in case it became necessary to occupy the Canaries, Azores, and possibly Cape Verde Islands. Raeder responded positively, provided that the navy could bring the materials and men there *before* the air force occupied the islands. "Führer asks to prove and prepare the entire question."[48]* Raeder still hoped that spectacular maritime successes against the British Royal Navy might prevent the United States from coming to the aid of the British in the immediate future.

Admiral Raeder's Mittelmeer alternative was short-lived. Germany's military leaders, steeped in planning for the eastern offensive, showed virtually no sympathy or understanding. And developments on the diplomatic front also militated against the navy's pet project. At first Admiral Raeder had been buoyed up by news on 27 September 1940 that Foreign Minister Joachim von Ribbentrop had concluded the German-Italian-Japanese Tripartite Pact, whereby each nation agreed to "give mutual support with all the political, economic and military means available, in the event that any one of the three . . . is attacked by a power that is not at present involved in the European war or the China-Japan conflict." While Ribbentrop (and later Raeder) viewed the pact as basically directed against Great Britain, the Führer opted for it only because he hoped it would prevent American involvement by threatening Washington with war across two oceans. Moreover, Hitler's highly publicized western tour on 20 October 1940 proved to be devoid of any substantial gains. On 23 October he met with General Franco at Hendaye and attempted to persuade the Spanish dictator to join the Tripartite Pact and declare war against Britain that winter; Franco's negative reply left the Führer "extremely disappointed, if not mad." Next day he met Pétain and Laval at Montoire, and although both men gave him vague assurances that Vichy France would defend North Africa against British encroachments, Hitler did not obtain a firm promise of military assistance. In fact, Pétain thereafter dispatched economist Louis Rougier to London (without informing Laval), in order to arrange with Prime Minister Winston Churchill a "modus vivendi" concerning British-French relations in Africa. Worse yet, the Führer's confrontation in Berchtesgaden on 12 November 1940 with Vyacheslav Molotov, the Russian foreign minister, came to nought. Hitler suggested a global arrangement: Japan would receive a free hand in the Pacific, Italy her *spazio vitale* in North

* Raeder's staff began to work on the plan to occupy the Atlantic islands on 15 October 1940. Bundesarchiv-Militärarchiv, Freiburg im Breisgau, West Germany, PG 32034 Case 114, p. 166.

Africa, Germany her *Lebensraum* in Central Africa and the "new order" in Europe, and Russia expansion into the Persian Gulf and India. The latter course of action especially would embroil Stalin with Great Britain, which in turn would make London more receptive to Hitler's "generous" offers of leaving continental Europe to Germany and overseas to Britain. But Molotov quickly grasped the meaning of Hitler's proposal and countered with a rejection of any global arrangement in favor of a series of limited agreements that would secure for Russia new areas in Finland, Poland and Bulgaria as well as control over the Dardanelles and even the waters between Denmark and Norway (Kattegat and Skagerrak). Hitler was furious. He now rejected totally Ribbentrop's anti-British and pro-Russian foreign policy and opted for war with Russia, to be followed by maritime victory over Great Britain and finally by a policy of "throw down the gauntlet" to America.[49] These diplomatic rebuffs also effectively finished Raeder's strategic alternative, the Mediterranean Sea proposal. Neither Vichy France nor Spain was prepared to provide major support for Germany — although Franco promised to provide one million volunteers if Berlin were ever attacked — and the negative results of the talks with Molotov decided Hitler to "solve" the "Russian question" the following spring by test of arms.

But the Führer had not forgotten the United States. On 29 October 1940 he informed his military leaders that he was most interested in the German plans to occupy the Atlantic islands "with an eye to the future war with America."[50] And on 14 November Hitler revealed for the first time the immediate short-term tactical reasons for his interest in these bases. "He saw in the Azores the only possibility for carrying out aerial attacks from a land base against the United States in order to force it to build up a large antiaircraft defense." The Führer's plan was simple: "to attack America, in case it entered the war, with a modern Messerschmidt [bomber] model with 12,600 km. range." This action would force the United States to "build up its nonexistent antiaircraft defense, instead of helping England in this matter." Hitler ordered "*immediate inquiry*" into harbor facilities on the Azores for the landing of airplane and heavy machinery parts. Admiral Raeder depicted the occupation as a "very risky operation, but which *can* succeed with luck."[51] He obviously was fascinated by the idea that the fleet of the "Z-Plan" would finally be given a place in German strategic calculations, and hence he raised no objections to this utterly fantastic scheme.* And while the strategic pos-

* There was one major flaw in Hitler's planning: in 1940–1941 Germany possessed only a few models of the Focke-Wulf 200C, the so-called Lufthansa four-engine "Condor" aircraft with a range of 2,500 miles, while the four-engine "Amerika-Bomber" (Messerschmidt Me 264), with a range of 9,000 miles and bomb load of

sibilities of the occupation of the Azores appealed to him, the admiral undoubtedly decided not to raise objections to the bomber tactics for fear of unnecessarily arousing his Führer's ire. Or did he perhaps for a fleeting moment believe that Hitler was about to accept his Mittelmeer proposal as a strategic alternative to the invasion of the Soviet Union?

A certain degree of resignation had probably overcome Admiral Raeder. The war at sea against Great Britain was failing. The United States aided that island empire with impunity. The Mediterranean concept was being scuttled without a fair hearing. And worst of all, "Führer is still inclined to pursue the struggle with Russia." In vain Raeder tried to get Hitler to agree to a "postponement until after the victory over England."[52] On 27 December 1940 the admiral again expressed "serious doubts against 'Barbarossa' before the defeat of England." But Hitler tolerated no interference from his naval commander in his plans for the Soviet Union:

> Generally speaking, the last continental opponent must be removed now under all possible circumstances due to current political developments (Russia's tendency to mix in Balkan affairs) [and] before it can come together with England. Therefore the army must receive the necessary strength. After that could result full concentration on air force and navy.

And it was precisely at this point, in November 1940, after his unsuccessful meeting with Molotov, that Hitler drew a long north-south border along the Ural Mountains on the large globe in his Berchtesgaden retreat.[53]

These discussions between Führer and admiral once again revealed the basic clash of strategy. There could be no doubt of the outcome: the next year would see a German blitz against the Soviet Union. It was expected to last several weeks and to be followed, after necessary armaments adjustments, by a concentrated aerial and naval assault on the two Anglo-Saxon maritime powers.

At this point one might well ask if Raeder's Mittelmeer concept was truly a viable alternative to the invasion of the Soviet Union. German

---

4,000 pounds, was first flown in December 1942; only one of these strategic bombers was ever built. Nor did Germany fare better with the Heinkel He 177, a four-engine bomber designed for a range of 3,400 miles with a payload of 13,200 pounds of bombs. Although 1,446 of these aircraft were built in three years, some fifty were lost during initial test flights, and only by January 1944 could even thirty-five be readied for an aerial assault against London. Generals Hans Jeschonnek and Ernst Udet had demanded that all German bombers be capable of steep dives, and hence precious years were wasted attempting to strengthen the He 177 sufficiently to absorb the great stress of high dives.

naval officers after 1945 stressed that it was. Some West German historians also see it as a realistic blueprint for victory over Great Britain.[54] Had the plan been implemented and had it succeeded, the Mediterranean Sea would have become an Axis lake. Great Britain's lifeline to India would have been severed and her Middle East oil supplies cut off. The Churchill government might have been toppled and Hitler could have negotiated his "understanding" with British leaders more sympathetic to his cause. On the other hand, mounting adversity might simply have strengthened Britain's will to persevere. German seizure of the Atlantic islands would invariably have brought about a crucial confrontation — and possibly war — with the United States. To be sure, all this retrospective speculation hinges upon whether Germany and Italy possessed the necessary naval power and ability to dislodge the Royal Navy from the Mediterranean Sea. But are these the right questions for historians to ask? Or is it not a classic case of putting the cart before the horse? For Hitler, and not Raeder, was responsible for Germany's military strategy and, ultimately, her fate.

Adolf Hitler had combined in his person as Führer the offices of chancellor and president of the German Reich; he was the supreme commander of all her armed forces; and after January 1939 the actual military chief of the three branches of the armed services. It was from this position of strength that he had imparted to his admirals and generals time and again his unbending will to crush the Soviet Union. In July 1940 he had informed them of the precise moment for the execution of this policy: spring 1941. In view of these facts, should it not have been Admiral Raeder's sole endeavor to coordinate naval planning with this massive and decisive undertaking? Instead, the admiral chased his elusive dream of Germany's naval control of the Mediterranean Sea and the Atlantic Ocean at a time when some 150 divisions were being assembled on her eastern border and her industry geared for army production. With criminal folly Führer and admiral pursued their separate policies independent of one another. In the end, Raeder succeeded only in whetting Hitler's appetite for the Atlantic islands and distracting him from his announced objective. Jost Dülffer, a West German historian, has squarely hit the mark: "There is no evidence to show that he [Raeder] even discerned Hitler's territorial goals in East Europe, or that he pondered over their implications for his naval program."[55]

More concrete and mundane matters also weighed heavily upon Admiral Raeder. He found the seaworthiness of his ships to be "shocking": during the first year of the war, the capital ships were at the front only 54 percent of the time and the protective destroyers a mere 40.3 percent. Mechanical breakdowns occurred with alarming frequency, while the specified cruising ranges for the ships fell far short of contract stipulations. The capital ships generally were one thousand sea miles short of expectation (*Gneisenau* 6,200 instead of 8,200); the heavy cruiser *Admiral Hipper* could traverse 4,430 sea miles and not the specified 7,900; the destroyers ranged between 1,800 and 2,400 sea miles, not the required 3,400.[56]

This notwithstanding, Raeder was anxious for renewed surface activity in the North Atlantic with an eye towards severing Britain's vital supply lines to America. He launched the second phase of the Atlantic surface war by dispatching *Admiral Scheer* on 23 October 1940 and *Admiral Hipper* on 27 November; the former scored a success against Convoy "HX 84," while the latter on 14 February 1941 put into Brest with only minor gains. Admiral Lütjens, fleet chief, on 28 December 1940 took Naval Group North (*Gneisenau* and *Scharnhorst*) out to sea in the first sortie of German capital ships into the Atlantic. But once again mechanical breakdowns set in and he docked in Trondheim only two days later. Undaunted, on 22 January 1941 Lütjens put out to sea once more, this time for two months. Operation Berlin was designed primarily to interrupt British maritime commerce and the admiral was ordered not to risk the two ships in engagements with heavy enemy escorts. Lütjens met with success, managing to elude the superior British Home Fleet and to sink 115,622 tons of enemy shipping.[57]

But the spring of 1941 was not a happy one for the German navy. Brest, where it hoped to base its capital ships, was heavily bombed by the British Royal Air Force on 5 February and again on 11 April. The battle cruiser *Gneisenau* on 6 April 1941 received still another torpedo hit and was once again immobilized. As a result, in April both *Admiral Scheer* and *Admiral Hipper* were recalled to Kiel in the Baltic Sea, thereby inaugurating the "strategic withdrawal" of the German fleet from its advanced bases on the Atlantic. Yet Raeder, ever mindful of the inactivity and inglorious end of the High Sea Fleet in 1914–1918, yearned for renewed surface action, and on 2 April began to lay plans for Operation Rheinübung, designed, like Operation Berlin, to interdict British shipping in the North Atlantic. The newly completed battleship *Bismarck* and heavy cruiser *Prinz Eugen* on 21 May 1941 left Gdingen (Gdynia) in the Baltic amidst the tones of folk music. Their fate is well known: on 27 May forces of the British Home Fleet and Force H (which had been at Oran) destroyed the most modern battleship in existence four hundred sea miles west of Brest, but not until *Bismarck* had demolished the battle cruiser *Hood* and damaged the battleship *Prince of Wales; Prinz Eugen* escaped and steamed to Brest, where she arrived on 1 June 1941.[58]

The loss of the *Bismarck* constituted a serious blow to Raeder's "double-pole" surface strategy. The day after she went down, the admiral deemed it "necessary to operate carefully now, as the German navy with its limited matériel cannot afford to lose any more surface units." The outcome of Operation Rheinübung in effect meant the end of all major surface activity until at least the fall of 1941. Moreover, Raeder had to replace Lütjens and his staff, lost with the *Bismarck*. Admiral Schniewind became the new fleet chief, and Vice Admiral Fricke replaced Schniewind as chief of staff of the Naval War Staff (Seekriegsleitung). Two new posts were also created: Vice Admiral Otto Ciliax became Commander of Capital Ships, and Vice Admiral Hubert Schmundt Commander of Cruisers. All hopes for surface raids into the Atlantic were dashed on 13 June, however, when the pocket battleship *Lützow* (ex *Deutschland*) was torpedoed; it was now calculated that the next sizable operation by surface vessels would have to wait until the end of January 1942.[59]

Nor did the submarine war provide sufficient compensation in 1940–1941 to offset these setbacks for the fleet. The German naval planners had in 1939 estimated that Great Britain possessed about 17 million tons of shipping and the United States an equal amount. By 1941 America had raised its merchant fleet to 27 million tons and the Germans — true to the Tirpitzean concept that the two Anglo-Saxon powers formed one indivisible bloc — lamented late in 1941 that the war had therefore actually brought an increase in shipping for Britain! As the United Kingdom required 50 million tons of imports annually, German naval planners in 1941 reasoned that U-boats would have to destroy no less than 800,000 to 1 million tons of shipping per month to curtail Britain's overseas trade and force her to the peace table. But this figure had not been reached with any regularity even during the summer of 1917, and sinkings in 1941 had risen from a paltry 92,702 tons in January to a high of about 300,000 tons in June; thereafter they declined again. And with the enormous demands made upon German industry by the army during the campaigns against Poland, the Low Countries and France, and the planned offensive against Russia as well as the continued construction since 1939 of surface vessels (*Bismarck*, *Tirpitz*, *Prinz Eugen*, and others), there remained little war material for U-boat construction. Rear Admiral Dönitz, who summed up the war at sea with the key words "*kill*" and "sink and burn!," had asked for twenty-nine new submarines per month, but in reality received in 1941 an average of fifteen per month. And even though losses remained low, at around 5 percent, in November 1941 there were still only eighty-four U-boats available.[60]

## Roosevelt Acts (1940)

While Adolf Hitler toyed with plans to seize the Atlantic islands, President Roosevelt had not been idle. His anti-Axis stance found support in a lively debate in the press concerning especially Hitler's ambitions in South America. The spirit of Senator Lodge and Admiral Dewey was not dead. As early as April 1938 Representative John J. McGrath of California had brought the attention of Admiral William D. Leahy, chief of Naval Operations, to the danger of German settlements in Brazil.[61] Two years later William L. Shirer reminded the American public that Germany posed a direct threat to the Americas. She might defeat the United States Navy, occupy Iceland, Greenland, Labrador, and Newfoundland, and thereafter advance against the American mainland. Or she might push off from Dakar for Argentina and Brazil.[62] Moreover, rumors ran rampant in the United States that Uruguay was about to come under the domination of local National Socialist groups. And other journalists, such as Edgar Ansel Mowrer and William Donovan, warned that Hitler might cripple the United States with the aid of a well-organized fifth column movement in America.[63] The American public was not immune to this cautionary rhetoric. A *Fortune* survey in July 1940 showed that 63 percent of those polled believed that German victory in Europe would be followed by an attempt to set foot in the Western Hemisphere. Worse yet, 43 percent expected a direct Axis attack on the United States.[64]*

But the mood of the country was isolationist. Consequently the President had to prepare slowly for a war he was sure the United States could not avoid. Though he hoped to the end to give support and avoid full engagement, Roosevelt nevertheless recognized that the total defeat of the antifascist nations of Europe would overthrow the balance of power and ultimately force the United States to come to grips with the newly created "Super Germany." Therefore, control of the world's major maritime arteries was of paramount importance. Roosevelt had amended the Neutrality Act in November 1939 to repeal the arms embargo and to make war materials available to belligerents on a cash-and-carry basis. The British Royal Navy ensured that only Great Britain could take advantage of this act. On 19 July 1940 the President signed the Two-Ocean Navy Expansion Act, which was to prepare the United States Navy for a two-flank war. Some 1,325,000 tons of warships,

* Some American generals also wanted to occupy Trinidad in order to head off the expected German move into South America. See Mark Skinner Watson *Chief of Staff: Prewar Plans and Preparations* (Washington 1950).

100,000 tons of auxiliary ships, and 1,500 naval airplanes were ordered for what was already the largest fleet in the world. This act, above all, demonstrated recognition of the fact that the survival of Great Britain was vital to the security of the United States. It was a suitable answer to the German naval plans presented to Hitler by Admiral Raeder on 11 July 1940. On 9 September the United States Navy placed under contract the construction of 210 warships, including seven battleships and twelve aircraft carriers. Here was the recognition by American naval planners that carriers and naval airplanes were the new backbone of the modern navy.

President Roosevelt also had to be acutely aware of developments in the Far East. The Japanese had by February 1931 overrun Manchuria and created the satellite state of Manchukuo; two years later Japan, along with Hitler Germany, withdrew from the League of Nations. Aggression was now given free rein. Premier Konoe Fumimaro in July 1937 opted for war with China, and Roosevelt's 1939 "moral embargo" speech did little to curb Japan's appetite because it left iron and oil shipments open. Chiang Kai-shek's forces were pushed back by the Japanese but not broken: Shantung province fell, Inner Mongolia was invaded, and most of China's important ports and major cities, including Canton, Hankow, Nanking, Peking, Shanghai, and Tientsin, fell to Emperor Hirohito's army by 1940. As Hitler was completing his triumphs in western Europe, Japan in the summer of 1940 moved into French Indochina and later that year joined Germany and Italy in the Tripartite Pact. Once again a limited ban on goods moving to Japan had little effect, and in April 1941, while Hitler was overrunning Greece and Yugoslavia, Japan concluded a nonaggression pact with Russia, which gave her a free hand to advance southwest against French, Dutch and British colonies. This strategy, mapped out by Foreign Minister Yosuke Matsuoka, was designed to realize Premier Konoe's Greater East Asia Co-prosperity Sphere. The United States, Great Britain and the Netherlands reacted to the Japanese advance into south Indochina in the summer of 1941 with a total embargo on all exports — especially vital supplies of iron, oil and rubber — to Japan. The latter now calculated that she could withstand such a blockade for only two years, and decided in September 1941 to break what her leaders called the ABCD (American, British, Chinese, Dutch) encirclement, by force if necessary. In General Hideki Tojo, Japan found a willing premier in October 1941.

Given these threatening developments in Europe and the Far East, Roosevelt inaugurated political discussions with Great Britain in 1941. The United States was, in fact, beginning to abandon strict neutrality for "nonbelligerency." On 29 January 1941 she opened talks with London designed to establish general guidelines for her possible entry into the war. On 11 March the United States alleviated Great Britain's financial crisis by extending aid under the Lend-Lease Act. Roosevelt introduced this bill with the homely analogy that in case of fire one lent his neighbor a fire hose without payment and asked only that the hose be returned after the fire had been put out. Senator Robert A. Taft countered for the isolationists with the argument that "lending war equipment is a good deal like lending chewing gum. You don't want it back."[65] In any case, the President announced that this measure meant "the end of compromise with tyranny." Sixteen days later staff talks produced the so-called ABC-1 Staff Agreement, which committed the United States to a "Europe first" strategy in the event that it became involved in warfare both in Europe and in Asia. Material adjustments brought further succor to beleaguered Britain. On 1 March the United States created the Support Force Atlantic Fleet, consisting of three destroyer flotillas to aid convoy duty. And on 18 April 1941 Admiral Ernest J. King, commander-in-chief of the United States Atlantic Fleet — acting in accordance with Roosevelt's declaration in July 1940 at the Pan-American Conference in Havana that the United States held herself responsible for the defense of the Western Hemisphere — through Operation Plan No. 3 drew a line of demarcation through the Atlantic Ocean. Hereby Greenland, the Azores, the Gulf of St. Lawrence, and the Caribbean Sea were declared war zones for "naval ships or aircraft of belligerents" such as Germany and Italy.[66] Each of these steps effectively crossed the strategic plans of the German Naval War Staff.

German naval leaders took note of these developments. Admiral Raeder was now fully convinced that the entry of the United States into the war on the British side was only a question of time. He began to press Hitler in the spring of 1941 for war with the United States "in order to achieve successes during this phase of relative weakness of the USA." These successes, "while not preventing the effective direct intervention of the United States in the European war, might, nevertheless, delay it."[67] Raeder especially desired such German successes before Roosevelt could create the fleet laid down in the Two-Ocean Navy Expansion Act. The official war diary of the German navy reveals the growing conviction in German naval circles that war with the United States was imminent. Lend-Lease was equated with "entry of the United States into the war." Churchill ceased to be the primary adversary. "Roosevelt is ever more becoming the antipode of Hitler." And the German naval attaché in Washington reported that the United States was now willing to abandon neutrality because of the influence upon American policy of "England and the Jewish, interventionist clique."[68] Ambassador Dieckhoff assured the Foreign Office that Lend-Lease was ineffective and merely a propagandistic venture.[69]

Whatever he may have thought about such views, Admiral Raeder believed that he possessed sufficient counterbalance to American naval power even if Hitler persisted in heading east before the final defeat of Great Britain. Japan was the key. Here Raeder's strategic concepts again ran tangent to those of the Führer. By striking at the Soviet Union, Hitler hoped to free Japan's back, thereby allowing her to take the offensive against the United States in the Pacific and divide the American war effort between two fronts. Raeder agreed:

> Should America's entry into the war on the side of England be brought about by such an initiative on Japan's part, then this would have to be accepted into the bargain because, as far as the navy is concerned, the sum of advantages outweighs that of disadvantages.[70]

Dizzying successes in western Europe caused Hitler briefly to abandon his usual cautious approach towards the United States. On 20 January 1941 he boasted to Benito Mussolini: "From America, even if it enters the war, I do not see any great danger."[71] The Führer assured the Japanese ambassador, Saburo Kurusu, on 3 February that Germany and the United States would remain enemies for at least one or two centuries.[72] On 14 April 1941 Hitler received the Japanese foreign minister, Yosuke Matsuoka, in Berlin. The latter inquired whether Germany could provide Japan with war materials in the event of a Japanese-American war:

> The Führer agreed to this and further pointed out that Germany also did not desire a conflict with the United States, but that it had figured it into its calculations . . . Germany had made its preparations so that no American could land in Europe. It would lead an energetic struggle against America with its U-boats and its air force.

Was the latter part of this statement alluding to his plan to send long-range bombers from the Azores against American cities? Hitler, going far beyond the requirements of the Tripartite Pact of 27 September 1940, the purpose of which had been primarily to keep the United States out of the present war by threatening it with a two-front war, assured Matsuoka that Germany would declare war immediately in case of a Japanese-American conflict, regardless of who started it.[73]* Foreign Minister von Ribbentrop was also active in the attempt to involve the

* Article 3 of the Tripartite Pact called for mutual assistance "with all . . . military means" only in the event of an American *attack* on one of the three Axis partners.

Japanese with the United States. Failure to fight the United States now in union with Germany, he argued, would isolate Japan against this "awesome Anglo-Saxon coalition" in the future.[74]

While the Führer and his admirals were mulling over the possible global ramifications of their strategic alternatives, German armies were busily subjecting the rest of Europe to Hitler's rule. In February 1941 the first units of General Erwin Rommel's Afrika Korps landed in Tripoli. The following month Operation Marita was launched; Yugoslavia capitulated on 17 March and Greece fell four days later. The island of Crete (Operation Merkur) was taken by paratroops on 1 June 1941. The German navy once again stood by while the Wehrmacht and the Luftwaffe earned their spurs. The greater part of Raeder's forces were tied down in Norway or in repair docks; *Admiral Graf Spee* and *Bismarck* rested on the bottom of the Atlantic Ocean. The commander-in-chief of the German navy now reluctantly resigned himself to Operation Barbarossa, the destruction of the Soviet Union.[75] And the plans for this undertaking indicated that the navy would receive a purely defensive task: to lay a mine belt across the harbor at Kronstadt in order to prevent Soviet vessels from escaping into the Baltic Sea and thereby threatening German fleet bases at Kiel and Gdynia.

With the hope that a Japanese-American conflict was in the making, Hitler directed the attention of his naval leaders once more towards the occupation of the Atlantic islands. On 22 May 1941 he brought up the occupation of the Azores in a most startling manner. "*Führer seeks the occupation in order to deploy long-range bombers against the United States*" (italics in the original). The sweet spring air of the Bavarian Alps must have exercised an intoxicating effect upon the Führer: he intended to let loose this aerial strike already in the fall of 1941.* To Raeder's interjection that Great Britain must first be defeated, the Führer replied evasively "that for the summer of 1941 the destruction of England-bound commerce must remain in the foreground for the navy."[76] In fact, Adolf Hitler had other more vital and far-reaching plans in mind.

The center of gravity of Hitler's plans, of course, was the invasion of the Soviet Union. Here was the Gordian knot which, when severed, would allow him freely to launch his *Weltblitzkrieg*. On 6 June 1941 he outlined the importance of Operation Barbarossa to Admiral Raeder:

Führer delivers explanations regarding his interpretation of the development of the situation in England and the influence of "Barbarossa" on same. Situa-

* The German air force plan to attack the United States in April 1942, recently discovered by an East German historian (see page 241), probably resulted from this decision.

tion in England is bad at this time. Collapse could result rapidly. Mid-July at the latest he could perceive the success of "Barbarossa" and its probable effect on the *overall situation.* [Italics in the original.][77]

On the day preceding the invasion of the Soviet Union, Hitler again instructed the navy to "avoid *every* incident with the United States until 'Barbarossa' unfolded itself. After a few weeks the situation would be cleared up" (italics in the original).[78]* The invasion, on 22 June 1941, the last major military campaign of the first phase of Hitler's overall program, was to culminate in a kind of *Weltblitzkrieg* in the Eastern Hemisphere with the following aims: (1) defeat of the Soviet Union in three or four months; (2) followed by a three-pronged attack via the Caucasus into Iran, via Bulgaria and Turkey into Syria and Iraq, and via Libya into Egypt, all resulting in the creation of a German Afghanistan directly threatening the British in India; (3) a Japanese offensive threatening India from the southeast, thereby avoiding the Philippines and resulting American involvement in the war; and (4) conquest of Gibraltar and northwest Africa "with offensive stance against America."[79] In this manner the war would lose its character of localized military campaigns and for the first time take on truly global dimensions. All of these plans were based on Hitler's precondition "that we must solve all continental European problems in 1941 because the USA will, by 1942, be in a position to intervene."[80]

In the predawn hours of 22 June 1941, almost 2 million German soldiers invaded the Soviet Union. Hermann Göring's Luftwaffe placed 2,770 aircraft, including 775 level and 310 dive bombers, in the field. Air Squadron 1, based in East Prussia, was deployed against Lithuania, Latvia and Estonia; Air Squadron 2 provided support for Army Group Center driving for Smolensk; and Air Squadron 4 was attached to Army Group South in a broad drive to the east from the Pripet Marshes to Romania. Both Generals Erhard Milch and Hans Jeschonnek had joined Göring earlier in an appeal to Hitler that Operation Barbarossa be postponed at least until some time after the fall of Britain. Milch and Jeschonnek were

* Hitler was not alone in this optimistic estimate. The initial operations plan against the Soviet Union, drawn up on 5 August 1940 by General Erich Marcks, predicted the defeat of the USSR and a German occupation as far as the Don–Central Volga line in nine weeks at best, at worst in seventeen. See Andreas Hillgruber *Deutschlands Rolle in der Vorgeschichte der beiden Weltkriege* (Göttingen 1967), 105. The navy accepted this army estimate at face value and incorporated it into its war diary on 30 December 1939, thereby showing that already at this early juncture it was not ignorant of the Führer's plans in the east (Bundesarchiv-Militärarchiv, Freiburg im Breisgau, West Germany, PG 32024 Case 104, p. 140). Hitler had cautioned Raeder against provoking incidents at sea with American ships as early as May 1941.

acutely aware that production of General Walther Wever's special "Ural" bombers had not progressed as planned, and the air force leaders above all wanted to avoid a two-front war after the heavy losses over Britain in 1940–1941.[81]

Admiral Raeder and the German navy shared this stance. The navy commander-in-chief had been apprised of the plan to attack Russia at least by July 1940, and in August that year Hitler had clearly pointed out to Raeder the danger he saw posed by Russia to German-occupied Norway. But the Führer cleverly assured Raeder that the war against Britain would remain the "primary" front at all times: "The focal point of naval operations will clearly be England — even during a campaign in the east." In addition to the aforementioned mining of Kronstadt harbor, the German navy — as in 1914–1918 — had to safeguard the transport of iron ore from Scandinavia to Germany's Baltic seaports, to secure the harbors of Gdingen (Gdynia) and Kiel against enemy raids, and to attempt small-scale sorties against Russian coastal positions in order to support major army operations in the Baltic states. The Soviet Baltic Sea fleet was not considered a formidable force, and Raeder hoped — as German admirals and generals had in 1917–1918 — that parts of it might eventually fall into his hands. "We can hope to obtain a large part of the Russian naval forces in more or less undamaged condition."[82]

The Naval War Staff was accordingly not overly concerned about Hitler's orders for Operation Barbarossa, and instead saw the Führer's Directive No. 32 of 11 June 1941 as the key to its conduct of the war. Entitled "Preparations for the Period after Barbarossa," the document depicted the war against the Soviet Union as only a temporary diversion from the struggle against Britain, and promised future armaments concentration on the navy ("Z-Plan") and the air force. The fall of European Russia would be followed by closer cooperation with Vichy France, especially in Africa against "Anglo-Saxon encroachments," and a German assault against British positions in the Mediterranean Sea and the Middle East. The Führer here had in mind a spearhead from Libya through Egypt and another from Bulgaria through Turkey, as well as a possible drive from the Caucasus into Iran. Operation Felix would be set in motion at the same time so that the western entrance to the Mediterranean Sea (Gibraltar) would be closed to Britain. And most important of all, Directive No. 32 once again assured Raeder that the Russian campaign remained merely a "secondary" operation. "Beside these possible operations against the British positions in the Mediterranean, the 'blockade of England' must, after completion of the eastern campaign, be renewed in full force by navy and air force." Here was the *raison d'être* of the "Z" fleet as well as the navy's apparently lackadaisical handling of the eastern campaign. But, as Michael Salewski has pointed out, the events of 22 June 1941 and 27 May 1941 (the sinking of the *Bismarck*) virtually ended all German surface operations against the "real enemy" Great Britain, and provided the latter with a much needed breathing spell.[83]

Initial German victories in the Soviet Union surpassed even Hitler's expectations. On 9 July he informed Raeder that naval armaments could already proceed at full speed; five days later the Führer officially shifted the emphasis in Germany's armaments production to the navy (U-boats) and the air force (Göring program).[84] At the same time Hitler again reminded Raeder "that it is all-important to him that the entry of the United States into the war be prevented for one to two months."[85] Confident of victory in the east in the near future, Hitler received the new Japanese ambassador, General Hiroshi Oshima, on 14 July 1941 at the Führer's East Prussia headquarters, the Wolfsschanze (Wolf's Lair) near Rastenburg. Adolf Hitler pontificated upon the future of the world amidst the sandy soil and scrub pine forests of East Prussia. He was unaware of the Japanese decision of 2 July 1941 to expand in the direction of the southeast rather than to invade the eastern Soviet Union, and hence he still counted upon a German-Japanese meeting in the winter of 1941 somewhere in Siberia. Under this fateful illusion Hitler gave the clearest definition to date of his ultimate plans concerning the United States. For one brief moment abandoning his original timetable, he urged that the two partners proceed against the United States across two oceans in his own lifetime:

> America is pressing with its new imperialist spirit sometimes into the European, sometimes into the Asian *Lebensraum.* Regarded from our point of view, Russia threatens in the East, America in the West; from Japan's point of view, in the West Russia, in the East America. Therefore he [Hitler] is of the opinion that we must jointly annihilate them. There are tasks in the lives of peoples that are hard. One cannot solve these tasks by closing one's self to them or by abandoning them until a future time.*

Now was the time to strike: "The Russian war has been won." Hitler closed the interview by stressing once again that:

> . . . if one must fight against the United States, then this should also occur under his leadership. He finds the idea of postponing something that can be

* In quotations from the "Führer Conferences" between Hitler and Raeder and from the diary of the Naval War Staff, Hitler appears to refer to himself in the third person because the records were kept in this manner by Captain Heinz Assmann, nephew of Vice Admiral Kurt Assmann in the war-technical division of the navy.

accomplished now cowardly. Every generation has the duty of relieving its children of that which can be done now.[86]

Thus flushed with spectacular successes in the east, Hitler temporarily abandoned his erstwhile cautious stance vis-à-vis the United States and joined his admirals in advocating the necessity of a German-American conflict.

## On the Brink (1941)

Though he obviously could not know of these considerations, Franklin D. Roosevelt was again taking all possible measures to thwart German plans regarding the United States. In fact, the United States was fast abandoning "nonbelligerency" in favor of a stage of "undeclared war." On 24 March 1941 Roosevelt allowed Great Britain to repair her vessels in United States ports, and six days later he ordered all German and Italian shipping in U.S. harbors seized. On 10–11 April the American Defense Zone was extended to the east coast of Greenland and to the Azores. Argentia, Newfoundland, formally became a United States base on 15 May, and by 1 June the United States Coast Guard set up the South Greenland Patrol with four warships. One month later the United States initiated aerial patrols of the northwest Atlantic from its base in Argentia. Roosevelt's most important decision, however, was the American relief of British forces on Iceland by the 1st Brigade of the United States Marine Corps, and the occupation of Greenland on 7 July 1941 through U.S. Task Force 19, consisting of four battleships, thirteen destroyers, and eight supply ships. And on 1 September 1941 the United States Navy was authorized to escort ships of any nation across the Atlantic, and Roosevelt committed two battleships, two heavy cruisers, and thirteen destroyers to the Denmark Strait Patrol.[87]* Thus Roosevelt dispatched to the patrol of these northern waters a force far greater than the entire German surface fleet. The Icelanders were not involved in this international naval chess play; nobody bothered to solicit their opinion, which was probably just as well for the United States because many of the natives sympathized with Hitler and his Nordic ideology. In any case, the United States was now virtually, even if not officially,

* Mexico, Costa Rica, Venezuela, Peru, and Ecuador also seized German ships in their ports. Germany estimated that it lost 12 ships (60,000 tons) in this manner. See Bundesarchiv-Militärarchiv, Freiburg im Breisgau, West Germany, PG 32123 Case 193, I SKL, Teil B VII, Handelsschiffahrt, 101, 107.

at war with Germany; because of the American naval bridge from Newfoundland via Greenland and Iceland to Great Britain, Germany's Atlantic naval strategy was effectively checkmated.

Admiral Raeder fully appreciated the significance of the American occupation of Iceland. Psychologically, it erased the initial exuberance of the German navy over early successes scored in the Soviet Union.[88]* Raeder's staff equated the American action with a declaration of war against Germany, arguing that this was merely the first step toward the occupation of the Azores, Dakar, and the Cape Verdes. Possibly North Africa would also come under American control. The "Battle of the Atlantic" would thereby be lost for Germany. The naval staff demanded "*immediate armed assault on all USA ships within our publicly proclaimed war zone*" (italics in the original), in short, war with the United States.[89] Fleet command now drafted operations plans for an "official" war with the United States. On 9 July 1941 Admiral Raeder asked the Führer for a declaration of war against the United States.[90] But Hitler was not to be swayed on this matter. He again reminded Raeder that he did not want to provoke the United States during the campaign in the east.[91] And on 14 July the Führer explained his stance on the American occupation of Iceland to Ambassador Oshima:

> We cannot get around the reckoning with America. One should not think that he has accepted the American occupation of Iceland because he is not acting at this moment. . . . If he, the Führer, is silent at this moment regarding Iceland, this does not mean that he has given it up. The Americans would have to get out, even if he would have to fight for years.[92]

On 25 July Hitler assured Admiral Raeder that the submarine war against the British Isles retained first priority. "Would only like to avoid that United States declares war during the eastern campaign." The time to settle accounts with the United States was not far off. "After the eastern campaign I reserve for myself the right to take severe action against the United States as well." If that country should become any more active in the European war, it would motivate the Führer to take further action: "As soon as the United States occupies Portuguese or

* The naval staff telegraphed its enthusiasm over the attack on the Soviet Union to all its Atlantic forces on 26 June. European solidarity, expressed in an anti-Bolshevik front, had gripped especially Germany, Italy, Finland, Romania, and Slovakia; Sweden and Turkey would soon follow suit. The reaction of the Vatican was "positive" and the isolationists in the United States were strengthened by this move. American Catholics especially, the navy argued, favored Hitler's attack on the Soviet Union. Bundesarchiv-Militärarchiv, Freiburg im Breisgau, West Germany, PG 32224 Case 276, I SKL, Teil C XVII, Besondere Fragen USA und Kriegführung gegen USA.

Spanish islands, I will march into Spain. From there I will bring tank and infantry divisions into North Africa in order to secure this [area]."[93] But, as we have seen, the German navy was perfectly unable, or unwilling, to understand the pivotal role that the Soviet Union assumed in Hitler's calculations. Raeder now began to doubt whether Hitler took the war at sea at all seriously.[94]

Civilian circles in Germany also castigated the American action in Iceland. The official National Socialist *Völkischer Beobachter* ran the following headline story: "Invasion of Iceland. Roosevelt provokes war. Stab-in-the-back attempt by the American President against Europe. Arm-in-arm with Bolshevik mass murderers." The paper claimed that Roosevelt had thereby irrevocably torn up the Monroe Doctrine.[95] Germany's diplomatic and military representatives in Washington were equally outraged. They saw the Iceland operation as the prelude to the creation of an American "blockade ring" girdling Europe. Chargé d'affaires Hans Thomsen and General von Boetticher reported that the Americans were hopelessly lost in "primitive strategic considerations," fantasy, and empty rhetoric. "They do not have the slightest idea of how to ease the German *threat* in the Atlantic during the German-Russian war" (italics in the original).[96] Nothing could better demonstrate their total lack of contact with reality.

Roosevelt's move into Iceland caused yet another division of opinion between the Führer and his admirals. Raeder now actively encouraged rapprochement with Vichy France, claiming that only with French naval support could Germany hope to carry on the Battle of the Atlantic and sever the lifeline between the United States and Great Britain.[97] The admiral's staff continued to stress that this was primarily an economic struggle, and it regarded Germany as the only block to American economic domination of the world.[98] Vulgar Marxist economic theories continued to blend with National Socialist racist ideology to produce the navy's evaluation of the Battle of the Atlantic. The "capitalist, imperialist robber economy of the United States," a cliché common to both Marxist and National Socialist rhetoric, threatened to enslave Europe. Hence only war with the United States could assure the survival of German-dominated Europe.[99] Time was with the Americans because of their vast industrial and manpower resources. The time to strike was now, before the United States could mobilize her vast war potential. The argument was not new. Germany had heard it throughout the Great War of 1914–1918. The economic "theories" of Hitler's admirals were deeply rooted in the Wilhelmian era.

Hitler, in turn, proved willing to grant his naval officers the *Stützpunkte* they had sought in the First World War: the entire Baltic region with the ports of Libau (Liepaja) and Reval (Tallin), and the French Channel ports and islands.[100] But he was not about to call on the French for help. The Führer still hoped to reach an "understanding" with Great Britain, and France with her colonial empire was the lure in that proposition. On 22 July 1941 Hitler expressed his conviction "that the end of this war will be the start of a permanent friendship with England."[101] And as late as December 1941 General Franz Halder noted: "Führer apparently still hopes to come to terms with England at France's expense."[102] In short, while the navy wanted to obtain bases at Bizerta, El Ferrol, Cadiz, Gibraltar, Casablanca, and Dakar[103] in order to challenge the Anglo-Saxon maritime powers for control of the Atlantic, Hitler continued to pursue his policy of coming to terms with Great Britain with the distant prospect of a subsequent Anglo-German offensive against the United States.*

By August 1941, however, the eastern campaign began to bog down. As a result, Hitler's optimistic utterances concerning the war against the United States disappeared. The plans for the immediate conquest of Gibraltar, northwest Africa, and the Atlantic islands (Operation Felix) were given up.† The Führer returned to his original timetable:

> I will not live to see it, but I am happy for the German *Volk* that it will one day witness how Germany and England united will line up against America. Germany and England will know what one has to expect from the other. And we will then have found the proper ally.[104]

On 25 October 1941 Hitler repeated the same point of view to the Italian foreign minister, Count Galeazzo Ciano:

> A future generation will have to occupy itself with the problem Europe-America. Then it will no longer be a matter of Germany or England, of fascism, national socialism, or opposite systems, but of the common interests of all of Europe within the European economic community with its African supplements.

A united Europe of 500 million Europeans would have to take up the struggle against 230 million Americans, of whom only some 60 million were Anglo-Saxons. "Hence the future will not belong to the ridiculous,

* Hitler abandoned his plans temporarily on 9 December 1941, arguing that France might prove an expedient ally against the United States for the moment. See Franz Halder *Kriegstagebuch* (Stuttgart 1962–1964), III, 337.

† Operation Felix was canceled by the military after Hitler's abortive attempt to bring Spain into the war during his meeting with Franco at Hendaye on 23 October 1940.

half-cultivated America, but to the resurrected Europe." History and tradition militated against American victory. "The older culture and the superior intellectual niveau of Europe would, in the end, emerge victorious."[105] Here was the complete return to Hitler's original program.

But Adolf Hitler was no longer the *arbiter mundi* that he still imagined himself to be. The initiative had slipped from his hands. From 10 to 15 August 1941 the British prime minister, Winston Churchill, met with President Roosevelt in Placentia Bay, Newfoundland. The outcome of this meeting was the Atlantic Charter, in which the two countries announced that in victory they sought no new territory, but the destruction of National Socialism in Europe. The two leaders further advocated an international organization to resolve future disputes at the conference table, and they agreed to strive for an equitable distribution of the world's wealth. Finally, to show the parallel with the First World War and President Woodrow Wilson's Fourteen Points, they proclaimed the right of self-determination to all nations and peoples. American material assistance to Great Britain began to increase significantly; on 27 August 1941 the first fourteen Liberty ships were launched, and a further 312, representing some 2.2 million tons, had been ordered. The "arsenal of democracy" was now virtually in a state of war with Germany.*

The Battle of the Atlantic also helped to draw the United States and Great Britain closer together. On 4 September the German submarine U-652 unsuccessfully tried to torpedo the American escort destroyer U.S.S. *Greer*, which had attempted to depth-charge the U-boat south of Ireland. Seven days later Roosevelt answered with his famous "shoot-on-sight order" against all Axis shipping in sea lanes "the protection of which is necessary for American defense." German and Italian ships were warned that they entered the American Defense Zone "at their own peril." The American decision on 1 September to escort merchant shipping across the Atlantic militated against peaceful relations with Germany on the high seas, and on 17 October the U.S.S. *Kearny* was damaged by a torpedo while escorting Convoy S.C. 48. Two weeks later the U.S.S. *Reuben James* was destroyed while acting as escort for Convoy H.X. 156; with her loss came the first casualties for the United States Navy in the Second World War. And on 7 and 11 November 1941 the American neutrality laws were altered to allow United States ships to be armed and to enter the German war zones around the British Isles.[106]

* In fact, Roosevelt was so anxious to bring the United States into the war that he resorted to a cheap propaganda trick. On 27 October he revealed the existence of a captured German map that supposedly showed that Germany would in the future set up five vassal states in South America and Central America. He was never able to produce the map for public inspection. Franklin D. Roosevelt *Public Papers and Addresses* (New York 1950), 1941 volume, pp. 439ff.

German naval leaders were hardly surprised by these developments — America's activity merely verified the navy's claim that Great Britain and the United States always had formed a joint interest group hostile to Germany. The navy's official war diary once more reflected the mood of Germany's admirals: they saw the Atlantic Charter as a "rough repetition of Wilson's Fourteen Points," Roosevelt's "shoot-on-sight order" as a "local, limited declaration of war," and the general expansion of American naval operations ("Azores, Cape Verdes, and Dakar") as the end not only of German surface raids in the Atlantic, but of dreams of African empire and of forcing Great Britain to the peace table through unrestricted submarine warfare.[107] "There no longer exists any difference between British and American ships."[108] Admiral Raeder's staff believed that Roosevelt could be forced to curtail his aggressive naval initiative only if met with equal force; strength and not concessions appealed to the American leader.[109] The same argument had, of course, been put forth once before, in 1916. Yet Raeder supported his staff's interpretation of United States naval policy as a "limited, local war," and he suggested that the only possible German reaction was to "answer each blatant act of war . . . with armed force." General Alfred Jodl offered Raeder his synopsis of how to handle the American menace: "One would have to draw a geographic line [through the Atlantic] and explain to the Americans that on one side of this line nothing would happen, but that on the other side they would risk the full dangers of war."[110] Of course, the United States had rejected precisely such a simplistic interpretation in the First World War—and ever since September 1939.

Seemingly handcuffed by Hitler's orders to avoid war with the United States during the Russian campaign* and by the American occupation of Greenland and Iceland, Germany's admirals decided to play their last trump: Japan. Rear Admiral Otto Groos and Vice Admiral Naokuni Nomura, head of the Japanese military mission to Germany, exchanged views on this matter throughout August 1941. The two men agreed that the Soviet Union and Great Britain would have to be defeated in the near future. "Then the Axis powers will be able to achieve peace and *prepare* themselves for a *future confrontation* with the *United States*" (italics in the original).[111] Admiral Raeder's staff felt confident in September that the Japanese would not reach agreement with the United States because they realized that "the conflict with the Anglo-Saxon powers cannot be avoided." German admirals regarded it as their

* Hitler cautioned Raeder again on 22 August against provoking "incidents" with United States ships. See Gerhard Wagner, ed. *Lagevorträge des Oberbefehlshabers der Kriegsmarine vor Hitler 1939–1945* (Munich 1972), 286. Admiral Karl Dönitz supported Hitler on this matter against Raeder. See ibid., 301.

duty to keep Japan aware of this fact so that she "will not miss her greatest historical moment."[112] Vice Admiral Kurt Fricke, Schniewind's successor as chief of staff of the Naval War Staff, went a step further. He openly encouraged Admiral Nomura to advise his government not to participate in the war against the Soviet Union (that is, attack Vladivostok) and to expand in the direction of Southeast Asia instead. Führer and admirals were once again working at cross purposes. Fricke reminded Nomura that Japan was "a nation of warriors" and that she was being tricked into inaction by "Anglo-Saxon bluff." Germany, on the other hand, was not fooled by "Anglo-Saxon bluff," but was transforming the Baltic and Black Seas into German "domestic lakes." The corner had been turned. "Russia's strength has already been broken." The admiral assured his Japanese colleague that Great Britain and the United States could never invade Europe. But time was working for the Americans. By 1945–1946 the United States would have her "two-ocean navy" and would then be able to meet and defeat each of the Axis powers in turn. The time to strike was now. Fricke urged the Japanese to provoke the United States at sea, fearing that Roosevelt could not be drawn into the "hot" war by "repeated incidents in the Atlantic or even engagements between American and German fleet units."[113] Foreign Minister von Ribbentrop seconded this initiative on 29 November by assuring Ambassador Oshima that a German-American war was unavoidable because "fundamental differences" existed between German and American vital interests.[114]

By late autumn 1941, then, Germany's naval planners were willing to accept the challenge of war with the United States. In October there was a final exchange of views between the Führer and his admirals concerning the war at sea against the United States. Hitler's special ambassador, Dr. Karl Ritter, visited the naval staff on 1 October 1941 only to be informed that the admirals were "dissatisfied" with the Führer's "overly cautious treatment of the United States." The Battle of the Atlantic was seriously impaired by Hitler's restrictions. The naval staff informed Ritter that Roosevelt would not declare war even if Germany torpedoed all shipping headed for the British Isles — again, an argument transplanted from the naval annals of 1916. Ritter, in turn, assured the admirals that the Führer only wanted to postpone the war with the United States until victory had been achieved in the east; this was expected in weeks. "Führer will later act according to the wishes of the navy."[115] And Hitler personally informed his admirals later that month that he was still looking for an "understanding" with Great Britain now that he had solved Germany's territorial needs in Europe.[116]

The German navy by the end of 1941 found itself in dire straits.

Surface "tip-and-run" operations in the Atlantic had virtually ceased since May–June 1941 in the wake of the loss of the *Bismarck* and torpedoing of the *Lützow*. And even though the battleship *Tirpitz* had finally joined the fleet, acute oil shortages in November 1941 led to a voluntary "temporary renunciation" of any future fleet sorties. On 5 November Raeder decided to dispatch the *Tirpitz* into the Arctic, an area that now became ever more a substitute for operations on the Atlantic; the battle cruisers *Gneisenau* and *Scharnhorst* were ordered to prepare for a possible departure from Brest to Norway or even home.[117] The navy obviously was completing its "strategic withdrawal" from the west, recognizing — albeit reluctantly — that continued fleet activity in the waters between Great Britain and the United States would result in further losses, as in the case of Operation Rheinübung. By December 1941 Admiral Raeder had to be aware that his fleet had lost initiative in the war at sea, and that he himself was almost in the position of the First World War naval chiefs, with a fleet unable to break through to the open Atlantic. In addition to the vastly superior British surface fleet, the Kriegsmarine had now to reckon with the entry of the United States Navy into the Atlantic in force in the very near future — if the events concerning the *Greer*, *Kearny* and *Reuben James* were at all indicative of things to come.

On 2 December 1941 the German navy monitored a rather curious British radio transmission. "A Japanese force of about sixteen vessels, including cruisers and aircraft carriers," was steaming on a southerly course past the Japanese Mandate islands* into the open Pacific.[118] And four days later the Kriegsmarine's war diary reported that the Battle of the Atlantic had become so intensive that a declaration of war between Germany and the United States remained only a formality.[119] In fact, events in the Pacific were soon to dictate the terms of the Battle of the Atlantic.

*The Mariana, Caroline and Marshall islands, formerly German possessions. Mandate over them was given to Japan by the League of Nations after the First World War.

NINE

# Germany and the United States at War (1941–1945)

> But my feelings against Americanism are feelings of hatred and deep repugnance. . . . Everything about the behavior of American society reveals that it's half Judaized, and the other half Negrified.
>
> — ADOLPH HITLER *January 1942*

THE JAPANESE ATTACK ON PEARL HARBOR ON 7 DECEMBER 1941 COMPLETELY surprised Hitler. That very morning he had still spoken about "achieving talks with England at the expense of France."[1] Upon hearing of the attack, the Führer reportedly "slapped his thighs, jumped to his feet as if electrified, and shouted 'Finally!' "[2] But world events had now progressed without Adolf Hitler. In a belated bid to regain the initiative, he rushed to Berlin and on 11 December 1941 declared war on the United States before a hastily assembled Reichstag. His speech was filled with all the vitriolic hatred that he could muster. There were the usual references to freemasons and Jews as the scourge of humanity, to the "plutocratic clique" that ruled the United States, to the fight against the Bolshevik and the "Anglo-Saxon, Jewish-capitalist world," and to Franklin D. Roosevelt and Woodrow Wilson, both "mentally ill."[3] Foreign Minister von Ribbentrop boasted: "A great power does not allow itself to be declared war on; it declares war itself."[4] Chargé d'affaires Hans Thomsen in Washington gloated that the United States had lost the military initiative in this war, and that Roosevelt's "date which will live in infamy" speech of 8 December showed once more that the American leader was totally inept as "Führer of a *nation*" (italics in the original).[5]

Hitler met the Japanese ambassador, Hiroshi Oshima, on 13 December 1941. The Führer had regained his composure and greeted his ally full of confidence. "You have given the proper declaration of war!" — a direct reference to the surprise attack on Pearl Harbor. The United States had deserved no better treatment. "The Japanese government has certainly not acted recklessly. It has, this he must admit, shown angelic patience towards this lout Roosevelt." Now the die was cast. "For Germany the entry of Japan [into the war] is a great relief."[6] Surely the racially inferior Americans would prove to be no major obstacle for the German and Japanese armed forces.

But what were Hitler's "real" motives* in declaring war on the United States at this point? He had counseled his naval leaders to utmost caution and restraint for two years; now he seemed lightheartedly to accept their advice. Certainly the decision was not freely arrived at; rather, it was the result of actions initiated by his eastern ally. In contrast to Hitler's other declarations of war, which usually came well after German troops had already invaded the country in question, this declaration remained unique in that it was the first given before hostilities commenced. When he declared war with Poland on 1 September 1939, Hitler's Wehrmacht had already violated that country's borders. The Führer's navy was steaming towards Norway and his army was across the Danish frontier on 7 April 1940, long before a declaration of war came from Berlin. The Low Countries and France experienced the German blitzkrieg on 10 May 1940, unaware of an official declaration of war. And the Soviet Union was invaded on 22 June 1941 without any official announcement of hostilities. The United States, therefore, proved to be the only exception to the Führer's pattern. And it was followed by no major action on Hitler's part. In short, it appeared totally out of character and tradition.

The Japanese offensive in the Pacific had indeed been a great relief to the German navy because it removed the fear — shared by Hitler as well as his admirals, even if somewhat unrealistically — of a Japanese-American rapprochement which would have allowed the United States Navy to concentrate all its forces in the Atlantic theater. Hence Hitler probably had in mind certain reasoning as he reached his fateful decision on 11 December 1941: he undoubtedly hoped to finish the eastern campaign in the spring of the following year and, in these circumstances, it seemed better to split the American naval forces from the start rather than have the United States concentrate all her forces against Japan, re-

* It may be recalled that the Tripartite Pact of 27 September 1940 had stipulated that Germany, Japan and Italy would come to one another's aid with "all the political, economic and military means available" if one of the three were "*attacked* by a power that is not at present involved in the European war or the China-Japan conflict." This certainly was not the case in December 1941. And the Führer's promise to Matsuoka in April 1941, that he would declare war immediately in case of a Japanese-American conflict, should not be taken as the gospel truth; Hitler at the time was primarily interested in luring the Japanese into the projected war against the Soviet Union, and this was the bait that he hoped would accomplish it. Moreover, how many times had Hitler kept his "word," especially in the field of diplomatic affairs?

sulting in all likelihood in a rapid defeat; failure to divide American forces between two oceans now would mean that the United States could early in 1942 deploy its naval as well as military strength in the European area alone. Hitler's decision to accept the war with the United States in the winter of 1941 thus can be seen as the "lesser of two evils."[7] The Führer believed that he still had the year 1942 at his disposal for the solution of the war against the Soviet Union. If that assumption proved correct, then the war with the western maritime powers could drag on until they realized the folly of their policy.*

The German navy initially reacted very positively to the declaration of war against the United States. Admiral Raeder had, of course, long urged this step on the Führer. On 11 December he confided to Hitler: "The situation in the Atlantic will be eased owing to the successful intervention of Japan." Raeder's staff officers were jubilant. "Roosevelt has lost his political game. . . . He has the war that he wanted, but under circumstances and at a time when it does not fit at all into his calculations." Few states could stay out of the conflict now that it had taken on global dimensions, and thus the final peace settlement could be a "*generous* realignment."[8] It would involve the fate of continents and span the entire globe.

However, Adolf Hitler quickly dampened the navy's enthusiasm over the Japanese offensive. The day after his declaration of war against the United States, the Führer informed Raeder, who wanted to renew surface operations early in 1942, that all German warships were to be relocated in Norway. Hitler ruled out further sorties into the Atlantic, and suggested that the battle cruisers *Gneisenau* and *Scharnhorst* be brought home through the English Channel. Raeder was against such a risky operation, which Hitler saw as the only alternative to the eventual destruction of the ships in Brest. But the Führer remained adamant and informed his naval commander-in-chief that failure to bring the ships home through the Channel would prompt him to order them to be paid off in Brest. For Hitler had been most impressed by the Japanese aerial destruction of seven battleships and 120 aircraft at Pearl Harbor. He now decreed capital ships to be obsolete and dismissed the strenuous objections of Raeder and Fricke to this stance with the observation that the remaining ships could be of use only in the defense of Norway.[9]

This turn of events hit Raeder hard. If carried out, Hitler's directive

* This is the meaning of Hitler's discussion with Admiral Raeder on 26 August 1942 in which the Führer explained that through "immediate total defeat of Russia" he could create an "easily defendable, blockade-safe *Lebensraum*," from which the war could continue for years to come. In this way he could lead the "struggle against the Anglo-Saxon naval powers" in order to make Great Britain and the United States "receptive to peace." Bundesarchiv-Militärarchiv, Freiburg im Breisgau, West Germany, PG 32186 Case 241, I SKL, Teil C VII, 216, 220.

meant the effective end of a German surface navy. Perhaps with this in mind, the Naval War Staff at the end of 1941 gave the following overall summation of the war at sea to date as well as prospects for the future:

The extension of the struggle to the distant oceans and the participation of a third major naval power will make the recognition of the decisive meaning of the terms maritime trade and maritime power part of the general body of knowledge of the last European. Hence the more painful it is for the German naval leadership that it cannot be the German navy that is delivering the decisive blows . . . indeed, that in its present condition, for which the war . . . came five years too soon, it is not even in a position to take decisive advantage in the Atlantic and in the Mediterranean of the significant easing of the burden that the Pacific brings with it.[10]

This inferiority complex soon changed to barely concealed jealousy. While Admiral Raeder huddled with his Führer in the frozen tundra wastes of East Prussia, the Japanese navy was sweeping the British Royal Navy from the seas in the Far East. The ego of the German naval leadership hardly was enhanced when the Japanese Admiralty accompanied its report of the sinking of the British capital ships *Repulse* and *Prince of Wales* (9 December 1941) with the ironic comment: "*Bismarck* is avenged."[11] Part of the problem, of course, was that the German admirals were, to a degree, prisoners of the past. They had earned their first taste of duty in the "yellow peril" era of Kaiser Wilhelm II. Moreover, their willing adherence to National Socialist racist ideology tended to strengthen earlier biases and confirm past prejudices. We have already seen that in the summer of 1940, flushed with victory over France, Rear Admiral Fricke had looked ahead to a possible conflict with Japan if that power attempted to establish her own "world empire." In November 1941 Raeder's paladins sadly noted that a Japanese-American war was being viewed in many quarters as a struggle between the yellow and the white races. German strategy had dictated the alliance with Japan, but National Socialist racism militated against support of "inferior" races. On 15 November 1941 German admirals had even nostalgically lamented that the Americans were withdrawing their gunboats from the Yangtze River. "Herewith the last ships of the white race disappear from the Yangtze, where they have served since 1900 to protect European and American lives."[12]

Quarrels soon beset the two partners. No sooner had Germany and Japan become allies against the United States than they bickered over the anticipated spoils of conquest. Fricke was informed by the Japanese on 17 December 1941 that they wished to divide the world at a line running north to south at 70° longitude. This border would begin in the Kara Sea and proceed south, running east of where the River Ob flows into the Kara Sea and west of Omsk, via Tashkent, between Bombay and Karachi, and on into the Indian Ocean. Fricke immediately rejected the plan because it would define Japan's future political sphere of interest, especially with regard to Asian Russia and India. "Tokyo (140° East) will thereby become the center of the globe from 70° East to 150° West (Hawaii)."[13] Obviously the admiral was dissatisfied with the share accorded Germany and Italy: the region stretching from 70° in Asian Russia to the coastal waters of the eastern United States. Admiral Raeder's staff also rejected the Japanese proposal for "political reasons." In addition, they firmly objected to a Japanese plan to occupy Madagascar because this would mean "expansion of the yellow sphere of influence beyond the 70° line."[14] In any event, the irony of the situation could hardly have been lost upon some of the more realistic planners in the two countries.* It was a Roman Catholic pope, Alexander VI, who in 1494 had drawn a similar dividing line for Spain and Portugal. And much of the globe remained to be conquered in 1941. General Halder later laconically commented: "These people [German admirals] dream in continents."[15]

In their distrust of Japanese motives and ambitions, German naval planners at least came closer again to the thoughts of their Führer. The alliance with Japan was, for Hitler, merely a temporary political expedient. "It goes without saying that we have no affinities with the Japanese."[16] But for the moment the United States was the immediate enemy, and Hitler therefore heaped his sarcasm and scorn upon the Americans. He discounted the fighting ability of the American soldiers, basing his calculations on his personal experiences in the First World War. "In any case, how could troops who had the dollar as their God be expected to fight to the utmost of their ability?"[17] And in January 1942 the Führer once more returned to his favorite theme:

> . . . one day England will be obliged to make approaches to the Continent. And it will be a German-British army that will chase the Americans from Iceland. I don't see much future for the Americans. In my view, it's a decayed country. And they have their racial problems, and the problem of social inequalities. . . . I like an Englishman a thousand times better than an American.

Hitler had now squared the circle. He had brought his strategic objectives, or so he imagined, in line with his racist ideology. His policy with regard to the United States was now also that strange composite of "vulgar Machiavellian foreign policy concepts" and "universal, racist-

* The pact was eventually signed on 18 January 1942.

ideological anti-Semitism." There would be no special treatment for the Americans when the Führer was ready to strike:

> But my feelings against Americanism are feelings of hatred and deep repugnance. I feel myself more akin to any European country, no matter which. Everything about the behavior of American society reveals that it's half Judaized, and the other half Negrified.[18]

But what about the war in December 1941? What apocalyptic events did Hitler have in store for the United States? Where would he strike? What action would Admiral Raeder take now that he had the war which he had long desired and worked for? Strangely, nothing happened on 11 December 1941. Only the Führer's visceral rhetoric was hurled across the Atlantic Ocean.

When the German military strike against the United States materialized, it turned out to be only a flea-flicker compared with previous actions. On 10 December 1941 Admiral Dönitz requested twelve large submarines for an attack upon maritime commerce off the eastern coast of the United States. Admiral Raeder, the man who had yearned for this war with the United States, two days later agreed to send six submarines in Operation Paukenschlag ("roll on the drum"; according to S. W. Roskill a "somewhat histrionic name"). Yet it was a further five weeks before five U-boats (1,100 tons each) managed to take up positions in American waters. Dönitz estimated that in January 1942 Germany possessed ninety-one submarines, of which only ten or twelve were at front stations at any given time. In addition to this exceedingly small force, the operation was also hampered by the need to maintain U-boats in the Mediterranean to protect vital supplies for Rommel's Afrika Korps against British air and fleet action, and by the long march from the Bay of Biscay to New York (three thousand nautical miles).[19]

The five boats arrived on 13 January 1942 in the waters between the Gulf of St. Lawrence and Cape Hatteras. Some fifty-four ships were destroyed in the Canadian Coastal Area in the next two months, while sinkings in American waters amounted to 470,000 tons in February and about 1.15 million tons to the end of April 1942; a single submarine (U-85) was lost during this period off the United States coast. The latter area, in fact, provided German U-boat skippers "a merry massacre," as Rear Admiral S. E. Morison put it. There existed on the eastern seaboard no coastal blackout, partial convoy was introduced only on 1 April 1942, lighted channel markers helped the Germans enter U.S. ports, and ships continued their unrestricted use of wireless.[20]

During March and April 1942, Dönitz dispatched six (and later eight) medium-size U-boats (750 tons) to the waters off New York, where they remained on patrol for two or three weeks at a time. But by April 1942 reports of German sinkings sharply declined because of the American decision to convoy all merchant shipping, and thereafter the undersea raiders sought their quarry in the safer waters of the Caribbean Sea and the Gulf of Mexico.[21] Operation Paukenschlag must surely be regarded as one of Hitler's most ineffective as well as misnamed undertakings.

In 1971, East German historian Olaf Groehler revealed the existence of a Luftwaffe plan entitled "Tasks for Long-Range Planes," drafted by Colonel Dietrich Schwenke on 27 April 1942 and submitted to Air Marshal Hermann Göring on 12 May. The Luftwaffe proposed to strike at American industrial sites as far inland as Indiana (Indianapolis) and Tennessee (Alcoa) with German bombers carrying 5.5 tons of bombs and based at Brest. The long-range bombers, possibly FW 200C, He 177 or Me 264 ("Amerika-Bomber") models, were to fly to the United States and back, stopping at the Azores to refuel. Unfortunately, it is not known what became of the proposal.[22] Yet it probably came about as a result of the Führer's plans, as discussed in November 1940 and May 1941, to deploy long-range bombers against American cities from the Azores (see pages 214–215, 223). Discovery of the 1942 plan confirms that Hitler had every intention of bringing the war to the United States once he had knocked the Soviet Union out of the campaign. (Or are there still those who would suggest that Hitler, Göring, Raeder, et al. were too "moral" to consider bombing civilian centers in the United States?) It is also interesting to note that the 1903–1906 plans to invade the area between Boston and New York (Operations Plan III) had by the spring of 1942 been translated into an aerial assault against United States cities. Obviously the aims had not changed, only the means.

The failure of Operation Barbarossa and especially the entry of the United States into the war in the winter of 1941 marked the irrevocable end of Adolf Hitler's master program. Instead of creating the Weltmacht with which Germany, stretching from the Urals to the Pyrenees and buttressed by its Central African colonial empire and Atlantic naval bases, would take up the struggle for world dominion with the Weltmacht America in the next generation, Hitler now found himself forced to defend a hastily improvised "Fortress Europe" against the Anglo-Saxon maritime powers as well as against expected Soviet counteroffensives. The long-range bombers would not be German and they would not head for United States cities from the Azores. On 3 January 1942 the Führer admitted his military impotence vis-à-vis the United States to Ambassador Oshima: "How one defeats the USA, he does not know yet."[23]* In fact,

* The reaction of the German people was judged to be much the same: "One expects primarily a defensive military policy with a dragging naval war lasting several

the German failure to end the war in the east victoriously in 1941 signified the reversal of all Hitler's strategic calculations. Russia would not be a "secondary" campaign, to be followed by navy and air force operations against the "primary" enemy Great Britain — as stipulated in Führer Directive No. 32 of 11 June 1941. Finally, the failure of the summer offensive in the Soviet Union in 1942, which Hitler termed his last chance to "alter destiny," made it fully clear to the Führer that "victory," as he put it to General Alfred Jodl, army chief of staff, "could no longer be realized."[24] Adolf Hitler's *Kampf* was over; that of Germany had begun in all earnest.

Admiral Raeder, who in November 1941 had still favored delaying construction of the Reich's only aircraft carrier (*Graf Zeppelin*), was impressed by the stunning Japanese naval air successes in December 1941 against the United States Navy at Pearl Harbor and the Philippines, and against the British capital ships *Prince of Wales* and *Repulse* in the Indian Ocean. The Naval War Staff on 10 December 1941 bitterly blamed the failure to develop a special naval air wing upon interservice rivalry, and specifically upon the Luftwaffe's insistence that all aircraft come under its jurisdiction. "It must in any case be recognized without any limitation that our own *independent Luftwaffe* has not managed in more than two years to accomplish against capital ships, that is, against the backbone of the enemy's sea power, what *the Japanese naval air wing managed to bring about in two days within the framework of a fleet operation*" (italics in the original).[25] But the critique is not fully justified. For this same entry in the naval diary reveals that Raeder's staff as late as December 1941 regarded capital ships in good Tirpitzean fashion as "the backbone of . . . sea power," and had until the last month of 1941 postponed completion of the carrier in favor of capital ship construction. Surely the navy's own failure to stress aircraft carrier development before December 1941 contributed to this acrimonious accusation of the Luftwaffe.

The enormous demands of the eastern campaign forced the German navy to turn over ever greater stocks of supplies and skilled laborers to the Wehrmacht, Luftwaffe, and Dönitz's submarines, with the result that neither the aircraft carrier *Graf Zeppelin* (scuttled on 24 April 1945 in Stettin, today Polish Szczecin) nor the heavy cruiser *Seydlitz* (destroyed on 10 April 1945 in Königsberg, today Russian Kaliningrad) was ever completed. Nor did any strategic improvements set in for the

years." Heinrich Boberach, ed. *Meldungen aus dem Reich. Auswahl aus den geheimen Lageberichten des Sicherheitsdienstes der SS 1939–1944* (Munich 1968), 184–85. Secret report No. 246 of the security forces (SD) of the SS. There was, however, "partial surprise" that Roosevelt had replaced Churchill as "world enemy No. 1."

German navy. As we have seen, the losses of the *Admiral Graf Spee*, *Blücher* and *Bismarck* virtually halted Atlantic sorties and, combined with Hitler's obsession (shared by Raeder) that Norway was "the zone of destiny" of the war, led early in 1942 to complete withdrawal of German surface vessels from the west. On 11 February 1942 Operation Cerberus, the return of the *Gneisenau*, *Scharnhorst* and *Prinz Eugen* from Brest to Wilhelmshaven, was completed through the English Channel — as Hitler had desired three months earlier. The undertaking was covered by 250 fighter aircraft provided by the Luftwaffe — a rare display of service cooperation — and though Vice Admiral Otto Ciliax managed to reach Germany with only relatively minor damage, a subsequent British air raid on 25 February 1942 damaged the *Gneisenau* (in dock) beyond repair. She was never to steam on the high seas again.*

The loss of now the fourth German capital ship in the war reduced the navy even further in importance in Hitler's opinion. In addition to the battleship *Tirpitz*, which had gone to Norway right after completion in November 1941, the Führer now ordered the remainder of his fleet there: the heavy cruiser *Prinz Eugen* arrived in Norway at the end of February 1942, and the *Admiral Hipper* one month later; the pocket battleships *Admiral Scheer* and *Lützow* came in May 1942; the cruisers *Köln* and *Nürnberg* in November 1942; and the battle cruiser *Scharnhorst* in January 1943. It was hoped that these ships would be able to intercept Allied convoys heading from Iceland to Archangel via the Bear Island–North Cape passage, but the *Prinz Eugen* was torpedoed and damaged en route to Norway. In August 1942 Hitler again denied Admiral Raeder permission to deploy any warship (*Scheer*) in the Atlantic Ocean, and hence *Scheer* and *Hipper* between August and November 1942 laid minefields and raided Allied commerce in the Barents Sea. *Tirpitz* was also used as a surface raider in March 1942, with the result that the Allied Arctic Ocean convoys were strengthened — as in 1917 after the cruisers *Brummer* and *Bremse* had raided the Norway-Scotland traffic — by the United States battleships *Washington* and *North Carolina*.[26]

German surface fleet operations in the Polar Sea were climaxed on 31 December 1942 by the inability of Vice Admiral Oskar Kummetz's task force, comprised of *Lützow*, *Hipper* and six destroyers, to deal effectively with the weakly guarded Convoy JW-51B near Bear Island. The German commander called the action off too early for fear of engaging British heavy units. It was too much for the Führer. On 6 January 1943 Hitler subjected Raeder to a ninety-minute tirade, calling Kummetz's action "typical of German ships, just the opposite of the British

* *Gneisenau* was later sunk as a blockade ship in Gdingen, today Polish Gdynia, in the Baltic Sea.

who, true to their tradition, fought to the bitter end." The Führer denounced the entire history of the German navy since the days of Tirpitz, and accused its leaders of lack of will and determination during both world wars. Raeder was given time to consider the Führer's views that all capital ships be laid up and their heavy guns used as shore batteries.[27]

It was the first time that the navy's commander-in-chief had been subjected to such a display of anger and ill will. The decision "to scrap the large ships" ran counter to Raeder's cherished notion of a balanced fleet, and Hitler's cut that "we cannot permit our large ships to ride idly at anchor for months" was in obvious reference to the navy's role in 1914–1918. The attack hurt Raeder deeply, for he had been almost frenzied since September 1939 in his efforts to deploy the surface ships against the enemy precisely because he was determined that the fleet would never again remain idle and possibly once more kindle rebellion, if not revolution. On 30 January 1943 Grand Admiral Erich Raeder resigned and was retired as inspector-general of the navy. He had suffered his Führer's abuse primarily because the latter was at that precise moment facing destruction of his Sixth Army at Stalingrad and the Afrika Korps in Tunisia — a potential loss of one-half million fighting men. And Hitler's (and the navy's) obsession with the strategic importance of Norway had proved to be fallacious when the Allies in November 1942 landed not in Norway but in northwest Africa. Hence the navy's chief had to bring Hitler the news of Kummetz's failure against Convoy JW-51B at a most inopportune moment.

Raeder's successor, Grand Admiral Karl Dönitz, on 26 February 1943 managed to persuade the Führer not to proceed with laying up the surface ships stationed in Norway, and to continue to deploy them against Allied shipping in northern waters. It was not a very difficult decision: the German collapse at El Alamein and the American landings in Morocco in November 1942, combined with the German surrender at Stalingrad on 31 January 1943, allowed the Allies to suspend Polar Sea convoys and to supply the Soviet Union via the Mediterranean Sea through the Persian Gulf with almost no losses.

Yet the remaining German heavy units were not secure even hidden in Norway's countless fjords. At the beginning of 1943 both *Scharnhorst* and *Prinz Eugen* were again ready for service in the Polar Sea; in September, the former combined with the *Tirpitz* to shell coal mines and dock facilities on Spitsbergen Island in the Arctic Ocean. But these were highly peripheral operations, and they received a decided setback late that year when British midget submarines managed to dynamite the *Tirpitz* in Alta Fjord and put her out of action for six months. Nevertheless, the Naval War Staff on 26 December 1943 decided to dispatch

Rear Admiral Erich Bey with *Scharnhorst* and five destroyers "to attack boldly and shrewdly" Convoy JW-55B. Bey was intercepted by British heavy escorts and could not get back to Norway; the battleship *Duke of York* and numerous destroyers sent the *Scharnhorst* to the bottom with the loss of almost 1,900 men.

By April 1944 the *Tirpitz* was ready for service, but attacks from British carrier-borne aircraft with thousand-pound bombs forced further repairs. In September she was again attacked, this time with six-ton bombs. The Naval War Staff now decided to station the world's most modern battleship in Tromso Fjord as a floating battery, surrounded by sand to prevent her capsizing under British air attacks. The effort was in vain; on 12 November 1944 the *Tirpitz*, hit with "blockbuster" bombs, capsized in Tromso Fjord, taking about 1,200 men with her.

The attempt to interdict Allied supply lines to Archangel, as requested by the army, thus ended as unsuccessfully as the earlier raids upon Allied commerce in the Atlantic. Between August 1944 and April 1945 the Soviet Union received about one million tons of war material via the Iceland-Archangel route, with which an additional sixty motorized divisions were equipped against the Wehrmacht. The German surface vessels were now withdrawn into the Baltic Sea for their final act: defense of the Reich. Here the ships became easy prey for Allied flyers. The Royal Air Force destroyed the pocket battleship *Admiral Scheer* in Kiel on 9 April 1945; the *Lützow* seven days later at Swinemünde (she was later scuttled and beached); and damaged the heavy cruiser *Admiral Hipper* at Kiel on 3 May 1945 (later also scuttled by her crew). The only German capital ship to survive the war was the heavy cruiser *Prinz Eugen*, which had been with the *Bismarck* during the fatal Operation Rheinübung in May 1941; she surrendered to the Allies in Copenhagen, and was destroyed in 1946 after taking part in atomic bomb tests at Bikini.[28]

The Reich had also hoped to interdict Allied supply convoys with her undersea raiders as in the First World War. In January 1942 Admiral Dönitz had a mere sixty-four submarines available for Atlantic sea duty, which meant that only ten or eleven boats were on station at any given time. Special "milch cows," large U-boats equipped as tankers with 250 to 340 tons of fuel, managed to extend operations, especially in the Caribbean, by two or three weeks. The introduction of the "Schnorkel," which allowed submarines to recharge their batteries while submerged, also enhanced the fighting ability of Dönitz's U-boat force. And in September 1942 the number of boats in the submarine branch of the navy finally passed the hundred mark. Allied merchant ship losses between June and November 1942 reached an average of 500,000 tons per month, but by December fell to 340,000 tons. U-boat losses during 1941 amounted to thirty-five, but climbed to eighty-seven in 1942.[29]

German naval setbacks in 1942, combined with the army's failure to defeat Russia in that year's summer offensive, convinced Hitler — as we have seen — that the war could no longer be won. On 8 September 1942 he told his military planners that he now regarded his position as similar to that of Hindenburg and Ludendorff in 1917–1918.[30] It was true that the navy's surface fleet had once again been unable to break Britain's iron control of the Atlantic, and Germany had once more to depend on U-boats as its last resort in the struggle with the "principal" enemy Great Britain. With regard to army affairs, however, Hitler's synopsis was not quite accurate: in 1917 Hindenburg and Ludendorff had at least knocked Czarist Russia out of the war; in 1942 Soviet Russia had blunted the German attacks and was planning her first major counteroffensives against the Wehrmacht. But in 1942, as in 1917, the German navy had obtained its war with the United States.

The period from the fall of 1942 to the summer of 1943 proved decisive for Germany. The battles of El Alamein, Stalingrad and Tunisia in November 1942 and January and May 1943 broke the back of the land war; Allied landings in northwest Africa in November 1942, Sicily in July 1943, and at Salerno in September 1943 placed German forces everywhere on the defensive. In 1940–1941 the Luftwaffe had been defeated over Britain, as now in Russia. Nor did the submarines fare better. In May 1943 they sank only 210,000 tons of Allied shipping while losing thirty-eight of 118 boats at sea; 237 submarines were destroyed that year. When U-boat sinkings after July 1943 averaged below 100,000 tons per month, Dönitz must have realized — as Admiral von Holtzendorff in the fall of 1917 — that the undersea effort had failed. His cherished U-boats were not even remotely approaching the figure of 700,000 to 1,000,000 tons of Allied shipping destroyed that the Naval War Staff late in 1941 had calculated necessary to defeat Great Britain alone. By the summer of 1943 it was estimated that only one enemy ship (about 5,500 tons) was being destroyed for every U-boat lost. But the navy's commander-in-chief kept up a brave front, and in September 1943 celebrated "the enormous strength which the Führer radiates, his unwavering confidence." Indeed, relations between the navy and Hitler had greatly improved since Dönitz succeeded Raeder in January 1943. The latter had attempted to restrict his dealings with the Führer to official business reports, while the former sought to strengthen his position by gaining favor with the Führer's intimate circle of advisers. Hence it is hardly surprising that Grand Admiral Dönitz in September 1943 concluded that it was "very clear that we are all very insignificant in comparison with him. . . . Anyone who believes that he can do better than the Führer is silly."[31]

But it would take more than the Führer's "enormous strength" or "unwavering confidence" to stem the tide of the war. The German navy was incapable of even attempting to oppose the Allied landings in France on 6 June 1944 (D-Day) and in southern France in August. The obsession of both Hitler and the Naval War Staff with the importance of Norway in this war once more contributed significantly to the success of the Allies. While Bergen was protected by thirty-four artillery batteries and Narvik by eighty as well as the entire German surface fleet, the 625-mile coastline between the estuary of the Somme and that of the Loire was protected by a mere thirty-seven heavy guns. This is even more incredible when one remembers that this stretch of French coast includes five major ports.[32]

The odds against submarine successes were also insurmountable in 1944. The approximately 140 operational U-boats were hunted by escort destroyers and reconnaissance aircraft over the entire width of the Atlantic with the newest radar devices. Submarine losses were 237 in 1943, 242 in 1944, and up to 151 in the first five months of 1945. Capital ships were used in 1945 solely to support the army's retreat in the Baltic states, with the result that submarines were left defenseless against the western Allies. During the six years of the Second World War, the submarine service built 1,113 boats, lost 996 at sea, and surrendered 153 in 1945. The U-boats destroyed 2,462 enemy ships — about 13 million tons — but, as in 1914–1918, were unable to influence decisively the outcome of the war. Human losses between 1939 and 1945 were staggering — 28,000 of 40,000 men (70 percent).[33]

The German navy in the Second World War did manage to fulfill Grand Admiral Raeder's fervent desire that it would not again remain idle in war nor again instigate rebellion and revolution. Most of its surface and undersea vessels, as we have seen, by the end of the war rested on the bottom of western seas. And though several army commanders supported the assassination attempt against Hitler on 20 July 1944, the navy remained loyal to its Führer and was thus spared the bloodletting that subsequently decimated the Prussian military nobility (*Junkers*). Joseph Goebbels had noted in his diary as early as 1932 that the navy was extremely sympathetic to the National Socialist cause, and Hitler had no reason ever to modify this judgment.

The war's end was now in sight. Hitler and Goebbels, before their suicide in the Berlin bunker on 30 April 1945, deluded themselves into believing that the death of Franklin D. Roosevelt on 12 April would save the Reich as that of the Empress Elizabeth of Russia in 1762 had saved Frederick the Great — the so-called miracle of the House of Hohenzollern. But no miracle came, and on 7 May 1945 Germany officially surrendered to the Allies at Rheims.

How different was this capitulation from that of 11 November 1918! Then the German army had stood on soil it had conquered in France, Belgium and Russia; now the army was utterly beaten and the Reich was occupied by Russian, British, American and French troops. Then the Imperial German Navy had been intact, the second largest fleet in the world; now the navy had only one capital ship, the *Prinz Eugen.* In June 1919 two minor officials of the German government were persuaded to sign the Versailles Treaty while Kaiser, generals and admirals absolved themselves of responsibility for the war and busied themselves with memoirs; this time Generals Keitel and Jodl had to sign the unconditional surrender — there could be no talk of a "stab in the back" in 1945. And perhaps because the navy this time understood, as Raeder had put it in 1939, how to "die gallantly," Adolf Hitler on 30 April 1945 had named Grand Admiral Karl Dönitz as his legal successor as "president of the Reich." With this act, the blemish of the rebellion of 1917 and the revolution of 1918 was removed from the German navy's record.

In 1919 the victorious Allies had demanded that the Kaiser be publicly arraigned and that "persons" to be specified, "accused of having committed acts in violation of the laws and customs of war," be brought before an Allied tribunal.[34] In mind here in addition to Tirpitz and Holtzendorff were submarine commanders who had indiscriminately torpedoed passenger liners on the high seas. But nothing came of this section of the Versailles Treaty, partly because the Allied and Associated Powers were not fully convinced of its legality, and partly because the Dutch government refused to hand over the exiled Kaiser. Articles 227–230 became just another part of the treaty to be exploited by German right-wing groups often led by generals and admirals who would have been affected under its stipulations.

In 1945 the victorious Allies were determined not to repeat the mistake of 1918–1919. This time the German military and naval leaders had to account for their wartime actions at an International Military Tribunal convened at Nuremberg. Grand Admirals Erich Raeder and Karl Dönitz were accused, with others, of "crimes against peace," "war crimes," and "crimes against humanity." Discovery of such German pestholes as Bergen-Belsen, Auschwitz, Treblinka and Dachau, and learning that millions of captured Europeans had been worked to death in German industries, stiffened the Allied resolve to bring to justice those responsible. The tribunal on 1 October 1946 found Admiral Raeder guilty on all three counts and decreed life imprisonment. Admiral Dönitz was found not guilty of crimes against peace but guilty on the other two counts and sentenced to ten years' imprisonment. The navy's use of slave labor for submarine construction late in the war especially tarnished Dönitz's record and weakened his argument that he was only following his Führer's orders. Raeder's relatively light sentence — army leaders Keitel and Jodl and the Luftwaffe's Göring were ordered hanged — resulted from his opposition to Operation Barbarossa.[35]

Raeder was released from Spandau prison in 1955 for medical reasons; he died at Kiel in 1960, and his rites were attended, albeit in civilian garb, by the first inspector-general of the West German navy, Vice Admiral Friedrich Ruge, as a sign of loyalty and continuity. Dönitz served out his term; released from Spandau in 1956, he resides in the fashionable village of Aumühle, just outside Hamburg and adjacent to Bismarck's estate at Friedrichsruh in the Saxon forest. Both men have written their memoirs.* Dönitz continues to hold court, especially for German, British, and American historians, and to draw royalties and pensions stemming from his wartime activities and his role as Hitler's successor. Such are the fortunes of war.

* It should be remembered, especially by United States historians, that Raeder's as well as Dönitz's memoirs were coordinated by a team of Admiralty Staff officers, headed by Admiral Erich Förste, to assure that no divergent views on major developments and decisions would appear. For this reason I have relied primarily upon the "Führer Conferences on Naval Affairs" and the official war diary of the Naval War Staff.

# IV

# Conclusion: Patterns of Conflict

# Conclusion: Patterns of Conflict

These people [German admirals] dream in continents.

— GENERAL FRANZ HALDER *12 June 1942*

IN THIS BOOK I HAVE ATTEMPTED TO SHOW TO WHAT DEGREE THE UNITED States constituted a significant factor in the strategic deliberations of the German navy from 1889 through the basic naval decisions of the Hitler period. It is hoped that by study of three periods of intense economic competition, colonial rivalry, naval construction, and war, some pattern of continuity — or discontinuity — will have emerged. Was there a definable set of beliefs and principles that guided German naval planners between 1889 and 1941? Or did Germany's naval policy simply evolve from isolated reactions at a given time to a specific set of circumstances?

Certain important themes and conflicts are clear. The first is the divergence between the eastern, land-oriented mentality of army officers and the western, maritime-oriented views of the naval hierarchy. During the First World War this conflict came to light most vividly during the Holtzendorff-Ludendorff feud over the future of the Black Sea region, when the navy bluntly declared that the fulcrum of the war was the Atlantic maritime arteries rather than the plains of Russia. And in 1940 the interservice differences were made manifest on the one hand by the army's (and Hitler's) plans to invade Russia (Operation Barbarossa) and on the other by the navy's Mediterranean program, which sought to establish Egypt, North Africa, Gibraltar, and the Atlantic islands as the pivot of German strategy.

There also existed during both world wars an overall lack of cooperation and planning between the two branches of the armed forces. Prior to 1914 both army and navy leaders developed their separate strategies independent of one another. The navy was apparently not fully aware in 1914 of the extent of the Schlieffen Plan; nor was it called upon in 1940–1941 to share the planning of Operation Barbarossa. The navy, in turn, developed its strategic objectives without consulting army leaders. It continued to view the war in the Atlantic as "its" war, and brooked no meddling from either Wehrmacht or Luftwaffe. The war against commerce bound for the British Isles continued to be regarded by the Naval War Staff as the "primary" objective of German strategic planning, while the eastern campaign — which incorporated Hitler's racial as well as military objectives — continued to be treated as a "secondary" theater. It was only during the last two years of the war, when the Reich was fighting a war of survival rather than conquest, that the navy began to deploy its remaining forces and to coordinate its planning with the demands of the other two branches of the armed services.

Both Wilhelm II and Adolf Hitler attempted, to varying degrees, to strike a balance between the programs recommended by each of the armed services, only thereby to overthrow their timetables and to face enemy coalitions that neither had desired nor counted on. Admiral von Tirpitz had before 1914 desired cooperation with Russia and Japan in the east in order to conduct with full energy the inevitable sea war against the so-called "Anglo-Saxon capitalist conspiracy" against Germany. Army leaders, on the other hand, had by 1910 become utterly convinced of the necessity for launching a preemptive strike — in the east as well as in the west, if need be — to maintain the Bismarck creation of 1871 in central Europe against what they considered to be encirclement by France and Russia. In the end, Germany managed to attain both: a naval war with the western maritime powers, and a major land war against France and Russia. The situation was much the same twenty-five years later. The navy wanted to maintain peace, or at least avoid major conflicts, until 1944–1945, when it would possess a surface fleet sufficient to challenge Great Britain's vital Atlantic sea lanes. Raeder's blueprint for German control of the Mediterranean again ran up against the army's (and Hitler's) alleged need to crush Germany's continental rivals before she could expand overseas. Thus by 1941, despite the Führer's claims that he had properly learned the lessons of the First World War, the Reich once again undertook both programs: war against the western maritime powers on the Atlantic, and a major land war against France and Russia. In the First World War Germany managed to defeat Russia, but not France, while in the Second World War the order was reversed; in neither conflict could her army defeat both continental opponents. The navy, on the other hand, did not in either war defeat a single major opponent.

This study furthermore reveals the fateful subjugation of political

(*Staatskunst*) to military (*Kriegshandwerk*) considerations. This was perhaps best illustrated by the decision in January 1917 to resume unrestricted submarine warfare, but it can also be witnessed in the attempts by German diplomats during both wars to warn the Reich's military and political leaders of the folly of unnecessarily provoking the United States. Neither Count Bernstorff, ambassador to the United States in the First World War, nor Hans Dieckhoff, ambassador in the Second, was able to make his counsel heard in high places. Both Wilhelm II and Adolf Hitler preferred to have their preconceived notions and biases confirmed by their diplomatic representatives abroad; independent, critical opinions and reports often resulted in the writer's loss of his post. The same cannot be said of the western democracies. The claims of dictators that they are better able to respond to crises notwithstanding, it was the British and American civilian leaders who proved most receptive to such innovative methods as convoying merchant shipping and who, in true Clausewitzean fashion, upheld the ascendancy of the political over the military point of view. Admiral Raeder, who early in the Second World War lamented that lack of firm political leadership had prevented a submarine victory over Great Britain in the First, proved unable to create a sizable U-boat fleet before his forced retirement in January 1943, or a respectable naval air wing with aircraft carriers — despite being able after 1933 to count upon "firm political leadership." It was the western powers, with civilian and government control of their military establishments, which managed to deploy about twenty aircraft carriers (to Germany's none) in 1939–1945. And these same democracies managed also to develop strategic bombers — the United States by 1943 outbuilt Germany's aircraft industry almost five to one — as well as the ultimate "secret weapon," the atom bomb. Neither Woodrow Wilson nor Franklin D. Roosevelt allowed military necessity, as presented by the United States Navy, to obfuscate their political aims. Wilson would not allow Admiral Benson to maintain the United States fleet in American ports for fear of a German assault in the Caribbean area in 1917, nor would Roosevelt entertain any strategy other than his "Europe first" concept in the event that the United States entered the Second World War. The very success of the antisubmarine war in the Atlantic attests to the close cooperation between air force and navy in Washington, while the high German U-boat losses in part are explained by the Reich's inability to coordinate naval and air strategy over the Atlantic and in France. Finally, Admirals Benson, Sims, and King never presumed to usurp the power of American statesmen and diplomats, in sharp contrast to officers such as Ludendorff, Hindenburg, Tirpitz, Holtzendorff, and, to a lesser extent, Raeder and Dönitz.

In addition, there was the failure of Germany's leaders from the

1890s through the 1940s to acquaint themselves with economic, military or social conditions in the United States. Around 1900 neither Admiral Koester nor Admiral Thomsen had any notion of the "size" of the United States; in 1917 as well as in 1941 Germany rushed into war without undertaking exhaustive studies of the capacity of the United States to conduct war. Admirals von Tirpitz, von Trotha, von Holtzendorff, and even von Müller dismissed American armed might and industrial power as negligible; Admiral von Capelle could assure General Ludendorff that not a single American troopship would ever reach Europe. Nor did Admirals Raeder, Fricke, Schniewind, or Carls possess sufficient basis in 1940–1941 to justify their frenzied efforts to extend the naval war against Great Britain also to the United States. And during the periods under investigation there was a general tendency to discount the fighting ability of the United States Navy, largely because of what were considered the low social origins of most American fighting men or, later on, because of their racial characteristics. From Lieutenant von Mantey in 1899 to Admiral Hebbinghaus in 1917, German naval officers scoffed at the "riffraff" that allegedly staffed the United States Navy. Nor did Admirals Raeder and Dönitz, both reared in the Tirpitzean school, regard the fighting ability of the United States Navy very highly — as manifest in their eagerness for conflict with this institution. But perhaps one should not lay blame primarily upon these men, for their leaders voiced the very same notions. Wilhelm II equated confusion, inefficiency and disorder with "Americanism" and had little regard for American officers; Adolf Hitler viewed the United States as "degenerate," with scarcely a third of its inhabitants from decent (Anglo-Saxon) racial stock, and soldiers who "had the dollar as their God."

Moreover, continuity can also be traced through several specific issues. There existed a continuity of thought among naval officers, who were recruited primarily from the German middle classes, that the United States was not really a free, independent power but rather part of an alleged "Anglo-Saxon conspiracy" designed to bottle Germany up in Europe and to keep her off the world's markets and seas. From Wilhelmian vulgar economic analysis to Hitlerean National Socialism, the United States was viewed as an inseparable ally of Great Britain. War with the United States was therefore regarded as inevitable; negotiations for alliance were ruled out from the start. Closely tied to this was the notion that in order to survive, the Reich had to extend her power and control beyond Europe. Both Wilhelm II and Adolf Hitler felt the need and desire to advance Germany from a major European to a world power (*Weltmacht*); both felt that there would be a sweeping redistribution of territories in the twentieth century, and both desired to see Germany ready to challenge especially Russia, Japan and the United States for the spoils. Popular slogans from the 1890s, such as "Our future lies with the seas," applied equally to the 1930s, and Tirpitz's opinion that Germany would be reduced to a "poor farming country" if she failed to acquire overseas possessions became an article of faith with almost every German naval officer between 1888 and 1941.

Throughout the period of this book the navy was also engaged in a frenzied attempt to "prove" to the German people and their leaders that a fleet was an essential component of power and status. The navy, unlike the army, had never been taken for granted in German history. Nor did it possess a long and proud tradition, such as the Prussian army's. On numerous occasions Germany's detrimental geographic position in the southeast corner of the North Sea, treaty obligations, hostile governments, or lack of sufficient funds, had militated against what Winston Churchill in 1912 termed a "luxury fleet." Yet each time the naval leadership had managed to maintain some semblance of sea power, and to persuade successive governments of its dire necessity. Partly from this stemmed its close-knit organization and incredible continuity of strategy and outlook, but also an artificial attempt to gauge all of its actions and policies by those of the world's first naval power, Great Britain. The Royal Navy between 1888 and 1945 was viewed by German naval planners as both example and rival. Ceremony, dress, terminology, etiquette, tactics, training, and so much more were taken straight from the Royal Navy. Yet sea power, as defined by Alfred Thayer Mahan and interpreted by two generations of German admirals, came down for almost sixty years to a maritime Armageddon between the British and German fleets. Naval policy, as the entire *Weltpolitik*, was reduced to an absurdly simple either-or formula: either a coastal fleet entailing voluntary renunciation of global naval strategy, or a mighty battle fleet designed to wring from Britain supremacy of the Atlantic sea lanes. There could be no middle ground. Whereas Tirpitz had planned such a decisive encounter in the central or southern North Sea for some time after 1920, Raeder, acting according to Admiral Wegener's 1916 concept, desired the supreme test around 1944–1945 in the waters west of the British Isles. In both wars the Atlantic Ocean (and not Norway) became a "zone of destiny" for the German navy.

Kaiser Wilhelm II and Adolf Hitler surprisingly shared a similar outlook vis-à-vis Great Britain and Germany in Europe and the world. Both men possessed what can only be termed a "love-hate" relationship with Britain. Wilhelm loved British hunts, ships, uniforms, regattas, and his "grandmama" (Queen Victoria), while at the same time wishing to crush "perfidious Albion" and to succeed her as the foremost European power. Hitler could speak on almost every occasion of his desire to reach an "understanding" with London, which according to Albert Speer ran "like a red thread" throughout his deliberations, yet at the same time plan for massive leveling of British civilian centers with his air force. Whereas the Kaiser regarded the American as "parvenu" in all his dealings, the Führer respected "an Englishman a thousand times more" than the "half Negrified" and "half Judaized" American. And both men held a high opinion of the Royal Navy, to the point of developing an inferiority complex over it. Wilhelm II repeatedly pointed to the long, victorious British naval tradition and especially to the days of Nelson and St. Vincent; Hitler in 1943 denounced the history of the German navy with the caustic remark that British ships at least "true to their tradition" fought to "the bitter end."

Within these fields there are yet additional concentric circles of continuity. Before both wars Germany drafted blueprints for sea power that clearly revealed the navy's desire to challenge not only Great Britain but also the United States for control of the western maritime arteries. Tirpitz's battle fleet of sixty capital ships (including thirty-eight dreadnoughts), conceived in a number of navy bills and supplements between 1898 and 1912 and to be automatically replaced every twenty years, and Raeder's "Z-Plan" of January 1939, calling for sixty-nine heavy units, were designed with an eye towards the ultimate objective of German control of the Atlantic. And in both wars naval planning agencies quickly concocted expansion plans that bordered on utopia; Commander Wegener's proposal of January 1916 found its parallel in Admiral Carls's program in the summer of 1940.

The issue of war aims also brings to light another aspect of continuity. During the First World War German admirals repeatedly expressed a wish to gain direct access to the Atlantic Ocean through annexation or occupation of the Belgian Channel ports, the Atlantic islands, the Murmansk coast, and the Faeroe Islands. Hitler's naval paladins expressed these same aspirations and partly realized them in May 1940 with the occupation of the Low Countries, France and Norway. Operation Felix was designed to seize not only Gibraltar but also the Atlantic islands, and thereby to fulfill another ambition stemming from the Wilhelmian era. Holtzendorff, Trotha and Levetzow ardently sought to establish German bases in the Mediterranean Sea and a German colonial empire in Central Africa; Raeder and his Naval War Staff echoed these demands some thirty years later. Not even the clamor for a German colony in South America, publicly raised by Gustav Schmoller and other economists and quickly accepted by Admirals von Tirpitz and Büchsel, was forgotten by Nazi planners almost half a century later; in both instances historical precedent for such a step was cited in the activities of the medieval house of Welser in Venezuela in the sixteenth century.

There were also certain strategic and tactical concepts that remained constant throughout this period. Both Tirpitz and Raeder created German sea power in line with Mahan's principle of the balanced fleet, with the battleships forming the locus of that sea power. From the 1890s to the bitter end of the Kriegsmarine in 1945, German naval planners steadfastly clung to the proposition that battleships were the principal unit of naval power, and they were deterred from this neither by the lack of a naval Cannae in 1914–1918 nor by the losses of the *Graf Spee*, *Blücher* and *Bismarck* in 1939–1941. Tirpitz and his staff chose to ignore the weapons of *guerre de course*, such as cruisers, submarines and naval aircraft; Raeder and his staff until the Japanese successes in December 1941 discounted the decisive influence of naval air power. In terms of strategy, German admirals gambled in 1941 as in 1917 that they could successfully end the war with an unrestricted submarine offensive against world shipping on the Atlantic Ocean before the United States could intervene effectively in Europe. Yet neither Admirals von Holtzendorff and von Capelle in 1917 nor Admirals Raeder and Dönitz in 1941 had created a force capable of such a crucial undertaking. In both instances the German calculations went awry: Holtzendorff's decisive figure of six hundred thousand tons in monthly sinkings was never reached with any consistency in 1917–1918, and the Naval War Staff's 1941 estimate that Great Britain could be forced to sue for peace if the U-boats could destroy between eight hundred thousand and one million tons of shipping per month was not even remotely achieved. Both times naval calculations culminated in defeat.

Not to be overlooked is the German desire for offensive strategy in the waters adjacent to the eastern seaboard of the United States. Operations Plan III of 1903–1906 envisaged a German naval strike via the Azores against Culebra and Puerto Rico, and from there against the eastern ports of the United States. Lieutenant von Mantey as well as Admirals von Tirpitz, von Diederichs, Büchsel, Thomsen, and von Koester had all ruled in favor of taking the action to the United States Navy. Admiral Carls's blueprint for German sea power in the summer of 1940 recommended that a permanent powerful German naval armada be stationed off the east and west coasts of the United States, while in the summer of 1942 the Luftwaffe translated Operations Plan III into a plan for aerial assault against American centers by German long-range bombers stationed in the Azores. During the First World War German admirals had, especially in 1917 and 1918, demanded submarine attacks against world shipping in American waters, and in the summer of 1918 had dispatched several undersea raiders to the waters between Boston and Baltimore. Operation Paukenschlag in January 1942 likewise brought about a half-dozen U-boats to the coastline between the Gulf of St. Lawrence and Cape Hatteras (North Carolina). In neither instance was the German force sufficient to achieve major results.

As the title of this book suggests, there was also a continuity of frustration. Between 1888 and 1905 German leaders felt hemmed in by lack of sufficient sea power with which to challenge the United States in Asia and South America. Yet in 1914 Admiral von Tirpitz saw his fleet forced into war at least five years before it would be completed and ready to stand a chance against the British Royal Navy. And in September 1939 Admiral Raeder felt similar frustration, lamenting that war had come once again five years too early, before the "Z-Plan" fleet was constructed; the navy, Raeder counseled, could only "die gallantly." Tirpitz in August 1914 had feverishly attempted to delay the outbreak of a general European war; Raeder in September 1939 attempted no such undertaking with his Führer.

It is to be hoped that this book will also temper the current fashion of analyzing the imperialism and accompanying navalism of the late nineteenth and early twentieth centuries strictly according to Marxist doctrine. To be sure, there were profits to be made in naval construction and overseas trade. But not for the German government. Colonies in Asia and Africa proved to be an economic burden, and the naval race greatly strained relations with the Reich's best trading partner, Great Britain. Not only monetary gain prompted Germany to seek a colonial empire and to protect it with a mammoth battle fleet; there were other factors equally at work. They included, among others, prestige, national honor, strategic deliberations (in the form of naval bases), and pure speculation. The desire for a colony in South America, for example, stemmed as much from the desire to find a home for excess German population as it did from profit motives — the Reich in 1889 housed about 47 million people on slightly over 200 thousand square miles, while the United States had little more than 60 million on almost 3 million square miles, and both possessed annual rates of population increase of 1.5 to 1.9 percent. In short, the phenomenon of imperialism is much too complex to be dismissed with a single causal explanation.

After the First World War, German admirals maintained that they could have won the war if the submarine offensive had been launched in its unrestricted form at an earlier date; after the Second World War German naval commanders argued that they could have won the war if the Führer had only accepted Raeder's Mediterranean program and not Operation Barbarossa. In neither instance do their complaints get at the core of the issue. Defeat in both wars was assured not by some single strategic or tactical omission or error, but rather by the combination of miscalculations outlined above. By clinging for more than half a century to Tirpitz's version of Mahan's fleet concept, by failing to bring military and naval policies into line with political policies before 1914 and during the First World War, by being unable, or unwilling, to coordinate naval, military and air strategy during the Battle of Britain, the Battle of the Atlantic and the attack on Russia in 1941, by remaining enmeshed in vulgar economic and primitive Darwinistic concepts . . . by all these methods German sailors, soldiers and statesmen brought their nation not the promised "great overseas policy" and much less the "Thousand-Year Reich," but twice defeat and ultimately division. Forgotten or rejected were Bismarck's principles of *Realpolitik*, the politics of the possible, in favor of what General Franz Halder called "dreams of empire." Twice in the twentieth century a nation of sixty millions in the heart of Europe attempted to extend its power and influence not only to the Urals and the Pyrenees, but also across the vast oceans to Asia, Africa and South America against the combined opposition of Russia, France, Great Britain and the United States. It is hardly surprising, given these realistic observations, that Germany failed both times. I have attempted to provide some insight into why the attempts were made, and specifically why both times the United States was brought into the conflict by apparently lighthearted German actions, only to turn the tide of war both times against the Reich.

This book, which basically ends with Adolf Hitler's declaration of war against the United States on 11 December 1941, has purposely not strayed into the postwar period. As is well known, West Germany (BRD) today is a western democracy with nearly twenty years of parliamentary rule, thereby surpassing in longevity the Weimar Republic (1919–1933). The Bonn regime is a signatory to major western defense and trade agreements; German industry is fully integrated into the Atlantic economic community, and specifically into the European Common Market. With regard to the United States, West Germany is her most reliable ally in Europe, while among the former Allies, especially France has turned her back on the nation that rescued her from permanent German rule in 1941–1945. And while these few observations in no way are intended to prophesy future German political developments, they should indicate at least a temporary reversal of the trends and concepts encountered earlier in this work. At the very least for this historian, it is a comforting thought that in 1972 a German-American historian (Konrad H. Jarausch) in *Die Zeit* could summarize the American image of Germany not with the goose step, Tiger tanks, U-boats, concentration camps, and the like, but with "Bratwurst — Beethoven — BMW."[1]

# Chapter Notes

BA-Koblenz: Bundesarchiv, Koblenz, West Germany (Federal Archive).

BA-MA: Bundesarchiv-Militärarchiv, Freiburg, West Germany (Federal Military Archive).

FO-Bonn: Auswärtiges Amt, Bonn, West Germany (Foreign Office).

*Grosse Politik: Die grosse Politik der europäischen Kabinette, 1871–1914: Sammlung der diplomatischen Akten des Auswärtigen Amtes* (Berlin 1922–1927), Johannes Lepsius, Albrecht M. Bartholdy, and Friedrich Thimme, eds.

Nachlass Stresemann: The National Archives, Washington, D.C. Nachlass des Reichsministers Dr. Gustav Stresemann. Microfilm T-120, 362 vols.

St. Antony's Papers: Records of the German Foreign Office Received by the Department of State from St. Antony's College.

## INTRODUCTION: THE NEWCOMERS

1 BA-Koblenz, Nachlass Bülow, No. 29. Memorandum on colonization from 1904.
2 Ibid., Nachlass Schwertfeger, No. 574. Trotha's speech in December 1902.
3 H. O. Meisner, ed. *Denkwürdigkeiten des Generalfeldmarschalls Alfred Grafen Waldersee* (Berlin 1923), II, 449.

# *Chapter Notes*

## I COMPETITION IN THE PACIFIC (1889–1899)

[1] Alfred Vagts *Deutschland und die Vereinigten Staaten in der Weltpolitik* (New York 1935), 2 vols. The major revisionist works dealing with German history in this period include: Hans-Ulrich Wehler *Bismarck und der Imperialismus* (Cologne 1969); Dirk Stegmann *Die Erben Bismarcks. Parteien und Verbände in der Spätphase des Wilhelminischen Deutschlands. Sammlungspolitik 1897–1918* (Cologne 1970); Volker R. Berghahn *Der Tirpitz-Plan. Genesis und Verfall einer innenpolitischen Krisenstrategie unter Wilhelm II* (Düsseldorf 1971); Klaus Wernecke *Der Wille zur Weltgeltung. Aussenpolitik und Öffentlichkeit im Kaiserreich am Vorabend des Ersten Weltkrieges* (Düsseldorf 1970); Helmut Böhme *Deutschlands Weg zur Grossmacht* (Cologne 1966). The revisionist "open door" interpretation of American diplomatic history is represented by, among others: William A. Williams *The Tragedy of American Diplomacy* (New York 1959); Walter LaFeber *The New Empire: An Interpretation of American Expansion 1860–1898* (New York 1963); Walter LaFeber *America, Russia, and the Cold War, 1945–1966* (New York 1967); Lloyd C. Gardner *Economic Aspects of New Deal Diplomacy* (Madison 1964); Thomas J. McCormick *China Market: America's Quest for Informal Empire, 1893–1901* (Chicago 1967).

[2] Vagts *Deutschland und die Vereinigten Staaten* I, 640.

[3] Cited in Paul M. Kennedy "The Partition of the Samoan Islands," unpublished dissertation, Oxford 1970, 65; now published: *The Samoan Tangle: A Study in Anglo-German-American Relations 1878–1900* (New York 1975).

[4] Vagts *Deutschland und die Vereinigten Staaten* I, 649–52.

[5] Cited in Kennedy "The Partition of the Samoan Islands," 73.

[6] FO-Bonn, Vereinigte Staaten von Amerika No. 5a. Acten betr. Marine-Angelegenheiten der Vereinigten Staaten, vol. 1. Hatzfeld to Bismarck, 30 January 1889; Bismarck to Hatzfeld, 1 February 1889.

[7] FO-Bonn, Ver. Staat. v. Amerika No. 16. Beziehungen der Vereinigten Staaten von Amerika zu Deutschland, vol. 1. Schurz to Arco, 3 February 1889; Bismarck to Arco, 24 February and 7 March 1889.

[8] Paul M. Kennedy "Bismarck's Imperialism: The Case of Samoa, 1880–1890," *Historical Journal*, XV (1972), 278.

[9] H. O. Meisner *Aus dem Briefwechsel des General-feldmarschalls Alfred Grafen von Waldersee* (Stuttgart and Berlin 1923), I, 227ff.

[10] Kennedy "Bismarck's Imperialism," 281–82.

[11] Vagts *Deutschland und die Vereinigten Staaten* I, 653.

[12] BA-MA, F 5174b Oberkommando der Marine. Acta betr. Vorbereitung der Operationspläne gegen Nordamerika, I, 2–13, 19a.

[13] Cited in Kennedy "Partition of the Samoan Islands," 81.

[14] Paul M. Kennedy "Anglo-German Relations in the Pacific and the Partition of Samoa: 1885–1899," *Australian Journal of Politics and History* (April 1971), 59. Memorandum by Lord Rosebury, 18 November 1892.

[15] Vagts *Deutschland und die Vereinigten Staaten* I, 694–95.

[16] Kaiser Wilhelm II *Ereignisse und Gestalten aus den Jahren 1878–1918* (Leipzig 1922), 60–62, 264.

[17] Vagts *Deutschland und die Vereinigten Staaten* I, 349.

[18] FO-Bonn, Amerika. Generalia No. 13. Kongresse behufs Zusammenschluss der Republiken des amerikanischen Kontinents und Zusammengehen der europäischen Staaten gegen Amerika, vol. 1. Foreign Office notes, 7 September 1896; Wilhelm II to Foreign Office, 9 September 1896. See also Preussen No. 1. Nr. 4b. Begegnung Seiner Majestät des Kaisers mit dem Kaiser von Russland, vols. 10 and 11.

[19] FO-Bonn, Amerika. Generalia No. 13, vol. 1. Hohenlohe's notes, 10 September 1896; Eulenburg to Foreign Office, 14 September 1896.
[20] Ibid. Wilhelm II to Hohenlohe, 20 October 1896.
[21] Ibid. Münster to Hohenlohe, 23 October 1896.
[22] Ibid. Marschall's notes, 1 February 1897.
[23] BA-Koblenz, Nachlass Bülow, No. 112. Wilhelm II to Hohenlohe, 1 August 1897.
[24] FO-Bonn, Amerika. Generalia No. 13, vol. 1. Bülow to Foreign Office, 11 August 1897.
[25] FO-Bonn, Spanische Besitzungen in Amerika No. 2 No. 1. Intervention der Europäischen Mächte zu Gunsten der Erhaltung Kubas für die spanische Monarchie, vol. 1. Ambassador Radowitz (Madrid) to Hohenlohe, 21 September 1897, with the Kaiser's marginalia.
[26] FO-Bonn, Ver. Staat. v. Amerika No. 1. Allgemeine Angelegenheiten der Vereinigten Staaten von Nord-Amerika, vol. 10. Holleben to Hohenlohe, 1 January 1898.
[27] Vagts *Deutschland und die Vereinigten Staaten* I, 354–57.
[28] FO-Bonn, Spanische Besitzungen in Amerika No. 2 No. 1, vol. 5. Wilhelm II's notes, 6 April 1898.
[29] FO-Bonn, Ver. Staat. v. Amerika No. 1, vol. 11. Holleben to Hohenlohe, 7 March 1900, with the Kaiser's marginalia.
[30] BA-Koblenz, Nachlass Bülow, No. 22. Radolin to Bülow, 8 July 1900.
[31] FO-Bonn, Amerika. Generalia No. 13, vol. 1. Holleben to Bülow, 19 January 1901.
[32] Ibid., vol. 2. Coerper to Tirpitz, 30 April 1901.
[33] Ibid. Holleben to Bülow, 4 June 1901.
[34] BA-Koblenz, Nachlass Hohenlohe-Schillingsfürst, Rep. 100, XXII, vol. 3. Staudt to Hohenlohe, 13 June 1901.
[35] FO-Bonn, Amerika. Generalia No. 13, vol. 2. Foreign Office notes, 10 August 1901.
[36] Vagts *Deutschland und die Vereinigten Staaten* I, 365.
[37] Ibid. 367.
[38] Bibliothèque Nationale, discussion M. Etienne and Wilhelm II, dated 1907. I am indebted to Professor William Cohen of Indiana University for this document.
[39] FO-Bonn, Ver. Staat. v. Amerika No. 6 No. 1. Amerikanische Staatsmänner, vol. 5. Count Albert von Quadt to Bülow, 29 August 1901. Fritz Fischer *Krieg der Illusionen. Die deutsche Politik von 1911 bis 1914* (Düsseldorf 1969), p. 201.
[40] BA-Koblenz, Nachlass Bülow, No. 91. Foreign Office (Baron Oswald von Richthofen) notes for Bülow on the Kaiser's talks with Czar Nicholas II, 12 November 1903, and Holstein to Bülow, 7 November 1899.
[41] See Winfried Baumgart "Zur Theorie des Imperialismus," *Aus Politik und Zeitgeschichte. Beilage zur Wochen Zeitung "Das Parlament,"* vol. 23/71 (5 June 1971), 3–11.
[42] Vagts *Deutschland und die Vereinigten Staaten* II, 1272.
[43] William R. Braisted *The United States Navy in the Pacific, 1897–1909* (Austin, Texas, 1958), 14, 20.
[44] Harold and Margaret Sprout *The Rise of American Naval Power* (Princeton 1943), 253.
[45] FO-Bonn, Spanische Besitzungen in Asien No. 1. Allgemeine Angelegenheiten der Philippinen, vol. 4. Tirpitz to "Admiral Berlin," 18 January 1897; Wilhelm II's marginal comments upon a report of 4 March 1897 by the German consul in Hong Kong.
[46] FO-Bonn, Ver. Staat. v. Amerika No. 16, vol. 1. White to Bülow, 8 December 1897.
[47] FO-Bonn, Spanische Besitzungen in Asien No. 1, vol. 6. Bülow to Wilhelm II, 2 March 1898; Holleben to Hohenlohe, 5 March 1898.
[48] Vagts *Deutschland und die Vereinigten Staaten* II, 1301.

[49] *Grosse Politik* XV, 28–29. Holleben to Hohenlohe, 22 April 1898, with the Kaiser's marginal notes.

[50] BA-Koblenz, Nachlass Bülow, No. 22, 255–59. Tirpitz to Bülow, 16 March 1898.

[51] FO-Bonn, Spanische Besitzungen in Amerika No. 2 No. 1, vol. 4. Bülow to Wilhelm II, 7 April 1898. Ibid. Deutschland No. 138. Die Kaiserlich Deutsche Marine vol. 1. Tirpitz to Wilhelm II, 24 April 1898.

[52] BA-MA, F 4324 Reichs-Marine-Amt. Krieg zwischen Spanien und Amerika, vol. 3. Knorr to Wilhelm II, 20 April 1898.

[53] Ibid. Notes for an imperial audience, 11 May 1898.

[54] FO-Bonn, Spanische Besitzungen in Asien No. 1, vol. 6. Bülow to London Embassy, 8 May 1898.

[55] Ibid. No. 1 Geheim (secret). Allgemeine Angelegenheiten der Philippinen, vol. 1. Krüger to Foreign Office, 12 May 1898; imperial audience notes, 14 May 1898; Bülow to Krüger, and Bülow to Hatzfeld (London), 18 May 1898.

[56] BA-MA, F 616/PG 65011 Reichs-Marine-Amt. Entsendung S.M. Schiffe nach den ostasiatischen Gewässern. Bülow to Tirpitz, 18 May 1898.

[57] Braisted *The United States Navy in the Pacific*, 33.

[58] BA-Koblenz, Nachlass Bülow, No. 112. Wilhelm II to Bülow, 20 May 1898.

[59] BA-MA, F 697/PG 65527 Reichs-Marine-Amt. Die Kreuzer-Division, vol. 6.

[60] FO-Bonn, Spanische Besitzungen in Asien No. 1, vol. 8. Holleben to Foreign Office, 13 June 1898, with the Kaiser's marginalia.

[61] Vagts *Deutschland und die Vereinigten Staaten* II, 1350.

[62] BA-MA, F 3419/PG 67346 Marine-Kabinett. Kolonien. Knorr to Wilhelm II, 1 July 1898.

[63] *Grosse Politik* XV, 44–45. Bülow to Holleben, 1 July 1898.

[64] FO-Bonn, Ver. Staat. v. Amerika No. 16, vol. 2. Dönhoff to Hohenlohe, 6 July 1898.

[65] Hermann Frhr. v. Eckardstein *Lebenserinnerungen und Politische Denkwürdigkeiten* (Leipzig 1919–1920), I, 311–12.

[66] BA-MA, F 697/PG 65527, vol. 6. Diederichs to Knorr, 9 August 1898. Braisted *The United States Navy in the Pacific*, 36.

[67] BA-MA, F 7537 Kommando des Kreuzergeschwaders. Philippinen. Manila. 2a. Diederichs to Berlin, 14 July 1898. The Kaiser noted "agreed" on the report and added: "Diederichs executed his functions with equal amounts of tact, seriousness, and energy." See Admiral Otto von Diederichs "A Statement of Events in Manila, May–October 1898," *Journal of the Royal United Services Institution*, vol. 59 (November 1914). The German version is in the March 1914 issue of *Marine-Rundschau*. Dewey has left his account in *The Autobiography of George Dewey, Admiral of the Navy* (New York 1913).

[68] BA-MA, F 4324 Reichs-Marine Amt. Krieg zwischen Spanien und Amerika, vol. 3. Diederichs to Berlin, 28 August 1898.

[69] *Grosse Politik* XV, 54–59.

[70] FO-Bonn, England No. 78 No. 1. Verhandlungen zwischen Deutschland und England und zwischen Deutschland und den Vereinigten Staaten von Amerika über eine ewentuelle Auftheilung des Kolonial-Besitzes anderer Staaten, vol. 3. Richthofen to Eulenburg, 12 July 1898.

[71] BA-Koblenz, Nachlass Bülow, No. 91. Holstein to Bülow, 25 July 1898.

[72] Braisted *The United States Navy in the Pacific*, 39.

[73] Vagts *Deutschland und die Vereinigten Staaten* II, 1385, fn. 2. Roosevelt to Spring Rice, 13 July 1897.

[74] Ibid. 1391.

[75] FO-Bonn, Ver. Staat. v. Amerika No. 16, vol. 5. Rebeur-Paschwitz to Tirpitz, 22 April 1899; Holleben to Foreign Office, 26 May 1899. A. Oskar Klaussmann, ed. *Kaiserreden. Reden und Erlasse, Briefe und Telegramme Kaiser Wilhelms des Zweiten. Ein Charakterbild des Deutschen Kaisers* (Leipzig 1902), 325.

[76] Most of the reports were included in FO-Bonn, Ver. Staat. v. Amerika No. 16, vols. 1–13.
[77] Vagts *Deutschland und die Vereinigten Staaten* II, 1380.
[78] Ibid. 1374, fn. 6.
[79] FO-Bonn, England No. 78 No. 1, vol. 3. Holleben to Foreign Office, 13 July 1898, with the Kaiser's marginalia.
[80] FO-Bonn, Ver. Staat. v. Nordamerika No. 1, vol. 10. Chargé Speck von Sternburg to Hohenlohe, 15 November 1898, with the Kaiser's marginalia.
[81] Kennedy "Partition of the Samoan Islands," 386. *Scientific American* 31 March 1900.
[82] FO-Bonn, England No. 78 No. 1, vol. 4. Richthofen to Eulenburg, 20 July 1898, with the Kaiser's marginalia.
[83] FO-Bonn, Deutschland No. 138 secret. Die Kaiserlich Deutsche Marine, vol. 2. Wilhelm II to Bülow, 29 October 1899.
[84] FO-Bonn, Ver. Staat. v. Amerika No. 16, vol. 6. Ambassador Metternich (at Castle Wilhelmshöhe) to Foreign Office, 8 August 1899.
[85] BA-MA, F 4324, vol. 3, Diederichs to Knorr, 2 and 28 August 1898; F 697/PG 65527, vol. 6, Diederichs to Knorr, 19 and 29 October 1898, 13 March 1899.
[86] BA-Koblenz, Nachlass Bülow, No. 111. Prince Henry to Wilhelm II, 11 July and 15 August 1898.
[87] BA-MA, F 3419/PG 67346, Tirpitz to Bülow, 7 January 1899; BA-Koblenz, Nachlass Hohenlohe-Schillingsfürst, Rep. 100, XII, A, vol. 16, Hohenlohe's notes of 1 May 1899.
[88] FO-Bonn, Deutschland No. 167. Kolonien und Flottenstationen (Generalia), vol. 2. Tirpitz to Bülow, 12 September 1899; Eckardstein *Lebenserinnerungen* II, 40, discussion with Tirpitz in October 1899.
[89] FO-Bonn, Spanische Besitzungen in Asien No. 1 secret, vol. 1. Foreign Office to Hatzfeld (London), 6 August 1898; *Grosse Politik* XV, 74, 75, 82, 88; FO-Bonn, Deutschland No. 167, vol. 1; FO-Bonn, Deutschland No. 138. Die Kaiserlich-deutsche Marine, vol. 14. Bülow to Krupp, 22 May 1898.
[90] FO-Bonn, Ver. Staat. v. Amerika No. 16, vol. 3. Holleben to Foreign Office, 11 August 1898.
[91] FO-Bonn, Deutschland No. 137 secret. Allgemeine Deutsche Politik, vol. 2. Bülow to Prince Henry, 14 March 1899.
[92] FO-Bonn, Südsee No. 5. Samoa-Inseln, vol. 2. Bülow to Foreign Office, 29 March 1899; Bülow to Holleben, 5 April 1899.
[93] Ibid. Bülow to Foreign Office, 1 April 1899, with the Kaiser's marginal comments.
[94] Kennedy "Partition of the Samoan Islands," 152–53.
[95] Vagts *Deutschland und die Vereinigten Staaten* I, 853, 858.
[96] Germany. Reichstag. Verhandlungen. Stenographische Berichte, vol. 167, 1758B.
[97] FO-Bonn, Südsee No. 5, vol. 6. Bülow's notes for 5 November 1899.
[98] Vagts *Deutschland und die Vereinigten Staaten* I, 871.
[99] FO-Bonn, Südsee No. 5, vol. 4. Tirpitz to Bülow, 11 October 1899.
[100] Ibid. Bendemann to Bülow, 11 October 1899.
[101] See Eckardstein *Lebenserinnerungen* II, 40.
[102] Germany. Reichstag. Verhandlungen. Stenographische Berichte, vol. 168, 3292C–3295B. Speech of 11 December 1899.
[103] BA-Koblenz, Nachlass Bülow, No. 91. Bülow's notes for Holstein concerning his visit to Great Britain, 24 November 1899.
[104] FO-Bonn, Ver. Staat. v. Amerika No. 11. Präsidenten der Vereinigten Staaten von Nord-Amerika, vol. 5, Holleben to Hohenlohe, 12 December 1899; FO-Bonn, Ver. Staat. v. Nordamerika 5a, vol. 16, Holleben to Hohenlohe, 6 December 1899.
[105] BA-Koblenz, Nachlass Bülow, No. 91. Bülow to Holstein, 24 November 1899.

# *Chapter Notes*

## 2 CONTINGENCY WAR PLANNING: BERLIN (1899–1900)

[1] Germany. Reichstag. Verhandlungen. Stenographische Berichte, 1897/98. 5. Session. 4. Sitzung, 46A, 60B, 60D. Bülow's speech is from 6 December 1897.

[2] See especially Volker R. Berghahn *Der Tirpitz-Plan. Genesis und Verfall einer innenpolitischen Krisenstrategie unter Wilhelm II* (Düsseldorf 1971).

[3] Cited in J. Meyer *Die Propaganda der deutschen Flottenbewegung 1897–1900* (Bern 1967), 45. W. Marienfeld "Wissenschaft und Schlachtflottenbau in Deutschland 1897–1906," *Beiheft 2: Marine-Rundschau* (April 1957), lists some 270 academicians who supported the naval propaganda.

[4] Cited in W. Marienfeld "Wissenschaft und Schlachtflottenbau," 31–32.

[5] Meyer *Propaganda der deutschen Flottenbewegung*, 23ff.

[6] Gerhard Ritter *Staatskunst und Kriegshandwerk. Das Problem des "Militarismus" in Deutschland* (Munich 1968), II, 185.

[7] Ludwig Dehio *Deutschland und die Weltpolitik im 20. Jahrhundert* (Munich 1955), 48. Even harsher verdicts are to be found in Theodor Schieder, ed. *Handbuch der Europäischen Geschichte* (Stuttgart 1968), VI, 218, and Rudolf Stadelmann "Die Epoche der deutsch-englischen Flottenrivalität," *Deutschland und Westeuropa. Drei Aufsätze* (Schloss Laupheim 1948), 101.

[8] See Holger H. Herwig "Admirals versus Generals: The War Aims of the Imperial German Navy 1914–1918," *Central European History* (September 1972), vol. 5, 210.

[9] Volker R. Berghahn "Zu den Zielen des deutschen Flottenbaus unter Wilhelm II," *Historische Zeitschrift* (1970), vol. 210, 61. On cruiser warfare see V. Bueb *Die "Junge Schule" der französischen Marine. Strategie und Politik 1875–1900* (Boppard 1971).

[10] Alfred Vagts "Hopes and Fears of an American-German War, 1870–1915," *Political Science Quarterly* (1940), vol. 54, Part I, 521, fn. 14.

[11] Cited in ibid., 522.

[12] Cited in Blanche E. C. Dugdale *Arthur James Balfour* (New York 1937), I, 291.

[13] BA-MA, F 3677 Inspektion des Bildungswesens der Marine. Winterarbeiten der Offiziere ausschl. Akademiker, I, 1, vol. 1. April 1893 – December 1904. "Themata für Winterarbeiten 1897/98."

[14] BA-MA, F 3677, vol. 1.

[15] BA-MA, F 5174b, vol. 1, 30–50.

[16] BA-MA, F 3677, vol. 1. North Sea naval station to the navy's Education Department, 11 September 1899; Vice Admiral Karcher to Rear Admiral Oldekop, 9 March 1897; Friedrich Forstmeier "Deutsche Invasionspläne gegen die USA um 1900," *Marine-Rundschau*, vol. 68 (1971), 346, 351.

[17] BA-MA, F 4909 Kommando der Marine-Station der Ostsee: Acta betr. Winterarbeiten (November 1895 – August 1900), p. 17, vol. 1.

[18] Harold and Margaret Sprout *The Rise of American Naval Power* (Princeton 1943), 240.

[19] BA-MA, F 5174b, vol. 1, 68–92. This citation also covers the next two paragraphs.

[20] Ibid., 100ff. This citation also covers the next paragraph.

[21] These theses, expounded especially by former naval officers such as Tirpitz, Trotha, Scheer, among others, have found their way into: Walther Hubatsch *Der Admiralstab und die Obersten Marinebehörden in Deutschland 1848–1945* (Frankfurt 1958); Albert Röhr *Handbuch der deutschen Marinegeschichte* (Oldenburg and Hamburg 1963); and especially Wahrhold Drascher "Zur Soziologie des deutschen Seeoffizierkorps," *Wehrwissenschaftliche Rundschau* (1962), vol. 12.

A counterargument is Holger H. Herwig *The German Naval Officer Corps 1890–1918: A Social and Political History* (Oxford 1973).

[22] BA-MA, F 5174b, vol. 1, 27–42. This citation covers also the next paragraph.

[23] BA-MA, F 5656 Admiralstab der Marine: Acta betr. Flottenerweiterungsprogramm (1899–1907), VI. 1. 3.

[24] Ibid. The original draft of Diederichs's reply is in BA-MA, F 5174b, vol. 1, 59–69, and dated 12 January 1900.

[25] BA-MA, F 5656, VI. 1. 3.

[26] BA-MA, F 7639 Admiralstab der Marine: Operationspläne (January 1897 – September 1899), vol. 3.

[27] BA-MA, F 5174b, vol. 1, 77–82. "Bericht des Marineattachés der Kaiserlichen Botschaft zu Washington No. 16: Rekognoszierung von Cape Cod Bay und Provincetown für ein Vorgehen gegen Boston." The report bore the remark "Original to His Majesty" on the cover. The report of 26 January 1900 was sent by Rebeur-Paschwitz directly to Tirpitz. Unfortunately, the records of the German naval attachés in Washington are not available before 1901, and hence it was impossible to find the original order requesting this information.

[28] BA-MA, F 2015/PG 65956 Admiralstab der Marine. Acta betr. Immediatvorträge, vol. 3, 288–91.

[29] BA-MA, F 5174b, vol. I, 85. J. A. S. Grenville and G. B. Young, *Politics, Strategy, and American Diplomacy: Studies in Foreign Policy, 1873–1917* (New Haven 1966), 305, state: "In December 1899 the Kaiser personally instructed Admiral Otto von Diederichs . . . and the now legendary Count Alfred von Schlieffen . . . to prepare a war plan against the United States."

[30] For the Navy Bill of 1900, see Volker R. Berghahn *Der Tirpitz-Plan*, 226ff.

[31] Stadelmann *Deutschland und Westeuropa*, 108. Berghahns "Zu den Zielen des deutschen Flottenbaus," 53, states that "soon after the First Navy Bill was passed Tirpitz informed the Kaiser that by 1902, at the latest, a further step would have to be taken" in naval construction.

[32] BA-Koblenz, Nachlass Bülow, No. 30. Bülow's notes probably from late in 1900 (n.d.). See Michael Stürmer "Machtgefüge und Verbandsentwicklung im wilhelminischen Deutschland," *Neue Politische Literatur* (1969), XIV, 505. The influence of the German Navy League upon domestic politics and the passage of the navy bills is analyzed by Eckart Kehr "Schlachtflottenbau und Parteipolitik 1894–1901," *Historische Studien* (Berlin 1930), vol. 197.

[33] Cited in E. von Mantey *Deutsche Marinegeschichte* (Charlottenburg 1926), 186.

[34] Michael Salewski " 'Neujahr 1900'—Die Säkularwende in zeitgenössischer Sicht," *Archiv für Kulturgeschichte* (1971), vol. 53, 346–47.

[35] Ibid., 354–55.

[36] Ibid., 379.

[37] Ibid., 359.

[38] Ibid., 361.

[39] Herwig, "Admirals versus Generals," 210–11.

[40] BA-Koblenz, Nachlass Bülow, No. 24. Notes for the budget commission, 27 March 1900.

[41] Ibid. Notes dated 28 March 1900.

[42] Ibid. Notes for the budget commission, 27 March 1900.

[43] FO-Bonn, Ver. Staat. v. Amerika No. 1, vol. 12. Rebeur-Paschwitz to Tirpitz, 9 November 1900.

[44] Johannes Penzler, ed. *Fürst Bülows Reden nebst urkundlichen Beiträgen zu seiner Politik* (Berlin 1907), I, 149, fn. 5.

[45] BA-MA, F 5174b, I, 84–89.

[46] Ibid., 89ff.

[47] Ibid., 96.

[48] Ibid., 98ff. This citation covers also the next paragraph.

[49] Ibid.

[50] FO-Bonn, Ver. Staat. v. Amerika No. 5. Militär-Angelegenheiten der Vereinigten Staaten von Nord-Amerika, vol. 11. Rebeur-Paschwitz to the Prussian Minister of War, Heinrich von Gossler, Military Report Nr. 34, 8 February 1901. See Yorck von Wartenburg *Weltgeschichte in Umrissen. Federzeichnungen eines Deutschen* (Berlin 1901), 501.
[51] BA-MA, F 5174b, I, 101ff.
[52] Ibid., 104.
[53] Ibid., 119ff.
[54] Ibid., 109.
[55] Ritter *Staatskunst und Kriegshandwerk*, II, 177, denounced Tirpitz's *Stützpunkt-politik* as a miserable failure. "The acquisition of Kiaochow remained an isolated incident, led to numerous diplomatic frictions, created a politically undesirable conflict of interest with the new great power Japan, and remained impossible to defend in case of war against this power as well as against England." For a discussion of Tirpitz's reasoning see Hubatsch *Der Admiralstab*, 88ff.
[56] Freiherr von Edelsheim *Operationen über See. Eine Studie von Freiherr von Edelsheim* (Berlin 1901). Translated into English as *Operations Upon the Sea: A Study* (New York 1914).
[57] Vagts "Hopes and Fears of an American-German War," *Political Science Quarterly* (March 1940), vol. 55, Part II, 63; Hubatsch *Der Admiralstab*, 108, fn. 33.
[58] *Militärwochenblatt Nr.* 72 (1901), 1917ff.; *Nr.* 77 (1901), 2045ff.
[59] Cited in Vagts "Hopes and Fears of an American-German War," *Political Science Quarterly*, vol. 55, Part II, 66.
[60] Cited in *Selections from the Correspondence of Theodore Roosevelt and Henry Cabot Lodge, 1884–1918* (New York 1925), I, 485, 487.
[61] Cited in ibid., 484. Roosevelt to Lodge, 27 March 1901.
[62] Vagts "Hopes and Fears of an American-German War," *Political Science Quarterly*, vol. 55, Part II, 57.
[63] FO-Bonn, Ver. Staat. v. Amerika No. 16, vol. 9. Holleben to Bülow, 2 August 1901.
[64] Ibid., No. 1, vol. 12. Quadt to Bülow, 31 October 1901.
[65] Ibid., No. 6, vol. 5. Quadt to Bülow, 20 October 1901, with the Kaiser's marginalia.
[66] BA-MA, F 5174b, I, 129–30. Date of the letter is 14 December 1901.
[67] Ibid., 131.
[68] Ibid., 132.
[69] Ibid., 137ff.
[70] Ibid., 154.
[71] BA-MA, Nachlass Levetzow, N 239, box 1, vol. 3. "Ost-Amerika 1902/03."

## 3 THE WAY WEST (1901–1906)

[1] FO-Bonn, Deutschland No. 167, vol. 3. "Die deutschen Kapitalanlagen in überseeischen Ländern," memorandum from June 1900. It is difficult either to verify or to refute these figures. The Foreign Office custom of classifying all Germans naturalized in Latin America within their criteria for foreign investments certainly padded the total. J. Fred Rippy, "German Investments in Latin America," *Journal of Business*, vol. 21 (April 1948), 64, estimates German holdings in 1918 at 677 million dollars (about 2.7 billion marks). German possession of Latin American government bonds in 1914, on the other hand, amounted to between 75 and 100 million dollars (p. 69). Rippy suggests that in 1918 there were approximately

850,000 "people of German blood" in Latin America — including Germans, Swiss, Austrians, and Russian Germans, among others (p. 65). Herbert Feis, *Europe, the World's Banker* (New York 1964), sets German investments in Latin America in 1914 at 3.8 billion marks (p. 74). However, Feis also gives an "aggregate total" for 1914 of 2.4 billion marks, or 600 million dollars (pp. 192–93, fn.). Unfortunately, I was unable to obtain a copy of the anonymous work *Die deutschen Interessen in Argentinien, Chile, Bolivien und Peru* (Berlin 1916). See also Raymond Mikesell, *Foreign Investments in Latin America* (Washington 1955), who accepts Rippy's figures for German investments.

[2] Alfred Vagts *Deutschland und die Vereinigten Staaten in der Weltpolitik* (New York 1935), II, 1475–76.

[3] FO-Bonn, Ver. Staat. v. Amerika No. 16, vol. 8. Prollius (Mexico) to Holleben, 19 January 1900; Holleben to Bülow, 12 February 1900; Bülow to Wilhelm II, 24 February 1900; Holleben to Hohenlohe, 18 May 1900; Holleben to Foreign Office, 7 January 1900, with the Kaiser's marginalia.

[4] Vagts *Deutschland und die Vereinigten Staaten* II, 1684.

[5] Ibid., 1716, 1720.

[6] FO-Bonn, Ver. Staat. v. Nordamerika No. 5a, vol. 18. Holleben to Bülow, 14 June 1901.

[7] Ibid., No. 16, vol. 10. Holleben to Bülow, 9 February 1902, with the Kaiser's marginal comments.

[8] Vagts *Deutschland und die Vereinigten Staaten* II, 1492.

[9] Ibid., 1493.

[10] Ibid., 1498.

[11] Ibid., 1504.

[12] Ibid., 1519–20.

[13] FO-Bonn, Deutschland No. 138, vol. 121, Prince von Schönburg to Bülow, 21 May 1902. Lamar Cecil *Albert Ballin: Business and Politics in Imperial Germany, 1888–1918* (Princeton 1967), 152–53, 156.

[14] See FO-Bonn, Deutschland No. 138 secret, vol. 4. Rebeur-Paschwitz to Tirpitz, 29 January 1900.

[15] FO-Bonn, Ver. Staat. v. Amerika No. 20a. Die Monroe-Doktrin, vol. 1. Rebeur-Paschwitz to the Naval Office, Report No. 224, 9 November 1900.

[16] FO-Bonn, Amerika. Generalia No. 13, vol. 1. Rebeur-Paschwitz to Tirpitz, 18 January 1901, concerning the trip of the *Wilmington* up the Orinoco and Amazon rivers with politicians and businessmen on board.

[17] FO-Bonn, Ver. Staat. v. Amerika No. 16, vol. 10. Rebeur-Paschwitz to Tirpitz, 21 January 1902.

[18] Vagts *Deutschland und die Vereinigten Staaten* II, 1794–95.

[19] FO-Bonn, Ver. Staat. v. Amerika No. 16, vol. 13. Ambassador Flöckher (Mexico) to Bülow, 18 April 1903.

[20] Vagts *Deutschland und die Vereinigten Staaten* II, 1640, 1704.

[21] Ibid., 1714, 1725.

[22] Ibid., 1728–29, 1738–39.

[23] Ibid., 1730.

[24] Ibid., 1735.

[25] FO-Bonn, Ver. Staat. v. Amerika No. 16, vol. 10. Bülow to Prince Henry, 30 January 1902.

[26] See *Harvard Graduate's Guide* (June 1902), 571. Also *Verhandlungen des Reichstags, 10. Legislaturperiode, II. Session, 124. Sitzung*, p. 3561.

[27] BA-Koblenz, Nachlass Bülow, No. 111. Holstein's notes, n.d. [1902].

[28] Ibid., 89–94. Holstein's notes for Bülow, 29 January 1902.

[29] Walter Görlitz, ed. *Der Kaiser . . . Aufzeichnungen des Chefs des Marinekabinetts Admiral Georg Alexander v. Müller über die Ära Wilhelms II.* (Göttingen 1965), 53–57.

[30] FO-Bonn, Ver. Staat. v. Amerika No. 1, vol. 13. Stiege to Wilhelm II, 24 August 1902.
[31] FO-Bonn, Ver. Staat. v. Amerika No. 20a, vol. 1. Richthofen to Tirpitz, 9 January 1903; Tirpitz to Richthofen, 13 January 1903. (Baron Oswald von Richthofen at the time was State Secretary of the Foreign Office.)
[32] Vagts *Deutschland und die Vereinigten Staaten* II, 1750–51.
[33] Ibid., 1754–55.
[34] Edward B. Parsons "The German-American Crisis of 1902–1903," *Historian*, vol. 33 (May 1971), 449–50.
[35] Vagts *Deutschland und die Vereinigten Staaten* II, 1758.
[36] Ibid., 1763, 1783.
[37] This thesis has recently been rediscovered by Hans-Ulrich Wehler; see numerous articles and books, specifically *Bismarck und der Imperialismus* (Cologne 1969).
[38] Vagts *Deutschland und die Vereinigten Staaten* II, 1525–26.
[39] Ibid., 1536–37.
[40] Ibid., 1541.
[41] BA-MA, F 5175, vol. 1, 74–77. Diederichs's notes for an imperial audience, 20 January 1902.
[42] Ibid., 51–52. Diederichs's notes for the audience with Wilhelm II and Bülow, 7 January 1902.
[43] Ibid., 3–4. Memorandum dated 24 August 1901.
[44] Parsons "German-American Crisis of 1902–1903," 447.
[45] H. O. Meisner, ed. *Denkwürdigkeiten des Generalfeldmarschalls Alfred von Waldersee* (Stuttgart/Berlin 1923), III, 202ff.
[46] Howard K. Beale *Theodore Roosevelt and the Rise of America to World Power* (New York 1962), 356–57.
[47] Norman Rich and M. H. Fisher, eds. *The Holstein Papers* (Cambridge 1963), IV, 245.
[48] BA-MA, F 5175, vol. 1, 248. Tirpitz to Bülow, 3 November 1902.
[49] BA-MA, F 7568 Kommando der ostamerikanischen Kreuzerdivision. Geheime O-Sachen. V, vol. 1, 202–208. Bülow to Wilhelm II, 1 September 1902.
[50] BA-MA, F 7567 Anlage III zum K.T.B. Vice Admiral Sir Archibald Douglas to Commodore Scheder, 20 December 1902; Scheder to Douglas, 20 December 1902.
[51] BA-MA, F 5179, vol. 2. Scheder to Wilhelm II, 24 January 1903; Scheder to Büchsel, 29 January 1903. For the German report see BA-MA, F 7568, vol. 2, Scheder to Wilhelm II, 21 January 1903, p. 127.
[52] BA-MA, F 5179, vol. 1. Büchsel to Scheder, 19 February 1903.
[53] FO-Bonn, Ver. Staat. v. Amerika No. 5a, vol. 20. Richthofen to Sternburg, 26 February 1903.
[54] Ibid., vol. 19. Holleben to Bülow, 29 October 1902.
[55] FO-Bonn, Ver. Staat. v. Amerika No. 16, vol. 11. Holleben to Foreign Office, 28 November 1902, with the Kaiser's marginalia.
[56] Vagts "Hopes and Fears of an American-German War," *Political Science Quarterly*, vol. 54, Part I, 532, fn. 39.
[57] Parsons "German-American Crisis of 1902–1903," 442.
[58] Ibid.
[59] Richard D. Challener *Admirals, Generals, and American Foreign Policy 1898–1914* (Princeton 1973), 84–85.
[60] See Harold and Margaret Sprout *The Rise of American Naval Power* (Princeton 1943), 258–62.
[61] Ibid., 259–60.
[62] Ibid., 258ff.
[63] Vagts *Deutschland und die Vereinigten Staaten* II, 1567.
[64] Ibid., 1568. The paper is dated 7 November 1902.
[65] BA-MA, F 2017/PG 65962, 209–11.

[66] FO-Bonn, Ver. Staat. v. Amerika No. 5a, vol. 20. Sternburg to Foreign Office, 12 March 1903.
[67] Vagts *Deutschland und die Vereinigten Staaten* II, 1595.
[68] FO-Bonn, Ver. Staat. v. Amerika No. 5a, vol. 20. Sternburg to Bülow, 2 March 1903.
[69] Vagts *Deutschland und die Vereinigten Staaten* II, 1611, fn. 1.
[70] BA-MA, F 619/PG 65029 Archiv der Marine. Friedensakten. Entsendung von Schiffen nach Amerika. Quadt to Bülow, 17 November 1902. *Army and Navy Journal* 15 November 1902.
[71] Vagts *Deutschland und die Vereinigten Staaten* II, 1634.
[72] Vagts "Hopes and Fears of an American-German War," *Political Science Quarterly*, vol. 55, Part II, 68ff.
[73] Ibid., 69, fn. 80.
[74] BA-MA, Nachlass Büchsel, N 168, vol. 8, 12–14.
[75] Ibid. This citation covers also the next paragraph. At the last moment Büchsel decided not to present these war aims during the audience. J. A. S. Grenville and G. B. Young, *Politics, Strategy, and American Diplomacy: Studies in Foreign Policy, 1873–1917* (New Haven 1966), 306, attribute these words to the Kaiser.
[76] BA-MA, F 5174b, I, 163–67.
[77] FO-Bonn, Ver. Staat. v. Amerika No. 16, vol. 12. Sternburg to Foreign Office, 20 February 1903; Schaefer to Berlin, 30 March 1903.
[78] BA-MA, F 2037/PG 66046 Reichs-Marine-Amt. Die Flottengesetz-Novelle II. Naval Office memoranda (Capelle) for the imperial audience, 2 November 1903.
[79] BA-MA, F 5174b, I, 180–83.
[80] Ibid., 190–91.
[81] Ibid., 43.
[82] See the "Denkschrift zu O-Plan III" in ibid., II, 1–5.
[83] See "Vorarbeit 4. Zusammensetzung des Trosses" in ibid., 205–17. The train included ships to carry coal, fresh water, ammunition, pumps, motorized vehicles, foodstuffs as well as specialized hospital and workshop ships. This memorandum listed in minute detail every phase of the operation from scouting the Azores to recoaling and communications.
[84] Ibid.
[85] Ibid., I, 193.
[86] Ibid., III, 95.
[87] Ibid., 76–89, 103.
[88] BA-MA, F 5174b, II, Admiralty Staff memorandum of 1 October 1905.
[89] Ibid., III, 139–67.
[90] Sprout *Rise of American Naval Power*, 272ff.
[91] BA-MA, F 5174b, III, 7–12.
[92] Ibid., 3, 168. Admiralty Staff memorandum, 10 September 1906.
[93] See Gerhard Ritter *Der Schlieffenplan. Kritik eines Mythos* (Munich 1956), 47ff.

## 4 CONTINGENCY WAR PLANNING: WASHINGTON (1900–1913)

[1] Cited in Alfred Vagts *Deutschland und die Vereinigten Staaten in der Weltpolitik* (New York 1935), II, 1706.
[2] Howard K. Beale *Theodore Roosevelt and the Rise of America to World Power* (New York 1962), 336.
[3] *Selections from the Correspondence of Theodore Roosevelt and Henry Cabot Lodge 1884–1918* (New York 1925), I, 487. Lodge to Roosevelt, 30 March 1901.
[4] Dexter Perkins *The Monroe Doctrine 1867–1907* (Baltimore 1937), 308.

[5] *Selections from the Correspondence of Roosevelt and Lodge*, II, 128. Lodge to Roosevelt, 3 June 1905.

[6] Ibid., I, 487. Lodge to Roosevelt, 30 March 1901.

[7] Beale *Theodore Roosevelt*, 136. See also Raymond A. Esthus *Theodore Roosevelt and the International Rivalries* (Waltham, Mass., 1970), 39. Roosevelt was convinced "that Britain was a friend and Germany a potential enemy."

[8] Howard C. Hill *Roosevelt and the Caribbean* (Chicago 1927), 33.

[9] Elting E. Morison, ed. *The Letters of Theodore Roosevelt* (Cambridge, Mass., 1951), III, 52. Roosevelt to George von Lengerke Meyer, 12 April 1901.

[10] Ibid., 465. Roosevelt to John Hay, 22 April 1903.

[11] Beale *Theodore Roosevelt*, 291, 293.

[12] *Selections from the Correspondence of Roosevelt and Lodge*, II, 136. Lodge to Roosevelt, 10 June 1905.

[13] Beale *Theodore Roosevelt*, 338–39.

[14] Ibid., 339.

[15] Ibid., 376, 378; Hans W. Gatzke "The United States and Germany on the Eve of World War I," I. Geiss and B. J. Wendt, eds. *Deutschland in der Weltpolitik des 19. und 20. Jahrhunderts* (Düsseldorf 1973), 278.

[16] D. Sommers *Haldane of Cloan: His Life and Times, 1856–1928* (London 1960), 203.

[17] Beale *Theodore Roosevelt*, 376.

[18] Perkins *The Monroe Doctrine*, 388. See especially Paul S. Holbo "Perilous Obscurity: Public Diplomacy and the Press in the Venezuelan Crisis, 1902–1903," *Historian*, vol. 32 (May 1970), 428–48.

[19] Vagts *Deutschland und die Vereinigten Staaten* II, 1521–22.

[20] Perkins *The Monroe Doctrine 1867–1907*, 391.

[21] Peter Karsten *The Naval Aristocracy: The Golden Age of Annapolis and the Emergence of American Navalism* (New York 1972), 266.

[22] Warner R. Schilling "Admirals and Foreign Policy 1913–1919," unpubl. diss., Yale University, 1954. University Microfilm (Ann Arbor, Michigan) No. 64–11,383, p. 37.

[23] Ibid., 37, 39.

[24] Josephus Daniels *The Wilson Era: Years of War and After, 1917–1923* (Chapel Hill, N.C., 1946), 507–508.

[25] Beale *Theodore Roosevelt*, 358.

[26] Schilling "Admirals and Foreign Policy," 28.

[27] Vagts "Hopes and Fears of an American-German War," *Political Science Quarterly*, vol. 54, Part I, 533; William R. Braisted *The United States Navy in the Pacific, 1897–1909* (Austin, Texas, 1958), 74, 151; Richard D. Challener *Admirals, Generals, and American Foreign Policy 1898–1914* (Princeton 1973), 47–48.

[28] Braisted *United States Navy in the Pacific, 1897–1909*, 244, 133.

[29] FO-Bonn, Ver. Staat. v. Nordamerika No. 5a, vol. 19. *New York Herald* interview with Beehler, 19 October 1902, with the Kaiser's marginal comments.

[30] Vagts *Deutschland und die Vereinigten Staaten* II, 1797.

[31] Vagts "Hopes and Fears of an American-German War," *Political Science Quarterly*, vol. 54, Part I, 525–26. Sigsbee to Secretary of the Navy, November 1901.

[32] FO-Bonn, Ver. Staat. v. Nordamerika No. 5a, vol. 21. Metternich to the Foreign Office, 23 November 1904, with the Kaiser's marginal comments.

[33] Schilling "Admirals and Foreign Policy," 29, fn. 46; 43.

[34] Ibid., 43. General Board to Secretary of the Navy, 13 February 1913 (Black War Plan).

[35] Braisted *United States Navy in the Pacific, 1897–1909*, 173; Harold and Margaret Sprout *The Rise of American Naval Power* (Princeton 1943), 260–61.

[36] Walther Hubatsch *Der Admiralstab und die Obersten Marinebehörden in Deutschland 1848–1945* (Frankfurt 1958), 92.

[37] Charles Carlisle Taylor *The Life of Admiral Mahan: Naval Philosopher* (New York 1920), 151.

[38] Braisted *United States Navy in the Pacific, 1897–1909,* 149–59.

[39] Ibid., 151, 170–71, 189, 239.

[40] Schilling "Admirals and Foreign Policy," 20, fn. 35.

[41] William R. Braisted *The United States Navy in the Pacific, 1909–1922* (Austin, Texas, 1971), 17–19.

[42] Schilling "Admirals and Foreign Policy," 39; 45, fn. 80.

[43] Braisted *United States Navy in the Pacific, 1909–1922,* 17–19.

[44] Hans W. Gatzke "The United States and Germany on the Eve of World War I," Geiss and Wendt, eds. *Deutschland in der Weltpolitik des 19. und 20. Jahrhunderts,* 282.

[45] The preceding and following excerpts are from the Black War Plan submitted by the General Board, and accepted by the Secretary of the Navy, Josephus Daniels, probably in July 1913. The technical aspects of the plan, highlighted by a number of extremely complicated mobilization timetables, had been developed by the Naval War College (*U.S. Department of the Navy, Naval History Division, Records of the General Board of the Navy, Operational Archives, Box 10, War Portfolios*). All citations in the next five paragraphs not otherwise annotated are from this collection. A detailed discussion of the plan is in Schilling "Admirals and Foreign Policy," 1–49. I would like to express my indebtedness to this earlier work, much of which forms the basis for the following discussion.

[46] Sprout *Rise of American Naval Power,* 311–12. Citation is from February 1914.

[47] General Board to Secretary of the Navy, 25 September 1912 (Black War Plan).

[48] J. A. S. Grenville claims that the board estimated the German strength at 750,000 troops ("Diplomacy and War Plans in the United States," *Transactions of the Royal Historical Society,* vol. 11, p. 17). See also Grenville and G. B. Young *Politics, Strategy, and American Diplomacy: Studies in Foreign Policy, 1873–1917* (New Haven 1966), 319.

[49] Grenville, in "Diplomacy and War Plans in the United States," *Transactions of the Royal Historical Society,* vol. 11, p. 17, states: "The chances of American success were rather gloomily rated about even" by the General Board. This claim is repeated in Grenville and Young *Politics, Strategy, and American Diplomacy,* 319.

[50] Schilling "Admirals and Foreign Policy," 46.

[51] Vagts "Hopes and Fears of an American-German War," *Political Science Quarterly,* vol. 55, Part II, 76.

## 5 GERMANY AND THE UNITED STATES AT WAR (1917–1918)

[1] See Paul M. Kennedy "Tirpitz, England and the Second Navy Law of 1900: A Strategical Critique," *Militärgeschichtliche Mitteilungen* (1970), No. 2, 33–57, and Volker R. Berghahn "Zu den Zielen des deutschen Flottenbaus unter Wilhelm II," *Historische Zeitschrift* (1970), vol. 210, 34–100.

[2] BA-MA, F 2045/PG 66079 Reichs-Marine-Amt. Zentralabteilung. Tirpitz to Loebell, 16 November 1905; BA-MA, Nachlass Heeringen, F 7619, vol. II, Tirpitz's memorandum of 8 February 1899.

[3] See Volker R. Berghahn and Wilhelm Deist "Kaiserliche Marine und Kriegsausbruch 1914. Neue Dokumente zur Juli-Krise," *Militärgeschichtliche Mitteilungen* (1970), No. 1, 37–58.

[4] Walter Görlitz, ed. *The Kaiser and His Court. The Diaries, Note Books and Letters of Admiral Georg Alexander von Müller Chief of the Naval Cabinet, 1914–1918* (New York 1964), 10–17; John C. G. Röhl *1914: Delusion or Design? The Testimony of Two German Diplomats* (London 1973), 28–32.

[5] Arthur J. Marder *From the Dreadnought to Scapa Flow: The Royal Navy in the Fisher Era, 1904–1919* (London 1965), II, 372–77.

[6] Karl-Heinz Janssen *Die graue Exzellenz. Zwischen Staatsräson und Vasallentreue. Aus den Papieren des kaiserlichen Gesandten Karl Georg von Treutler* (Frankfurt/Berlin 1971), 192.

[7] Karl E. Birnbaum *Peace Moves and U-Boat Warfare: A Study of Imperial Germany's Policy Towards the United States April 18, 1916 – January 9, 1917* (Stockholm 1958), 26.

[8] Ibid., 31.

[9] FO-Bonn, Der Weltkrieg No. 18 secret adh. I. Verhandlungen . . . U-Krieg, vol. 1.

[10] Ibid. Tirpitz to Bethmann Hollweg, 31 January 1916.

[11] Ibid., vol. 2. Tirpitz's memorandum for Bethmann Hollweg, 8 February 1916.

[12] BA-MA, F 3580/PG 68122 Kais. Marine-Kabinett. Krieg 1914/15, vol. 1, 11–12. Protocol of a meeting of Tirpitz, Bethmann Hollweg, Jagow, and Pohl. BA-MA Nachlass Hollweg, F 5790, vol. 3, 1915.

[13] FO-Bonn, Der Weltkrieg No. 18 secret adh. I. Verhandlungen . . . U-Krieg, vol. 5. Crown Prince Wilhelm to Bethmann Hollweg, 23 May 1916.

[14] Birnbaum *Peace Moves and U-Boat Warfare*, 174–75.

[15] Janssen *Die graue Exzellenz*, 210.

[16] Holtzendorff to Hindenburg, 22 December 1916, Auswärtiges Amt. Abteilung A. Akten. Krieg 1914. "Unterseebooten Krieg gegen England und andere feindliche Staaten." Der Weltkrieg No. 18 Geheim, Records of the German Foreign Office Received by the Department of State from St. Antony's College (later cited as St. Antony's Papers), reel 8, frame 52/2.

[17] David F. Trask *Captains and Cabinets: Anglo-American Naval Relations, 1917–1918* (Columbia, Missouri, 1972), 69.

[18] Birnbaum *Peace Moves and U-Boat Warfare*, 317–18.

[19] BA-MA, Nachlass Levetzow, N239, box 15, vol. 2. Notes on his discussion with Bethmann Hollweg, 8 January 1917.

[20] Rudolf von Valentini *Kaiser und Kabinettschef. Nach eigenen Aufzeichnungen und dem Briefwechsel des Wirklichen Geheimen Rats Rudolf v. Valentini* (Oldenburg 1931), 145ff.

[21] Adolphe Laurens *Histoire de la guerre sous-marine allemande (1914–1918)* (Paris 1930), 244. For a German account of the Pless conference, see Arno Spindler *Wie es zu dem Entschluss zum uneingeschränkten U-Boots-Krieg 1917 gekommen ist* (Göttingen n.d.), 37–43.

[22] Walter Görlitz, ed. *Regierte der Kaiser? Kriegstagebücher, Aufzeichnungen und Briefe des Chefs des Marine-Kabinetts Admiral Georg Alexander von Müller 1914–1918* (Göttingen 1959), 249, 251.

[23] Erich Ludendorff *Urkunden der Obersten Heeresleitung über Ihre Tätigkeit, 1916–1918* (Berlin 1922), 21.

[24] St. Antony's Papers, reel 8, frame 104. Bernstorff to Bethmann Hollweg, 14 January 1917.

[25] Ibid., frames 206–208. Bethmann Hollweg to Bernstorff, 16 January 1917.

[26] Ibid., frame 189. Lersner to Foreign Office, 16 January 1917.

[27] FO-Bonn, Mexico, No. 16 secret (Geheim) Legationsrat Dr. Goeppert. Zimmermann to Eckardt, 13 January 1917. For the telegram from the Foreign Office to Bernstorff in Washington on 16 January 1917, see Barbara W. Tuchman *The Zimmermann Telegram* (New York 1965), 11, 185–86.

[28] Trask *Captains and Cabinets*, 44.

[29] BA-MA, Nachlass Hipper, N 162, vol. 6, 24. Diary entry 4 February 1917. See also ibid., vol. 4, 3, diary entry 1 September 1915.

[30] BA-MA, Nachlass Souchon, N 156, vol. 19. Letter to his wife, 6 February 1917. See also ibid., letter to his wife, 9 October 1916.

[31] Ibid., vol. 20. Letters to his wife, 10 and 21 April, 1 May 1917.

[32] BA-MA, Nachlass Hollweg, F 5790, vol. 3. Tirpitz to Bethmann Hollweg, 6 August 1915.

[33] BA-MA, Nachlass Tirpitz, N 253, vol. 221. Tirpitz to the Prussian ambassador in Karlsruhe (von Eisendecher), 13 July 1916.

[34] BA-MA, Nachlass Vanselow, F 7612. Ludendorff to Stinnes, 15 September 1916.

[35] BA-MA, F 3583/PG 68132 Kais. Marine-Kabinett. Oberste Stellen der Marine. Wilhelm's marginal notes, 24 August 1915.

[36] BA-MA, Nachlass Levetzow, N 239, box 3, vol. 4. Boy-Ed to Holtzendorff, 26 June 1916.

[37] L. E. Hill, ed. "The Papers of Ernst von Weizsäcker." Letters to his father, 7 February and 9 September 1916. These papers will shortly be published by the Propyläen Verlag (Ullstein) in West Berlin. I am indebted to Professor Hill for making them available to me.

[38] Janssen *Die graue Exzellenz*, 248. Zech to Treutler, 20 December 1917. Karl Dietrich Erdmann, ed. *Kurt Riezler. Tagebücher, Aufsätze, Dokumente* (Göttingen 1972), 395, 402, 422.

[39] For the decision to resume unrestricted submarine warfare see especially Arno Spindler *Wie es zu dem Entschluss zum uneingeschränkten U-Boots-Krieg 1917 gekommen ist* (Göttingen n.d.); Birnbaum *Peace Moves and U-Boat Warfare;* Herrmann Bauer *Reichsleitung und U-bootseinsatz* (Lippoldsberg 1956); R. H. Gibson and Maurice Prendergast *The German Submarine War, 1914 to 1918* (London 1931); A. Laurens *Histoire de la guerre sous-marine allemande;* Andreas H. Michelsen *Der U-Bootskrieg 1914–1918* (Leipzig 1925); Kurt Naudé *Der Kampf um den uneingeschränkten U-Boot-Krieg 1914 bis 1917. Ein Beitrag zu dem Problem "Politik und Kriegführung"* (Hamburg 1941). An English language account is Henry Newbolt *Naval Operations* (London 1928), 5 vols. These volumes are part of the British official history of World War I: *History of the Great War Based on Official Documents.*

[40] Karl Galster *England, Deutsche Flotte und Weltkrieg* (Kiel 1925), 144; Michelsen *Der U-Bootskrieg*, 48–49. Estimates of submarines available for duty on 1 February 1917 vary. Michelsen's figure is 111 (ibid., 125). The most recent estimate is 105, given by Robert M. Grant *U-Boats Destroyed: The Effect of Anti-Submarine Warfare, 1914–1918* (London 1964), 41, and by Arno Spindler *Der Handelskrieg mit U-Booten* (Berlin 1941), IV, 1.

[41] Grant *U-Boats Destroyed*, 72.

[42] BA-MA, Nachlass Büchsel, N 168, vol. 7, 67. Memorandum of 12 March 1916.

[43] Holger H. Herwig *The German Naval Officer Corps: A Social and Political History 1890–1918* (Oxford 1973), 192–93.

[44] Galster *England, Deutsche Flotte und Weltkrieg*, 121. See also Walther Hubatsch *Der Admiralstab und die Obersten Marinebehörden in Deutschland, 1858–1945* (Frankfurt 1958), 171, and Kurt Assmann *Deutsche Seestrategie in zwei Weltkriegen* (Heidelberg 1957), 42–43.

[45] Trask *Captains and Cabinets*, 69.

[46] St. Antony's Papers, reel 11, vol. 39, frame 1. Holtzendorff to Zimmermann, 15 April 1917.

[47] Ibid., vol. 40, frame 23. Holtzendorff to the Kaiser, 24 April 1917.

[48] Ibid., vol. 39, frames 140–41. Grünau to Foreign Office.

[49] BA-MA, F 7864 Admiralstab der Marine. Amerika. Ludendorff's discussion with Captain von Bülow, 29 March 1917.

[50] BA-MA, F 1139 Befehlshaber der Ostseestreitkräfte, Heft 1, Politisches, 83–90. Boy-Ed to Prince Henry, 17 March 1917. See also Nachlass Levetzow, N 239, box 3, vol. 6.

[51] BA-MA, Nachlass Levetzow, N 239, box 19, vol. 2. Lieutenant Dr. Richard Fuss before the Industrial Club, 31 March 1917.

[52] St. Antony's Papers, reel 11, vol. 39, frames 80–81. Zimmermann to Grünau, 18 April 1917.

[53] Ibid., vol. 43, frame 155. Holtzendorff to Foreign Office, 22 May 1917.
[54] The National Archives, Washington, D.C. Nachlass des Reichsministers Dr. Gustav Stresemann. Microfilm T-120, cont. 3066, serial 6879, frame H 131736. Hereafter cited as Nachlass Stresemann.
[55] BA-MA, Nachlass Levetzow, N 239, box 3, vol. 6. Boy-Ed to Usslar, 17 April 1917.
[56] BA-MA, F 7864 Admiralstab der Marine. Allgemeines. Holtzendorff to all commanders, 21 April 1917.
[57] BA-Koblenz, Berichte von Holtzendorff, R1/vol. 12. Arndt von Holtzendorff to Ballin, 20 April 1917.
[58] Ibid. Arndt von Holtzendorff to Ballin, 9 June 1917.
[59] St. Antony's Papers, reel 12, vol. 48, frame 183. Hindenburg to Bethmann Hollweg, 29 June 1917.
[60] Ibid., frames 187–91. Bethmann Hollweg to Hindenburg, 25 June 1917.
[61] Arno Spindler *Der Handelskrieg mit U-Booten* IV, 224; Grant *U-Boats Destroyed*, 41.
[62] Klaus Epstein *Matthias Erzberger and the Dilemma of German Democracy* (Princeton 1959), 186.
[63] Walther Rathenau *Tagebuch, 1907–1922* (Düsseldorf 1967), 220–21.
[64] Ludendorff *Urkunden der Obersten Heeresleitung*, 413. See also Herbert Michaelis et al., eds. *Ursachen und Folgen vom Deutschen Zusammenbruch 1918 und 1945 bis zur staatlichen Neuordnung Deutschlands in der Gegenwart* (Berlin n.d.), II, 27.
[65] St. Antony's Papers, reel 12, vol. 50, frames 35d to 35g. Memorandum on submarine warfare in American waters, 14 July 1917.
[66] Fritz Fischer *Griff nach der Weltmacht. Die Kriegszielpolitik des kaiserlichen Deutschland 1914/1918* (Düsseldorf 1964), 455–57. Report of the Kreuznach conference, 23 April 1917.
[67] Richard Kühlmann *Erinnerungen* (Heidelberg 1948), 480, 482. See also Gerhard Ritter *Staatskunst und Kriegshandwerk. Das Problem des "Militarismus" in Deutschland* (Munich 1965–1968), IV, 70.
[68] BA-Koblenz, Berichte von Holtzendorff, R1/vol. 13. Notes on the private talk between Wilhelm II and Admiral von Holtzendorff, 20 July 1917.
[69] BA-MA, F 7864 Admiralstab der Marine. Amerika. Kühlmann to Lersner, 26 August 1917, with the Kaiser's marginalia.
[70] Holger H. Herwig and David F. Trask "The Failure of Imperial Germany's Undersea Offensive against World Shipping, February 1917 – October 1918," *Historian*, vol. 33 (August 1971), 620.
[71] Spindler *Der Handelskrieg mit U-Booten* IV, 399–400.
[72] Ibid., 396. See also St. Antony's Papers, reel 13, vol. 55, frames 45–47. Holtzendorff to Kühlmann, 8 and 28 October 1917.
[73] See Herwig *The German Naval Officer Corps*, 224–26.
[74] Hubatsch *Admiralstab und Oberste Marinebehörden*, 177.
[75] Reinhard Scheer *Germany's High Sea Fleet in the World War* (London 1920), 328.
[76] Ibid., 335; Michelsen *Der U-Bootskrieg*, 131; Gerald D. Feldman *Army, Industry, and Labor in Germany, 1914–1918* (Princeton 1966), 444.
[77] St. Antony's Papers, reel 13, vol. 53, frames 62–63, Kühlmann to Hindenburg, 7 September 1917. Ibid., vol. 54, frames 78–84, Holtzendorff to Foreign Office, 8 October 1917. Ibid., vol. 57, frame 200, Holtzendorff to Foreign Office, 15 December 1917.
[78] BA-MA, Nachlass Levetzow, N 239, box 19, vol. 2. Levetzow's version of the memorandum is from 2 February 1916.
[79] BA-MA, Nachlass Hollweg, F 7589, vol. 1. Hollweg's study is undated, but internal evidence points to its conception in the year 1916.
[80] BA-MA, Nachlass Vanselow, F 7612, "Kriegsziele der Marine." Memorandum by Admiral von Holtzendorff, 26 November 1916.

[81] Ibid. See also Fischer *Griff nach der Weltmacht*, 416–18.

[82] BA-MA, Nachlass Tirpitz, N 253, vol. 178, 100. Tirpitz to Ludendorff, 30 December 1916.

[83] BA-MA, Nachlass Levetzow, N 239, box 19, vol. 2. Trotha's memorandum, "Aufgaben der Marine nach dem Kriege," 1 July 1917. For a general discussion of these war aims see especially K. H. Jarausch "The Illusion of Limited War: Chancellor Bethmann Hollweg's Calculated Risk, July 1914," *Central European History*, vol. 2 (March 1969), 48–76; W. Schieder, ed. *Erster Weltkrieg. Ursachen, Entstehungen und Kriegsziele* (Cologne 1969); F. Klein et al., eds. *Deutschland im Ersten Weltkrieg* (East Berlin 1968); Klaus Wernecke *Der Wille zur Weltgeltung. Aussenpolitik und Öffentlichkeit in Deutschland am Vorabend des Ersten Weltkrieges* (Düsseldorf 1969). The major monographs on this subject include Fischer *Griff nach der Weltmacht;* Ritter *Staatskunst und Kriegshandwerk;* Andreas Hillgruber *Deutschlands Rolle in der Vorgeschichte der beiden Weltkriege* (Göttingen 1967); and, more peripherally, Fritz Fischer *Krieg der Illusionen. Die deutsche Politik von 1911 bis 1914* (Düsseldorf 1969).

[84] Hans Gatzke *Germany's Drive to the West: A Study of German War Aims During the First World War* (Baltimore 1950), 229–30.

[85] BA-MA, F 2022/PG 65984 Admiralstab der Marine. Immediatvorträge, vol. 31, 62–63.

[86] BA-MA, Nachlass Tirpitz, N 253, vol. 167. Memorandum of 19 February 1918 entitled "Kriegslage." For the Fatherland Party and Tirpitz, see Karl Wortmann *Geschichte der deutschen Vaterlands-Partei 1917–1918* (Halle/Saale 1926), and George E. Etue, Jr. "The German Fatherland Party 1917–1918," unpub. diss., University of California, Berkeley, 1959.

[87] BA-MA, F 591/PG 69257 Admiralstab der Marine. Schwarzes Meer. Hopman to Vanselow, 27 May 1918. For the Holtzendorff-Ludendorff feud, see Herwig "War Aims of the German Navy 1914–1918," *Central European History*, vol. 5, 226; Winfried Baumgart *Deutsche Ostpolitik 1918. Von Brest-Litovsk bis zum Ende des Ersten Weltkrieges* (Vienna/Munich 1966) and "Neue Quellen zur Beurteilung Ludendorffs. Der Konflikt mit dem Admiralstabschef über die deutsche Schwarzmeerpolitik im Sommer 1918," *Militärgeschichtliche Mitteilungen*, 1969, No. 2, 161–77.

[88] BA-MA, Nachlass Keyserlingk, N 161, vol. 3, 19–30.

[89] BA-MA, F 4055/PG 64725 Anlage zum KTB der Seekriegsleitung. See also BA-MA, Nachlass Levetzow, N 239, box 22, vol. 17. Protocol of the 21 September 1918 meeting with Bartenwerffer.

[90] BA-MA, F 589/PG 69246. Admiralty Staff memorandum entitled "Amerikanische Stützpunkte und Auslandshäfen in Europa."

[91] Ibid. Memorandum from April 1918.

[92] Harold and Margaret Sprout *The Rise of American Naval Power* (Princeton 1943), 363–66; Girard L. McEntee *Military History of the World War* (New York 1943), 381, 386.

[93] BA-MA, F 2022/PG 65984, vol. 31, p. 35.

[94] BA-MA, Nachlass Tirpitz, N 253, vol. 161. Summary of Germany's "Kriegslage," 19 February 1918.

[95] Erich Ludendorff *Meine Kriegserinnerungen 1914–1918* (Berlin 1919), 332.

[96] St. Antony's Papers, reel 13, vol. 59, frame 175. Ludendorff to Foreign Office, 22 January 1918.

[97] Baumgart *Deutsche Ostpolitik 1918*, 24–27, 68; Holger H. Herwig "German Policy in the Eastern Baltic Sea in 1918: Expansion or Anti-Bolshevik Crusade?," *Slavic Review*, vol. 32 (June 1973), 339–41.

[98] Wilhelm Groener *Lebenserinnerungen: Jugend; Generalstab; Weltkrieg* (Göttingen 1957), 565.

[99] St. Antony's Papers, reel 14, vol. 62, frames 162–63. Holtzendorff to Foreign Office, 26 February 1918.

[100] Scheer *Germany's High Sea Fleet,* 335.

[101] Ludendorff *Meine Kriegserinnerungen,* 491; Erich Ludendorff *Kriegsführung und Politik* (Berlin 1922), 207.

[102] Otto Groos *Seekriegslehren im Lichte des Weltkrieges* (Berlin 1929), 227–28.

[103] Rear Admiral Wülfing von Ditten "Die amerikanische Waffen- und Truppentransporte im Weltkriege," *Marine-Rundschau,* vol. 34 (1929), 548–58; McEntee *Military History of the World War,* 381.

[104] Schultess' Europäischer Geschichtskalender, Neue Folge. Erster Teil, vol. 34 (1918), 147–49. Capelle to Hauptausschuss des Reichstages, 17 to 18 April 1918.

[105] Groos *Seekriegslehren im Lichte des Weltkrieges,* 139; Galster *England, Deutsche Flotte und Weltkrieg,* 122; Marder *From the Dreadnought to Scapa Flow* V, 143–56.

[106] On the submarine cruisers see Michelsen *Der U-Bootskrieg,* 65–66; Spindler *Der Handelskrieg mit U-Booten* IV, 2; Gibson and Prendergast *The German Submarine War,* 218–19.

[107] St. Antony's Papers, reel 14, vol. 62, frame 172. Holtzendorff to Kühlmann, 3 March 1918.

[108] Ibid., frames 182, 191. Kühlmann to Foreign Office, 5 March 1918.

[109] Karl Graf von Hertling *Ein Jahr in der Reichskanzlei. Erinnerungen an die Kanzlerschaft meines Vaters* (Freiburg 1919), 115–16.

[110] St. Antony's Papers, reel 14, vol. 62, frame 194. Lersner to Foreign Office, 7 March 1918.

[111] Ibid., vol. 65, frame 43. Berkheim to Foreign Office, 25 June 1918.

[112] BA-MA, F 2022/PG 65984, vol. 31, 72. Holtzendorff's imperial audience on 1 April 1918.

[113] St. Antony's Papers, reel 14, vol. 65, frame 27. Berkheim to Foreign Office, 23 June 1918. Ibid., frame 35, Hindenburg to Hertling, 24 June 1918. Ibid., frame 38, Grünau to Foreign Office, 24 June 1918.

[114] Ibid., frame 89. Grünau to Foreign Office, 28 June 1918.

[115] Ibid., frame 110. Protocol of discussion, 2 July 1918.

[116] Hertling *Ein Jahr in der Reichskanzlei,* 115–16.

[117] BA-MA, Nachlass Müller, N 159, vol. 7, pp. 9–9a, 10, 12, 18, entries for 25 June, 4 and 31 July 1918. See also Scheer *Germany's High Sea Fleet,* 332; St. Antony's Papers, reel 14, vol. 65, frame 129, Grünau to Foreign Office, 18 July 1918; ibid., frames 214–24, discussion on the American blockade, 29 July 1918; ibid., vol. 66, frame 1, Hertling to Foreign Office, 1 August 1918.

[118] Nachlass Stresemann, cont. 3077, serial 6912, frame H 136101. Admiral Dick to Stresemann, 27 June 1918.

[119] Walther Rathenau *Briefe* (Dresden 1926), II, 54.

[120] Gibson and Prendergast *German Submarine War,* 306–307, 310.

[121] BA-MA, Nachlass Keyserlingk, N 161, vol. 19, 138. See also Scheer *Germany's High Sea Fleet,* 337, 344; Michelsen *Der U-Bootskrieg,* 132; Herwig *German Naval Officer Corps,* 238–39.

[122] BA-MA, Nachlass Hipper, N 162, vol. 8, 27. Diary entry for 29 August 1918.

[123] Erich Matthias and Rudolf Morsey, eds. *Der Interfraktionelle Ausschuss* (Düsseldorf 1959), II, 571. Discussion of 13 September 1918.

[124] Nachlass Stresemann, cont. 3077, serial 6910, frames H 135694–95. Stresemann to Zöphel, 3 September 1918.

[125] Junius Alter, ed. *Ein Armeeführer erlebt den Weltkrieg. Persönliche Aufzeichnungen des Generalobersten v. Einem* (Leipzig 1938), 426.

[126] BA-MA, Nachlass Hipper, N 162, vol. 9, 2. Diary entry for 7 October 1918.

[127] BA-MA, Nachlass Levetzow, N 239, box 4, vol. 9. Trotha to Levetzow, 8 October 1918. For the planned naval "death ride" see Wilhelm Deist "Die Politik der Seekriegsleitung und die Rebellion der Flotte Ende Oktober 1918," *Vierteljahrshefte für Zeitgeschichte* (October 1966), XIV/4, 353–55.

[128] BA-MA, Nachlass Levetzow, N 239, box 22, vol. 3. Memorandum n.d., but probably between 15 and 20 October 1918.
[129] Herwig *German Naval Officer Corps*, 248.
[130] Ditten "Die amerikanische Waffen- und Truppentransporte," 497–509.
[131] John Wilber Jenkins *Our Navy's Part in the Great War* (New York 1919), 27. For a critical analysis of the German plan see Herwig *German Naval Officer Corps*, 248–49.
[132] Herwig *German Naval Officer Corps*, 257–62; Alfred Niemann *Revolution von Oben — Umsturz von Unten. Entwicklung und Verlauf der Staatsumwälzung in Deutschland 1914–1918* (Berlin 1927), 385.
[133] Gibson and Prendergast *German Submarine War*, 330–31. Records of the German Foreign Ministry, Whaddon Hall microfilms, serial No. 9246H, frames E 653456–458. For the surrender of the U-boats see Gibson and Prendergast *German Submarine War*, 275–80, 330–32; Grant *U-Boats Destroyed;* Hans Hugo Sokol *Österreich-Ungarns Seekrieg 1914–1918* (Vienna 1933), IV, 737, 743.
[134] For the events at Scapa Flow see "Denkschrift über Britische Völkerrechtsverletzungen begangen an der Besatzung der in Scapa Flow versenkten deutsche Flotte" (Berlin 1921), German Naval Record Collection of the U.S. Naval History Division, Washington, D.C. (Tambach collection), TA-112D 64936; Galster *England, Deutsche Flotte und Weltkrieg*, 166; Marder *Dreadnought to Scapa Flow* V, 275–93; Seth P. Tillman *Anglo-American Relations at the Paris Peace Conference* (Princeton 1960), 172; Herwig *German Naval Officer Corps*, "Epilogue," passim.
[135] BA-MA, Nachlass Levetzow, N 239, box 18, vol. 1, 42–43. Trotha to Captain von Bülow, 9 July 1918.
[136] Herwig *German Naval Officer Corps*, 265; BA-MA, Nachlass Michaelis, N 164, vol. 6, 39.
[137] Hill, ed. "Papers of Ernst von Weizsäcker." Letter to his father, 5 October 1918.
[138] Fischer *Krieg der Illusionen*, 1.

## 6 UNITED STATES STRATEGY (1917–1918)

[1] Warner R. Schilling "Admirals and Foreign Policy 1913–1919," unpubl. diss., Yale University, 1954, 49.
[2] Ibid., 49a.
[3] Ibid., 57.
[4] Josephus Daniels *The Wilson Era: Years of War and After, 1917–1923* (Chapel Hill 1946), I, 241–43.
[5] Martin Kitchen "Militärische Unternehmungen gegen Kanada im Ersten Weltkrieg," *Militärgeschichtliche Mitteilungen* (1970), No. 1, 27–30; F. von Bernhardi *Der kommende Krieg* (Berlin 1911).
[6] Kitchen "Militärische Unternehmungen gegen Kanada," 33–35.
[7] Michael Dorman *The Secret Service Story* (New York 1967), 128–31.
[8] Ibid., 132.
[9] Schilling "Admirals and Foreign Policy," 54.
[10] Ibid., 55a.
[11] Ibid., 56; Frank Freidel *Franklin D. Roosevelt: The Apprenticeship* (Boston 1952), 293–94; David F. Trask *Captains and Cabinets: Anglo-American Naval Relations, 1917–1918* (Columbia, Missouri, 1972), 45. Professor Trask kindly shared his research notes with me, but I have here decided to refer to his book rather than to the archival collections.
[12] Freidel *Roosevelt: The Apprenticeship*, 240–47.

[13] William R. Braisted *The United States Navy in the Pacific, 1909–1922* (Austin, Texas, 1971), 184–85.
[14] Schilling "Admirals and Foreign Policy," 58.
[15] Ibid., 59.
[16] See especially Trask *Captains and Cabinets,* 285; Braisted *The United States Navy in the Pacific, 1909–1922,* 171–208.
[17] Trask *Captains and Cabinets,* 44.
[18] Ibid., 47–48. Benson to Daniels, February 1917.
[19] Ibid., 55. Schilling "Admirals and Foreign Policy," 77–78.
[20] Schilling "Admirals and Foreign Policy," 81.
[21] Trask *Captains and Cabinets,* 58. Admiral Badger to Daniels, 5 April 1917.
[22] Schilling "Admirals and Foreign Policy," 64.
[23] Ibid., 87–88.
[24] French Ministry of Marine, Service Historique de la Marine, Es file, box 13, memorandum of 16 April 1917. I am indebted to Professor David F. Trask for this document.
[25] William Sowden Sims *The Victory at Sea* (Garden City, New York, 1920), 374–76. In collaboration with Burton J. Hendrick.
[26] Ibid., 376–84.
[27] Ray Stannard Baker *Woodrow Wilson: Life and Letters* (New York 1939), vol. VII, 34, 51.
[28] Schilling "Admirals and Foreign Policy," 89.
[29] Herwig and Trask "The Failure of Imperial Germany's Undersea Offensive," *Historian,* vol. 33, 614–15.
[30] E. David Cronon, ed. *The Cabinet Diaries of Josephus Daniels, 1913–1921* (Lincoln, Nebraska, 1963), 105. Daniels diary, 25 February 1917.
[31] Ibid., 146. Daniels diary, 4 May 1917. It is not clear whether Wilson knew of the British initiative at this time.
[32] Herwig and Trask "The Failure of Imperial Germany's Undersea Offensive," 615.
[33] Sims *Victory at Sea,* 386, 390.
[34] Trask *Captains and Cabinets,* 88. Sims to Pratt, 6 June 1917.
[35] Sims *Victory at Sea,* 191.
[36] Herwig and Trask "The Failure of Imperial Germany's Undersea Offensive," 617.
[37] Schilling "Admirals and Foreign Policy," 102. General Board to Secretary of the Navy, 13 July 1917.
[38] Trask *Captains and Cabinets,* 90. Sims to Pratt, 3 July 1917.
[39] Carroll Kilpatrick, ed. *Roosevelt and Daniels: A Friendship in Politics* (Chapel Hill 1952), 36–37; Schilling "Admirals and Foreign Policy," 101–103. Decision of 6 July 1917.
[40] Charles Seymour, ed. *The Intimate Papers of Colonel House* (Boston 1928), III, *Into the World War,* 190–93; Trask *Captains and Cabinets,* 172–74.
[41] St. Antony's Papers, reel 12, vol. 51, frames 127–29. Holtzendorff to Zimmermann, 3 August 1917.
[42] Trask *Captains and Cabinets,* 135. Page to Daniels, September [?] 1917.
[43] Herwig and Trask "The Failure of Imperial Germany's Undersea Offensive," 623. Spring Rice to Balfour, 25 October 1917.
[44] Cronon, ed. *Cabinet Diaries,* 235. Daniels diary, 10 November 1917.
[45] Seymour, ed. *Intimate Papers of Colonel House,* III, 269, 299.
[46] Herwig and Trask "The Failure of Imperial Germany's Undersea Offensive," 624. Planning Section Problem No. 2, 12 January 1918.
[47] Schilling "Admirals and Foreign Policy," 111–14. London Planning Section, Memorandum 21, submitted by Sims to the Navy Department, 11 May 1918.
[48] Trask *Captains and Cabinets,* 286–89.
[49] Schilling "Admirals and Foreign Policy," 121–22. Office of Naval Intelligence Report, 1 June 1918: General Board to Secretary of the Navy, 10 September 1918.

[50] Dudley W. Knox *A History of the United States Navy* (New York 1936), 405–407.
[51] Herwig and Trask "The Failure of Imperial Germany's Undersea Offensive," 633.
[52] Trask *Captains and Cabinets*, 363. Sims to Navy Department, 13 November 1918.
[53] Schilling "Admirals and Foreign Policy," 129.
[54] Ibid., 177. London Planning Section, Memorandum, 18 October 1918.
[55] Ibid., 131, General Board to Secretary of the Navy, 24 January and 22 August 1918; Richard D. Challener *Admirals, Generals, and American Foreign Policy 1898–1914* (Princeton 1973), 45.
[56] Schilling "Admirals and Foreign Policy," 135. Pratt to Sims, 15 August 1918.
[57] Ibid., 230. London Planning Section, Memorandum 65, 4 November 1918.

## 7 BACKGROUND: HITLER, RAEDER, AND THE UNITED STATES

[1] For the provisions of the Versailles settlement, see: *U.S. Senate, 67th Congress, 4th Session. Treaties, Conventions, International Acts, Protocols, and Agreements Between the United States of America and Other Powers 1910–1923* (Washington, D.C., 1923), 3331–3522.
[2] W. H. Tantum IV and E. J. Hoffschmidt *The Rise and Fall of the German Air Force (1933–1945)* (Old Greenwich, Connecticut, 1969), 13.
[3] Walther Hubatsch *Der Admiralstab und die Obersten Marinebehörden in Deutschland 1848–1945* (Frankfurt 1958), 201ff; Michael Salewski *Die deutsche Seekriegsleitung 1935 bis 1945* (Frankfurt 1970), I, 83–90, 108–12.
[4] Klaus Hildebrand *The Foreign Policy of the Third Reich* (Berkeley and Los Angeles 1973), passim; Hans-Adolf Jacobsen *Nationalsozialistische Aussenpolitik 1933–1938* (Frankfurt 1968), 424–28.
[5] See Alan Bullock *Hitler: A Study in Tyranny* (London 1964), 503, for Hitler's answer on 28 April 1939 to Roosevelt's request that Germany promise not to attack a number of European states.
[6] Adolf Hitler *Zweites Buch* (Stuttgart 1961), 127, 129, 130, 173. For Hitler's views on the United States see: Saul Friedländer *Hitler et les Etats Unis (1939–1941)* (Geneva 1963); James V. Compton *The Swastika and the Eagle: Hitler, the United States, and the Origins of World War II* (Boston 1967; German version *Hitler und die USA: Die Amerikapolitik des Dritten Reiches und die Ursprünge des Zweiten Weltkrieges*, Oldenburg and Hamburg 1968); Hermann Rauschning *Hitler Speaks: A Series of Political Conversations with Adolf Hitler on His Real Aims* (London 1939); Alton Frye *Nazi Germany and the American Hemisphere, 1933–1941* (New Haven 1967); Hans J. Trefousse *Germany and American Neutrality 1939–1941* (New York 1951); Fritz T. Epstein "Germany and the United States: Basic Patterns of Conflict and Understanding," *Issues and Conflicts* (Kansas 1959); Gerhard L. Weinberg "Hitler's Image of the United States," *American Historical Review*, vol. 69 (July 1964), 1006–21; Andreas Hillgruber "Der Faktor Amerika in Hitlers Strategie 1938–1941," *Aus Politik und Zeitgeschichte. Beilage zur Wochenzeitung "Das Parlament,"* B19/66 (11 May 1966), 1–21.
[7] English language sources: Compton *The Swastika and the Eagle*, 16–23; Rauschning *Hitler Speaks*, 75–79.
[8] Cited in Compton *Hitler und die USA*, 24, 25. For the "revisionist" school on Roosevelt and World War II see: Charles A. Beard *President Roosevelt and the Coming of the War, 1941* (New Haven 1948); Charles C. Tansill *Back Door to War* (Chicago 1952); William Henry Chamberlin *America's Second Crusade* (Chicago 1950); Harry Elmer Barnes, ed. *Perpetual War for Perpetual Peace* (Caldwell, Idaho, 1953); Frederic R. Sanborn *Design for War: A Study of Secret*

*Power Politics, 1937–1941* (New York 1951); Bruce M. Russett *No Clear and Present Danger: A Skeptical View of the U.S. Entry into World War II* (New York 1972).

[9] Max Domarus *Hitlers Reden und Proklamationen* (Würzburg 1963), IV, 1808.

[10] Albert Speer *Erinnerungen* (Frankfurt 1969), 319.

[11] Martin Bormann *Le testament politique de Hitler* (Paris 1959), 122. Introduced by H. R. Trevor-Roper and A. François-Poncet.

[12] Ernst Hanfstaengl *Zwischen Weissen und Braunem Haus. Erinnerungen eines politischen Aussenseiters* (Munich 1970), 41, 46–47, 66.

[13] Compton *Hitler und die USA*, 123.

[14] Hanfstaengl *Zwischen Weissen und Braunem Haus*, 280, 316.

[15] Ibid., 57.

[16] Ibid., 177.

[17] Hermann Rauschning *Gespräche mit Hitler* (New York 1940), 67–70.

[18] Cited in Compton *Hitler und die USA*, 217.

[19] BA-Koblenz, R 43 II. Reichskanzlei 1468. Dieckhoff to Foreign Office, 2 February and 22 March 1938.

[20] Ibid., 1467b. Rechenberg's tract is from May 1937. See also Hans-Heinrich Lammers (Chancery chief) to Rechenberg, 6 October 1937.

[21] Ibid. Rechenberg's second treatise is from September 1941. Hitler's reaction is recorded by Dr. Meerwald, Chancery, to Rechenberg, 16 September 1941.

[22] Ibid., 1470. Colin Ross to Hitler, 15 January 1941.

[23] BA-Koblenz, Büro des Staatssekretärs. USA, vol. 5. Boetticher to Foreign Office, 11 March 1941.

[24] Ibid., vol. 10. Special adviser, Ambassador Krümmer, to Ernst von Weizsäcker, 18 November 1941.

[25] Adolf Hitler *Mein Kampf* (Munich 1933), 741.

[26] Cited in Andreas Hillgruber *Hitlers Strategie. Politik und Kriegführung 1940–1941* (Frankfurt 1965), 556.

[27] Speer *Erinnerungen*, 166–75.

[28] Andreas Hillgruber *Deutschlands Rolle in der Vorgeschichte der beiden Weltkriege* (Göttingen 1967), 68. See also: A. J. P. Taylor *The Origins of the Second World War* (London 1961); David L. Hoggan *Der Erzwungene Krieg* (Tübingen 1961); Walter Görlitz *Der Zweite Weltkrieg 1939–1945* (Stuttgart 1952); H. R. Trevor-Roper "Hitlers Kriegsziele," *Stationen der deutschen Geschichte 1919–1945* (Stuttgart 1962); Günter Moltmann "Weltherrschaftsideen Hitlers," *Europa und Übersee. Festschrift für Egmont Zechlin* (Hamburg 1961), 197–240.

[29] The foregoing analysis of Hitler's "program" is taken from Hillgruber *Hitlers Strategie*, passim, which is summarized in Hillgruber *Deutschlands Rolle in der Vorgeschichte*, 68–83.

[30] Rauschning *Gespräche mit Hitler*, 12.

[31] H. R. Trevor-Roper, ed. *Hitler's Table Talk, 1941–1944* (London 1953), 28, 661.

[32] Moltmann "Weltherrschaftsideen Hitlers," 214–17.

[33] Gerhard L. Weinberg "German Colonial Plans and Policies 1938–1942," *Geschichte und Gegenwartsbewusstsein. Historische Betrachtungen und Untersuchungen. Festschrift für Hans Rothfels* (Göttingen 1963), 462.

[34] Klaus Hildebrand *Vom Reich zum Weltreich. Hitler, NSDAP und koloniale Frage 1919–1945* (Munich 1969).

[35] Rauschning *Gespräche mit Hitler*, 61–66.

[36] Moltmann "Weltherrschaftsideen Hitlers," 209–12.

[37] Hitler *Zweites Buch*, 171.

[38] Hanfstaengl *Zwischen Weissen und Braunem Haus*, 184.

[39] Cited in Jost Dülffer "Hitler und die Marineführung. Marineplanungen 1920 bis 1939," unpubl. diss., Freiburg University, 1971, 219. Raeder to the German naval delegate in Geneva (Admiral Baron Albrecht von Freyberg-Eisenberg-Allmen-

dingen), 25 March 1933. Dülffer's work is now in print: *Weimar, Hitler und die Marine; Reichspolitik und Flottenbau 1920–1939* (Düsseldorf 1973).

[40] See especially Salewski *Die deutsche Seekriegsleitung* I, 485ff.

[41] Hitler *Zweites Buch*, 169, 171.

[42] Dülffer "Hitler und die Marineführung," 233–34.

[43] BA-MA, PG 32187 Case 242. I SKL (Seekriegsleitung). Teil C VII. Entry for 11 January 1943. (These Naval War Staff records in the German Federal Military Archive in Freiburg carry the British classification PG from their date of capture, 1945, to that of their return to Germany, 1965; the British numbers will eventually all be replaced by German codes. According to popular legend, PG derives from "Pinched from the Germans.") See also Michael Salewski "Das Ende der deutschen Schlachtschiffe im Zweiten Weltkrieg," *Militärgeschichtliche Mitteilungen*, 2/1972, 53–73.

[44] Cited in Dülffer "Hitler und die Marineführung," 237.

[45] Cited in ibid., 289–90.

[46] Hitler *Mein Kampf*, 722.

[47] Hitler *Zweites Buch*, 171ff.

[48] Dülffer "Hitler und die Marineführung," 516.

[49] Ibid., 602.

[50] Ibid., 608.

[51] Salewski *Die deutsche Seekriegsleitung* I, 44–45.

[52] See especially Michael Salewski "Selbstverständnis und historisches Bewusstsein der deutschen Kriegsmarine," *Marine-Rundschau*, vol. 67 (1970), 65–88, and Salewski *Die deutsche Seekriegsleitung* I, 486ff.

[53] Cited in Dülffer "Hitler und die Marineführung," 533.

[54] Salewski *Die deutsche Seekriegsleitung* I, 45–50. This citation also covers the next paragraph.

[55] Ibid., 43; S. W. Roskill *The War at Sea 1939–1945* (London 1954), I, 590–92; Paul Auphan and Jacques Mordal *The French Navy in World War II* (Annapolis 1959), 389.

[56] Friedrich Ruge *Der Seekrieg 1939–1945* (Stuttgart 1956), 29. Slightly different figures are given by Anthony Martienssen *Hitler and His Admirals* (New York 1949), 13.

[57] See especially Hillgruber *Hitlers Strategie*, 35ff, 147ff, and Dülffer "Hitler und die Marineführung," 600ff, in support of this argument. See also Salewski's different view in *Die deutsche Seekriegsleitung* I, 59ff.

[58] Salewski *Die deutsche Seekriegsleitung* I, 65–66, 77–78.

[59] Ibid., 488.

## 8 ONCE MORE WORLD WAR (1939–1941)

[1] Andreas Hillgruber *Hitlers Strategie. Politik und Kriegführung 1940–1941* (Frankfurt 1965), 17ff.

[2] Andreas Hillgruber *Deutschlands Rolle in der Vorgeschichte der beiden Weltkriege* (Göttingen 1967), 98.

[3] Gerhard Wagner, ed. *Lagevorträge des Oberbefehlshabers der Kriegsmarine vor Hitler 1939–1945* (Munich 1972), 19–21. This publication contains the "I SKL. Teil C VII. Überlegungen des Chefs der SKL und Niederschriften über Vorträge und Besprechungen beim Führer," PG 32184 Case 239ff. An English version, "The Führer Conferences on Naval Affairs," was published in 1948 in *Brassey's Naval Annual*. The war diary of the SKL recorded Raeder's reaction to the start of the war on 7 November 1939. See BA-MA, PG 32023 Case 103, p. 43.

[4] Hermann von Lindheim "Wie Hitler versuchte, den Eintritt der USA in den Zweiten Weltkrieg zu verhindern," *Wehrforschung*, vol. 1 (May/June 1972), 87.
[5] BA-MA, PG 32184 Case 239. I SKL. Teil C VII. "Überlegungen des Chefs der SKL und Niederschriften über Vorträge und Besprechungen beim Führer. September 1939 – Dezember 1940," p. 13.
[6] Ibid., 99.
[7] Ibid., 146–47. Entry for 21 May 1940.
[8] Generaloberst Franz Halder *Kriegstagebuch* (Stuttgart 1962–1964), I, 227.
[9] J. Rohwer and G. Hümmelchen *Chronik des Seekrieges 1939–1945* (Oldenburg/ Hamburg 1968), 66.
[10] Friedrich Ruge *Der Seekrieg 1939–1945* (Stuttgart 1956), 37.
[11] BA-MA, PG 32611 Case 535. Denkschrift der SKL über den verschärften Seekrieg gegen England vom 15. X. 1939.
[12] Cited in Wagner, ed. *Lagevorträge*, 52–54. Entry for 23 November 1939.
[13] Michael Salewski *Die deutsche Seekriegsleitung 1935 bis 1945* (Frankfurt 1970), I, 92, 125, 158–59; S. W. Roskill *The War at Sea 1939–1945* (London 1954), I, 604–605.
[14] Salewski *Die deutsche Seekriegsleitung* I, 160–64.
[15] Ibid., 167–73.
[16] Rohwer and Hümmelchen *Chronik des Seekrieges*, 35, 37, 51. See Hans-Dietrich Loock *Quisling, Rosenberg und Terboven* (Stuttgart 1970), 209, 234, for the influence of Wegener upon Raeder.
[17] Alan Bullock *Hitler: A Study in Tyranny* (New York 1958), 536; Andreas Hillgruber and Gerhard Hümmelchen *Chronik des Zweiten Weltkrieges* (Frankfurt 1966), 9–12.
[18] Hillgruber and Hümmelchen *Chronik des Zweiten Weltkrieges*, 13–15; Paul Auphan and Jacques Mordal *The French Navy in World War II* (Annapolis 1959), 392–93, 111, 131.
[19] BA-MA, PG 32184 Case 239. I SKL. Teil C VII, 146–47.
[20] Ibid., 150.
[21] Salewski *Die deutsche Seekriegsleitung* I, 201–11.
[22] Ibid., 212.
[23] Ibid., 218, 222–23, 246; Walther Hubatsch, ed. *Hitlers Weisungen für die Kriegführung 1939–1945. Dokumente des Oberkommandos der Wehrmacht* (Frankfurt 1962), 53ff.
[24] Cited in Hillgruber *Deutschlands Rolle in der Vorgeschichte*, 103–105.
[25] BA-Koblenz, R 43 II. Reichskanzlei 1470, pp. 3–4. German News Service report of the Wiegand interview.
[26] Albert Speer *Erinnerungen* (Frankfurt 1969), 85, 86.
[27] Verbal communication to the author in May 1970 and July 1972.
[28] BA-MA, PG 32025 Case 105. Kriegstagebuch Seekriegsleitung. I Abteilung. Teil A (III M 1000), p. 13. Entry for 3 January 1940.
[29] BA-MA, PG 32029 Case 109, pp. 222 and 272–73. Entries for 22 and 27 May 1940.
[30] BA-MA, PG 32030 Case 110, p. 186. Entry for 18 June 1940.
[31] Michael Salewski "Selbstverständnis und historisches Bewusstsein der deutschen Kriegsmarine," *Marine-Rundschau*, vol. 67, 82.
[32] BA-MA, PG 32228 Case 282. I SKL. Teil Cc. Flottenaufbau nach dem Kriege. Juli–November 1943. This citation covers also the next paragraph.
[33] BA-MA, PG 32228 Case 282. I SKL. Teil Cc. Memorandum by Fricke and Wagner dated 3 June 1940.
[34] Ibid. These figures also stem from the Fricke/Wagner program.
[35] Ibid. Schniewind's memorandum is dated 6 July 1940.
[36] Salewski *Die deutsche Seekriegsleitung* I, 236–37. Salewski tried to minimize the importance of these plans with the chapter heading "The Alternative to Reality: Dreams and Utopias."
[37] Gerhard L. Weinberg "German Colonial Plans and Policies 1938–1942," *Geschichte*

*und Gegenwartsbewusstsein . . . Festschrift für Hans Rothfels* (Göttingen 1963), 473–74.

[38] Halder *Kriegstagebuch* II, 21. Entry for 13 July 1940.

[39] Cited in Gerhard L. Weinberg "Hitler's Image of the United States," *American Historical Review*, vol. 69, 1014. Halder *Kriegstagebuch* II, 49, records similar sentiments on 22 July 1940. Even the date of the campaign against Russia was announced: "Spring 1941."

[40] BA-MA, PG 32184 Case 239. I SKL. Teil C VII, 151.

[41] Ibid., 158.

[42] BA-MA, PG 32033 Case 113, p. 23. Entry for 3 September 1940.

[43] F. H. Hinsley *Hitler's Strategy* (Cambridge 1951), 65.

[44] Ibid., 111.

[45] Salewski "Selbstverständnis und historisches Bewusstsein," 83.

[46] See Salewski *Die deutsche Seekriegsleitung* I, 271–87, 293–304, for Raeder's Mediterranean program. The documents are in Wagner, ed. *Lagevorträge*, 136–41.

[47] BA-MA, PG 32184 Case 239. I SKL. Teil C VII, 207–209.

[48] Ibid., 225. See also Halder *Kriegstagebuch* II, 185, 187.

[49] Hillgruber *Hitlers Strategie*, 319–21; Klaus Hildebrand *The Foreign Policy of the Third Reich* (Berkeley and Los Angeles 1973), passim.

[50] Cited in Günter Moltmann "Weltherrschaftsideen Hitlers," *Europa und Übersee. Festschrift für Egmont Zechlin* (Hamburg 1961), 199. Memorandum by Major von Falckenstein, air force liaison officer with army headquarters.

[51] BA-MA, PG 31748 Case 277. I SKL. Teil Ca. Grundlegende Fragen der Kriegführung, May 1939 – November 1943, p. 370.

[52] BA-MA, PG 32184 Case 239. I SKL. Teil C VII, 243–44; Speer *Erinnerungen*, 194–95.

[53] BA-MA, PG 32184 Case 239. I SKL. Teil C VII, 290–91.

[54] See, for example: Ruge *Der Seekrieg;* Erich Raeder *Mein Leben* (Tübingen 1956–1957); Lothar Gruchmann "Die 'verpassten strategischen Chance' der Achsenmächte im Mittelmeerraum 1940 bis 1941," *Vierteljahrshefte für Zeitgeschichte*, vol. 18 (October 1970), 456–75.

[55] Jost Dülffer "Hitler und die Marineführung. Marineplanungen 1920 bis 1939," unpubl. diss., Freiburg University, 1971, 596. (Now in print: *Weimar, Hitler und die Marine: Reichspolitik und Flottenbau 1920–1939*, Düsseldorf 1973.)

[56] Salewski *Die deutsche Seekriegsleitung* I, 381–82.

[57] Ibid., 383–86.

[58] Ibid., 387–95, 455.

[59] Ibid., 398, 400–401, 449, 450, 455–56, 463.

[60] Ibid., 265, 405, 436–39.

[61] BA-Koblenz, Vereinigte Staaten von Amerika 38 No. 3. Flottenrüstung Ver. Staat. v. Amerika. Ambassador Dieckhoff to Foreign Office, 1 April 1938. McGrath was speaking before the Congressional Naval Committee.

[62] Moltmann "Weltherrschaftsideen Hitlers," 219. Shirer's reports are from December 1940.

[63] Ibid.

[64] Manfred Jonas *Isolationism in America* (Ithaca, New York, 1966), 213.

[65] John E. Wiltz *From Isolation to War, 1931–1941* (New York 1968), 85–86.

[66] S. E. Morison *History of United States Naval Operations in World War II* (Boston 1947–1962), I, *The Battle of the Atlantic, 1939–1943*, 27–51, 61. See also D. F. Drummond *The Passing of American Neutrality, 1937–1941* (Ann Arbor 1955); W. L. Langer and S. E. Gleason *The Undeclared War, 1940–1941* (New York 1953); Robert A. Divine *The Reluctant Belligerent: American Entry into World War II* (New York 1965), *The Illusion of Neutrality* (Chicago 1962), and *Roosevelt and World War II* (Baltimore 1969).

[67] Cited in Salewski *Die deutsche Seekriegsleitung* I, 489.

[68] BA-MA, PG 32036 Case 116, p. 232, entry for 20 December 1940; PG 32037 Case

117, p. 253, entry for 20 January 1941; and PG 32038 Case 118, p. 336, entry for 25 February 1941.

69 BA-Koblenz, Büro des Staatssekretärs. USA, vol. 5. Dieckhoff to Foreign Office, 10 March 1941.

70 BA-MA, PG 32186 Case 240. I SKL. Teil C VII, 35. Raeder based his analysis on a lengthy memorandum on this subject by Admiral Otto Groos on 14 January 1941. BA-MA, PG 32220–21 Case 272. I SKL. Teil C XV, Zusammenarbeit mit Japan.

71 Cited in Hans-Adolf Jacobsen *1939–1945. Der Zweite Weltkrieg in Chronik und Dokumenten* (Darmstadt 1959), 190. For Hitler's views on Japan see Theo Sommer *Deutschland und Japan zwischen den Mächten 1935–1940* (Tübingen 1962); Ernst L. Presseisen *Germany and Japan: A Study in Totalitarian Diplomacy, 1933–1941* (Den Haag 1958); Frank W. Iklé *German-Japanese Relations, 1936–1940* (New York 1956); Herbert Feis *The Road to Pearl Harbor* (Princeton 1962); P. W. Schroeder *The Axis Alliance and Japanese-American Relations 1941* (Ithaca, New York, 1958); John Toland *The Rising Sun: The Decline and Fall of the Japanese Empire, 1936–1945* (New York 1970); J. Menzel-Meskill *Hitler and Japan: The Hollow Alliance* (New York 1966); Bernd Martin *Deutschland und Japan im Zweiten Weltkrieg* (Göttingen 1969); and especially Andreas Hillgruber "Japan und der Fall 'Barbarossa'. Japanische Dokumente zu den Gesprächen Hitlers und Ribbentrops mit Botschafter Oshima von Februar bis Juni 1941," *Wehr-Wissenschaftliche Rundschau*, vol. 18 (June 1968), 312–36.

72 James V. Compton *Hitler und die USA. Die Amerikapolitik des Dritten Reiches und die Ursprünge des Zweiten Weltkrieges* (Oldenburg and Hamburg 1968), 214.

73 Cited in Andreas Hillgruber, ed. *Staatsmänner und Diplomaten bei Hitler. Vertrauliche Aufzeichnungen über Unterredungen mit Vertretern des Auslandes 1939–1941* (Munich 1969), 256.

74 BA-Koblenz, Büro des Staatssekretärs. USA, vol. 6. Ribbentrop to Foreign Office, 11 May 1941. See especially P. W. Schroeder *The Axis Alliance and Japanese-American Relations 1941* (Ithaca, New York, 1958) and R. J. C. Butow *Tojo and the Coming of War* (Princeton 1961).

75 Salewski "Selbstverständnis und historisches Bewusstsein," 84.

76 BA-MA, PG 32185 Case 240. I SKL. Teil C VII, 103.

77 Ibid., 170.

78 Ibid., 185.

79 Ibid., 117–18.

80 Cited in Andreas Hillgruber "Der Faktor Amerika in Hitlers Strategie 1938–1941," *Aus Politik und Zeitgeschichte. Beilage zur Wochenzeitung "Das Parlament,"* B19/66, p. 15.

81 W. H. Tantum IV and E. J. Hoffschmidt *The Rise and Fall of the German Air Force (1933 to 1949)* (Old Greenwich, Connecticut, 1969), 161, 165.

82 Salewski *Die deutsche Seekriegsleitung* I, 361–66; Hubatsch, ed. *Hitlers Weisungen für die Kriegführung*, 84. Führer Directive No. 21.

83 Salewski *Die deutsche Seekriegsleitung* I, 339; Hubatsch, ed. *Hitlers Weisungen für die Kriegführung*, 129ff.

84 Hubatsch, ed. *Hitlers Weisungen für die Kriegführung*, 136ff.

85 BA-MA, PG 32185 Case 240. I SKL. Teil C VII, 188.

86 Cited in Hillgruber, ed. *Staatsmänner und Diplomaten bei Hitler*, 301–302.

87 Morison *History of United States Naval Operations in World War II* I, 62–82; Roskill *The War at Sea 1939–1945* I, 612–13.

88 See Wagner, ed. *Lagevorträge*, 236, 263. War diary entries throughout May 1941 and for 21 June 1941.

89 BA-MA, PG 32043 Case 123. I SKL. Teil A, 99–101, 102. Entry for 8 July 1941.

90 Salewski *Die deutsche Seekriegsleitung* I, 494.

91 See Wagner, ed. *Lagevorträge*, 271. Entry for 25 July 1941.

92 Cited in Hillgruber, ed. *Staatsmänner und Diplomaten bei Hitler*, 299, 303.

[93] BA-MA, PG 32185 Case 240. I SKL. Teil C VII, 205–209.
[94] Salewski *Die deutsche Seekriegsleitung* I, 494.
[95] BA-Koblenz, R 43 II. Reichskanzlei, 1470. *Völkischer Beobachter*, No. 190, 9 July 1941.
[96] BA-Koblenz, Büro des Staatssekretärs. USA, vol. 7. Thomsen and Boetticher to OKW, 10 July 1941. See also their letters for July 1941.
[97] See the navy's memorandum, "Stand Schlacht im Atlantik," for Hitler on 25 July 1941. Wagner, ed. *Lagevorträge*, 274–75.
[98] See BA-MA, PG 32224 Case 276. I SKL. Teil C XVII. Besondere Fragen USA. Memorandum from October 1941.
[99] Salewski *Die deutsche Seekriegsleitung* I, 486–87. See especially the memorandum by Lieutenant Commander Alfred Kranzfelder on this subject on 10 May 1941.
[100] Wagner, ed. *Lagevorträge*, 283. Raeder's discussion with Hitler on 22 August 1941.
[101] Henry Picker, ed. *Hitlers Tischgespräche im Führerhauptquartier 1941–1942* (Stuttgart 1963), 136.
[102] Halder *Kriegstagebuch* III, 333. Entry for 7 December 1941, the day of the Japanese attack on Pearl Harbor.
[103] Ibid., 227. Entry for 13 September 1941.
[104] Cited in Picker, ed. *Hitlers Tischgespräche*, 145.
[105] Cited in Hillgruber, ed. *Staatsmänner und Diplomaten bei Hitler*, 319–20.
[106] Morison *History of United States Naval Operations in World War II* I, 79–80; Roskill *The War at Sea 1939–1945* I, 612–13.
[107] BA-MA, PG 32043 Case 123, p. 234, entry for 16 July 1941; PG 32044 Case 124, p. 225, entry for 14 August 1941; PG 32045 Case 125, pp. 205–206, entries for 13 September 1941.
[108] Wagner, ed. *Lagevorträge*, 290. Raeder's discussion with Hitler on 17 September 1941.
[109] BA-MA, PG 32045 Case 125, pp. 205–206, entry for 13 September 1941.
[110] Ibid. 258, entry for 16 September 1941.
[111] The admirals exchanged several notes, especially on 6 and 16 August 1941. BA-MA, PG 32116 Case 184. I SKL. Teil B V; and PG 32220–21 Case 272, I SKL. Teil C XV.
[112] BA-MA, PG 32045 Case 125, p. 304, entry for 19 September 1941, and p. 456, entry for 27 September 1941.
[113] BA-MA, PG 32220–21 Case 272. I SKL. Teil C XV. Fricke to Nomura, 15 October 1941.
[114] Cited in Compton *Hitler und die USA*, 214.
[115] BA-MA, PG 32046 Case 126, p. 4, entry for 1 October 1941.
[116] Ibid., 478. Entry for 28 October 1941.
[117] Salewski *Die deutsche Seekriegsleitung* I, 467.
[118] BA-MA, PG 32048 Case 128, p. 17. Entry for 2 December 1941.
[119] Ibid., 83–84. Entry for 6 December 1941.

## 9 GERMANY AND THE UNITED STATES AT WAR (1941–1945)

[1] Franz Halder *Kriegstagebuch* (Stuttgart 1962–1964), III, 333.
[2] Max Domarus, ed. *Hitlers Reden und Proklamationen* (Würzburg 1963), IV, 1791.
[3] Ibid., 1807, 1810.
[4] Cited in Gerhard L. Weinberg "Hitler's Image of the United States," *American Historical Review*, vol. 69, p. 1017.

[5] BA-Koblenz, Büro des Staatssekretärs. Krieg Amerika, vol. 1. Thomsen to Foreign Office, 7 and 10 December 1941.

[6] Cited in Andreas Hillgruber, ed. *Staatsmänner und Diplomaten bei Hitler . . . 1939–1941* (Munich 1969), 337–39.

[7] Andreas Hillgruber *Deutschlands Rolle in der Vorgeschichte der beiden Weltkriege* (Göttingen 1967), 124.

[8] BA-MA, PG 32048 Case 128, pp. 101–103. Entry for 7 December 1941.

[9] Michael Salewski *Die deutsche Seekriegsleitung 1935–1945* (Frankfurt 1970), I, 468.

[10] BA-MA, PG 32048 Case 128, p. 102. War diary entry for 7 December 1941.

[11] Ibid., 178. Entry for 11 December 1941.

[12] BA-MA, PG 32047 Case 127, p. 373, entry for 21 November 1941, and p. 442, entry for 25 November 1941.

[13] BA-MA, PG 32220–21 Case 272. I SKL. Teil C XV. Fricke's memorandum of 17 December 1941.

[14] BA-MA, PG 32048 Case 128, p. 295, entry for 19 December 1941, and p. 342, entry for 22 December 1941.

[15] Halder *Kriegstagebuch* III, 455. Entry for 12 June 1942.

[16] H. R. Trevor-Roper, ed. *Hitler's Secret Conversations 1941–1944* (London 1953), 196. Entry for 7 January 1942.

[17] Cited in Hillgruber, ed. *Staatsmänner und Diplomaten bei Hitler*, 337–39.

[18] Trevor-Roper, ed. *Hitler's Secret Conversations*, 196. Entry for 7 January 1942.

[19] BA-MA, PG 32048 Case 128, p. 159, entry for 10 December 1941; PG 32049 Case 129, p. 423, entry for 23 January 1942. See also Karl Dönitz *Zehn Jahre und zwanzig Tage* (Frankfurt 1967), 192–210; S. W. Roskill *The War at Sea 1939–1945* (London 1956), II, 94–96.

[20] See Friedrich Ruge *Der Seekrieg 1939–1945* (Stuttgart 1956), 253–55; S. E. Morison *History of United States Naval Operations in World War II* (Boston 1947–1962), I, *The Battle of the Atlantic, 1939–1943*, 125.

[21] Roskill *The War at Sea 1939–1945* II, 94–96; Ruge *Der Seekrieg 1939–1945*, 253–55.

[22] Olaf Groehler in the *Democratic German Report* (an English language publication of the East German government), vol. 21 (October 4, 1972), 144; the article is expanded in his book *Geschichte des Luftkrieges 1910 bis 1970* (Berlin 1975).

[23] Cited in Hans-Adolf Jacobsen *1939–1945: Der Zweite Weltkrieg in Chronik und Dokumenten* (Darmstadt 1959), 255.

[24] Cited in Andreas Hillgruber "Der Faktor Amerika in Hitlers Strategie 1938–1941," *Aus Politik und Zeitgeschichte. Beilage zur Wochenzeitung "Das Parlament,"* B19/66, p. 21.

[25] BA-MA, PG 32048 Case 128, p. 164. Entry for 10 December 1941.

[26] See Ruge *Der Seekrieg 1939–1945*, 264–75; F. H. Hinsley *Hitler's Strategy* (Cambridge 1951), 196–98, 215.

[27] Roskill *The War at Sea 1939–1945* II, 353; Hinsley *Hitler's Strategy*, 218–19. This citation covers also the next paragraph.

[28] The events of the last two years of war are summarized from Ruge *Der Seekrieg 1939–1945*, 279–84, and the end of the German surface vessels from Roskill *The War at Sea 1939–1945* III, part II, 457.

[29] See Ruge *Der Seekrieg 1939–1945*, 253–55, 295, 297; Roskill *The War at Sea 1939–1945* II, 474–75.

[30] Hillgruber *Deutschlands Rolle in der Vorgeschichte der beiden Weltkriege*, 126.

[31] Roskill *The War at Sea 1939–1945* III, part I, 364; Hinsley *Hitler's Strategy*, 230; Ruge *Der Seekrieg 1939–1945*, 304–307.

[32] Ruge *Der Seekrieg 1939–1945*, 362.

[33] Dönitz *Zehn Jahre und zwanzig Tage*, 483–84; Ruge *Der Seekrieg 1939–1945*, 384; Roskill *The War at Sea 1939–1945* III, part II, 471–72.

[34] *U.S. Senate, 67th Congress, 4th Session. Treaties, Conventions, International Acts, Protocols, and Agreements Between the United States of America and Other Powers 1910–1923* (Washington 1923), 3418–19.

[35] *Trial of the Major War Criminals Before the International Military Tribunal* (Nuremberg 1947), I, 310–17, 365. The statement concerning Raeder is from Salewski *Die deutsche Seekriegsleitung* I, 361.

## CONCLUSION: PATTERNS OF CONFLICT

[1] Konrad H. Jarausch "Die unheimlichen 'Germans': Das problematische Deutschlandbild amerikanischer Akademiker," *Die Zeit* 18 July 1972, p. 8.

# Select Bibliography

THE GERMAN NAVY ARCHIVE (MARINEARCHIV), NOW IN FREIBURG, WEST Germany, at the Federal Military Archive (Bundesarchiv-Militärarchiv), forms the documentary basis for this work. Originally in Berlin as an integral part of the High Command, the Navy Archive was moved early in November 1944, because of heavy Allied air raids, to Tambach Castle near Coburg in Bavaria. It was stored in the swimming pool there and was, by order of Admiral Karlgeorg Schuster, chief of the Navy History Office, to be destroyed rather than surrendered if Germany lost the war. About two hundred liters of gasoline and several cords of wood were gathered for this purpose, but in the severe winter of 1944–1945 the staff used the combustible material for heat rather than archival destruction. By 7 May 1945 Washington knew of the capture of these vital records, and over the next two years 3,900 reels of microfilm copies of the material were made in London. The records were returned — excluding the submarine logs, which are held in Great Britain — between 1959 and 1965 in eight large shipments totaling 110 tons. I have throughout the book used the original documents in Freiburg. The microfilm copies, the so-called Tambach Archive, are now at the National Archives in Washington, D.C., as: German Naval Record Collection of the U.S. Naval History Division, TA 112.

A number of works cited below in the bibliography must be singled out as of special value to this study because I relied on them heavily to sketch in some of the historical background for the documentary sections. They include, for the period prior to 1914 with regard to German-

American relations, especially Alfred Vagts, J. A. S. Grenville and G. B. Young; for the First World War, Karl Birnbaum, Carl-Axel Gemzell (whose book arrived only during the final stage of this study), Klaus Schwabe, and Bernd Stegemann, just to mention a few. Not surprisingly, the National Socialist era has drawn the largest contingent of analysts: Fritz T. Epstein, Saul Friedländer, Alton Frye, James V. Compton, Andreas Hillgruber, Günter Moltmann, Joachim Remak, H. J. Trefousse, Klaus Hildebrand, Hans-Adolf Jacobsen, F. H. Hinsley, Theodor Schieder, and many others.

The "Tirpitz" fleet has found its share of investigators, from Walther Hubatsch to Jonathan Steinberg and Volker R. Berghahn; the "Raeder" fleet has most recently undergone detailed study by Jost Dülffer for the period prior to the outbreak of the Second World War, and Michael Salewski for the war years. Harold and Margaret Sprout pioneered the political history of the United States Navy in the period before 1918; Peter Karsten has provided the first partial analysis of the Annapolis "naval aristocracy"; Richard D. Challener has traced the relations between American admirals and generals in terms of foreign policy from 1898 to 1914; Warner R. Schilling and David F. Trask have analyzed the United States Navy's role during the First World War; and Samuel Eliot Morison has provided epic treatment of the American navy during the Second World War.

Finally, a word on the literature of the Hitler era, which over the last few years has inspired a virtual flood of printer's ink for works ranging from fairly standard biographies to outlandish psychohistories. If the reader misses such listings in the bibliography, it is because I have opted for providing him or her with the benefits of the scholarly analyses of the period found below and in the chapter notes.

## PRIMARY SOURCES

### (I) *Unpublished Archival Collections*

(1) Koblenz, West Germany. Bundesarchiv (Federal Archive)

R. 1 Reichsinstitut für Geschichte des neuen Deutschland. Berichte v. Holtzendorff an Ballin. 16 vols.
R 43/II. Akten der neuen Reichskanzlei

Personal Papers (Nachlass)

Nl Bülow
Nl Bötticher
Nl Gessler
Nl Hertling
Nl Hohenlohe-Schillingsfürst
Nl Schwertfeger

## *Select Bibliography*


Barnes, Harry Elmer, ed. *Perpetual War for Perpetual Peace*. Caldwell, Idaho, 1953.

Baumgart, Winfried. *Deutsche Ostpolitik 1918. Von Brest-Litowsk bis zum Ende des Ersten Weltkrieges*. Vienna and Munich 1966.

Beale, Howard K. *Theodore Roosevelt and the Rise of America to World Power*. New York 1962.

Beard, Charles A. *President Roosevelt and the Coming of the War, 1941*. New Haven 1948.

Bemis, Samuel Flagg. *A Diplomatic History of the United States*. New York 1942.

Berghahn, Volker R. *Der Tirpitz-Plan. Genesis und Verfall einer innenpolitischen Krisenstrategie unter Wilhelm II*. Düsseldorf 1971.

Birnbaum, Karl E. *Peace Moves and U-Boat Warfare: A Study of Imperial Germany's Policy towards the United States April 18, 1916–January 9, 1917*. Stockholm 1958.

Böhme, H. *Deutschlands Weg zur Grossmacht*. Cologne 1966.

Braisted, William R. *The United States Navy in the Pacific, 1897–1909*. Austin 1958.

———. *The United States Navy in the Pacific, 1909–1922*. Austin 1971.

Bueb, V. *Die "Junge Schule" der französischen Marine. Strategie und Politik 1875–1900*. Boppard 1971.

Bülow, Bernhard von. *Deutsche Politik*. Berlin 1917.

Bullock, Alan. *Hitler: A Study in Tyranny*. London 1964.

Butow, R. J. C. *Tojo and the Coming of War*. Princeton 1961.

Cambell, C. S. *Anglo-American Understanding 1898–1903*. Baltimore 1957.

Cecil, Lamar J. R. *Albert Ballin: Business and Politics in Imperial Germany, 1888–1918*. Princeton 1967.

Challener, Richard D. *Admirals, Generals, and American Foreign Policy 1898–1914*. Princeton 1973.

Chamberlin, William Henry. *America's Second Crusade*. Chicago 1950.

Compton, James V. *The Swastika and the Eagle: Hitler, the United States, and the Origins of World War II*. Boston 1967. German version: *Hitler und die USA: Die Amerikapolitik des Dritten Reiches und die Ursprünge des Zweiten Weltkrieges*. Oldenburg and Hamburg 1968.

Daniels, Josephus. *The Wilson Era: Years of War and After, 1917–1923*. Chapel Hill 1946.

Dehio, Ludwig. *Deutschland und die Weltpolitik im 20. Jahrhundert*. Munich 1955.

DeJong, L. *Die deutsche Fünfte Kolonne im Zweiten Weltkrieg*. Stuttgart 1959.

Divine, Robert A. *The Reluctant Belligerent: American Entry into World War II*. New York 1965.

———. *The Illusion of Neutrality*. Chicago 1962.

———. *Roosevelt and World War II*. Baltimore 1969.

Dorman, Michael. *The Secret Service Story*. New York 1967.

Drummond, D. F. *The Passing of American Neutrality, 1937–1941*. Ann Arbor 1955.

Dugdale, Blanche E. C. *Arthur James Balfour*. New York 1937. 2 vols.

Dülffer, Jost. "Hitler und die Marineführung. Marineplanungen 1920 bis 1939." Unpubl. diss., Freiburg 1971. Later published as: *Weimar, Hitler und die Marine; Reichspolitik und Flottenbau 1920–1939*. Düsseldorf 1973.

Edelsheim, Franz Freiherr von. *Operationen über See. Eine Studie von Freiherr von Edelsheim*. Berlin 1901. Translated into English as *Operations Upon the Sea: A Study*. New York 1914.

Etue, George E. Jr. "The German Fatherland Party 1917–1918." Unpubl. diss., University of California, Berkeley 1959.

Esthus, Raymond A. *Theodore Roosevelt and the International Rivalries*. Waltham 1970.

Feis, Herbert. *The Road to Pearl Harbor*. Princeton 1962.

———. *Europe, the World's Banker, 1870–1914*. New York 1964.

Feldman, Gerald D. *Army, Industry, and Labor in Germany, 1914–1918*. Princeton 1966.

Fischer, Fritz. *Griff nach der Weltmacht. Die Kriegszielpolitik des kaiserlichen Deutschland 1914–1918*. Düsseldorf 1964.

———. *Krieg der Illusionen. Die deutsche Politik von 1911 bis 1914*. Düsseldorf 1969.

Fraenkel, Ernst. *Amerika im Spiegel des deutschen politischen Denkens*. Cologne 1959.

Freidel, Frank. *Franklin D. Roosevelt: The Apprenticeship*. Boston 1952.

Friedländer, Saul. *Hitler et les Etats Unis (1939–1941)*. Geneva 1963.

Frothingham, Thomas G. *The Naval History of the World War*. Cambridge 1926. 3 vols.

Frye, Alton. *Nazi Germany and the American Hemisphere, 1933–1941*. New Haven 1967.

Galster, Karl. *England, Deutsche Flotte und Weltkrieg*. Kiel 1925.

Gardner, Lloyd C. *Economic Aspects of New Deal Diplomacy*. Madison 1964.

Gatzke, Hans W. *Germany's Drive to the West: A Study of German War Aims During the First World War*. Baltimore 1950.

Gelber, Lionel M. *The Rise of Anglo-American Friendship*. London 1938.

Gemzell, Carl-Axel. *Organization, Conflict, and Innovation: A Study of German Naval Strategic Planning, 1888–1940*. Lund 1973.

Gibson, R. H., and Maurice Prendergast. *The German Submarine War, 1914 to 1918*. London 1931.

Görlitz, Walter. *Der Zweite Weltkrieg 1939–1945*. Stuttgart 1952.

Grant, Robert M. *U-Boat Intelligence, 1914–1918*. Hamden, Connecticut, 1969.

———. *U-Boats Destroyed: The Effect of Anti-Submarine War, 1914–1918*. London 1964.

Grantham, Dewey W. *Theodore Roosevelt*. Englewood Cliffs, New Jersey, 1971.

Gregory, Ross. *Walter Hines Page: Ambassador to the Court of Saint James's*. Lexington 1970.

Grenville, J. A. S., and G. B. Young. *Politics, Strategy, and American Diplomacy: Studies in Foreign Policy, 1873–1917*. New Haven 1966.

Groos, Otto. *Seekriegslehren im Lichte des Weltkrieges*. Berlin 1929.

Hale, Oron J. *Publicity and Diplomacy with Special Reference to England and Germany 1890–1914*. London 1940.

Hallgarten, George W. F. *Imperialismus vor 1914*. Munich 1963. 2 vols.

Hanfstaengl, Ernst. *Zwischen Weissen und Braunem Haus. Erinnerungen eines politischen Aussenseiters*. Munich 1970.

Hendrick, Burton J. *The Life and Letters of Walter Hines Page*. Garden City, New York, 1922. 3 vols.

Herwig, Holger H. *The German Naval Officer Corps 1890–1918: A Social and Political History*. Oxford 1973.

Hildebrand, Klaus. *Vom Reich zum Weltreich. Hitler, NSDAP und koloniale Frage 1919–1945*. Munich 1969.

———. *Nationalsozialistische Aussenpolitik*. Stuttgart 1970.

Hill, Howard C. *Roosevelt and the Caribbean*. Chicago 1927.

Hillgruber, Andreas. *Hitlers Strategie. Politik und Kriegführung 1940–1941*. Frankfurt 1965.

———. *Deutschlands Rolle in der Vorgeschichte der beiden Weltkriege*. Göttingen 1967.

———. *Kontinuität und Diskontinuität in der deutschen Aussenpolitik von Bismarck bis Hitler*. Düsseldorf 1969.

Hillgruber, Andreas, and Gerhard Hümmelchen. *Chronik des Zweiten Weltkrieges*. Frankfurt 1966.

Hinsley, F. H. *Hitler's Strategy*. Cambridge 1951.

Hoggan, David L. *Der Erzwungene Krieg*. Tübingen 1961.

Hubatsch, Walther. *Der Admiralstab und die Obersten Marinebehörden in Deutschland 1848–1945*. Frankfurt 1958.

———. *Die Ära Tirpitz.* Göttingen 1955.
Iklé, Frank W. *German-Japanese Relations, 1936–1940.* New York 1956.
Jacobsen, Hans-Adolf. *1939–1945: Der Zweite Weltkrieg in Chronik und Dokumenten.* Darmstadt 1959.
———. *Nationalsozialistische Aussenpolitik 1933–1938.* Frankfurt 1968.
Jenkins, John Wilber. *Our Navy's Part in the Great War.* New York 1919.
Jonas, Manfred. *Isolationism in America.* Ithaca 1966.
Karsten, Peter. *The Naval Aristocracy: The Golden Age of Annapolis and the Emergence of Modern American Navalism.* New York 1972.
Kehr, Eckart. "Schlachtflottenbau und Parteipolitik 1894–1901. Versuch eines Querschnitts durch die innenpolitischen, sozialen und ideologischen Voraussetzungen des deutschen Imperialismus," *Historische Studien,* Berlin 1930, vol. 197.
Kennedy, Paul M. "The Partition of the Samoan Islands, 1898–1899." Unpubl. diss., Oxford 1970. Later published as: *The Samoan Tangle: A Study in Anglo-German-American Relations 1878–1900.* New York 1975.
Kilpatrick, Carroll, ed. *Roosevelt and Daniels: A Friendship in Politics.* Chapel Hill 1952.
Klein, F. et al., eds. *Deutschland im Ersten Weltkrieg.* East Berlin 1968.
Knox, Dudley W. *A History of the United States Navy.* New York 1936.
Langer, William L. *The Diplomacy of Imperialism 1890–1902.* New York 1951.
———. *European Alliances and Alignments.* New York 1931.
Langer, William L., and S. E. Gleason. *The Undeclared War, 1940–1941.* New York 1953.
———. *The Challenge to Isolation, 1937–1940.* New York 1952.
Laurens, A. *Histoire de la guerre sous-marine allemande (1914–1918).* Paris 1930.
LaFeber, Walter. *The New Empire: An Interpretation of American Expansion 1860–1898.* New York 1963.
———. *America, Russia, and the Cold War, 1945–1966.* New York 1967.
Loock, Hans-Dietrich. *Quisling, Rosenberg und Terboven.* Stuttgart 1970.
Lowe, C. J. *The Reluctant Imperialists.* London 1967. 2 vols.
Mantey, E. von. *Deutsche Marinegeschichte.* Charlottenburg 1926.
Marder, Arthur J. *From the Dreadnought to Scapa Flow: The Royal Navy in the Fisher Era, 1904–1919.* London 1961–1970. 5 vols.
———. *The Anatomy of British Sea Power.* London 1940.
Marienfeld, W. "Wissenschaft und Schlachtflottenbau in Deutschland 1897–1906," *Beiheft 2: Marine-Rundschau* (April 1957).
Martienssen, Anthony. *Hitler and His Admirals.* New York 1949.
Martin, Bernd. *Deutschland und Japan im Zweiten Weltkrieg.* Göttingen 1969.
McCormick, Thomas J. *China Market: America's Quest for Informal Empire, 1893–1901.* Chicago 1967.
McEntee, Girard L. *Military History of the World War.* New York 1943.
Menzel-Meskill, J. *Hitler and Japan: The Hollow Alliance.* New York 1966.
Meyer, J. *Die Propaganda der deutschen Flottenbewegung 1897–1900.* Bern 1967.
Michelsen, Andreas H. *Der U-Bootskrieg 1914–1918.* Leipzig 1925.
Mikesell, Raymond. *Foreign Investments in Latin America.* Washington 1955.
Morison, Elting E. *Admiral Sims and the Modern American Navy.* Boston 1942.
Naudé, Kurt. *Der Kampf um den uneingeschränkten U-Boot-Krieg 1914 bis 1917. Ein Beitrag zu dem Problem 'Politik und Kriegführung.'* Hamburg 1941.
Newbolt, Henry. *Naval Operations.* London 1928. 5 vols. (Part of the British official history of the First World War: *History of the Great War Based on Official Documents.*)
Niemann, Alfred. *Revolution von Oben — Umsturz von Unten. Entwicklung und Verlauf der Staatsumwälzung in Deutschland 1914–1918.* Berlin 1927.
Peters, Evelene. *Roosevelt und der Kaiser. Ein Beitrag zur Geschichte der deutsch-amerikanischen Beziehungen 1895–1906.* Leipzig 1936.

Perkins, Dexter. *The Monroe Doctrine 1867–1907*. Baltimore 1937. (Revised edition, Boston 1963.)
Presseisen, Ernst L. *Germany and Japan: A Study in Totalitarian Diplomacy, 1933–1941*. The Hague 1958.
Rauschning, Hermann. *Gespräche mit Hitler*. New York 1940.
Ritter, Gerhard. *Der Schlieffenplan. Kritik eines Mythos*. Munich 1956.
———. *Staatskunst und Kriegshandwerk. Das Problem des "Militarismus" in Deutschland*. Munich 1965–1968. 4 vols.
Röhl, John C. G. *1914: Delusion or Design? The Testimony of Two German Diplomats*. London 1973.
Röhr, Albert. *Handbuch der deutschen Marinegeschichte*. Oldenburg and Hamburg 1963.
Ruge, Friedrich. *Der Seekrieg 1939–1945*. Stuttgart 1956.
Russett, Bruce M. *No Clear and Present Danger: A Skeptical View of the U.S. Entry into World War II*. New York 1972.
Ryden, G. H. *The Foreign Policy of the United States in Relation to Samoa*. New Haven 1933.
Salewski, Michael. *Die deutsche Seekriegsleitung 1935 bis 1945*. Frankfurt 1970.
Sanborn, Frederic R. *Design for War: A Study of Secret Power Politics, 1937–1941*. New York 1951.
Scheer, Reinhard. *Germany's High Sea Fleet in the World War*. London 1920.
Schieder, Theodor. *Hermann Rauschnings "Gespräche mit Hitler" als Geschichtsquelle*. Opladen 1972.
———, ed. *Handbuch der europäischen Geschichte*. Stuttgart 1968.
Schieder, W., ed. *Erster Weltkrieg. Ursachen, Entstehungen und Kriegsziele*. Cologne 1969.
Schilling, Warner R. "Admirals and Foreign Policy 1913–1919." Unpubl. diss., Yale University 1954.
Schroeder, P. W. *The Axis Alliance and Japanese-American Relations 1941*. Ithaca, New York, 1958.
Sims, W. S., and B. J. Hendrick. *The Victory at Sea*. Garden City, New York, 1920.
Sommer, Theo. *Deutschland und Japan zwischen den Mächten 1935–1940*. Tübingen 1962.
Sommers, D. *Haldane of Cloan: His Life and Times, 1856–1928*. London 1960.
Spindler, Arno. *Wie es zu dem Entschluss zum uneingeschränkten U-Boots-Krieg gekommen ist*. Göttingen n.d.
Sprout, Harold and Margaret. *The Rise of American Naval Power*. Revised edition, Princeton 1966.
Stadelmann, Rudolf. *Deutschland und Westeuropa. Drei Aufsätze*. Schloss Laupheim 1948.
Stegmann, Dirk. *Die Erben Bismarcks. Parteien und Verbände in der Spätphase des Wilhelminischen Deutschlands. Sammlungspolitik 1897–1918*. Cologne 1970.
Stegemann, Bernd. *Die Deutsche Marinepolitik 1916–1918*. Berlin 1970.
Steinberg, Jonathan. *Yesterday's Deterrent: The Birth of the Tirpitz Battle Fleet*. London 1965.
Tansill, Charles C. *Back Door to War*. New York 1952.
Tantum, W. H., IV, and E. J. Hoffschmidt. *The Rise and Fall of the German Air Force (1933 to 1945)*. Old Greenwich, Connecticut, 1969.
Taylor, A. J. P. *The Origins of the Second World War*. London 1961.
Taylor, Charles Carlisle. *The Life of Admiral Mahan: Naval Philosopher*. New York 1920.
Tillman, Seth P. *Anglo-American Relations at the Paris Peace Conference*. Princeton 1961.
Tirpitz, Alfred von. *Der Aufbau der deutschen Weltmacht*. Stuttgart and Berlin 1924.

Toland, John. *The Rising Sun: The Decline and Fall of the Japanese Empire, 1936–1945*. New York 1970.

Trask, David F. *Victory Without Peace. American Foreign Relations in the Twentieth Century*. New York 1968.

———. *Captains and Cabinets: Anglo-American Naval Relations, 1917–1918*. Columbia, Missouri, 1972.

———. *The United States in the Supreme War Council: American War Aims and Inter-Allied Strategy, 1917–1918*. Middletown, Connecticut, 1961.

Trefousse, Hans J. *Germany and American Neutrality 1939–1941*. New York 1951.

Tuchman, Barbara W. *The Zimmermann Telegram*. New York 1965.

*Untersuchungen zur Geschichte des Offizierkorps. Anciennität und Beförderung nach Leistung*. Stuttgart 1962.

Vagts, Alfred. *Deutschland und die Vereinigten Staaten in der Weltpolitik*. New York 1935. 2 vols.

Wartenburg, Yorck von. *Weltgeschichte in Umrissen. Federzeichnungen eines Deutschen*. Berlin 1901.

Watson, Mark Skinner. *Chief of Staff: Prewar Plans and Preparations*. Washington 1950.

Wehler, Hans-Ulrich. *Bismarck und der Imperialismus*. Cologne and Berlin 1969.

Wernecke, Klaus. *Der Wille zur Weltgeltung. Aussenpolitik und Öffentlichkeit im Kaiserreich am Vorabend des Ersten Weltkrieges*. Düsseldorf 1970.

Williams, William A. *The Tragedy of American Diplomacy*. New York 1959.

Wiltz, John E. *From Isolation to War, 1931–1941*. New York 1968.

Woodward, E. L. *Great Britain and the German Navy*. Oxford 1935.

Wortmann, Karl. *Geschichte der deutschen Vaterlands-Partei 1917–1918*. Halle an der Saale 1926.

Ziekursch, Johannes. *Politische Geschichte des neuen deutschen Kaiserreiches*. Frankfurt 1930. 3 vols.

Zimmermann, A. *Geschichte der deutschen Kolonialpolitik*. Berlin 1914.

### (II) *Articles and Special Chapters in Anthologies*

Baumgart, Winfried. "Zur Theorie des Imperialismus," *Aus Politik und Zeitgeschichte. Beilage zur Wochenzeitung "Das Parlament,"* vol. 23/71, 3–11.

———. "Neue Quellen zur Beurteilung Ludendorffs. Der Konflikt mit dem Admiralstabschef über die deutsche Schwarzmeerpolitik im Sommer 1918," *Militärgeschichtliche Mitteilungen, 1969*, No. 2, 161–177.

Berghahn, Volker R. "Zu den Zielen des deutschen Flottenbaus unter Wilhelm II.," *Historische Zeitschrift*, vol. 210 (1970), 34–100. This article is expanded in Berghahn's book *Der Tirpitz-Plan* (see entry on page 297).

Berghahn, Volker R., and Wilhelm Deist. "Kaiserliche Marine und Kriegsausbruch 1914," *Militärgeschichtliche Mitteilungen*, 1/1970, 37–58.

Bogatsch, Rudolf. "Politische und militärische Probleme nach dem Frankreichfeldzug," *Vollmacht des Gewissens*, vol. II (Frankfurt and Berlin 1965), 11–146.

Deist, Wilhelm. "Die Politik der Seekriegsleitung und die Rebellion der Flotte Ende Oktober 1918," *Vierteljahrshefte für Zeitgeschichte*, vol. XIV (October 1966), 341–368.

Diederichs, Admiral Otto von. "A Statement of Events in Manila, May–October 1898," *Journal of the Royal United Services Institution*, vol. 59 (November 1914).

Ditten, Wülfing von. "Die amerikanische Waffen- und Truppentransporte im Weltkriege," *Marine-Rundschau*, vol. 34 (1929), 548–58.

Drascher, Wahrhold. "Zur Soziologie des deutschen Seeoffizierkorps," *Wehrwissenschaftliche Rundschau*, vol. 12 (1962), 555–569.

Dülffer, Jost. "Das deutsch-englische Flottenabkommen vom 18. Juni 1935," *Marine-Rundschau*, vol. 69 (1972), 641–59.

Epstein, Fritz T. "Germany and the United States: Basic Patterns of Conflict and

Understanding," *Issues and Conflicts* (Lawrence, Kansas, 1959). Edited by G. L. Anderson.

Forstmeier, Friedrich. "Deutsche Invasionspläne gegen die USA um 1900," *Marine-Rundschau,* vol. 68 (1971), 344–51.

Gatzke, Hans W. "The United States and Germany on the Eve of World War I," *Deutschland in der Weltpolitik des 19. und 20. Jahrhunderts* (Düsseldorf 1973), 271–86. Edited by I. Geiss and B. J. Wendt.

Grenville, J. A. S. "Diplomacy and War Plans in the United States, 1890–1917," *Transactions of the Royal Historical Society,* vol. 11 (1961), 1–21.

Gruchmann, Lothar. "Die 'verpassten strategischen Chance' der Achsenmächte im Mittelmeerraum 1940 bis 1941," *Vierteljahrshefte für Zeitgeschichte,* vol. 18 (October 1970), 456–75.

Herwig, Holger H. "Prelude to *Weltblitzkrieg:* Germany's Naval Policy Towards the United States of America, 1939–1941," *Journal of Modern History,* vol. 43 (December 1971), 649–68.

———. "German Policy in the Eastern Baltic Sea in 1918: Expansion or Anti-Bolshevik Crusade?," *Slavic Review,* vol. 32 (June 1973), 339–357.

———. "Admirals versus Generals: The War Aims of the Imperial German Navy 1914–1918," *Central European History,* vol. 5 (September 1972), 203–28.

Herwig, Holger H., and David F. Trask. "The Failure of Germany's Undersea Offensive Against World Shipping, February 1917 – October 1918," *Historian,* vol. 33 (August 1971), 611–36.

———. "Naval Operations Plans Between Germany and the United States of America 1898–1913: A Study of Strategic Planning in the Age of Imperialism," *Militärgeschichtliche Mitteilungen,* 2/1970, 5–32.

Hillgruber, Andreas. "Japan und der Fall 'Barbarossa.' Japanische Dokumente zu den Gesprächen Hitlers und Ribbentrops mit Botschafter Oshima von Februar bis Juni 1941," *Wehr-Wissenschaftliche Rundschau,* vol. 18 (June 1968), 312–36.

———. "Der Faktor Amerika in Hitlers Strategie 1938–1941," *Aus Politik und Zeitgeschichte. Beilage zur Wochenzeitung "Das Parlament,"* B19/66, 1–21.

Holbo, Paul S. "Perilous Obscurity: Public Diplomacy and the Press in the Venezuelan Crisis, 1902–1903," *Historian,* vol. 32 (May 1970), 428–48.

Jarausch, Konrad H. "The Illusion of Limited War: Chancellor Bethmann Hollweg's Calculated Risk, July 1914," *Central European History,* vol. 2 (March 1969), 48–76.

Kennedy, Paul M. "Anglo-German Relations in the Pacific and the Partition of Samoa: 1885–1899," *Australian Journal of Politics and History* (April 1971), 56–72.

———. "Bismarck's Imperialism: The Case of Samoa, 1880–1890," *Historical Journal,* vol. 15 (1972), 261–283.

———. "Tirpitz, England and the Second Navy Law of 1900: A Strategical Critique," *Militärgeschichtliche Mitteilungen,* 1970, No. 2, 33–57.

Kitchen, Martin. "Militärische Unternehmungen gegen Kanada im Ersten Weltkrieg," *Militärgeschichtliche Mitteilungen,* 1970, No. 1, 27–36.

Lindheim, Hermann von. "Wie Hitler versuchte, den Eintritt der USA in den Zweiten Weltkrieg zu verhindern," *Wehrforschung,* vol. 1 (1972), 87–91.

Livermore, Seward W. "Theodore Roosevelt, the American Navy, and the Venezuelan Crisis of 1902–1903," *American Historical Review,* vol. 51 (April 1946), 452–71.

Moltmann, Günther. "Weltherrschaftsideen Hitlers," *Europa und Übersee. Festschrift für Egmont Zechlin* (Hamburg 1961), 197–240.

Parsons, Edward B. "The German-American Crisis of 1902–1903," *Historian,* vol. 33 (May 1971), 436–52.

Rippy, J. Fred. "German Investments in Latin America," *Journal of Business,* vol. 21 (April 1948), 63–73.

Salewski, Michael. "Das Ende der deutschen Schlachtschiffe im Zweiten Weltkrieg," *Militärgeschichtliche Mitteilungen,* 2/1972, 53–73.

——. "Selbstverständnis und historisches Bewusstsein der deutschen Kriegsmarine," *Marine-Rundschau*, vol. 67 (1970), 65–88.

——. " 'Neujahr 1900' — Die Säkularwende in zeitgenössischer Sicht," *Archiv für Kulturgeschichte*, vol. 53 (1971), 335–81.

Stürmer, Michael. "Machtgefüge und Verbandsentwicklung im wilhelminischen Deutschland," *Neue Politische Literatur*, vol. 14 (1969), 490–507.

Vagts, Alfred. "Hopes and Fears of an American-German War, 1870–1915," *Political Science Quarterly*, vol. 54 (December 1939), 514–35, and vol. 55 (March 1940), 53–76.

Wehler, Hans-Ulrich. "1889: Wendepunkt der amerikanischen Aussenpolitik. Die Anfänge des modernen Panamerikanismus — Die Samoakrise," *Historische Zeitschrift*, vol. 201 (August 1965), 86–109.

Weinberg, Gerhard L. "German Colonial Plans and Policies 1938–1942," *Geschichte und Gegenwartsbewusstsein. Historische Betrachtungen und Untersuchungen. Festschrift für Hans Rothfels* (Göttingen 1963), 462–91.

——. "Hitler's Image of the United States," *American Historical Review*, vol. 69 (July 1964), 1006–21.

# Index

# Index

# Index

# Index

# Index